Software Design, Automated Testing, and Maintenance

A Practical Approach

Software Design, Automated Testing, and Maintenance
A Practical Approach

Daniel M. Hoffman
University of Victoria, Victoria, Canada

Paul A. Strooper
University of Queensland, Brisbane, Australia

INTERNATIONAL THOMSON COMPUTER PRESS
I(T)P An International Thomson Publishing Company

London • Bonn • Boston • Johannesburg • Madrid • Melbourne • Mexico City • New York • Paris
Singapore • Tokyo • Toronto • Albany, NY • Belmont, CA • Cincinnati, OH • Detroit, MI

Copyright © 1995 International Thomson Computer Press

I(T)P™   A division of International Thomson Publishing Inc.
The ITP Logo is a trademark under license.

Printed in the United States of America
For more information, contact:

International Thomson Computer Press
20 Park Place, Suite 1001
Boston, MA 02116
USA

International Thomson Publishing Group
Königswinterer Strasse 418
53227 Bonn
Germany

International Thomson Publishing Europe
Berkshire House 168-173
High Holborn
London WCIV 7AA
England

International Thomson Publishing Asia
221 Henderson Road #05-10
Henderson Building
Singapore 0315

Thomas Nelson Australia
102 Dodds Street
South Melbourne, 3205
Victoria, Australia

International Publishing Japan
Hirakawacho Kyowa Building, 3F
2-2-1 Hirakawacho
Chiyoda-ku, 102 Tokyo
Japan

Nelson Canada
1120 Birchmount Road
Scarborough, Ontario
Canada MIK 5G4

International Thomson Editores
Campos Eliseos 385, Piso 7
Col. Polanco
11560 Mexico D. F. Mexico

International Thomson Publishing Southern Africa
Bldg. 19, Constantia Park
239 Old Pretoria Road, P.O. Box 2459
Halfway House, 1685 South Africa

1 2 3 4 5 6 7 8 9 10 QEBFF 01 00 99 98 97 96 95

Library of Congress Cataloging-in-Publication Data
(available upon request)

ISBN 1-850-32206-6

Contents

List of Figures

List of Tables

Preface

Many Software Engineering survey texts are available on the market. These texts have become the de facto standard for teaching the undergraduate Software Engineering courses required in most Computer Science departments. While survey texts are useful for reference, serious problems arise when they are used to teach the fundamentals of Software Engineering.

- *Too many topics, too little depth.* Survey texts present a little about a lot of topics, from *algebraic specification* to *Z*. The examples are superficial and the notations are inconsistent from one topic to the next. Consequently, the students never achieve much skill with any particular technique. Little of practical value is gained.

- *Designed for experts.* Survey books can work well with a Software Engineering expert as instructor; the course is based on his or her personal experience and the text is used as auxiliary reading. In practice, the instructor is frequently not a Software Engineering expert. Many departments have no such expert; few have enough to teach all the course sections required. For the non-expert, a survey text offers too little support. There is too much material to teach. Research topics are mixed with practical methods, and no clear distinction is made between the two. The examples are few and mostly trivial. The exercises are hard to grade fairly and efficiently, especially if the grading is done by a teaching assistant. With only survey texts available, most non-experts dread the prospect of teaching Software Engineering.

- *Software maintenance not taught effectively.* It is well known that maintenance is a critical topic. Working programmers spend most of their time maintaining existing systems, not writing new ones. Teaching maintenance is extremely difficult with a survey text. Maintenance assignments are simply not an option without a target system to maintain. Consequently, only general maintenance principles can be taught.

Our goal is to complement the broad surveys found in most texts with a more focused approach. Rather than survey Software Engineering research and practice, we pursue mastery of a small set of fundamental concepts and skills.

We present practical methods, ready for use in industry now. We focus on maintenance, emphasizing reading over writing and modification over new development. We show how to design, document, and test software to reduce maintenance costs.

In developing these themes, we make extensive use of a fully worked, nontrivial case study. Intentionally, the case study is small by industrial standards. It is carefully constructed to be as simple as possible while still being sufficiently complex to illustrate the methods. Despite its small size, it gives rise to surprisingly subtle issues in specification, design, verification, and maintenance. We have made the case study available online, so students can get hands-on experience running and modifying the code, documentation, and automated test scripts. As a result, the text is well-suited for classroom use and for self-study.

Scaling Up

Scalability is an important concern in Software Engineering education. Too often, the methods taught are not applicable in industry. We know that the methods we teach scale up because they are scaled-down versions of methods in industrial use now:

- Our work products are based on the those used in the *Software Cost Reduction* project led by David Parnas [1, 2].

- Our notations and inspection methods are based on those used in the *Cleanroom* method pioneered by Harlan Mills [3, 4].

- Our methods for system testing follow standard practice in industry. Because automated module testing is not a standard industrial practice, our approach to module testing is novel. Nonetheless, it has seen industrial application [5, 6, 7].

Object-Oriented Programming

We take a practical approach to object-oriented programming (OOP). OOP is based on encapsulation, inheritance, and polymorphism, as supplied by languages such as C++ and SmallTalk. In this text, we use Base Class Object-Oriented Programming (BCOOP). BCOOP uses only encapsulation and can be carried out using C, Pascal, and even FORTRAN; the separate compilation facilities of these languages provide adequate support for encapsulation. While inheritance and polymorphism are important concepts, there are significant advantages to BCOOP. From a teaching perspective, it is critical to recognize the complexity of full OOP. Because an entire course can be devoted to teaching just the required language features, we cannot teach full OOP without sacrificing essential Software Engineering material. Of the three concepts—encapsulation, inheritance, and polymorphism—encapsulation is certainly the most important concept and the one that should be taught first. From an industrial perspective, BCOOP is also attractive. It applies to the huge quantity of existing code in C, Pascal, and FORTRAN; it is well-understood, having been studied extensively for over 20 years. In contrast, industrial use of full OOP is still relatively limited; the languages, tools, and techniques change frequently and development is full of surprises. The payoff for success is high, but so is the risk of failure. BCOOP provides an attractive migration path, using, for example, BCOOP and C now, and full OOP and C++ later. In summary, we teach OOP throughout the text, but only the BCOOP subset.

Tool Support

We also take a practical approach to Software Engineering tools, to make the text readily accessible to a wide audience and to focus on fundamental principles and techniques, rather than particular tool features. Thus, we rely on the "software development environment" available on today's UNIX systems. We store and access system configurations using the UNIX file system and the *vi* editor; we build executable programs using the C compiler and the *make* utility; and we make use of standard libraries, primarily *stdio* and *curses*. We also use a simple test driver generator, developed by the authors because no equivalent tool could be found on the market.

Text Organization

The text is organized as follows: Chapter 1 provides a broad survey of Software Engineering issues, principles, and methods. A variety of lifecycle approaches are described. Project management, development methods, quality assurance, and tools are discussed. Chapter 2 presents a carefully selected set of documentation principles and work products, based on the "rational approach" proposed by Parnas [1]. Chapter 2 also covers inspection and testing, the two verification methods in widespread use in industry today.

Chapter 3 presents the discrete mathematics concepts used to support the work products of Chapter 2. Sets, relations, functions, logic, and finite state machines (FSMs) are covered. Chapter 3 also presents *Module State Machines*, a special kind of FSM designed for specifying software modules. In this chapter, and throughout the text, we focus on *specification functions*: functions that arise naturally in software specifications. To represent specification functions, we rely heavily on the *multiple assignment statement* and *conditional rule* popularized by Mills and others in the Cleanroom approach [3].

Chapter 4 introduces the SHAM system: the example used throughout the text. SHAM (Strooper-Hoffman Abstract Machine) provides a load-and-go interpreter for a toy assembly language. Two versions of SHAM are presented;

BSHAM is batch oriented, while ISHAM provides an interactive interface. SHAM is small enough to learn easily and yet complex enough to present challenging problems in design and verification.

Each of Chapters 5–10 covers a different work product. Each chapter presents the work product purpose, required format, and inspection procedures, illustrated in detail on examples from SHAM.

Part III contains a single chapter, summarizing the key ideas and discussing practical considerations: what happens when these techniques are applied to large systems under realistic conditions? Inevitably, principles are compromised, work products are omitted, and the development chronology does not follow the ideal. Part III also contains a discussion of polymorphism and inheritance in C++.

Internet Access

Substantial supporting materials are available online, including the contents of Appendices A–F, a full set of overhead slides, and the PGMGEN testing tool described in Chapter 10. To retrieve copies using FTP, find a machine on the Internet and type:

```
% ftp godot.uvic.ca
Name (godot.uvic.ca:...): anonymous
Password:<your email address for our log file>
...
ftp> cd pub/dhoffman/SDATM
ftp> get README
```

(For those without Internet name server access, use IP address 142.104.88.101.) Consult the README file for information on the available materials.

The authors can be reached by electronic mail at dhoffman@csr.uvic.ca and pstroop@cs.uq.oz.au.

Acknowledgments

This text is based on the course *CSC 365—Software Engineering* as taught at the University of Victoria for the past 10 years. The students of CSC 365 have made significant contributions to the text by finding errors and, more importantly, by showing us what works and what does not in Software Engineering education. Many others have also contributed to this project. In particular, we would like to thank David Carrington, Helen Cheung, Byron Ehle, Maarten van Emden, Jerome Hoffman, Hausi Müller, Kelvin Ross, Terry Shepard, Peter Walsh, and Colin Wortley.

Software Design, Automated
Testing, and Maintenance

A Practical Approach

Part I

Background

Chapter 1

Introduction

1.1 The Software Engineering Problem

We all depend on computers in many aspects of our business and leisure activities. Today's companies cannot run without computer-based information systems. The telephone network could not operate without computers. Computers are widely used in safety-critical applications including medical devices, automobiles, aircraft, and industrial process control. In these types of applications, software failures can cause injury or loss of life. It is difficult to picture the consequences if all the world's computers were to fail now. While this event is unlikely, imagining it highlights the extent to which computers have permeated our lives. Because the influence of computer systems is so widespread, it is important that these systems be useful, affordable, and reliable. While both hardware and software are essential, hardware development is far more advanced. Despite important and difficult open problems, the power and reliability of hardware are impressive and improving; the costs are low and dropping. As the weak link, software is the critical factor in achieving the required system characteristics.

Thus, we all depend on well-engineered software. But what exactly is *Software Engineering*? It is significantly different from *solo programming*, where the same person is both developer and maintainer, there is one version—the current one—and the user is the programmer or someone nearby. Software Engineering is well characterized as *multi-person/multi-version* programming [8].

In *multi-person* programming, the systems are too big to be developed by one person. Teams are required, consisting of tens or hundreds of people. The systems are in operation for years after development and must be maintained, typically by people who are not part of the development team. With programming teams, precise specification of the product is critical so that the team members agree on the characteristics of the system being built. The development task must be divided into modules so that the work can be split among the different developers. Precise specification of the modules is also critical so

3

that they interact correctly. Finally, each module and the full system must be verified against its specification. Without verification, adequate reliability is unattainable.

Multi-person systems invariably have multiple versions as well. Often the same system must run on different platforms, distinguished by differences in the hardware and operating system. After installation, modifications are inevitable to fix errors and to adapt to changes in user requirements and in the underlying platform. Successful development of multi-version systems depends on the ability to predict the types of changes likely to occur and to develop systems for which those changes are easy to make. Careful control of the multiple versions is also essential. Multiple copies of code and documentation must be stored, retrieved, and modified, at reasonable cost.

Because of the special difficulties involved in managing large teams and developing and maintaining a number of system versions, multi-person/multi-version programming is fundamentally different from solo programming.

1.2 Software Engineering Principles

Basic principles play a key role in handling the difficult problems that arise in multi-person/multi-version programming. The most important principle in software engineering—and in problem-solving generally—is *separation of concerns* [9]. A problem that is too complex to be solved directly is decomposed into subproblems. Subproblems that are still too difficult to solve directly are further decomposed. The decomposition is most useful if the subproblems are independent or nearly so. Thus, considerable effort in software engineering is devoted to (1) the search for decompositions that maximize the independence of the subproblems and (2) careful documentation of the dependencies that remain.

In addition to the general principle of separation of concerns, this text is dominated by four broad themes:

1. *The central role of documentation.* Our approach is based on a single set of documents supporting design, implementation, and maintenance. Precise system and module specifications play a key role: providing the foundation for the important practice of *implementation to specification*.

2. *Systematic verification.* We use two complementary methods of verification. Inspections are applied to all work products using the inspection procedure now standard in industry. Testing is applied to executable work products at both the system and module level. We emphasize automated testing and isolation of the module under test.

3. *Effective use of mathematics.* We have selected a small set of mathematical concepts. Notations based on these are used extensively in our specification documents. While we make frequent use of mathematical concepts and notations, our approach is not highly formal. We use both formal

notations and prose, choosing whichever seems clearer and simpler. Our inspections are proof-based, in the sense that the reader's job is to present a convincing logical argument. For example, when inspecting an implementation, the reader must show that it satisfies the specification. This proof orientation has a substantial impact on the inspections and on the specification documents that support them.

4. *Reducing the cost of maintenance.* While most texts deal with maintenance as a separate phase, we view maintenance as redevelopment. Maintenance then consists of partially repeating the development phases, modifying the original work products to reflect the fix or enhancement. Our design method is based on *information hiding*, whereby maintenance costs are reduced by planning for likely changes to the system. Our testing is automated so that the tests can be repeated after every change to the implementation. Finally, we emphasize maintenance in our teaching. Most assignments focus on reading code and documentation, and on making changes to existing code and documentation. Course projects carry a change through from specification to testing, updating and verifying all the relevant work products along the way.

1.3   Software Lifecycle

1.3.1   Software tasks

Throughout the "life" of a software system there are many phases of development and change. Even after a system is delivered, it continually evolves and changes. Therefore, to properly manage a software project, we must model the *lifecycle* of a software system. Many lifecycle models have been proposed, based on the tasks involved in developing and maintaining a software system. Below we briefly describe each of these tasks.

Requirements analysis. The first task in every software project is a careful analysis of the problem to be solved. This involves determining the needs of the user and is typically accomplished through a dialogue between the user and the developer of the system. Clearly this is an important task; no matter how well you build a system, if it is not what the user needs then it is not useful. It is also a complicated task: often the user does not know exactly what he or she wants the system to do and cannot clearly communicate what he or she knows. In particular, when a task is first automated, it is difficult to predict how the new system will be used. Communication problems arise when the developer and the user have widely varying backgrounds. Computer systems are developed for an enormous variety of problem domains; software developers cannot be·experts in all these domains. To accurately analyze user needs, however, considerable expertise is required in the particular domain for which the system is built.

Requirements analysis involves a wide variety of issues, including the purpose, benefits, and cost of the proposed system. The specific requirements are often grouped into *functional* and *non-functional* requirements. The functional requirements specify the system inputs and the outputs. The non-functional requirements include all other constraints under which the system must be delivered and operate. These include constraints on cost, delivery date, maintainability, performance, and user friendliness.

Another aspect of requirements analysis, which is just as important, is determining whether it is feasible to build a software system to satisfy the requirements. This involves estimating the cost of developing and maintaining the system, and determining the benefits of the system. These costs and benefits must then be compared to determine if it is worthwhile to implement the system.

Requirements specification. Based on the needs identified during requirements analysis, the required behavior of the delivered system is determined and recorded. Note the distinction between the requirements analysis and the requirements specification tasks. During requirements analysis we determine the user needs; during requirements specification we precisely define a particular system to satisfy those needs.

In the literature, many widely varying notations have been proposed for requirements specification. These range from informal specifications using natural language to highly formal notations. The major advantage of informal, natural language specifications is that they can be read and understood without special training. Consequently, they can be used to communicate between the developer and the user. However, such specifications are often vague and ambiguous, contain inconsistencies and omissions, and are hard to maintain. Structured notations, such as PSL [10], organize the specification into sections but still rely on natural language to specify the behavior. This makes finding specific information easier and it allows for some consistency and completeness checking. These notations often lack a precisely defined meaning, however, and are therefore hard to reason about. The same holds for diagrammatic notations such as dataflow diagrams and entity-relationship diagrams. Formal notations, such as Z [11] and VDM [12], have a precisely defined meaning. Their major disadvantage is their complexity, which means that special training is required to understand them. Most programmers do not have the training to use these formal notations. Moreover, users rarely have the background to understand these formal notations, and it is therefore hard to determine if a requirements specification correctly reflects the user's needs.

Architectural design. The requirements analysis and specification tasks determine and record *what* has to be built. The architectural design is the first task that addresses the problem of *how* to build the system. This is accomplished by decomposing the system into modules and by determining how these modules will interact.

This task is motivated by the principle of separation of concerns. When faced with a complex development task, we subdivide it into components, which we call *modules*. Modules that are still too complex to implement directly are then further subdivided into other modules, and so on. In general, separation of concerns is effective only if the components are relatively independent and if we can specify and control the unavoidable interactions between the components. For software systems, this translates into modules with minimal and controlled interaction.

Detailed design. For each module, the details of the interface are specified. In many cases, the interface consists of procedures and functions used to access the module. For example, a stack module may have calls to push and pop stack elements and calls to return the top element and the depth of the stack. When such a *call-based* interface is used, the detailed design specifies the behavior of the access routines.

In addition, the detailed design specifies the internal data structures and the algorithms that will be used to implement the module. For example, the detailed design of a stack might specify that the stack will be implemented as an array.

The difference between architectural design and detailed design can again be explained in terms of the separation between *what* we build, and *how* we build it. During architectural design, we determine *what* service each module provides. During detailed design, we determine *how* this service will be provided.

Implementation. During implementation, source code is developed for each module, according to the internal data structures and algorithms specified in the detailed design. Note that the implementation is the only product that is required to run the system. Other tasks also produce documents and even source code, such as test code, but these are created primarily for use by the developer.

Testing. During testing, we verify that the system performs the required service. During *module testing*, each module is tested individually. During *integration testing*, we verify that groups of modules and subsystems interact correctly. During *system testing*, we verify that the entire system behaves as specified in the requirements specification. Finally, during *acceptance testing*, we verify that the system satisfies the user's needs.

Maintenance. While it may seem that the developer's job is done after a system is delivered and installed, in fact it has just begun. Studies show that, on average, more than half of the total cost of a software project is incurred during maintenance [13]. Here, for simplicity, we refer to maintenance as all the change activity that occurs after delivery of the system.

Since the cost associated with maintenance is so high, it is worthwhile to examine the different types of maintenance that take place. *Corrective maintenance* involves the removal of errors from the system; the functionality of the system is changed to match the requirements specification. *Adaptive maintenance* involves modifying the system in reaction to changes in the system environment, such as the hardware or the operating system. Here, the functionality of the system changes little or not at all. *Perfective maintenance* involves changes requested by the user or the developer to improve the quality of the system. This includes changes to both the functional and non-functional requirements of the system. Data gathered on existing systems suggest that corrective and adaptive maintenance each account for less than 20 percent of the total maintenance cost, while perfective maintenance accounts for over 50 percent [14]. This means that, even if we can produce a software system free of errors, a large proportion of the overall cost will still be devoted to adaptive and perfective maintenance. Consequently, reducing the maintenance cost should be an important consideration during software development.

1.3.2   The waterfall model

The tasks just described appear in one form or another in most large software projects. A lifecycle model attempts to capture how these tasks interrelate and in what order they are performed. A simple model is the *waterfall model* in which each task has a well-defined starting and ending point and a task is not started until the previous task is completed. For example, under the waterfall model, a project starts with requirements analysis. After requirements analysis is completed, the requirements specification task is begun, with no option of going back to requirements analysis. Figure 1.1 illustrates why this model is called the waterfall model: one task flows into the next, without the option of going back upstream to a previous task.

Clearly the waterfall model is an oversimplification; it does not allow feedback from a task to previous tasks. For example, during requirements specification, errors will be found in the requirements analysis necessitating further requirements analysis. Even if we were able to perform all the tasks free of errors, feedback is still required because the user requirements and the environment in which the system operates frequently change both during and after development.

A second problem with the waterfall model is that a phase is not started until a previous phase is completed. This has the disadvantage that it takes a long time before any deliverable products can be shown to the user. If the user then finds that the system does not satisfy his or her needs, much of the effort involved in producing the system will be wasted.

To address the issue of feedback, we allow iterative interaction between the various tasks. Figure 1.2 illustrates this iterative waterfall model. Note that the feedback may involve several tasks. For example, it is common that during development the requirements of the system change. This results in a change to the requirements, and the change then propagates forward through all the tasks in the lifecycle.

1.3.3   Other models

The iterative waterfall model addresses the problem of feedback. We now briefly describe two other models that support feedback and also reduce the time between the start of a project and the delivery of a system to the user.

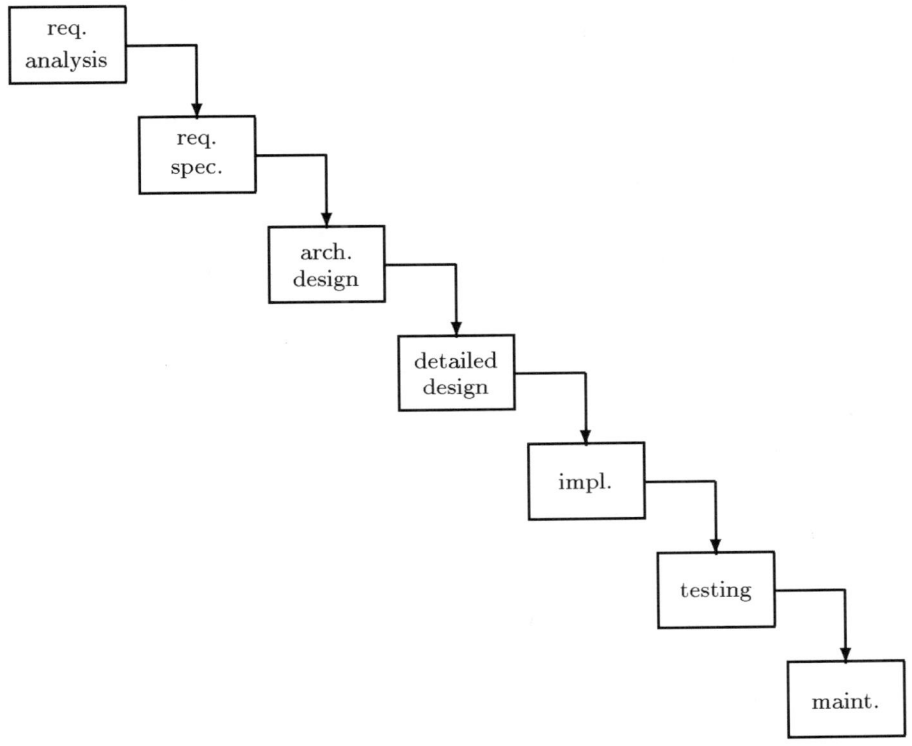

Figure 1.1   Waterfall model of the software lifecycle

The motivation behind the *evolutionary model* is that it is impossible to build a large software system right the first time. As Brooks [15, page 116] points out, with a software system, "plan to throw one away; you will, anyhow." This suggests that the first version of a system should be a trial system whose purpose is to help understand the requirements of the system. Such a preliminary version is called a *prototype* and often does not include the full functionality of the eventual system. After the prototype is used to better understand the requirements, it is discarded and the real system is built.

Building a system version primarily for learning purposes is known as *prototyping*. The *evolutionary model* takes this approach further and models the software lifecycle as a continual evolution from one version of the system to the next. After the initial version of the system is built, each version evolves from the previous one by changes resulting from a better understanding of the requirements and changes to the environment in which the system operates.

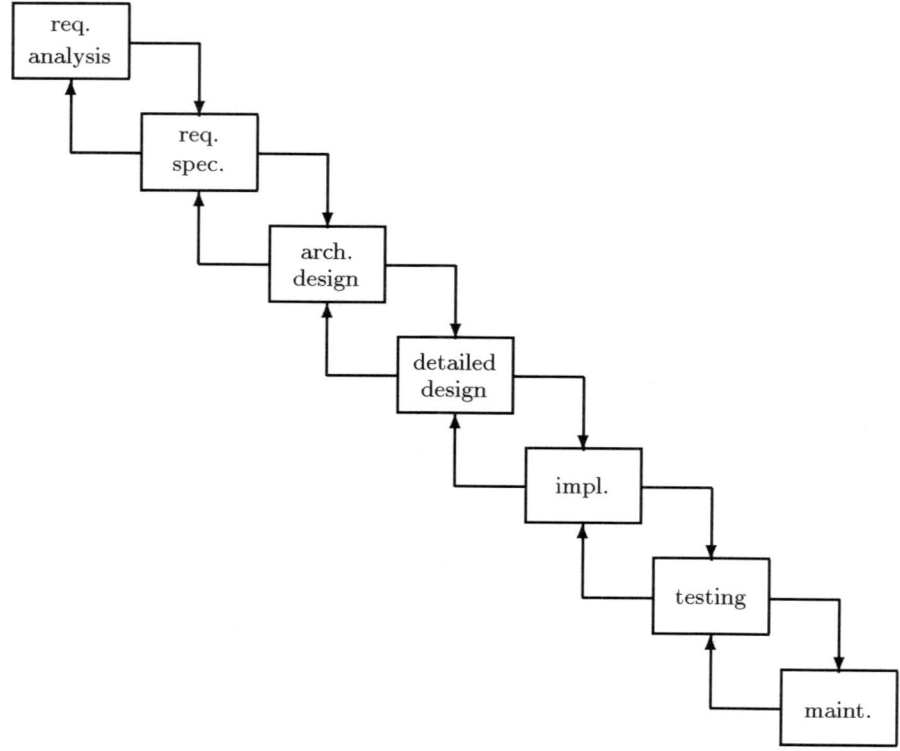

Figure 1.2   Iterative waterfall model of the software lifecycle

Note that the evolutionary model does not specify how each version of the system is constructed; the waterfall model can be used for that. That is, for each new version, we first determine the changes to the requirements and then incorporate the changes through the various tasks in the waterfall model. In this way, maintenance is modeled as redevelopment, since we perform the same tasks for maintenance as we performed for the development of the system.

The *spiral model* of the software lifecycle can be viewed as a special case of the evolutionary model. The spiral model is guided by the risk associated with each change to the current system. For example, a small well-understood change represents a small risk, whereas a substantial and poorly understood change represents a large risk.

As its name suggests, the spiral model is cyclic. During each cycle of the spiral, the following four steps are performed:

1. The objectives for the change from the current version are determined, and

alternatives for implementing the change are identified.

2. The alternatives are evaluated, and potential risks associated with each alternative are identified.

3. The best alternative is implemented, and the results of the change are verified.

4. The results from the current cycle are reviewed, and a plan is constructed for the next cycle.

The spiral model addresses both development and maintenance of a software system. As with the evolutionary model, maintenance is modeled as redevelopment.

1.3.4   Our model

Since, in reality, the progression from one task or one version to the next will vary from one project to the next, we do not favor any particular model of the software lifecycle. Instead, we emphasize the deliverables of a software project. In particular, we discuss seven *work products* that are created for each software system, but we do not concern ourselves overly with the order in which these work products are produced. However, we present the deliverables in a linear fashion, following the order of the waterfall model. This is the best order for explaining and understanding the work products, even though during development the work products are frequently created in a different order.

In the remainder of this text, we do not treat the requirements analysis task in detail. Although it is an important task, it is also very complex and varies widely from one project to the next. Moreover, we believe that it is difficult to appreciate the key requirements analysis issues until you have seen and used at least one requirements specification.

We present no work products associated only with maintenance, because we view maintenance as redevelopment, as in the evolutionary and spiral models. In our approach, maintenance involves updating the seven work products. In addition, maintenance is a major motivator for much of what we do during development:

- The work products serve as vital documentation during maintenance. It is therefore essential that the work products are updated during maintenance; otherwise they quickly become outdated and unreliable.

- During requirements specification, we attempt to anticipate likely changes to the system. These likely changes are then used during the architectural design to ensure that it will be easy to incorporate them later on.

- During testing, we emphasize cheap repeatability of test cases through automation so that it is easy to run all our test cases after every change to the system.

- Throughout the text, we emphasize maintenance in the exercises, which for a large part involves changing parts of our model system. This is partly the motivation for using a model system, without which it is impossible to obtain an appreciation of the considerable effort involved with maintenance.

1.4   The Big Picture

Software engineering is a broad field. On the one hand, it must address technical issues such as methods and tools to develop software systems. On the other hand, it is concerned with managerial issues relating to delivering software systems on time and within budget, including human and organizational factors. Obviously, it is impossible to cover all these topics in depth in a single text. However, it is important to realize where the material that we cover in this text fits in the "big picture."

1.4.1   Software project management

Many considerations are necessary for managing a software project. *Estimating* and *scheduling* are critical for achieving the basic control necessary to ensure that a software system is delivered on time and within budget. *Configuration management* is essential for controlling the many work products and versions of a system that exist in a typical software project.

During project estimation, we attempt to determine the resources required for completing a project and hence the cost associated with the project. This involves estimating both the human resources and the system resources, such as equipment and software tools. Since human resources typically dominate the cost of a software project, they are the most important consideration during estimation. While it is possible to make accurate estimates for projects that are similar to previous projects, it is very hard to do so for a very different system or even for a similar system in a new application domain. Estimation models such as COCOMO [13] may assist with software project estimation, but even these models must be calibrated to the individual organization and type of project at hand.

After an estimate has been made, the manager must determine a schedule for completing the project. This involves determining a start and end date, and resource allocation for each task. Although the software lifecycle model provides an initial decomposition of the tasks to be performed, a finer decomposition is required to develop an accurate schedule. Notations such as PERT charts can be used to record the various task interdependencies. Usually, many tasks cannot be started until other tasks are completed. For example, a module cannot be implemented until its interface is determined. Bar graphs or Gantt charts are useful for recording the schedule. Once the project gets under way, progress must be monitored and compared with the schedule. If the project falls behind schedule, remedial action may be required. This may involve allocating additional resources to the project, increasing the productivity of existing staff in some way, or rescheduling the project.

Configuration management addresses the multi-version aspect of a software engineering project. In a typical project, the system is maintained in many different files and directories, and complex relationships exist between the files. The problem is further complicated by frequent changes. The consequences of poor configuration management include: finding the same error twice because it was not fixed in all versions, inconsistency between documentation and code, and loss of documentation or code. Such problems are unavoidable unless considerable attention is paid to configuration management.

In a software system, a configuration includes all the work products associated with the system. This includes not only the system that is delivered to the user, but also the documentation and support code maintained by the developer. A configuration may also include different versions of executable files for different hardware and operating systems.

To appreciate the problems associated with configuration management, it is important to realize the enormous number of objects that are part of a typical software project. Even a small system may contain over a hundred files. For realistically sized systems, this number will increase to thousands or tens of thousands. Problems associated with configuration management are therefore similar to the ones faced by a modern library in storing and tracking books. Such libraries often contain more than a million volumes. Without careful inventory, many of the books will inevitably end up lost. Even the storage of books requires strict organization and careful attention; if a book is placed on the wrong shelf, it may be lost for all intents and purposes.

The three major tasks in configuration management are (1) the storage of objects, (2) the building of systems, and (3) the verification of the configuration. The objects in a configuration must be stored in such a way that they can easily be accessed and changed. A number of issues arise. Several people may attempt to access or update an object at the same time. Sometimes not all objects are stored in the same location or even on the same system. Multiple versions of the same object may exist. The building of systems involves providing support for the construction of products from the objects in a configuration. A typical example is the construction of an executable file from several source files. Finally, the verification of a configuration involves ensuring that the current configuration is consistent and conforms to the configuration plan.

1.4.2 Software development methods

A wide variety of methods are in use for developing software products. We briefly review four of these methods: structured analysis and design, object-oriented programming, the Cleanroom approach, and formal methods.

Structured analysis and structured design (SA/SD) is a family of design methods. These methods rely heavily upon graphical representations, such as *dataflow diagrams* and *entity-relationship diagrams*, and are widely used in industry. Object-oriented analysis and design is an extension of SA/SD.

Object-oriented programming is based on *encapsulation*, *inheritance*, and *polymorphism*, as supplied by languages such as SmallTalk and C++. *Encapsulation* insulates parts of the system from changes in other parts. For example, in an object-oriented language, the services of a stack would be encapsulated in a stack object that can be accessed through a standard interface, but that hides the internal data structures used to implement the stack. Consequently, the implementation data structure can be easily changed from, for example, an array to a linked list, without affecting other parts of the system. *Inheritance* is a mechanism by which the services of one object can be extended or changed, without having to reimplement the entire object. *Polymorphism* allows us to provide the same service for objects of different types. For example, instead of having to implement a stack of integers and a stack of strings separately, we can develop a single implementation that can store integers or strings.

The *Cleanroom* method is based upon an evolutionary model of the software lifecycle. In the Cleanroom approach, software development consists of a sequence of executable product increments. These increments accumulate over the development lifecycle and eventually result in the final product.

Three key components distinguish the Cleanroom approach from other approaches to incremental development.

1. The specifications describe the required behavior as functions that are structured so that they can be easily composed.

2. Program units are designed and implemented to satisfy the specification functions. However, these program units are never executed by the developers, who rely solely on logical argument to convince themselves that the software correctly implements the specification.

3. After a system increment is completed, it is certified through independent, statistically based testing, as is often done in other areas of engineering and manufacturing. It is statistically based because the test cases are chosen randomly from a frequency distribution intended to closely resemble the actual usage to come.

The Cleanroom approach is based on error prevention rather than error detection, and empirical studies [16] show encouraging results. When compared with more traditional approaches to software development, fewer defects are found in software produced with the Cleanroom approach. What is interesting is that during these studies both quality and productivity improved.

Formal methods provide specification notations with precisely defined mathematical meanings and proof methods. It is then possible to manipulate the specification mechanically to establish, for example, consistency and completeness. In principle, it is possible to formally verify that a system implementation satisfies its specification.

Examples of formal methods include model-based specification languages such as Z [11] and VDM [12]. These languages specify software behavior in terms of a model of the state, using mathematical objects such as sets and sequences. The algebraic [17] and trace [18] methods define the behavior directly in terms of sequences of calls on the software.

Since formal specifications have a precisely defined meaning, they can support rigorous reasoning. The trend in software engineering research is toward documents that are as formal as possible. Sophisticated mathematics is needed to achieve this formality; even simple systems often have complex specifications. Industrial software developers typically find these specifications unreadable. Moreover, no figures are available for the cost of reading, writing, verifying, and maintaining formal specifications for industrial systems. The result is a crippling standoff; formal methods researchers insist on complete formality, and practicing programmers continue to rely on the code alone.

Effective documentation depends on a more balanced view, based on two ideas. First, *formality is not a suitable engineering goal*. While it is a powerful means for achieving engineering goals, such as reliability, it is dangerously inappropriate as an end in itself. There is no inherent value to the customer in formality, only in the other characteristics that may, or may not, be best achieved by formal methods. Second, *the principal purpose for documentation is communication between people*. Therefore, formality should be used when it facilitates this communication, and avoided otherwise.

Consider, for example, the sequence of integers $s = \langle s[0], s[1], \ldots, s[n-1] \rangle$ and the following two assertions.

1. s contains no duplicates

2. $(\forall i, j \in [0, n-1])(i \neq j \rightarrow s[i] \neq s[j])$

Which is better? The answer depends on the audience. The first assertion is shorter and would be preferred by many programmers. The second one is more precise and might appeal to readers with logic training.

1.4.3 Software quality assurance

Software has a reputation for poor quality; a reputation that is, to a large extent, justified. Errors are common in software systems, and often the systems are hard to use. The software developers themselves suffer from this poor quality. The systems they produce are hard to understand and maintain, translating into high maintenance costs. It is therefore not surprising that software quality assurance, the attempt to ensure that a system meets some quality standard, is an important consideration in every software project.

- Correctness: extent to which system performs its specified service
- Reliability: likelihood of failure during actual use
- Robustness: how well a system behaves under unexpected circumstances
- Maintainability
    - Readability: ease with which software can be understood
    - Modifiability: ease with which software can be modified
    - Verifiability: ease with which software can be verified
- User friendliness: ease with which the system can be used
- Performance: time and space efficiency of the software
- Portability: ease with which software can be moved to other platforms

Figure 1.3   Software qualities

The list of qualities that must be considered for a software system is large. Figure 1.3 shows a partial list.   The qualities that are most important will vary from one project to another. Below we briefly expand on correctness, reliability, and robustness; three qualities that are important in any software project.

Correctness refers to the extent to which the system behavior corresponds to the requirements specification. While it is a fact of life that no non-trivial software system is completely correct, it is useful to establish correctness as an important goal. *Reliability* focuses on the actual use of the system over time. One approach for expressing reliability is *mean-time between failures*: the average time between two successive failures of the system. A system may have errors but still be highly reliable if the errors appear only on inputs that never occur in actual use. *Robustness* addresses how well a system behaves under unexpected circumstances, such as incorrect user input and hardware failures. For example, many text editors allow the user to recover much of an edit session after the system goes down unexpectedly, even if the user did not explicitly save any information while editing.

Determining whether a system meets the user's needs involves two tasks: verification and validation. *Verification* determines whether a system meets its requirements specification. *Validation* determines whether the requirements specification adequately captures the user's needs. Since a lot more is known about verification than about validation, we focus on verification. Four approaches to verification are testing, walkthroughs, inspections, and formal verification.

Testing is the execution of a program to reveal errors in its behavior. We already discussed the various levels of testing that must be performed: module testing, integration testing, system testing, and acceptance testing. Note that acceptance testing is a form of validation, and the other three are a form of verification.

Both *walkthroughs* and *inspections* are verification methods that are based on peer review. During a walkthrough, a person walks through a work product based on certain scenarios, with the intention of finding errors in the work product. For example, a walkthrough of a piece of code may involve selecting some test cases and "hand-executing" the code for those test cases. Inspections are more structured and focus on particular inspection criteria, such as ensuring that every loop in a program terminates. By focusing on particular criteria, there is a better chance of detecting violations of these criteria.

Formal verification involves formally proving that a system meets its specification. While testing, walkthroughs, and inspections are widely applied in industry, formal verification has had little industrial application. However, because the idea is so appealing, formal verification is, and will remain, an active research topic.

1.4.4 Software measurement

Measurement plays a critical role in software estimation and in determining and improving the quality of software. To verify and improve on the estimates we make, we must compare our estimates to figures from actual projects. Similarly, if we want to improve the quality of our software, we can use measurement to assess both the current state of affairs and the impact of changes.

The first step in measurement is determining precisely what to measure. For software systems, one important aspect is the work products, such as specifications, source code, and object code. Less obviously, we must also measure properties of the process by which the software is created, such as how many people work on a project and for how long.

We can roughly subdivide the properties suitable for measurement into three categories. The first is a notion of size, which measures properties of work products. Here the notion of size is quite variable, ranging from something as simple as the number of lines in a file to notions of complexity of a piece of source code. The second is a notion of effort, which measures properties of human involvement. Typically this measurement is expressed as a number of person-months or person-years expended on a project. The third category involves measurements of the number of defects in a work product, which relates to the quality of the product.

To improve the products or the processes by which the products are created, an organization must go through a continual cycle guided by measurement. During the first phase of the cycle, information is gathered by measuring properties of the current products and processes. This information is then analyzed, and potential areas of improvement are identified. Finally, the products and processes are changed to implement the improvements. During the next cycle, new measurements will indicate whether or not the improvements have had their desired effect.

A *metric* is a quantifiable measurement that is intended to capture relevant information. Many metrics have been proposed for software systems. There are the obvious ones such as the number of source lines in a system and the number of person-years expended on a project. More elaborate ones include the cyclomatic complexity [19] and the Halstead metric [20], which measure the complexity of a piece of code based on its syntactic structure. There are also metrics for other tasks and products in the software lifecycle. For example, metrics such as statement, branch, and path coverage measure how many statements, branches, and paths are executed in a program by a set of test cases. This is intended to measure how well the test cases exercise the program.

The two most important considerations for a metric are (1) how well it captures the quality of interest and (2) how expensive it is to calculate. For many proposed metrics, the first consideration is a serious concern. For example, it is not clear that there is a significant relationship between the statement coverage achieved by a test suite and the quality of the test suite.

1.4.5   Software tools

In this section, we discuss the tools used by software engineers for constructing software systems. There is a large list of standard tools that are essential and used in every project. These tools include editors, compilers, debuggers, file systems, and standard libraries. The list of other tools is virtually endless. We briefly review the tools that are now in common use in industry.

Configuration management tools are essential for storing the large number of objects involved and for building systems from those objects. Luckily, this area of software management has great potential for automation since it is largely a bookkeeping task. Configuration management tools allow developers to build systems from the objects in the configuration. For example, based on dependency files and time stamps, the UNIX *make* facility can determine which object files must be recompiled and linked to generate an executable program. There are also tools for version control, which, in their simplest form, track multiple versions of a file. Since storing all the versions separately is typically unaffordable, these tools maintain the versions by storing differences between successive versions. Examples of simple version control tools are the UNIX RCS and SCCS utilities.

Common *testing tools* include coverage measurement tools, file comparators, and keystroke capture and playback tools. Coverage tools measure which parts of the source code were executed by a set of test cases. For example, the UNIX tool *tcov* measures which statements in a source file were executed. More sophisticated coverage tools measure characteristics such as branch and path coverage.

Since many systems produce files as output, a number of testing tools exist for comparing files. The expected output for a test case can be stored in one file and automatically compared with the actual output from the test case, which is saved in another file. The UNIX utility *diff* does a line by line comparison of two files. More sophisticated comparison tools are able to ignore certain aspects of the output, such as differences in the number of whitespaces.

Although it is hard to completely automate the testing of interactive applications, a number of tools exist to facilitate this task. A keystroke capture and playback tool is like a tape recorder for the characters entered from the keyboard. During the capture phase, the characters typed by the tester are recorded. During testing, the keystrokes entered by the tester are played back in the same sequence and at the same rate as the original sequence. Keystroke capture and playback tools are often used in conjunction with tools to compare screen images. During the recording session, the tester may save the current content of the screen. During the playback phase, the new screen contents can be compared with the saved one.

The goal of Computer-Aided Software Engineering (CASE) is the automation of software engineering activities. The first generation of CASE tools consisted primarily of tools to support structured analysis and structured design. These include graphical editors for dataflow diagrams and entity-relationship diagrams, as well as estimating and scheduling tools. The current trend in CASE tools is to move towards *software development environments*: integrated collections of tools. Such environments include tools to support the planning, development, and maintenance of a software project.

1.5 Bibliographic Notes

Pressman [21] provides a good overview of industrial software engineering issues and practices. Ghezzi et al. [22] survey most of the known software engineering methods and provide an excellent bibliography.

Much has been written on the topics excluded from this text. DeMarco [23] and Yourdon and Constantine [24] describe structured analysis and design; Ward and Mellor [25] show how to adapt these methods to real-time systems. Boehm [26, 27] discusses prototyping and its impact on the software development lifecycle. The Cleanroom approach is explained in detail by Dyer [4]. Jones [12] and Spivey [11] show how to apply formal methods to software engineering using VDM and Z, respectively. A great deal has been written about object-oriented programming, in SmallTalk [28], Ada [29], Eiffel [30], and C++ [31].

Techniques for project scheduling and management, including metrics, are presented by Humphrey [32] and Grady [33]. Babich [34] focuses on configuration management.

Chapter 2

Software Engineering Fundamentals

It is easy for me to single out the one factor that led to our relative success: we were all engineers and had been trained to organize our thinking along engineering lines. We had a need to rationalize the job; to define a system of documentation so that others would know what was being done; to define interfaces and police them carefully; ... [H. D. Benington]

2.1 Introduction

This chapter presents the Software Engineering concepts that will be used in the chapters to come. Section 2.2 describes the central role of documentation and presents the principles of effective documentation. Section 2.3 defines the seven work products—code and documentation—that are the output of our software development phases. A key role is played by specifications: descriptions of the required behavior of a system or component. In Section 2.4, we cover verification: demonstrating the correctness of a work product. Verification through testing and inspection is discussed. Finally, Section 2.5 discusses software cost estimation.

2.2 Documentation Principles

2.2.1 Current practice

In the software industry today, many programmers view documentation as a necessary evil. They believe it has little value and produce it reluctantly and with as little effort as possible. Only the production source code is taken seriously. Often there is little or no documentation written, especially regarding system internals. In other cases, there are shelves full of documentation, but it is so hard to use that it remains unused. Frequently different sets of documentation are produced for each development phase: one set for analysis, another for implementation, and yet another for maintenance. The relationship between the sets of documentation is uncontrolled and poorly understood.

This approach causes numerous difficulties. The documentation is incomplete and inaccurate, a serious problem. A deeper problem is that the documentation is unplanned and undisciplined. Inappropriate assumptions are made about the knowledge and goals of the reader. It is hard to find specific facts. The terminology is confusing and inconsistent, and key concepts are undefined or vaguely defined. Multiple terms are used for a single concept; distinct concepts are described by the same term. Due to poor organization, the documents are hard to maintain and, therefore, are not maintained. Producing independent sets of documentation for each development phase is expensive and ineffective. Significant redundancy is inevitable. Because the documents are used only once, they contain many errors. Only repeated use will reveal these errors and provide the motivation to remove them.

2.2.2   Planned documentation

Careful planning is required to avoid the problems just described. Before the first document is written, a document structure must be defined, specifying the roles of all the documents and the relationships between them. This structure forms an information taxonomy: a set of classification rules providing, for each relevant fact, the document and section in which that fact will be stored. Such a structure makes documents easier to create, use, and maintain. The document structure must be explicitly defined and clearly understood. A good document structure will encourage documentation designed for *reference use*, so that specific facts are easy to find; *ease of review*, so that errors can be found and corrected; and *ease of change*, so that the documents can be kept consistent with the code.

For each document, criteria must be developed specifying the scope, purpose, and other required characteristics of the document itself. These criteria guide document writers by establishing clear goals, help reviewers determine what constitutes an error, and tell readers what information to expect in a given document. Document criteria must provide at least the following information:

- *Audience*: the intended readers. Successful technical communication depends on knowing the characteristics of your audience.

- *Prerequisites*: knowledge the reader is assumed to have before reading the document. The prerequisites determine which concepts must be defined and which should not be defined.

- *Purpose*: knowledge the reader can acquire from the document.

Specification documents play a central role in disciplined software development. These documents focus on the observable behavior of a system or component. Among the readers of a specification, four roles naturally arise. Consider specification S and implementation I.

- The *designer* decides on I's observable behavior and records it in S.

- The *developer* creates an implementation I to satisfy S.

- The *verifier* determines whether I does in fact satisfy S.

- The *user* reads S to learn how to use I.

While most documentation is created during system development, it is critical to keep the maintainer in mind. Typically, the maintainer is not a member of the development team and is not present at project meetings. He or she therefore depends heavily on the documentation. Further, because it is so expensive, maintenance is a prime target for cost savings.

2.2.3 Triple-purpose documents

We have described the problems associated with producing different sets of documentation for each development phase. To avoid these problems, we use triple-purpose documents: a *single* set of documents for design, implementation, and maintenance.

Initially, these documents are the focus of the design effort. They record design decisions independently of the implementation and serve as the basis for design reviews, revealing many errors before implementation. During implementation the same documents support parallel development, telling users what they can expect, telling implementors what must be done, and serving as the basis for correctness during testing. During maintenance the documents are used again. They support analysis of change requests, provide a structure in which to record changes, and aid in training new staff.

With the same documents used in design, implementation, and maintenance, less documentation is required. Further, this approach supplies the repeated use needed to discover errors and to motivate their removal.

2.2.4 Summary

Industrial documentation suffers from problems so serious that programmers rely almost exclusively on the code. To remedy these problems, the documents must be designed as carefully as the code they support. The same set of documents must be used for design, implementation, and maintenance.

Our design methodology is based on the central role of documentation. It is, in some ways, more important than the code. Discard the code and keep the documents, and you can recreate the code quickly and capably. Discard the

Table 2.1   *stack* interface syntax

Routine name	Inputs	Outputs	Exceptions
s_init			
s_push	*integer*		full
s_pop			empty
g_top		*integer*	empty
g_depth		*integer*	

documents and keep the code, and the resulting system will be hard to control and expensive to maintain.

2.3   Work Products

Our design method is based on seven *work products*: a generic term for deliverables, including documentation, code, and data files. We begin by defining the essential terms, and then describe the work products.

2.3.1   Terminology

We define a *module* as a programming work assignment and a *module interface* (hereafter just *interface*) as the set of assumptions that programmers using the module are permitted to make about its behavior. We view a module as a black box, accessible only through a fixed set of *access routines*. We divide the access routines into three groups: (1) *set* routines that modify the internal module state, (2) *get* routines that return values computed from the module state, without modifying it, and (3) *set-get* routines that do both. Intuitively, set routines correspond to pure procedures, get routines to pure functions, and set-get routines to functions with side effects. In access routine names, we use the prefix s_ to indicate set access routines, g_ to indicate get routines, and sg_ to indicate set-get routines.

Under certain circumstances, an access routine call may be illegal: issuing the call will generate an *exception*. The module implementation is required to *detect* the occurrence of an illegal call and to *signal* the module user that the associated exception has occurred. These ideas are illustrated on a *stack* module (see Table 2.1), providing a pushdown integer stack with a maximum of MAXSIZ elements. The module behaves as follows: s_init initializes the stack, with no elements. s_push(i) pushes i onto the stack, signaling the exception full if the stack contains MAXSIZ elements. g_top returns the value of the top stack element and s_pop discards this element; both calls signal empty if the stack has no elements. g_depth returns the number of elements in the stack.

2.3.2 Work product definitions

The seven work products are described below in the order in which they would be developed under ideal circumstances. Here the descriptions are brief; each work product is described and illustrated in detail in Part II.

1. *Requirements Specification*: describes the required behavior of an application program in terms of its observable inputs and outputs. Both normal and abnormal behavior are specified. To reduce maintenance costs, expected changes in the system's required behavior and environment are recorded. Since most systems are too large to be implemented by a single person, the development task is decomposed into modules.

2. *Module Guide*: describes and motivates the module decomposition. For each module, the Module Guide provides two items: (1) a sketch of the service offered by the module and (2) a description of the expected changes that might impact the module.

3. *Module Interface Specification*: precisely describes the services that each module provides. Interface specifications are *black box*; that is, no mention is made of internal data structures and algorithms.

4. *Module Internal Design*: specifies the internal data structures, or *module state*, in the syntax of the implementation programming language. The effect of each access routine is also specified, in terms of the module state.

5. *Module Implementation*: the production source code and the build procedures.

6. *Test Plan*: describes the strategy used for selecting test cases, for executing the tests, and for checking the output for correctness.

7. *Test Implementation*: consists of the source code, data files, and manual procedures required for testing. We make heavy use of scaffolding so that modules can be tested in isolation. Where practical, tests are automated so that they can be repeated cheaply and accurately.

The work products are summarized in Figure 2.1. In terms of the lifecycle described in Section 1.3, the Module Guide is an architectural design work product and the Module Interface Specification and Module Internal Design are detailed design work products.

A given system will consist of multiple instances of each of these work products. Typically one or more Requirements Specifications and one Module Guide are developed per system, and one Module Interface Specification, Module Internal Design, Module Implementation, Test Plan, and Test Implementation are required for each module. A Test Plan and Test Implementation are also required for system testing. For example, the SHAM System has two Requirements Specifications, one Module Guide, nine instances of work products 3–5,

1. Requirements Specification
   Specification of the required system behavior.
2. Module Guide
   Description of and motivation for the module decomposition.
3. Module Interface Specification
   Specification of the required behavior of each module.
4. Module Internal Design
   Specification of the module internal data structures.
5. Module Implementation
   Production source code.
6. Test Plan
   Strategy for selecting and executing tests.
7. Test Implementation
   Source code, data files, and manual procedures required for testing.

Figure 2.1   Work product summary

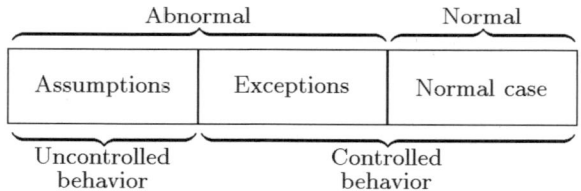

Figure 2.2   The specification trichotomy

and ten instances of work products 6 and 7. Note that only one of the seven work products—the Module Implementation—is delivered code; the others are, in fact, overhead. While so much overhead may seem disturbing, it is needed to control software development and maintenance.

2.3.3   The specification trichotomy

In specification work products, it is important to distinguish between normal and abnormal situations. A key step is establishing the *specification trichotomy*, a division of the possible situations into (1) implementor's assumptions, (2) exceptions, and (3) normal cases. The assumptions describe the abnormal situations that the implementation need not handle and the exceptions describe the abnormal situations that must be detected and signaled; the remaining cases are considered normal. The specification trichotomy is illustrated graphically in Figure 2.2.

When developing specifications, we begin by deciding which situations will be normal and which will be abnormal. There are two main reasons to consider a user request abnormal:

1. *Inherently illegal requests.* The request is inherently illegal or undefined. For example, a call to *g_top* when the stack is empty is an inherently illegal request.

2. *Resource limitations.* The request cannot be satisfied due to resource limitations. For example, a call to *s_push* is illegal if there is no more memory available.

Once the normal/abnormal division has been established, we must subdivide the abnormal cases into implementor's assumptions and exceptions. Assumptions arise for two main reasons:

1. *Undetectable violations.* The request is illegal, but not in a way that the implementor can detect. For example, when a pointer is passed as a function parameter, there may be no way to determine whether the pointer value is a legal address.

2. *Cost considerations.* The illegality is detectable, but the cost of detection is too high. For example, checks for illegal array subscripts are usually omitted from production code for performance reasons.

In SHAM, we take a conservative approach, preferring exceptions to implementor's assumptions when exception detection is feasible.

It is important to realize that establishing the specification trichotomy involves making influential decisions. For example, deciding that a given case should be considered normal may make the software more useful but may also significantly increase development cost or degrade performance.

2.4 Verification

Verification is the task of showing that a work product is free from errors. For example, we may verify that a system meets its Requirements Specification or that a Module Implementation obeys an indenting convention. The work product criteria define the required characteristics of each work product and thus determine what constitutes an error. Systematic verification is critical in software engineering, to reveal errors and to enforce adherence to standards. Without verification, errors will be numerous, and standards will be ignored.

There are substantial benefits to discovering errors as early as possible. Generally speaking, the later an error is discovered the more the cost to fix it. Suppose, for example, that the Requirements Specification has an error. If it is revealed while verifying the specification, only the specification must be changed. However, if the error is discovered during system testing, design and code changes are frequently needed as well.

It is useful to divide errors into two classes. A *failure* is the occurrence of incorrect system behavior, that is, an incorrect output. A *fault* is an error in the work product itself. There are two complementary approaches to verification, distinguished by the errors revealed and the techniques applied. *Inspection* is designed to find faults through human review. *Testing* is designed to find failures using program execution.

2.4.1   Inspection

Software inspections are based on peer review by small teams and have been widely used in industry with impressive success. For example, over 2.5 million lines of code have been inspected at Bell-Northern Research (BNR), a Canadian developer of telephone switching equipment [35]. On average, one fault was found per person-hour invested. While this may seem expensive, inspection was two to four times as effective as testing. Further, it cost BNR an average of 4.5 person-days to fix a fault discovered after installation in the field. Clearly, early fault discovery pays off.

The inspection process is structured: roles are assigned to each team member and specific steps are followed. The *moderator* plays the most important role, controlling all meetings and ensuring that the conduct is professional and the criticism constructive. The *reader* paraphrases the work product line by line, attempting to convince the inspection team that it is fault-free. The *recorder* produces a written record of the faults found. The remaining team members are the *inspectors*; they listen, seeking faults in the work product or in the reader's paraphrasing. Inspection teams are small, typically consisting of three to five people. Usually the reader is *not* the author of the work product; the author tends to paraphrase too quickly. Also, having a non-author as reader helps ensure that the work product will be comprehensible.

The inspection process consists of five steps:

1. *Overview meeting.* This brief meeting provides an overview of the work product and its context. Copies of the work product are distributed to all team members.

2. *Preparation.* Each team member studies the work product.

3. *Inspection meeting.* The reader paraphrases the work product, line by line. Questions from the inspectors are pursued only until a fault has been identified. In this meeting, there is no discussion of who is to blame for the fault or of how the fault will be removed. Normally inspection meetings do not exceed two hours in length, due to the intense concentration required.

4. *Rework.* The faults discovered in the inspection meeting are removed by the author.

5. *Follow-up.* The moderator ensures that the rework has been completed. If many changes were made, the moderator normally requires reinspection of the entire work product.

Our inspections are proof-based in the following sense: For each work product, we establish a specific set of criteria. In an inspection meeting, the reader is obliged to show that the work product satisfies the criteria. In many cases this obligation is best accomplished with a "proof"—a logical argument that the work product has the required characteristics. For example, when inspecting a Requirements Specification, the reader must show that the specification is complete; every input has been considered and dealt with. Typically, the proof is presented informally, in the style normally used for communication between programmers. The proof orientation of our inspections has a substantial impact on work product design; the documents are structured to make the inspection-meeting proofs as simple as possible.

In summary, inspection is a systematic approach for fault detection. The primary benefits are early fault discovery—because specifications as well as code can be inspected—and feedback to developers on error-prone habits. Inspection is also an effective educational technique; new staff members can learn programming techniques and documentation standards by attending inspection meetings.

2.4.2 Testing

According to Dijkstra "Program testing can be used to show the presence of bugs, but never their absence" [36]. As a consequence, testing alone cannot provide much confidence. Testing is, however, quite valuable as an independent check on code that has been carefully designed and inspected.

For software testing, we adapt two important concepts from hardware testing. *Controllability* refers to the ease with which an arbitrary input may be applied to a system or module. *Observability* refers to the ease with which the output may be observed.

Test scaffolding is code whose purpose is testing the production system or its components. Consider a module M. A *driver* is test code written to call access routines provided by M. A *stub* is test code that serves as a substitute for an access routine called by M.

There are three principles underlying effective and affordable testing.

1. *Building and maintaining test suites.* Often tests are developed during or after implementation and are discarded after acceptance. It is important to plan testing early in development, so that testability can be used to influence system design, and to deliver and maintain tests along with the production code. A system should not be considered complete until both production code and test code are complete. Without testing in place, the system may appear finished, but it is a maintenance problem in disguise.

2. *Isolating the module under test.* It is typically difficult to thoroughly test a module M while it is installed in a production system. M's access routines are often not directly accessible. If M is a general-purpose module, some of its access routines may not be called at all in a particular production system. Errors in other modules may appear to be errors in M. Conversely, errors in M may be masked by errors in other modules. In short, when M is running in its production environment, controllability and observability are often poor. Using test scaffolding, M may be tested in isolation from the production environment. In practice, modules are best tested with a mixture of scaffolding and production code; the critical tradeoff is between the benefits realized through isolation and the cost of developing and maintaining the scaffolding.

3. *Applying design for testability.* While stubs and drivers can improve controllability and observability, the module decomposition and the module interfaces also have a significant effect on testability. In VLSI design, interchip communication is extremely expensive, and so it is minimized. In software, there is no such physical limitation. For example, there is no time or space cost in communication through global variables. Yet, experience has shown that uncontrolled module interactions significantly increase test cost. Like poor performance, poor testability must be viewed as a design weakness.

2.4.3   Inspection versus testing

Testing and inspection closely complement each other: the advantages of one are the disadvantages of the other. Testing operates by examination of run-time behavior and has two principal advantages:

1. Much of the testing task can be automated. While test development is largely manual, tests can often be run with minimal labor cost.

2. The results are guaranteed, in the sense that they come from actual execution of production code.

Testing has three main disadvantages:

1. The results are specific, applying only to program behavior on the test inputs. Because there is normally an extremely large number of possible inputs, most are never tested.

2. When failures are found, they are symptoms. Debugging is needed to locate the fault in the program source, and the debugging is expensive.

3. Testing can be applied only to executable work products.

The primary advantages of inspections are:

Table 2.2   Testing versus inspection

	Testing	Inspection	
Pro	Many tasks are automatable. Results are guaranteed.	Automation is difficult. Results are suspect.	Con
Con	Results are specific. Debugging is still required. Executable work products only.	Results are general. No debugging is required. Executability not required.	Pro

1. The results are general, often applying to all inputs.

2. The errors found are faults in the work product itself. No debugging is needed to trace from the failure to the fault.

3. Any work product can be inspected; executability is not a requirement.

The primary disadvantages are:

1. Significant benefits from automation are unlikely, at least in the near term.

2. The results are questionable, because inspection of complex code is itself complex and, therefore, error-prone.

The dual nature of testing and inspection is summarized in Table 2.2.

2.5   Estimation

Because multi-version, multi-person software projects are so expensive and because the software industry is so competitive, accurate cost estimates are extremely important.

2.5.1   Estimating concepts

Estimating the cost of a complex task typically requires three steps:

1. Break the task into subtasks. Estimates are best done on relatively small subtasks, so the subtasks may themselves need to be broken down.

2. Provide a cost estimate for each subtask. Important costs to consider include person-hours, calendar time, and machine resources.

3. Generate the task cost by summing the subtask costs.

Initially, the estimates will be mere guesses, and significant cost overruns will be common. (Schedule pressure makes overestimates rare.) There are three ways of achieving more accurate estimates:

1. Sketch—partially solve—the task until you have a good understanding of the work remaining. Generally, more detailed sketches produce more accurate estimates.

2. Base your estimate on actual cost figures from a similar, previous project. Obviously, this approach depends on the availability of cost figures from past projects. Thus, it pays to record actual costs carefully.

3. Practice. With experience, the accuracy of your estimates will improve substantially.

2.5.2   Software estimating

Estimates are frequently demanded as part of the requirements analysis phase and rightly so. Unfortunately, an accurate estimate is difficult to produce at this time. With a good requirements specification, much better estimates are possible; while much is still unknown, the developer's obligation is precisely and completely defined. The module decomposition step is critical for the estimator as well as for the developer; it identifies the modules and their services. Then, for each module M, five subtasks are immediate: the development of M's interface specification, internal design, implementation, test plan, and test implementation. Frequently, these tasks are small enough to be estimated directly. Of course, errors in the module decomposition may cause serious errors in the estimate.

During maintenance, estimating is often simpler because the existing work products suggest much of the task breakdown. For example, given a change request, the following steps can be used:

- Sketch the changes to the requirements specification and review these with the user to be sure that the request is well understood.

- Determine the modules affected by the change. The module guide is specifically designed to make this task as easy as possible.

- For each affected module, review the five work products associated with that module and estimate the change cost for each.

In summary, during both new development and maintenance, a disciplined work product structure significantly eases the estimator's task.

2.6   Summary

We discuss the central role of documentation in Software Engineering above, and we describe the severe problems resulting from current approaches to documentation. The importance of human-readable system descriptions is emphasized. We argue for triple-purpose documents, for design, implementation, and maintenance and introduce the seven work products used in this text. We discuss verification, using the complementary techniques of inspection and testing. Specification documents play a key role here: without them there is no basis for correctness. Finally, we present a simple procedure for estimating and show how the seven work products support accurate estimates during development and maintenance. In the next chapter, we consider the mathematical concepts underlying the seven work products.

2.7 Bibliographic Notes

Our approach to software design and documentation owes much to the writings [1, 8, 37] and lectures of David Parnas, and to others who have applied Parnas's methods [2, 38, 39]. Royce [40] and Boehm [27] describe alternative software development lifecycles.

Software inspection was developed by Fagan [41] and widely applied in industry by Russell [35] and many others. Our inspection strategy was heavily influenced by Harlan Mills; we use his characterization of "proof" and his common-sense approach to the use of mathematical notation in proofs [3]. Dyer [4] describes a similar approach to proofs in inspection meetings. Jackson and Hoffman present the results of an industrial experiment in proof-based inspection of Module Interface Specifications [39].

Among the many books on software testing, the practical text by Myers [42] is perhaps the best known. Howden [43] presents the theoretical foundations for many testing techniques.

Chapter 3

Mathematical Fundamentals

The power of a formal notation should manifest itself in the achievements we could never do without it. [E. W. Dijkstra]

3.1 Introduction

The purpose of this chapter is to supply the mathematics needed to read, write, and verify the work products introduced in Chapter 2. We focus on *specification functions*: functions that arise naturally in software specifications. For specification functions, the best known description is large and complex. Typically, this description is not a monolithic formula but instead a collection of simple formulas each applicable to a different situation. Frequently, specifying the different situations takes as much effort as specifying the behavior required in each situation. Thus, the task of partitioning the function domain strongly influences the specification effort, the choice of notation, and the verification arguments. The mathematics is simple and familiar; only the function representation is new.

Section 3.2 defines functions in terms of sets and relations. Section 3.3 presents logic, the language of conditions. Logic plays a critical role in partitioning the domain of a specification function. Section 3.4 presents a simple type scheme for defining structured objects: sets, sequences, and tuples. Sections 3.5 and 3.6 describe the multiple assignment statement and conditional rules, programming-language-like constructs with simple functional semantics. Section 3.7 introduces Finite State Machines (FSMs), a powerful specification construct defined in terms of sets and functions. Section 3.8 presents Module State Machines (MSMs), a special kind of FSM designed for specifying software modules.

To make the text reasonably self-contained, we have included an introduction to sets, relations, and logic in this chapter. Most of this material can be found in any textbook on discrete mathematics, such as Piff [44]. Similarly, we use standard notations for representing sets, sequences, and tuples. The reader already familiar with this material can skip over the first few sections of this chapter and read only Sections 3.5, 3.6, 3.7, and 3.8.

3.2   Functions

3.2.1   Sets

A *set* is an unordered collection of elements. The distinguishing characteristics of a set are that the number of occurrences as well as the order of the elements are not defined; an element either belongs to a set or it does not. When an element x belongs to a set S, we write $x \in S$, and when it does not, we write $x \notin S$.

There are several ways to define a set. We can enumerate the elements in the set: $\{x_1, x_2, \ldots, x_n\}$ denotes the set with elements $x_1, x_2, \ldots, x_n$ where $n \geq 0$. We can use a logical condition: $\{x \mid p(x)\}$ denotes the set of all elements x that satisfy $p(x)$. For example, $\{4, 2, 1, 3\}$ and

$$\{x \mid x \text{ is an integer between 1 and 4 inclusive}\}$$

denote the same set. A third way to define a set is with an integer range of the form $[i..j]$, which denotes the set $\{x \mid x \text{ is an integer and } x \geq i \text{ and } x \leq j\}$. For example, $[2..4] = \{2, 3, 4\}$ and $[7..4] = \{\}$.

3.2.2   Relations

A *binary relation* is a set of ordered pairs. In this text, the only type of relations we consider are binary relations. For a relation R, the *domain* of R is the set of all values appearing as the first component of an element in R. The *range* of R is the set of the second components. If we let $\langle x, y \rangle$ denote an ordered pair, then the domain of a relation R is $\{x \mid \langle x, y \rangle \in R\}$, and the range is $\{y \mid \langle x, y \rangle \in R\}$.

Since a relation is a set, we can define it in the same way as we did with sets. For example, $\{\langle 0, 1 \rangle, \langle 0, 2 \rangle, \langle 2, 3 \rangle\}$ is a relation with domain $\{0, 2\}$ and range $\{1, 2, 3\}$. When a relation contains an infinite number of elements, we can no longer enumerate the elements, but we can define the relation with a rule. For example,

$$\{\langle x, y \rangle \mid x \text{ and } y \text{ are integers and } x < y\}$$

defines the familiar *less-than* relation. In this case, both the domain and the range consist of the set of integers.

3.2.3 Functions

A *function* is a relation in which each element in the domain appears exactly once as the first component of an ordered pair in the relation. Since a function is a relation, we can define a function in the same way as a relation. We can enumerate the elements; for example, $\{\langle 0, 1\rangle, \langle 1, 2\rangle, \langle 2, 3\rangle\}$ is a function. However, not all relations are functions: $\{\langle 0, 1\rangle, \langle 0, 2\rangle, \langle 1, 2\rangle\}$ is not, because 0 is the first component of both $\langle 0, 1\rangle$ and $\langle 0, 2\rangle$. We can also define a function with a rule. For example,

$$\{\langle x, y\rangle \mid x \text{ is an integer and } y = x^2\}$$

is a function. On the other hand,

$$\{\langle x, y\rangle \mid y \text{ is an integer and } y^2 = x\}$$

is not a function, because both $\langle 4, 2\rangle$ and $\langle 4, -2\rangle$ are in this set.

A function associates each element of the domain with a unique element of the range. For function f, we often write $f(a) = b$ when $\langle a, b\rangle \in f$ and say that b is the *output* of the function f for the *input* a. Thus, for

$$f = \{\langle x, y\rangle \mid x \text{ is an integer and } y = x^2\}$$

we have $f(0) = 0$ and $f(2) = 4$. Using this notation, we can define a function by giving a rule that computes the value for each of the inputs. For example, we can define f by the rule $f(x) = x^2$.

When we define a function by a rule, the domain and range of the function may not be clear. For example, the function f defined by $f(x) = x^2$ could be defined over the natural numbers, the real numbers, etc. To reduce ambiguity, we introduce a notation to restrict the domain and range. The expression

$$f : T_1 \to T_2$$

states that the domain of f is a subset of T_1 and the range of f is a subset of T_2. For example, the expressions

$$f : integer \to integer \text{ and } f(x) = x^2$$

define the integer square function; the domain of f is the integers and the range is the set of non-negative integers.

Functions can have more than one input or output. This does not violate our original definition: each function is a set of ordered pairs. It means that one or both of the components of the ordered pair can be a composite object, such as another ordered pair. Many common mathematical functions have more than one input. For example, the addition function over the integers is defined by

$$\{\langle\langle x_1, x_2\rangle, y\rangle \mid x_1 \text{ and } x_2 \text{ are integers and } y = x_1 + x_2\}$$

Table 3.1   Truth table for the logical connectives

p	q	$\neg p$	$p \wedge q$	$p \vee q$	$p \to q$	$p \leftrightarrow q$
true	true	false	true	true	true	true
true	false	false	false	true	false	false
false	true	true	false	true	true	false
false	false	true	false	false	true	true

A clockwise rotation by $\pi/2$ radians of a point in two-dimensional Euclidean space can be defined by the function

$$\{\langle \langle x_1, y_1 \rangle, \langle x_2, y_2 \rangle \rangle \mid x_1, y_1, x_2, \text{ and } y_2 \text{ are integers and } x_2 = y_1 \text{ and } y_2 = -x_1\}$$

This function takes a pair of numbers as input, and produces a pair of numbers as output.

Some functions have as output a truth value. Consider the function

$$\{\langle x, y \rangle \mid x \text{ is an integer and } y = (x > 0)\}$$

Some pairs belonging to this function are $\langle 0, false \rangle$, $\langle -1, false \rangle$, and $\langle 1, true \rangle$. As another example, consider the function *not*: $\{\langle true, false \rangle, \langle false, true \rangle\}$.

3.3   Logic

3.3.1   Logical expressions

A *logical expression* is a statement whose truth can be determined. An example of such a statement is $5 < 7$. Each logical expression has a *truth value* associated with it: either *true* or *false*. For example, the truth value of $5 < 7$ is *true* and that of $7 < 5$ is *false*.

True and *false* are the simplest types of logical expressions. We can form more complex expressions from simpler ones by using the standard *logical connectives*: $\neg, \wedge, \vee, \to$, and $\leftrightarrow$. The *truth table* in Table 3.1 defines the meaning of these logical connectives. There is a row in the truth table for each assignment of truth values to p and q. The columns of the truth table define the truth values for each of the logical connectives, given the truth values for p and q. For example, since both $7 < 5$ and $2 + 2 = 5$ are *false*, the truth value of $((7 < 5) \to (2 + 2 = 5))$ is *true*, as is indicated by the last entry under $p \to q$.

With logical expressions, we can make the definition of sets, relations, and functions more precise and compact. For example, we can define the set $[1..10]$ by the expression

$$\{x \mid x \text{ is an integer and } (x \geq 1) \wedge (x \leq 10)\}$$

Table 3.2 Truth table for $\neg(\neg p \vee \neg q)$

p	q	$\neg p$	$\neg q$	$\neg p \vee \neg q$	$\neg(\neg p \vee \neg q)$
true	*true*	*false*	*false*	*false*	*true*
true	*false*	*false*	*true*	*true*	*false*
false	*true*	*true*	*false*	*true*	*false*
false	*false*	*true*	*true*	*true*	*false*

Although the expression

$$\{x \mid x \text{ is an integer and } (x \geq 1) \vee (x \leq 10)\}$$

is similar, it defines quite a different set: the set of all integers.

So far we have been careful with the placement of parentheses in logical expressions. To avoid an abundance of parentheses, we define a *precedence* on the logical connectives. The order of precedence, in decreasing order, is: $\neg$, $\wedge$, $\vee$, $\rightarrow$, and $\leftrightarrow$. Sequences with the same logical connective are evaluated left to right. Thus $p \wedge q \vee r \wedge s$ represents $(p \wedge q) \vee (r \wedge s)$, and $p \wedge q \wedge r$ represents $(p \wedge q) \wedge r$.

Consider the expression $\neg(\neg p \vee \neg q)$. Given any pair of truth values for p and q, we can calculate the truth value for the entire expression: replace p and q by their truth values, and simplify the expression with the rules from the truth table. We can do this for all pairs of truth values for p and q, and summarize this information in the truth table shown in Table 3.2. Each column contains the truth values of a subexpression, with the final column representing the truth value of the expression itself. Note that the entries in the last column are the same as for $p \wedge q$. This means that $\neg(\neg p \vee \neg q)$ and $p \wedge q$ are *logically equivalent*.

3.3.2 Quantifiers

In software engineering, we rely heavily on the use of variables, and we often need to use variables inside logical expressions. Once we introduce variables, we have to concern ourselves with the *type* of a variable. Although variable types is the subject of Section 3.4, we need to briefly discuss it here. One problem that arises is that the expression $5 < x$ is not defined for all values of x; for example, it is not defined when x is the color red. To circumvent this problem, we associate with each variable a *type*: a set of values from which the variable can take its values. In many cases, the type of a variable is clear from the context. When it is not, the type needs to be stated explicitly.

Once we introduce variables, it is useful to *quantify* a logical expression over a given variable. We therefore introduce the *universal quantifier* $\forall$ and the *existential quantifier* $\exists$ as shown in Table 3.3. In this table, the set S denotes the type of the variable x. When the type of a variable is clear from its context

Table 3.3   Quantifiers

Quantifier	Meaning
$(\forall x \in S)(p(x))$	for all $x \in S$, $p(x)$ is *true*
$(\exists x \in S)(p(x))$	there exists an $x \in S$ such that $p(x)$ is *true*

we can omit the set S and abbreviate the quantified statements as $(\forall x)(p(x))$ or $(\exists x)(p(x))$. When we want to quantify over more than one variable it is convenient to group these variables together. For example, we use $(\forall x, y \in S)(p(x, y))$ as a shorthand for $(\forall x \in S)((\forall y \in S)(p(x, y)))$.

The expression $(\exists x \in S)(p(x))$ is *true* if and only if there exists a value v of type S such that $p(v)$ is *true*. The expression $(\forall x)(p(x))$ is *true* if and only if $p(v)$ is *true* for all values v of type S. For example, $(\exists x \in$ integers$)(x < 7)$ is *true*, because there exists an integer x (e.g., 5) such that $x < 7$. The expression $(\forall x \in$ integers$)(x < 7)$ is *false*, because $x < 7$ does not hold when, for example, $x = 9$.

We can also nest quantifiers. Thus, if x and y are both integers, then $(\forall x)(\exists y)(y < x)$ is *true*. If they are both natural numbers, then the expression is *false*, since there is no natural number smaller than 0. On the other hand, $(\exists x)(\forall y)(x \leq y)$ is *true* for the natural numbers, but *false* for the integers. Another example of a nested quantified statement is the definition of the limit of a function: $\lim_{x \to x_0} f(x) = L$ is defined as

$$(\forall \epsilon \in \text{positive reals})(\exists \delta \in \text{reals})(|x - x_0| < \delta \to |f(x) - L| < \epsilon)$$

where $|x|$ denotes the absolute value of x.

Two remarks about variables in quantified statements: first, the truth value of a quantified statement is independent of the name of the variable used in the quantifier. In other words, just as in many programming languages, variables are merely place holders. Second, the scope of a variable in a quantified expression extends only to the smallest subexpression following it. Parentheses may be used to extend that scope. Thus, $(\forall x \in S)p(x) \wedge q(x)$ and $(\forall x \in S)(p(x) \wedge q(x))$ are not logically equivalent. The first one is equivalent to $(\forall y \in S)p(y) \wedge q(x)$. Performing a similar renaming for the second expression produces $(\forall y \in S)(p(y) \wedge q(y))$.

A variable is *bound* in an expression if it appears in the scope of a quantifier. A variable is *free* if it is not bound to any quantifier. For example, in $(\forall y \in S) \, p(y) \wedge q(x)$, the variable y is bound, and x is free. Strictly speaking, we can only talk about the occurrence of a variable being bound or free. For example, in $(\forall x \in S) \, p(x) \wedge q(x)$, the first occurrence of x is bound, and the second one is free.

When an expression contains a free variable, we often cannot determine the truth value of that expression. For example, we cannot determine if $x < 7$ is *true* or *false*, without knowing a value for x. If a logical expression contains no free variables, then its truth value is defined. We have already determined that $(\forall x \in \text{integers})(x < 7)$ is *false* and that $(\exists x \in \text{integers})(x < 7)$ is *true*.

3.4 Types

In this section, we define precisely what we mean by a "type" and we introduce the types and operations that are used in this text. Many other types and operations are possible.

3.4.1 Defining types

A *type* is a set of values—any precisely defined set is a type. We distinguish *primitive types* and *user-defined types*. The primitive types are *integer*, *boolean*, *char* (character), and *string*. To define a user-defined type, the set of values belonging to the type has to be given. A convenient way of defining new types is with *type constructors*, which allow us to build more complex types from simpler ones. The type constructors that are used in this text are *set*, *sequence*, and *tuple*.

If T is a type, then

$$x_1, x_2, \ldots, x_n : T$$

specifies that variables $x_1, x_2, \ldots, x_n$ are of type T where $n \geq 1$. For example, the statements

$$x: integer$$
$$a, b, c : string$$

define the integer variable x and the string variables a, b, and c.

To define a user-defined type, we use a *type definition*, which is of the form

$$T = d$$

where T is the name of the new type, and d is its definition. For example,

$$color = \{red, white, blue\}$$

defines the new type *color* as the set $\{red, white, blue\}$. We can now declare variables of type *color*. For example,

$$x : color$$

defines a variable x of this type.

Table 3.4   Operations on *integer*

Operation	Meaning
$+, -, \times, /$	addition, subtraction, multiplication, integer division
$=, \neq$	equal, not equal
$<, \leq, \geq, >$	less than, less than or equal, greater than or equal, greater than

Table 3.5   Operations on *strings* (s, s_1, and s_2 are strings)

Operation	Meaning
$s[i..j]$	substring of s from position i to position j
$s_1 \parallel s_2$	concatenation of s_1 and s_2
$=, \neq$	equal, not equal
$\in, \notin$	member, non-member
$s[i]$	i-th character of s
$\mid s \mid$	length of s

3.4.2   Primitive types

The *integer* type is the infinite set $\{\ldots, -2, -1, 0, 1, 2, \ldots\}$. The operations on integer variables are shown in Table 3.4.

The *boolean* type is the set $\{true, false\}$. The operations on boolean variables are the logical connectives shown in Table 3.1.

The *char* type consists of the set of ASCII characters. To represent a character constant, we enclose it in single quotes. The only operations on character variables are equality ($=$) and inequality ($\neq$).

The *string* type consists of all finite sequences of characters. To represent a string constant, we enclose it in double quotes. For example, "" is the empty string and "abc" contains the characters 'a', 'b', and 'c'. The operations on string variables are shown in Table 3.5. Positions in strings are zero-relative. For the substring operation, if $i > j$, then $s[i..j]$ is defined as the empty string.

For example, if $x =$ "abcd" and $y =$ "ef", then

$$x[0..3] = \text{"abcd"} \qquad x[3..3] = \text{"d"} \qquad x[3..1] = \text{""}$$
$$x \parallel y = \text{"abcdef"} \qquad y \parallel x = \text{"efabcd"}$$
$$\text{'c'} \in x \qquad \text{'c'} \notin y$$
$$x[0] = \text{'a'} \qquad x[3] = \text{'d'}$$
$$\mid x \mid = 4 \qquad \mid x[1..2] \mid = 2 \qquad \mid y \mid = 2$$

3.4.3   Sets

A *set* is an unordered collection of elements of the same type. To declare a set of type T, we use the expression *set of T*.

Table 3.6   Operations on *sets*

Operation	Meaning
$\cup, \cap, -, \times$	union, intersection, difference, Cartesian product
$=, \neq$	equal, not equal
$\in, \notin$	member, non-member
$\lvert s \rvert$	size of set s

We have already seen various ways to define sets. We can enumerate the elements in the set: $\{x_1, x_2, \ldots, x_n\}$ denotes the set with elements $x_1, x_2, \ldots, x_n$, where $n \geq 0$. We can use a logical expression: $\{x \mid p(x)\}$ denotes the set of elements x that satisfy $p(x)$. And we can define a set with an integer range of the form $[i..j]$, which denotes the set $\{x \mid x \in integer \wedge x \geq i \wedge x \leq j\}$.

For example,

$$T = set \; of \; \{red, green, blue\}$$

defines the type T as the power set (the set of all subsets) of $\{red, green, blue\}$. Three possible values for variables of type T are $\{\}$, $\{red\}$, and $\{red, blue\}$. The declaration

$$x : set \; of \; integer$$

defines the variable x as a set of integers. Among the possible values for x are $\{\}$ and $\{1, 3, 5, 7, 9\}$.

The operations on set variables are shown in Table 3.6. For sets a and b, set union, intersection, difference, and Cartesian product are defined as follows.

$$
\begin{aligned}
a \cup b &= \{x \mid x \in a \vee x \in b\} \\
a \cap b &= \{x \mid x \in a \wedge x \in b\} \\
a - b &= \{x \mid x \in a \wedge x \notin b\} \\
a \times b &= \{\langle x, y \rangle \mid x \in a \wedge y \in b\}
\end{aligned}
$$

For example, if $a = \{1, 2, 3\}$ and $b = \{2, 3\}$, then

$$
\begin{aligned}
a \cup b = b \cup a &= \{1, 2, 3\} \\
a \cap b = b \cap a &= \{2, 3\} \\
a - b &= \{1\} \qquad\qquad\qquad b - a = \{\} \\
a \times b &= \{\langle 1, 2 \rangle, \langle 1, 3 \rangle, \langle 2, 2 \rangle, \langle 2, 3 \rangle, \langle 3, 2 \rangle, \langle 3, 3 \rangle\} \\
1 &\in a \qquad\qquad\qquad\qquad\;\; 1 \notin b \\
\lvert a \rvert &= 3 \qquad\qquad\qquad\qquad\;\; \lvert b \rvert = 2
\end{aligned}
$$

3.4.4   Sequences

A *sequence* is an ordered collection of elements of the same type. Since the elements of a sequence are ordered, an element can occur more than once in a sequence. A sequence is sometimes referred to as a *list*, and it is similar to the *array* used in many programming languages. To declare a sequence of type T, we use the expression *sequence of* T.

We use an expression of the form $\langle x_0, x_1, \ldots, x_n \rangle$ where $n \geq 0$ to represent the sequence with elements $x_0, x_1, \ldots, x_n$. Thus, $\langle \rangle$ represents the empty sequence and $\langle 1, 3, 5 \rangle$ represents a sequence with three elements. The positions in a sequence are zero-relative. For example, the element in position 1 in list $\langle 1, 3, 5 \rangle$ is 3, and 1 is the element in position 0.

The declaration

$$T = sequence\ of\ \{red, green, blue\}$$

defines the type T as the set of all sequences of elements from $\{red, green, blue\}$. Three possible values for variables of type T are $\langle \rangle$, $\langle red \rangle$, and $\langle red, blue, red \rangle$. The declaration

$$x : sequence\ of\ integer$$

defines the variable x as a sequence of integers. Among the possible values for x are $\langle \rangle$ and $\langle 1, 3, 1, 3, 1 \rangle$.

The definitions above are for variable-length sequences. To define a fixed-length sequence of type T with length l, we use the expression *sequence* $[l]$ *of* T, where l is a positive integer. Similarly, fixed-size arrays of arbitrary dimensions can be defined by expressions of the form

$$sequence\ [l_1, l_2, \ldots, l_n]\ of\ T$$

which is shorthand for

$$sequence\ [l_1]\ of\ sequence\ [l_2]\ of\ \ldots\ sequence\ [l_n]\ of\ T$$

The operations on sequences are shown in Table 3.7.   If $a = \langle 1, 2, 3, 4 \rangle$ and $b = \langle 5, 3 \rangle$, then

$$
\begin{array}{lll}
a[0..3] = \langle 1,2,3,4 \rangle & a[3..3] = \langle 4 \rangle & a[3..1] = \langle \rangle \\
a \parallel b = \langle 1,2,3,4,5,6 \rangle & b \parallel a = \langle 5,6,1,2,3,4 \rangle & \\
3 \in x & 3 \notin y & \\
a[0] = 1 & a[3] = 4 & \\
|a| = 4 & |a[1..2]| = 2 & |b| = 2
\end{array}
$$

Note that the operations on sequences are the same as the operations on strings. This is not surprising, since a string is a sequence of characters.

We have seen that sequences and strings have many things in common. They also have a common problem. The operations $s[i]$ and $s[i..j]$ on strings and

Table 3.7   Operations on *sequences* (s, s_1, and s_2 are sequences)

Operation	Meaning
$s[i..j]$	subsequence of s from position i to position j
$s_1 \parallel s_2$	concatenation of s_1 and s_2
$=, \neq$	equal, not equal
$\in, \notin$	member, non-member
$s[i]$	i-th element of s
$|s|$	length of s

sequences are not always defined. For example, for any string or sequence s, the value $s[-1]$ is undefined. Similarly, if $|s| = 2$, then $s[2]$ is undefined. In general, $s[i]$ is undefined if $i \notin [0..|s|-1]$; $s[i..j]$ is undefined if $i \notin [0..|s|-1] \vee j \notin [0..|s|-1]$. Care is required to avoid such undefined values.

Special problems arise with logical expressions on sequences. Suppose that we want to write an expression that is *true* for a sequence of integers s if and only if all the values in s are non-negative. A first attempt could be

$$(\forall i \in integer)(s[i] \geq 0)$$

However, when $i = -1$, $s[i]$ is undefined, and $s[i] \geq 0$ is neither *true* nor *false*. To solve the problem we explicitly restrict the type of the variable in the quantified statement, as in

$$(\forall i \in [0..|s| - 1])(s[i] \geq 0)$$

3.4.5   Tuples

A *tuple* is a collection of elements of possibly different types. Each tuple has one or more *fields* associated with it, and each field has a unique identifier called the *field name*. In some programming languages, a tuple is referred to as a *record* or a *structure*. To declare a tuple, we use an expression of the form

$$tuple\ of\ (f_1 : T_1, f_2 : T_2, \ldots, f_n : T_n)$$

where $n \geq 1$, f_i is the field name, and T_i is the field type of i-th field. If all fields are of the same type t, then we use the abbreviated form

$$tuple\ of\ (f_1, f_2, \ldots, f_n : T)$$

For example, the declaration

$$pair = tuple\ of\ (id : integer, val : string)$$

Table 3.8   Operations on *tuples*

Operation	Meaning
$=, \neq$	equal, not equal
$t.f$	value of field f of tuple t

defines the type *pair* to be a tuple with two fields: the first field has the name *id* and contains an integer, and the second field has the name *val* and contains a string.

To define the value of a tuple, we use an expression of the form $\langle x_1, x_2, \ldots, x_n \rangle$ where $n \geq 1$ and x_i is an expression of the same type as the i-th field in the tuple. For example, $\langle 4, \texttt{"cat"} \rangle$ is a value of type *pair*.

The operations on tuples are shown in Table 3.8.   For example, if x is a variable of type *pair* and $x = \langle 4, \texttt{"cat"} \rangle$, then $x.id = 4$ and $x.val = \texttt{"cat."}$

3.4.6   Examples

With type constructors, we can build types of arbitrary complexity. For example,

$$T = set\ of\ pair$$

defines the type T as a set of *pairs*. We could equally well declare T by the expression

$$T = set\ of\ tuple\ of\ (id : integer, val : string)$$

Examples of values of this type are $\{\}$ and $\{\langle 1, \texttt{"cat"} \rangle, \langle 3, \texttt{"dog"} \rangle\}$.

We can now define functions on variables of this type. The function

$$f : T \to boolean,\ \text{where}\ f(S) = (\forall x \in S)(x.id > 0)$$

returns *true* if and only if the field *id* for all the tuples in the set S is greater than 0. For example, $f(\{\}) = true$, $f(\{\langle 1, \texttt{"cat"} \rangle, \langle 3, \texttt{"dog"} \rangle\}) = true$, and $f(\{\langle 1, \texttt{"cat"} \rangle, \langle 0, \texttt{"dog"} \rangle\}) = false$.

3.5   The Multiple Assignment Statement

The *multiple assignment* statement assigns values to variables. The general form of the multiple assignment statement is

$$v_1, v_2, \ldots, v_n := e_1, e_2, \ldots, e_n$$

where $n \geq 1$, the v_is are distinct variables, and each e_i is an expression of the same type as v_i. To evaluate the above statement, first compute the values of

Table 3.9   Examples of multiple assignment statements

Assignment	Before		After	
	x	y	x	y
$x, y := 0, 10$	1	2	0	10
	4	7	0	10
$x, y := 10, x$	1	2	10	1
	4	7	10	4
$x, y := y, x$	1	2	2	1
	4	7	7	4

all the expressions e_i and then assign these values simultaneously to the corresponding variables v_i. When $n = 1$ we have the more familiar single assignment statement, which assigns a value to a single variable.

Some examples of multiple assignment statements are

$$x, y := 0, 10$$
$$x, y := 10, x$$
$$x, y := y, x$$

The first assignment statement assigns 0 to x and 10 to y. The second one assigns 10 to x and assigns the value of x to y. Note that this does not have the same effect as performing the single assignments $x := 10$ and $y := x$ one after the other. The third assignment interchanges the values of x and y. Table 3.9 shows the effect of these three multiple assignment statements for different values of x and y.

The multiple assignment statement is a convenient tool for defining the meaning of pieces of code. We define the *state* of a program to be the values of the variables in the program at a given time. To represent a state, we define an order to the variables and use a tuple of the form $\langle v_1, v_2, \ldots, v_n \rangle$ to represent the values of the variables, where n is the number of variables in the program. For example, if program P contains the integer variables x, y, and z, then a state is represented by a triple $\langle v_1, v_2, v_3 \rangle$ where v_1 represents the value of x, v_2 the value of y, and v_3 the value of z. The *state space* is the set of all states. Thus, the state space for program P is

$$\{\langle v_1, v_2, v_3 \rangle \mid v_1 \in integer \land v_2 \in integer \land v_3 \in integer\}.$$

Note that to interpret a tuple in the state space, we need to know not only the variables in the program, but also the order in which these variables are represented.

We can now view the multiple assignment statement as a function on the state space of the program. In the following, we assume that the state space consists of triples of values for variables x, y, and z. For example, the assignment $x := y + 1$

Table 3.10   Meaning of example multiple assignment statements

Assignment	Meaning
$x, y := 0, 10$	$\{\langle\langle x_1, y_1, z_1\rangle, \langle x_2, y_2, z_2\rangle\rangle \mid x_2 = 0 \land y_2 = 10 \land z_2 = z_1\}$
$x, y := 10, x$	$\{\langle\langle x_1, y_1, z_1\rangle, \langle x_2, y_2, z_2\rangle\rangle \mid x_2 = 10 \land y_2 = x_1 \land z_2 = z_1\}$
$x, y := y, x$	$\{\langle\langle x_1, y_1, z_1\rangle, \langle x_2, y_2, z_2\rangle\rangle \mid x_2 = y_1 \land y_2 = x_1 \land z_2 = z_1\}$

defines the function

$$\{\langle\langle x_1, y_1, z_1\rangle, \langle x_2, y_2, z_2\rangle\rangle \mid x_2 = y_1 + 1 \land y_2 = y_1 \land z_2 = z_1\}$$

Both the input and output of this function are integer triples. The first value of the output triple is the second value of the input triple incremented by one, and the second and third values of the output triple are the same as those of the input triple. Note that in this representation, we have considerable freedom in the choice of variable names. For example, we could also use

$$\{\langle\langle a, b, c\rangle, \langle d, e, f\rangle\rangle \mid d = b + 1 \land e = b \land f = c\}$$

to define the meaning of the above assignment statement. Table 3.10 shows the functions defined by the multiple assignment statements in Table 3.9.

Consider the sequence of assignments

$$x := y + 1$$
$$y := x \times z$$

We can express the meaning of this sequence of assignments as the function

$$\{\langle\langle x_1, y_1, z_1\rangle, \langle x_2, y_2, z_2\rangle\rangle \mid x_2 = y_1 + 1 \land y_2 = (y_1 + 1) \times z_1 \land z_2 = z_1\}$$

which is the same function as defined by the multiple assignment statement $x, y := y + 1, (y + 1) \times z$. In general, for *any* sequence of assignments, we can find a multiple assignment statement that defines the same function.

3.6   Conditional Rules

A *conditional rule* is an expression of the form

$$(c_1 \Rightarrow r_1 \mid c_2 \Rightarrow r_2 \mid \ldots \mid c_n \Rightarrow r_n)$$

where $n \geq 1$, the c_is are logical expressions, and the r_is are rules. We call $c_i \Rightarrow r_i$ the *i*-th *component* of the rule, c_i a *condition*, and r_i a *rule*. To apply the above conditional rule, evaluate the conditions in order, starting with c_1; for the first c_i that evaluates to *true*, apply rule r_i. If no condition evaluates to *true*, then the conditional rule is undefined.

We can use a conditional rule to define the value of a function. For example, we can define the minimum function with the rule

$$min(x, y) = (x \le y \Rightarrow x \mid x > y \Rightarrow y)$$

Sometimes it is useful to nest one conditional rule inside another. For example, we can define a lexicographic order on pairs of integers $\langle x, y \rangle$ with the rule

$$\langle x_1, y_1 \rangle < \langle x_2, y_2 \rangle = (\;\; x_1 < x_2 \Rightarrow true \mid$$
$$x_1 = x_2 \Rightarrow (y_1 < y_2 \Rightarrow true \mid y_1 \ge y_2 \Rightarrow false) \mid$$
$$x_1 > x_2 \Rightarrow false)$$

This rule is equivalent to the simple conditional rule

$$(\;\; x_1 < x_2 \Rightarrow true \mid$$
$$x_1 = x_2 \wedge y_1 < y_2 \Rightarrow true \mid$$
$$x_1 = x_2 \wedge y_1 \ge y_2 \Rightarrow false \mid$$
$$x_1 > x_2 \Rightarrow false)$$

which can be shown from the definition of conditional rule.

Another application of a conditional rule is to define the meaning of a program, i.e., a function on the state space of the program. For example, we can define the meaning of the statement

$$\text{if } (x < y) \text{ then } z := x \text{ else } z := y$$

which assigns the minimum of x and y to z, with the conditional rule

$$(x < y \Rightarrow z := x \mid x \ge y \Rightarrow z := y)$$

Similarly, we can express the meaning of a piece of code that sorts the variables x and y with the conditional rule

$$(x < y \Rightarrow x, y := x, y \mid x \ge y \Rightarrow x, y := y, x)$$

For long conditional rules, it is often clearer to express the conditional rule as a table. Translating a conditional rule to tabular form is straightforward. For example, Table 3.11 contains the tabular form of the conditional rule

$$min(x, y) = (x \le y \Rightarrow x \mid x > y \Rightarrow y)$$

In the tabular form, we use one row for each component; the first column contains the condition, and the second column the rule. Similarly, Table 3.12 shows the tabular form of the conditional rule

$$(x < y \Rightarrow x, y := x, y \mid x \ge y \Rightarrow x, y := y, x)$$

In this case, we use two columns to define the rule part. The tabular form

Table 3.11   Tabular form for conditional rule defining minimum function

Condition	$min(x,y)$
$x \leq y$	x
$x > y$	y

Table 3.12   Tabular form for conditional rule defining sorting of two variables

Condition	$x :=$	$y :=$
$x < y$	x	y
$x \geq y$	y	x

becomes particularly attractive for nested rules, where we can use indenting in the condition column to indicate the nesting. For example, Table 3.13 contains the tabular form of the conditional rule

$$\langle x_1, y_1 \rangle < \langle x_2, y_2 \rangle = (\; x_1 < x_2 \Rightarrow true \;|$$
$$x_1 = x_2 \Rightarrow (y_1 < y_2 \Rightarrow true \;|\; y_1 \geq y_2 \Rightarrow false) \;|$$
$$x_1 > x_2 \Rightarrow false)$$

We end this section by pointing out the difference between the logical connective "$\rightarrow$" and a conditional rule with one component. In the following, we assume that x and y are *integer* variables. The conditional rule

$$(x < y \Rightarrow false)$$

defines a function on pairs of integers $\langle x, y \rangle$ that is *false* if $x < y$, and not defined otherwise. The logical expression

$$x < y \rightarrow false$$

Table 3.13   Tabular form for conditional rule defining lexicographic order

Condition		$\langle x_0, y_0 \rangle < \langle x_1, y_1 \rangle$
$x_0 < x_1$		*true*
$x_0 = x_1$		
	$y_0 < y_1$	*true*
	$y_0 \geq y_1$	*false*
$x_0 > x_1$		*false*

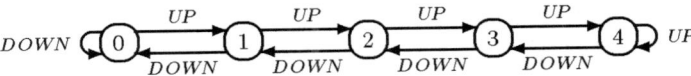

Figure 3.1   Counter finite state machine

is defined for all values of x and y; it is *false* if $x < y$, and *true* otherwise. The following conditional rule is equivalent:

$$(x < y \Rightarrow false \mid x \geq y \Rightarrow true)$$

3.7   Finite State Machines

In this section, we consider various kinds of *Finite State Machines* (FSMs) that differ in the way they produce output. However, every FSM contains at least the following four components:

- S: a finite set of *states*.

- s_0: the *initial state* $(s_0 \in S)$.

- I: a finite set of *inputs*.

- $T : S \times I \rightarrow S$: the *transition function*, where $T(s, x)$ defines the new state for input x while in state s.

For example, Figure 3.1 shows the states and transitions for an FSM that models a counter that is incremented by the input *UP* and decremented by the input *DOWN*. When the counter reaches its maximum value, 4, the input *UP* has no effect, and when its value is 0, the input *DOWN* has no effect. In this case, the set of states S is $\{0, 1, 2, 3, 4\}$, the initial state s_0 is 0, the set of inputs I is $\{UP, DOWN\}$, and the transition function T is defined by the conditional rule in Table 3.14.

So far, we have only considered inputs, states, and transitions of an FSM. When we use an FSM for software specification, we are interested in describing the input/output behavior of the software. As a result, we are not really interested in the states and the transitions of the FSM: the sole purpose of the states and transitions is to define the input/output behavior. We will now look at two methods for associating outputs with an FSM. We can then use FSMs for software specification by requiring that, for each input sequence, the software produces the same output as the FSM.

The first type of output that an FSM can produce is called an *event output*, which is an output associated with a transition of an FSM. That is, we can associate a set of event outputs O_E with an FSM and define an event-output

Table 3.14   Transition function for counter finite state machine

Condition	$T(s, x)$
$x = DOWN$	
$\quad s = 0$	0
$\quad s \in [1..4]$	$s - 1$
$x = UP$	
$\quad s \in [0..3]$	$s + 1$
$\quad s = 4$	4

Table 3.15   Event-output function for counter finite state machine

Condition	$E(s, x)$
$s = 0$	
$\quad x = DOWN$	$ALARM$
$\quad x = UP$	$NORMAL$
$s \in [1..3]$	$NORMAL$
$s = 4$	
$\quad x = DOWN$	$NORMAL$
$\quad x = UP$	$ALARM$

function $E : S \times I \rightarrow O_E$, where $E(s, x)$ is the event output associated with the transition corresponding to state s and input x.

For example, Table 3.15 defines an event-output function for the counter FSM shown in Figure 3.1. The set of event outputs O_E is $\{ALARM, NORMAL\}$. The event-output function E defines the event output as $ALARM$ when the input is $DOWN$ and the counter cannot be decremented any further, or when the input is UP and the counter has reached its maximum value. In all other cases, E defines the output as $NORMAL$. Intuitively, the $ALARM$ output signifies a failure of the FSM to properly maintain the count of UP and $DOWN$ events.

The second type of output is called a *condition output*, which is an output associated with a state. In this case, we associate a set of condition outputs O_C with an FSM and define a condition-output function $C : S \rightarrow O_C$ where $C(s)$ is the condition output associated with state s.

Table 3.16 defines a condition-output function for the counter FSM shown in Figure 3.1. The set of condition outputs O_C is $\{NORMAL, WARNING\}$. The condition-output function C defines the condition output as $WARNING$ when the counter is at its minimum or maximum value, and as $NORMAL$ in all other cases. Intuitively, the $WARNING$ output signifies that the next input may cause the FSM to fail.

Table 3.16   Condition-output function for counter finite state machine

Condition	$C(s)$
$s = 0$	$WARNING$
$s \in [1..3]$	$NORMAL$
$s = 4$	$WARNING$

In summary, every FSM has a set of inputs, a set of states, an initial state, and a state transition function. In addition, the types of FSMs we are interested in also have event outputs, condition outputs, or both. Since event outputs are associated with transitions, they are instantaneous and available only during the transition. Therefore, event outputs are well suited to model the output of functions in software. Condition outputs, on the other hand, are associated with states and their value is unchanged until the next transition. Therefore, condition outputs are well suited to model screen output.

The type of FSM defined in this section is known as a *Mealy machine* if it has an event-output function and as a *Moore machine* if it has a condition-output function. There are many other types of finite state machines, such as non-deterministic state machines or state machines based on final states rather than output functions. Some of the FSMs that we will consider in this text are non-deterministic: more than one transition or output is possible for a given state and/or input. To define a non-deterministic FSM, we replace one or more of the transition, event-output, or condition-output functions by relations. In the next section, we consider MSMs: a special kind of FSM designed for specifying software modules.

3.8   Module State Machines

Module state machines (MSMs) provide the mathematical basis for three work products: Module Interface Specification, Module Internal Design, and Module Implementation. Here we describe a language for specifying MSMs and illustrate the language features on two examples.

3.8.1   Specification sections

An MSM consists of a state declaration and one section for each access routine, describing its behavior in terms of the state. The **state variables** section defines the specification state space by declaring a collection of typed variables. The **access routine semantics** section contains one subsection for each access routine. Each subsection contains two entries, whose form depends on whether the access routine is a set, get, or set-get routine.

Table 3.17 *list* module state machine—access routines

Routine name	Input	Output	Exception
s_init			
s_add	*integer*		full
	integer		pos
s_del	*integer*		pos
s_val	*integer*		pos
	integer		
g_val	*integer*	*integer*	pos

- *Set access routine entries.* A **transition** and an **exceptions** entry are required. The **transition** entry specifies a state transition: new values for the state variables expressed in terms of the old values. The transition is usually specified by a multiple assignment statement, with state variables on the left-hand side. In some cases, it is important to explicitly distinguish between the new and old state values. For state variable x, $pre(x)$ refers to x's value just before the transition; $post(x)$ refers to its value just after. The **exceptions** entry specifies the situations in which each exception must be signaled. The exceptions are specified by an assignment to the special variable exc, or by "none," indicating that no exception is ever signaled.

- *Get access routine entries.* An **output** and an **exceptions** entry are required. The **output** entry describes the access routine return value, specified by an assignment to the special variable *out*. The **exceptions** entry is as for set routines.

- *Set-get access routine entries.* A **transition-output** and an **exceptions** entry are required. The **transition-output** describes a state transition and an output. The transition is specified as in the **transition** section of a set call; the output is specified as in the **output** section of a get call. The **exceptions** entry is as for set routines.

3.8.2 Example: list module

Consider the *list* module, which provides access to a list of at most N integers. List elements are accessed by position (zero-relative), and elements may be added and deleted at any position. The access routines for *list* are shown in Table 3.17. **s_init** initializes the module, with the list empty. **s_add**(i, x) inserts x at position i, and **s_del**(i) deletes the element at position i. **s_val**(i, x) replaces the value at position i with x, and **g_val**(i) returns the value at position i.

The **access routine semantics** are shown in Figure 3.2. The state is the single variable s, holding the list contents. **s_init** assigns the empty list to s and

state variables
s : sequence of integer

access routine semantics
s_init:
      transition: $s := \langle\rangle$
      exceptions: none
s_add(i, x):
      transition: $s := s[0..i-1] \parallel \langle x \rangle \parallel s[i..|s|-1]$
      exceptions: $exc := (|s| = N \Rightarrow \mathtt{full} \mid i \notin [0..|s|] \Rightarrow \mathtt{pos})$
s_del(i):
      transition: $s := s[0..i-1] \parallel s[i+1..|s|-1]$
      exceptions: $exc := (i \notin [0..|s|-1] \Rightarrow \mathtt{pos})$
s_val(i, x):
      transition: $s[i] := x$
      exceptions: $exc := (i \notin [0..|s|-1] \Rightarrow \mathtt{pos})$
g_val(i):
      output: $out := s[i]$
      exceptions: $exc := (i \notin [0..|s|-1] \Rightarrow \mathtt{pos})$

Figure 3.2 *list* module state machine—semantics

never signals an exception. s_add(i, x) inserts x immediately following $s[i-1]$ and signals the exception **full** if s has N elements and the exception **pos** if i is out of range. Note that insertions are permitted at position $|s|$, even though this position is one beyond the end of s. s_del(i) removes $s[i]$, signaling **pos** if i is out of range. s_val(i, x) simply assigns x to $s[i]$ and g_val(i) returns $s[i]$. Both signal **pos** if i is out of range.

Table 3.18 shows two examples of an *execution table*: a tabular description of the "execution" of a *trace*—a sequence of calls—by an MSM. There is one row for each call in the trace, and a column for the call, the new state, the output, and the exception associated with the call. In table (a), the elements are stored in the order they are added. In table (b), the s_add position parameter causes the elements to be stored in the reverse order.

3.8.3 Additional specification rules

In the description of MSMs above, several important issues have been ignored.

- *Non-determinism.* For a given access routine call, is more than one new state permitted? Is more than one output or exception permitted? We normally use an MSM as a specification. In this role, non-determinism indicates that the implementor has some freedom in the observable behavior of the implementation.

(a)

Table 3.18   *list* module state machine—execution tables ($N = 3$)

	Call	New state	Output	Exception
(1)	s_init	$\langle\rangle$	—	—
(2)	s_add(0, 10)	$\langle 10 \rangle$	—	—
(3)	s_add(1, 20)	$\langle 10, 20 \rangle$	—	—
(4)	s_add(2, 30)	$\langle 10, 20, 30 \rangle$	—	—
(5)	g_val(2)	$\langle 10, 20, 30 \rangle$	30	—

(b)

	Call	New state	Output	Exception
(1)	s_init	$\langle\rangle$	—	—
(2)	s_add(0, 10)	$\langle 10 \rangle$	—	—
(3)	s_add(0, 20)	$\langle 20, 10 \rangle$	—	—
(4)	s_add(0, 30)	$\langle 30, 20, 10 \rangle$	—	—
(5)	g_val(2)	$\langle 30, 20, 10 \rangle$	10	—

- *Exception semantics.* When an exception occurs, are there any constraints on the new state or output?

- *Completeness.* Are there calls for which no transition or output is specified? In other words, are there traces for which there is no specified behavior?

Different answers to these questions give rise to different MSM definitions. We next provide one set of answers: the ones used for all MSMs in this text.

- *Non-determinism.* MSMs are non-deterministic in a number of ways. For set calls, the transition may be non-deterministic, for get calls the output may be non-deterministic, and for set-get calls both the transition and output may be non-deterministic. However, for all access routines, the exception behavior must be deterministic.

- *Exception semantics.* When an exception occurs, we constrain the state transition, but not the output. Suppose that call C causes an exception. If C is a set call, then no state transition occurs. If C is a get call, then the output is *dontcare*: any output of the correct type is permitted. If C is a set-get call then no transition occurs and the output is *dontcare*.

- *Completeness.* MSMs must be complete. Whenever the **exceptions** entry does *not* indicate an exception, the **transition**, **output**, or **transition-output** entry must provide the normal-case behavior.

These rules are summarized in Table 3.19.

Table 3.19   Module state machines—semantics summary

Call	Normal case	Exceptions
set	**transition** specifies 1 or more states.	**exceptions** specifies 0 or 1 exception(s). **transition** ignored: no state change.
get	**output** specifies 1 or more outputs.	**exceptions** specifies 0 or 1 exception(s). **output** ignored; any output permitted.
set-get	**transition-output** specifies 1 or more state/output pairs.	**exceptions** specifies 0 or 1 exception(s). **transition-output** ignored: no state change; any output permitted.

Table 3.20   *elist* module state machine—access routines

Routine name	Input	Output	Exception
g_exval	*integer*	*boolean*	
g_pos	*integer*	*integer*	val
s_delval	*integer*		val
sg_val		*integer*	empty

3.8.4   Example: extended list module

The *elist* (extended list) module provides extensions to the *list* module, illustrating the rules described in the previous section. The *elist* module supports the access routines shown in Table 3.20, as well as the *list* access routines. The semantics for the *list* access routines are unchanged. The semantics for the new access routines are shown in Figure 3.3 and paraphrased as follows: g_exval(x) returns *true* or *false* according to whether x is in s. g_pos(x) returns the position of x in s and signals **val** if x does not occur in s. If x occurs in more than one position, then any one of these positions is a correct *out* value. s_delval(x) deletes the element with value x and signals **val** if x does not occur in s. Again, if x occurs in more than one position, then any one of these may be deleted. Note the use of *pre* in the **transition** entry to ensure that it is clear which version of s is intended. sg_val returns the value of some element of s and deletes it, signaling **empty** if s has no elements. Both the transition and the output are non-deterministic.

Table 3.21 shows execution tables illustrating the rules for exception semantics, assuming $N = 3$. In table (a), the s_add call in line 5 generates the exception **full**. There is no change in state, even though the expression in the **transition** entry is defined. Table (b) shows a g_val call causing exception **pos**. While the output 0 is shown, any other integer is equally correct.

Table 3.22 shows execution tables illustrating the rules for non-deterministic transitions and outputs. In table (a), the g_pos call returns 0; 2 is also accept-

access routine semantics
g_exval(x):
    output: $out := x \in s$
    exceptions: none
g_pos(x):
    output: $out := i$ where $(i \in [0..|s| - 1] \wedge s[i] = x)$
    exceptions: $exc := (x \notin s \Rightarrow$ **val**$)$
s_delval(x):
    transition: $s := s[0..i - 1] \parallel s[i + 1..|s| - 1]$, where $pre(s)[i] = x$
    exceptions: $exc := (x \notin s \Rightarrow$ **val**$)$
sg_val:
    transition-output: $s, out := s[0..i - 1] \parallel s[i + 1..|s| - 1], s[i]$
                                 where $i \in [0..|pre(s)| - 1]$
    exceptions: $exc := (|s| = 0 \Rightarrow$ **empty**$)$

Figure 3.3   *elist* module state machine—semantics

Table 3.21   *elist* module state machine—execution tables $(N = 3)$

(a)

	Call	New state	Output	Exception
(1)	s_init	$\langle\rangle$	—	—
(2)	s_add$(0, 10)$	$\langle 10 \rangle$	—	—
(3)	s_add$(1, 20)$	$\langle 10, 20 \rangle$	—	—
(4)	s_add$(2, 30)$	$\langle 10, 20, 30 \rangle$	—	—
(5)	s_add$(3, 40)$	$\langle 10, 20, 30 \rangle$	—	full

(b)

	Call	New state	Output	Exception
(1)	s_init	$\langle\rangle$	—	—
(2)	s_add$(0, 10)$	$\langle 10 \rangle$	—	—
(3)	s_add$(1, 20)$	$\langle 10, 20 \rangle$	—	—
(4)	g_val(2)	$\langle 10, 20 \rangle$	0	pos

Table 3.22 *elist* module state machine—execution tables $(N = 3)$

(a)

	Call	New state	Output	Exception
(1)	s_init	$\langle\rangle$	—	—
(2)	s_add(0, 10)	$\langle 10\rangle$	—	—
(3)	s_add(1, 20)	$\langle 10, 20\rangle$	—	—
(4)	s_add(2, 10)	$\langle 10, 20, 10\rangle$	—	—
(5)	g_pos(10)	$\langle 10, 20, 10\rangle$	0	—

(b)

	Call	New state	Output	Exception
(1)	s_init	$\langle\rangle$	—	—
(2)	s_add(0, 10)	$\langle 10\rangle$	—	—
(3)	s_add(1, 20)	$\langle 10, 20\rangle$	—	—
(4)	s_add(2, 10)	$\langle 10, 20, 10\rangle$	—	—
(5)	s_delval(10)	$\langle 10, 20\rangle$	—	—

(c)

	Call	New state	Output	Exception
(1)	s_init	$\langle\rangle$	—	—
(2)	s_add(0, 10)	$\langle 10\rangle$	—	—
(3)	s_add(1, 20)	$\langle 10, 20\rangle$	—	—
(4)	s_add(2, 10)	$\langle 10, 20, 10\rangle$	—	—
(5)	sg_val	$\langle 10, 10\rangle$	20	—

able. Similarly, in table (b) the **s_delval** call shows a new state of $\langle 10, 20\rangle$; $\langle 20, 10\rangle$ is also correct. Table (c) illustrates transition-output non-determinism. While the new state/output pair shown is $\langle 10, 10\rangle/20$, the pairs $\langle 10, 20\rangle/10$ and $\langle 20, 10\rangle/10$ are also correct.

3.9   Summary

We discussed the mathematics needed for specifying functions that naturally arise in software specifications. The notations use the familiar notions of sets and relations, and the standard logical connectives and quantifiers.

We rely on a simple type scheme based on the primitive types integer, boolean, char, and string, and three type constructors: sets, sequences, and tuples. Sets provide unordered collections of elements of the same type, sequences provide ordered collections of elements of the same type, and tuples provide collections of elements of possibly different types. These type constructors can be combined to build types of arbitrary complexity.

The *multiple assignment statement* and the *conditional rule* are two specification constructs with simple functional semantics. The multiple assignment statement is a generalization of the familiar (single) assignment statement, and the conditional rule is similar to the case statement provided by some programming languages. For long and complex conditional rules, it is often clearer to express the rule in tabular format. Tabular conditional rules are used heavily in SHAM Requirements Specifications.

The Finite State Machine (FSM) is a powerful specification construct. Each FSM has a set of inputs, a set of states, an initial state, and a state transition function. The FSMs we are interested in also have outputs. A Module State Machine (MSM) is a special kind of FSM designed for specifying software modules. MSMs form the mathematical basis for three work products: Module Interface Specification, Module Internal Design, and Module Implementation.

3.10   Bibliographic Notes

Textbooks on discrete mathematics such as Piff's [44] cover many of the topics discussed in this chapter. In addition, many texts discuss each of these topics in more detail. Sets, relations, and functions are covered in the classic set theory text by Halmos [45]. Hodges [46] provides a good introduction to logic, and Enderton [47] covers the topic in depth. Our types and type constructors are generalizations of the types found in programming languages such as Pascal [48]. A more formal treatment of types can be found in the literature on algebraic specifications [49], the Z notation [11], and functional programming [50]. The multiple assignment statement and conditional rule are taken directly from the text by Linger et al. [3]. Finite State Machines are covered in most texts on automata theory [51]. Output automata, such as our Module State Machines, and equivalences between pairs of output automata are described in more depth by Nelson [52] and Hoffman and Jones [53].

Part II

Work Products

Chapter 4

Introduction

And now I see with eyes serene, the very pulse of the machine.
[W. Wordsworth]

4.1 The SHAM System

4.1.1 Purpose

The raison d'être of SHAM, the Strooper-Hoffman Abstract Machine, is to demonstrate methods for specifying, designing, implementing, and testing software systems. The important considerations for selecting SHAM as an example are that:

1. SHAM is sufficiently complex to demonstrate the methods.

2. SHAM is easy to learn, so that the emphasis can be on teaching the methods, rather than on teaching SHAM.

3. SHAM is entertaining enough that the reader is encouraged to read the remainder of this book.

However, no effort was made to make SHAM "realistic," in the sense of a useful, complex, or even industry-like system. SHAM is indeed a sham.

To make reasonable decisions about what services to include in SHAM, it helps to define a hypothetical purpose for it. In the remainder, we assume that SHAM is a simple assembler used for teaching the basic aspects of primitive von Neumann–style programming, where both program and data are stored in memory, and the processor operates in a simple fetch-and-execute cycle. In setting out the requirements for SHAM, we follow an ASAP approach, which in this case stands for "as simple as possible." Despite its simplicity, SHAM is sufficiently complex to demonstrate the methods, and surprisingly subtle specification, design, and verification issues arise.

4.1.2   Overview of services offered

As explained in Chapter 1, during the *Requirements Analysis* phase of a software project the basic services offered by the system are determined. While this text does not cover the Requirements Analysis phase in detail, we briefly discuss the key requirements decisions made for SHAM.

We focus on the following questions.

- *What is the register and memory model?* We must decide how many registers there are, and how they are used. For example, we must decide if index registers are supported. Similarly, we must decide on the memory model; for example, is virtual memory supported?

- *What is the instruction format?* We must decide whether an instruction occupies one, two, or more memory locations, what types of operands are allowed, and how the operands are stored.

- *What instructions are supported?* We need instructions to support memory access, arithmetic functions, branching, and miscellaneous tasks such as input/output.

- *What is the user interface?* Does SHAM operate in batch or interactive mode? A good case can be made for both modes of operation. A batch version is simpler to implement and is terminal-independent, so that SHAM can run in many different environments. However, an interactive version can demonstrate key issues relating to keyboard and terminal support in software specification, design, and verification. Moreover, an interactive version is more intuitive for the user, better serving our hypothetical purpose of teaching von Neumann–style programming.

Possible answers to these questions are discussed in most books on computer architecture [54]. We now discuss the decisions that were made for SHAM. Clearly these decisions are somewhat arbitrary, but in our decisions we are guided by the ASAP principle.

- *Register and memory model.* SHAM has two registers: the accumulator, *acc*, and the program counter, *pc*. A flat memory model is used with a single memory array, accessed through integer addresses. Neither index registers nor virtual addressing is supported.

- *Instruction format.* Each instruction is stored in a single memory location. Only numeric operands are supported and, for instructions with an operand, the operand also occupies a single memory location. Only unsigned decimal values are supported.

- *Instruction set.* Table 4.1 shows the SHAM instructions. Note that there is no way to read input in SHAM; input values must be hard-coded into the program using *LOADCON*.

Table 4.1 SHAM instruction set

Instruction	Operand	Description
Memory access		
LOAD	a	load value at address a into *acc*
STORE	a	store *acc* at address a
Arithmetic		
ADD	a	add value at address a to *acc*
SUBTRACT	a	subtract value at address a from *acc*
Branch		
BRANCH	a	branch to address a
BRANCHZERO	a	branch to address a if $acc = 0$
BRANCHPOS	a	branch to address a if $acc > 0$
Miscellaneous		
LOADCON	i	load integer i into *acc*
PRINT		print value of *acc*
HALT		terminate SHAM

- *User interface.* Since a batch and an interactive interface to SHAM are both useful, we provide two versions. BSHAM offers a batch interface; the source program is stored in a file and run in a load-and-go fashion. The only output produced by this version is error messages and integers printed with the *PRINT* instruction. The second version, ISHAM, provides an interactive interface; the registers and memory are displayed on the screen and the user single-steps through program execution.

It is clear that after a system such as SHAM is placed into production, changes will be requested. Some of the likely changes are influenced by the above decisions. For example, it is easy to imagine that the user would want more instructions, index registers, or symbolic addresses. Another source for change requests is the user interface. For example, changes to the syntax of the SHAM input file or the screen format for the interactive version are likely to be requested. These, and other, likely changes are documented in the Requirements Specification, so they can be taken into account when designing the system.

4.1.3 Overview of work products

Section 2.3 discusses the seven work products that we use in the development of SHAM. In the following chapters, we describe each of these work products in detail; we now review the particular instances of each of the work products that exist for SHAM. There is one Requirements Specification for SHAM, but it contains two parts. The first part defines the behavior of BSHAM, the batch version, and the second part defines the behavior of ISHAM, the interactive version. Since there are few differences between the two versions, the second part is written as an addendum to the first and defines only the ways in which the interactive version is different.

There is one Module Guide for SHAM; it defines the modules for both BSHAM and ISHAM. There are nine modules in SHAM. Three of these, *absmach*, *load*, and *token*, are used in exactly the same way in BSHAM and ISHAM. Two modules, *exec* and *sham*, are used in both versions, but in slightly different ways in each version. And four modules, *keybdin*, *scndr*, *scngeom*, and *scnstr*, are used only in ISHAM. Finally, there are two modules, *stack* and *symtbl*, that are not part of SHAM proper, but that we frequently use for illustration.

For most of the SHAM modules, there is a Module Interface Specification, a Module Internal Design, a Module Implementation, a Test Plan, and a Test Implementation. However, for some modules one or more of the work products are omitted; only the Module Implementation is always present. For example, for some modules there is no Test Implementation because the module is best tested during system testing. Finally, there is a Test Plan and a Test Implementation for the system testing of both the BSHAM and the ISHAM systems.

4.1.4 Document conventions and notations

Each work product has its own conventions and notations; these are explained in the appropriate chapters. However, certain conventions and notations are used in all work products.

There is an abbreviation for each of the work products: RS for Requirements Specification, MG for Module Guide, MIS for Module Interface Specification, MID for Module Internal Design, MI for Module Implementation, TP for Test Plan, and TI for Test Implementation.

By default, all identifiers are shown in *italics*. The one exception to this rule is that all code fragments (from the Module Implementation and the Test Implementation) are shown in `typewriter font`.

In the MG, a unique prefix is defined for each SHAM module. For example, the prefix for the *stack* module is `ps_`, for "pushdown stack." The prefix for module M is used on all identifiers exported by M. Thus, the initialization access routine for *stack* is called `ps_s_init`. The prefix of an identifier is always included when the identifier appears in a work product. However, for readability, we omit the prefix when we reference the identifier in the text, unless this leads to confusion. For example, we use `s_init` if it is clear that we are referring to the initialization routine for *stack*.

4.2 Overview of Part II

The remaining chapters in Part II discuss the work products in detail. Chapter 5 explains how the required behavior of a system is captured in the Requirements Specification. The module decomposition of a system, which is recorded in the

Module Guide, is described in Chapter 6. Chapter 7 discusses the design of module interfaces, and the Module Interface Specification that is used to record this design. The Module Internal Design specifies the internal data structures of a module and is discussed in Chapter 8 and the Module Implementation is discussed in Chapter 9. Finally, Chapter 10 discusses the testing phase and its associated work products, the Test Plan and the Test Implementation.

Chapter 5

Requirements Specification

Observability is the essence of specification.

5.1   Introduction

The goal of the Requirements Specification (hereafter "RS") is to precisely specify the required behavior of a software system. The idea is to make the "what decisions" explicitly up front, not implicitly during design and implementation. The RS supports the four roles described in Section 2.2. Here the *users* are the end users, and the *designers* are the requirements engineers. The *developers* are the staff who write the Module Guide, Module Interface Specifications, Module Internal Designs, and Module Implementations. The *verifiers* are the inspectors and testers, especially the system testers.

To support these four groups of people, a well-organized reference document is needed. The RS defines all the required system behavior in one place, accurately and consistently. Both normal and exceptional behavior are specified. The RS supports the software development process in a number of important ways:

- *Serves as a contract between the users and the developers.* The requirements typically include too many details to memorize and frequently contain decisions hammered out in intense negotiations. A written record is critical.

- *Ensures that developers need not decide what is best for users.* It is not feasible for every developer to be an expert in the application area. However, the RS can provide the developer with the information needed to make good design decisions.

- *Provides essential support for independent verification.* Often, a developer and verifier disagree on system correctness. The RS provides an authoritative source for resolving these disputes.

- *Supports estimates of time and resources.* Without a detailed description of the required behavior, accurate cost estimation is rarely possible.

- *Provides protection against personnel turnover.* In software development, frequent turnover is a fact of life. If the requirements information is stored only in a developer's head, then that information leaves when the developer leaves.

- *Supports the maintainer.* Many maintainers were not members of the original development team, and therefore they rely heavily on the RS to obtain the required system behavior.

In the remainder of this chapter, we define the RS work product, review in detail the BSHAM and ISHAM RSs, and describe the verification of RSs. The full BSHAM RS and ISHAM RS may be found in Appendix A.

5.2   Work Product Definition

It pays to recognize the type of information commonly recorded in an RS and to define a standard document structure to organize that information. When properly designed, standardized documents are easier to write, read, verify, and maintain.

5.2.1   Document sections

Our RSs are based on finite state machines (FSMs) and are divided into seven sections. The **Overview** section provides a brief description of both the system specified and the specification document itself. The required hardware and software environment and the notational conventions used in the document are also defined.

The **Environment variables** section defines variables that are used to model relevant aspects of the system's environment. An environment variable declaration specifies a name, a type, and an interpretation: the relationship between the variable value and the environment. Environment variables are divided into two groups: *input* variables—which the system may read, but not modify—and *output* variables—which may be written but not read. For example, the ISHAM screen can be modeled with the output environment variable *scn*:

> *scn : sequence* [24][80] *of char*
>> $scn[r][c]$ is the character at screen row r and column c,
>> with numbering zero-relative and beginning at the upper-left corner.

According to the declaration, $scn[23][0] = \text{'x'}$ is true if there is an 'x' in the lowest, leftmost position of the terminal screen.

The **State machine** section is the core of the specification and defines one or more FSMs (see Section 3.7). In practice, the FSM descriptions are rarely completely formal; such descriptions are too long and cumbersome to justify their development and maintenance cost. Instead, parts of the FSM are described formally, while other parts are sketched or omitted entirely. Generally, we sketch or omit what is obvious or unimportant. Rather than strive for complete formality, we ensure that the description is complete and precise enough that the required behavior is clear. In principle, from the RS description, the reader should be able to construct a completely formal FSM.

Constants, types, and functions, using the concepts and notations presented in Chapter 3, make the RS easier to understand and maintain. For example, in the **Functions** section of the BSHAM RS, a function is used to compactly specify the text for exception messages.

In a successful system, change is inevitable. Changes in the application area, the need for improved performance, and upgrades to the hardware and software environment all force systems to be modified. The knowledge of what changes are likely is extremely valuable to the designer, because it allows him or her to structure the system so that those changes are inexpensive to make. Such *design for change* is the focus of Chapter 6. To support design for change, each RS contains an **Expected changes** section, describing the changes likely to be requested after system development is complete.

While it is not possible to predict all future changes, certain types of changes occur often and can be predicted well enough to support design for change. For example, input and output formats—for files, reports, and terminal screens—change frequently, as user needs change and become better understood. New system features are added, and old ones modified or deleted. The underlying hardware and software platform is subject to frequent change. Nowadays, hardware may be replaced every few years, and new operating system versions may well arrive annually. Users and developers can often suggest additional changes. For example, payroll personnel know that tax calculations change frequently. The developer applies his or her knowledge of the technology; it is the developer's job to know when a new operating system version is arriving and how it differs from the current version.

Of the seven sections just described, only the **State machine** section needs further discussion.

5.2.2 The state machine section

The **State machine** section is divided into the following five subsections.

1. **Inputs**. The inputs are defined, usually in terms of the input environment variables. In practice, inputs vary widely in form, including commands from the keyboard, lines from a file, or even entire files or directories.

Overview: overview of the system and the RS; notational conventions

Environment variables: declarations of variables modeling the environment

State machine: definition of the FSM on which the RS is based
    Inputs: inputs, in terms of the input environment variables
    Outputs: outputs, in terms of the output environment variables
    States: declarations of variables storing the system state
    Initial state: an initial value for each state variable
    Transitions and outputs: new state and outputs, for each state/input pair

Constants: auxiliary constants

Types: auxiliary types

Functions: auxiliary functions

Expected changes: a list of changes likely after development is complete

Figure 5.1   Requirements specification sections

2. **Outputs**. This section defines the outputs, usually in terms of the environment variables. As with the inputs, considerable variety is encountered in practice. Both event and condition outputs (see Section 3.7) may be specified.

3. **State variables**. The state space is defined in terms of state variables. Each variable is declared by providing its name and type.

4. **Initial state**. The initial state is specified by providing a value for each state variable.

5. **Transitions and outputs**. This section specifies the outputs and new state corresponding to each input and old state. Exceptions are explicitly defined, as conditions on the input and old state. Unless stated otherwise, when an exception occurs the transition is "none": no change in any state variable.

The RS document sections are summarized in Figure 5.1.

5.3   BSHAM Requirements Specification

The BSHAM RS describes the required behavior of the batch version of the SHAM system. The dataflow diagram in Figure 5.2 shows the interaction between the `bsham` program and its environment. A box indicates a data source

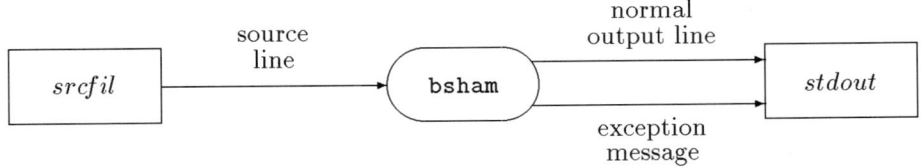

Figure 5.2 BSHAM dataflow diagram

or sink, an oval an executable program, and an arrow a discrete dataflow. Thus, **bsham** reads source program lines from *srcfil* and writes normal output lines and exception messages to *stdout*.

The BSHAM RS must specify, in detail, what normal and exceptional output is produced for each possible *srcfil*. The RS focuses on the following areas:

- *Language syntax—source and object.* What are the legal instructions and operands, input format, and source-code-to-object-code mapping?

- *Registers and main memory.* What are the word size and memory size?

- *Language semantics.* What is the effect of each instruction on memory, the registers, and the program output?

- *Exceptions.* Under what conditions do exceptions occur? What action must be taken?

Even though the service offered by the BSHAM system is simple, developing a detailed RS is challenging. The remainder of this section describes the key parts of the BSHAM RS; the full document may be found in Appendix A.

5.3.1 RS section: Overview

This section provides an overview of the BSHAM system, briefly described in Chapter 4. BSHAM runs on Sun/3 and Sun/4 workstations running SunOS. It is implemented in the C programming language and requires the UNIX/C standard libraries [55]. A simple naming convention is used throughout the RS, as follows. All identifiers are shown in *italics*. The names of constants and abbreviations are all uppercase. The others are all lowercase, except for types, whose names end in '*T*'.

5.3.2 RS section: Environment variables

As suggested by Figure 5.2, there are two environment variables, declared as follows.

srcfil : *string*
> The file name passed on the command line.

stdout : *string*
> UNIX stdout.

5.3.3   RS section: State machine

BSHAM behavior is specified using two FSMs: one for each of the load and execution phases. The load-phase FSM reads the source program a line at a time, and loads the object-code version into BSHAM's main memory. Exception messages are issued as needed. If the load phase is exception-free, then the execution-phase FSM begins running. It continues until a *HALT* instruction is reached or an exception occurs.

5.3.3.1   Command-line invocation

BSHAM is invoked by typing

```
bsham srcfil
```

on the command line. Input is read from *srcfil* and output is written to *stdout*.
   The required response to command-line exceptions is specified using a type and a function, shown in Table 5.1. The type *excidT* introduces identifiers for command-line, load-phase, and execution-phase exceptions. The function *excmsg* specifies the message text corresponding to each exception identifier. Some messages include the illegal token (*tok*) or the location (*loc*) in the source or object code. As Table 5.1 shows, there are two command-line exceptions. If the *srcfil* argument is not present

$$excmsg(NOFILEXC, 0, "")$$

is written to *stdout*. If *srcfil* is unreadable (or does not exist)

$$excmsg(FILSYSEXC, 0, srcfil)$$

is written to *stdout*. If there are any command-line exceptions, BSHAM execution terminates.

5.3.3.2   Load phase

The specification of the load phase depends on the constants and types shown in Figure 5.3. *MAXLINLEN* is the maximum length of a *srcfil* input line, *MAXINT* is the largest integer that can fit in a memory word, and *MEMSIZ* is the total number of words of main memory. The set of legal memory addresses, and the set of legal register or memory values are specified by *shamaddrT* and *shamintegerT*, respectively.

Table 5.1   BSHAM exceptions—*excidT* and *excmsg*

$excidT = \{FILSYSEXC, NOFILEXC,$
$\quad\quad BLANKLINEXC, MISSINGOPEXC, NOMEMEXC,$
$\quad\quad OPFMTEXC, SOURCEEXC,$
$\quad\quad ADDREXC, ARITHEXC, NOOPEXC, OBJECTEXC\}$

$excmsg : excidT \times integer \times string \rightarrow string$

if *id* is	then *excmsg(id, loc, tok)* is
Command-line messages	
FILSYSEXC	`Command line error. Cannot open file:` *tok*
NOFILEXC	`Command line error. No file name specified`
Load-phase messages	
BLANKLINEXC	`Load exception at` *loc*`. Blank line illegal`
MISSINGOPEXC	`Load exception at` *loc*`. Operand missing`
NOMEMEXC	`Load exception at` *loc*`. Program too large`
OPFMTEXC	`Load exception at` *loc*`. Illegal operand:` *tok*
SOURCEEXC	`Load exception at` *loc*`. Illegal instruction:` *tok*
Execution-phase messages	
ADDREXC	`Execution exception at` *loc*`. Illegal operand:` *tok*
ARITHEXC	`Execution exception at` *loc*`. Arithmetic overflow`
NOOPEXC	`Execution exception at` *loc*`. Operand not accessible`
OBJECTEXC	`Execution exception at` *loc*`. Illegal instruction:` *tok*

Constants

Name	Value
MAXLINLEN	100
MAXINT	999
MEMSIZ	100

Types

$shamaddrT = [0..MEMSIZ - 1]$
$shamintegerT = [0..MAXINT]$

Figure 5.3   Constants and types

Table 5.2   Language syntax table

Mnemonic	I.source	I.object	Operand type
Memory access			
LOAD	load	0	*shamaddrT*
STORE	store	1	*shamaddrT*
Arithmetic			
ADD	add	2	*shamaddrT*
SUBTRACT	sub	3	*shamaddrT*
Branch			
BRANCH	br	4	*shamaddrT*
BRANCHZERO	brz	5	*shamaddrT*
BRANCHPOS	brp	6	*shamaddrT*
Miscellaneous			
LOADCON	loadcon	7	*shamintegerT*
PRINT	print	8	
HALT	halt	9	

The SHAM instructions and their arguments are shown in the Language Syntax Table (Table 5.2). The first column contains the instruction mnemonic used in this document. Column two contains the string that must be used in *srcfil*, and column three contains the object-code form generated by BSHAM. The last column shows the type of the instruction operand, if any. In this table and throughout the RS, *I.source* and *I.object* refer to instruction *I*'s source-code string and object-code integer, respectively. Thus, *SUBTRACT.source* is **sub** and *SUBTRACT.object* is 3; *SUBTRACT* takes a single operand of type *shamaddrT*.

At load time, the contents of *srcfil* are scanned a line at a time, converted to object-code form, and loaded into main memory. Each line in *srcfil* must contain exactly one BSHAM instruction. Input lines must not exceed *MAXLINLEN* characters—BSHAM behavior is unpredictable on longer lines. On each input line, tokens must be separated by one or more blanks. Object-code instructions are loaded contiguously, beginning at address 0. Instructions without an operand occupy a single memory location. Instructions with an operand occupy two consecutive memory locations: the instruction code in the first location and the operand in the second.

The load-phase FSM is shown in Figure 5.4. The **Inputs** and **Outputs** are self-explanatory. The **States** entry declares one variable; main memory is represented by an array of *MEMSIZ* integers. Initially, all the memory elements contain zero. The **Transitions and outputs** entry describes the processing of the *n*th line in *srcfil*. If the line is exception-free and *mem* is not full, then the object code specified by the Language Syntax Table (Table 5.2) is loaded.

Inputs

Each input is a line from *srcfil*, read in the order it appears in *srcfil*.

Outputs

Normal-case output and exception messages are written to *stdout*.

States

$mem : sequence \ [0..MEMSIZ - 1] \ of \ shamintegerT$

Initial state

Every element of *mem* is set to 0.

Transitions and outputs

For line L, with line number n:

if the Load-phase Exception Table specifies an exception then

write the specified message to *stdout*

else

if no previous line had an exception then

if there is room in *mem* then

load the object code form of L into *mem*

else

write $excmsg(NOMEMEXC, n, "")$ to *stdout*

Figure 5.4 Load-phase FSM

Table 5.3 illustrates normal-case behavior for the **BSHAM** load phase. The first column shows the source code for a trivial BSHAM program that computes and prints the value of $2 + 2$. For each *mem* address in column two, column three contains the object-code value specified by the Language Syntax Table. The remaining four columns will be discussed below under the execution phase.

The load-phase exception behavior is specified using a tabular conditional rule, the *excmsg* function already described, and several new types. The types are shown in Figure 5.5. The type *sourceT* enumerates the source code instructions whose string values are shown in Table 5.2; *op0sourceT* and *op1sourceT* partition *opsourceT* into the zero and one-operand instructions. In the Load-phase Exception Table (Table 5.4) the normal case and exception situations are defined by the conditions in column one. The message text is specified in column two, where **Normal case** indicates that no exception is to be signaled.

Table 5.5 shows a purposely flawed program, and the specified exception messages. Consider the first line of Table 5.5 in terms of Table 5.4. Here:

$$L = \texttt{br 115}, \ K = 2, \ T_1 = \texttt{br}, \ and \ T_2 = \texttt{115}.$$

We follow the conditional rule in the Load-phase Exception Table (Table 5.4), top-down and noting only the conditions that are true. We find that

$$K > 0, \ T_1 \in op1sourceT, \ K > 1, \ T_1 \neq LOADCON.source, \ T_2 \notin shamaddrT$$

Table 5.3   Example: the $2 + 2$ program

srcfil	Object code		'After' values			
	Address	Value	pc	acc	$mem[8]$	$stdout$
loadcon 2	0	7	2	2	0	$\langle\rangle$
	1	2				
store 8	2	1	4	2	2	$\langle\rangle$
	3	8				
add 8	4	2	6	4	2	$\langle\rangle$
	5	8				
print	6	8	7	4	2	$\langle 4\rangle$
halt	7	9	7	4	2	$\langle 4\rangle$

$sourceT = \{LOAD.source, STORE.source, ADD.source, SUBTRACT.source,$
$\qquad BRANCH.source, BRANCHZERO.source, BRANCHPOS.source,$
$\qquad LOADCON.source, PRINT.source, HALT.source\}$

$op0sourceT = \{HALT.source, PRINT.source\}$

$op\_sourceT = sourceT - op0sourceT$

Figure 5.5   Types for classifying source code instructions

Table 5.4   Load-phase exception table

Let L be the current line, with line number n (numbered one-relative).
Let $T_1, T_2, \ldots, T_K$ be the tokens in L.

Condition	Message
$K = 0$ (L is blank)	$excmsg(BLANKLINEXC, n, "")$
$K > 0$	
$\quad T_1 \in op0sourceT$	Normal case
$\quad T_1 \in op1sourceT$	
$\qquad K = 1$	$excmsg(MISSINGOPEXC, n, "")$
$\qquad K > 1$	
$\qquad\quad T_1 = LOADCON.source$	
$\qquad\qquad T_2 \in shamintegerT$	Normal case
$\qquad\qquad T_2 \notin shamintegerT$	$excmsg(OPFMTEXC, n, T_2)$
$\qquad\quad T_1 \neq LOADCON.source$	
$\qquad\qquad T_2 \in shamaddrT$	Normal case
$\qquad\qquad T_2 \notin shamaddrT$	$excmsg(OPFMTEXC, n, T_2)$
$\quad T_1 \notin sourceT$	$excmsg(SOURCEEXC, n, T_1)$

Table 5.5   Example: load-phase exceptions

srcfil	Exception message
br 115	Load exception at 1. Illegal operand: 115
lode 7	Load exception at 2. Illegal instruction: lode
add	Load exception at 3. Operand missing
add 5 8	

Thus $excmsg(OPFMTEXC, 1, 115)$ is indicated. Figure 5.1 shows that the message text is

> Load exception at 1. Illegal operand: 115.

Note that the last instruction in Table 5.5 generates no exception message, even though *ADD* takes only one operand. While it might seem that a correct *srcfil* line must have exactly one or two tokens, careful examination of the Load-phase Exception Table (Table 5.4) will show that *srcfil* lines of three, four, or more tokens may be correct; it is only the first one or two tokens that are significant. This provides BSHAM with a crude commenting feature, as shown in the sample programs in the BSHAM RS.

If there are any load-time exceptions, BSHAM execution terminates at the end of the load phase.

5.3.3.3   Execution phase

The execution phase is based on the Language Semantics Table (Table 5.6). This table specifies the effect of each exception-free BSHAM instruction on the values of *mem*, *acc*, and *pc*. We illustrate its use with three examples.

1. Suppose that $pc = 5$, $acc = 10$, $mem[5] = 1$, and $mem[6] = 50$. Because $pc = 5$, the current instruction is $mem[5]$ and its operand is $mem[6]$. According to the Language Syntax Table (Table 5.2), $mem[5]$ contains the object-code value for a *STORE* instruction. Referring to the Language Semantics Table, we see the following multiple assignment statement for *STORE.object*:

$$mem[op], pc := acc, (pc + 2) \bmod MEMSIZ$$

where $op = mem[pc + 1]$. Substituting the current values for *op*, *pc*, and *acc*, and simplifying, we get

$$mem[50], pc := 10, 7$$

Thus, the *STORE* instruction at address 5 copies the accumulator to the address in $mem[6]$. All other *mem* locations and *acc* remain unchanged.

2. Suppose that $pc = 5$, $acc = 10$, $mem[5] = 2$, $mem[6] = 50$, and $mem[50] = 5$. According to the Language Syntax Table, $mem[5]$ is an ADD instruction. The Language Semantics Table contains the following multiple assignment statement for $ADD.object$:

$$acc, pc := acc + mem[op], (pc + 2) \bmod MEMSIZ.$$

Substituting the current values for acc, op, and pc and simplifying, we get

$$acc, pc := 15, 7.$$

Thus, the ADD instruction at address 5 adds the value at address $mem[6]$ to the accumulator. All mem values remain unchanged.

3. Suppose that $pc = 5$, $mem[5] = 5$, and $mem[6] = 5$. According to Table 5.2, $mem[5]$ is a $BRANCHZERO$ instruction. The Language Semantics Table contains the following conditional multiple assignment statement for $BRANCHZERO.object$:

$$pc := (acc = 0 \Rightarrow op \mid acc > 0 \Rightarrow (pc + 2) \bmod MEMSIZ).$$

Substituting the current values for op and pc, and simplifying, we get

$$pc := (acc = 0 \Rightarrow 5 \mid acc > 0 \Rightarrow 7).$$

Thus, if $acc = 0$ then the $BRANCHZERO$ instruction will cause an infinite loop; otherwise, it will have no effect beyond advancing the pc to the next instruction.

Given the Language Semantics Table, the execution-phase FSM is straightforward (see Figure 5.6). There are no **Inputs**; only the mem values collected during the load phase are needed. The **Outputs** are integers generated by $PRINT$ instructions and execution-phase exception messages. The **States** are the same as for the load-phase FSM. The **Initial state** consists of the mem values as they were when the load phase completed processing the last line in $srcfil$, and the initial value of acc and pc is 0. According to the **Transitions and outputs** section, the FSM executes the instructions in $mem[pc]$ until an exception occurs or $mem[pc] = HALT.object$. Note that, while the load phase may generate multiple exception messages, the execution phase halts on the first exception.

We illustrate the execution-phase FSM by again using Table 5.3. Columns four through seven show the values of pc, acc, $mem[8]$, and $stdout$ after the instruction in each row has completed execution. The algorithm is simple: $LOADCON$ puts 2 in the accumulator, which is then stored at address 8, added to the accumulator, and printed. As column two shows, the object code instructions occupy words 0–7, and address 8 is the first available location for data. Note that the $HALT$ instruction has no effect on the state variables.

Table 5.6   Language semantics table $(op = mem[pc + 1])$

Instruction at $mem[pc]$	Effect on mem, acc, and pc
Memory access	
$LOAD.object$	$acc, pc := mem[op], (pc + 2) \bmod MEMSIZ$
$STORE.object$	$mem[op], pc := acc, (pc + 2) \bmod MEMSIZ$
Arithmetic	
$ADD.object$	$acc, pc := acc + mem[op], (pc + 2) \bmod MEMSIZ$
$SUBTRACT.object$	$acc, pc := acc - mem[op], (pc + 2) \bmod MEMSIZ$
Branch	
$BRANCH.object$	$pc := op$
$BRANCHZERO.object$	$pc := (acc = 0 \Rightarrow op$ $\mid acc > 0 \Rightarrow (pc + 2) \bmod MEMSIZ)$
$BRANCHPOS.object$	$pc := (acc > 0 \Rightarrow op$ $\mid acc = 0 \Rightarrow (pc + 2) \bmod MEMSIZ)$
Miscellaneous	
$LOADCON.object$	$acc, pc := op, (pc + 2) \bmod MEMSIZ$
$PRINT.object$	$pc := (pc + 1) \bmod MEMSIZ$
$HALT.object$	no change to acc, pc, mem

Inputs
>   None.

Outputs
>   Normal-case output and exception messages are written to *stdout*.

States
> $mem : sequence\ [0..MEMSIZ - 1]\ of\ shamintegerT$
> $acc : shamintegerT$
> $pc : shamaddrT$

Initial state
> $mem, acc, pc :=$ (the final value from the load phase FSM)$, 0, 0$

Transitions and outputs
>   for the instruction beginning at $mem[pc]$:
>>   if the Execution-phase Exception Table specifies an exception then
>>>   write the specified message to *stdout*
>>>   terminate SHAM
>>   else if $mem[pc] = HALT.object$ then
>>>   terminate SHAM
>>   else
>>>   if $mem[pc] = PRINT.object$ then
>>>>   write to *stdout* : acc || newline
>>>   modify mem, acc, and pc as shown in the Language Semantics Table

Figure 5.6   BSHAM execution-phase FSM

$$objectT = \{LOAD.object, STORE.object, ADD.object, SUBTRACT.object,$$
$$BRANCH.object, BRANCHZERO.object, BRANCHPOS.object,$$
$$LOADCON.object, PRINT.object, HALT.object\}$$

$$op0objectT = \{HALT.object, PRINT.object\}$$

$$op1objectT = objectT - op0objectT$$

Figure 5.7   Types for classifying object code instructions

As for the load phase, the execution-phase exception behavior is defined using a tabular conditional rule, the *excmsg* function, and several types. The types are shown in Figure 5.7. The type *objectT* enumerates the object code instructions whose integer values are shown in Table 5.2; *op0objectT* and *op1objectT* partition *opobjectT* into the zero and one-operand instructions. In the Execution-phase Exception Table (Table 5.7), the normal-case and exception situations are defined by the conditions in column one. The message text is specified in column two, where **Normal case** indicates that no exception is to be signaled. The execution-phase exceptions are subtle; this table deserves careful study. We next walk through the exceptions defined in the table. For convenience, let $i = mem[pc]$ and $op = mem[pc + 1]$.

1. *ARITHEXC*: signaled if i is an *ADD* (or *SUBTRACT*) instruction and the result of the addition (or subtraction) is not a legal integer. The result is not representable in the accumulator.

2. *ADDREXC*: signaled if i is a one-operand instruction requiring an address, and *op* is not a legal address. If the address is illegal, then the operand cannot be retrieved from *mem*.

3. *NOOPEXC*: signaled if i is a one-operand instruction in the last word of *mem*. Here, *op* is needed but undefined.

4. *OBJECTEXC*: signaled if i is not a legal instruction. In this case, no line in the Language Semantics Table applies.

Table 5.8 explores a BSHAM program that generates *ADDREXC*. Column one shows the source code, columns two and three the object code, and columns four, five, and six, the values of *pc*, *acc*, and *mem*[5] after each instruction has been executed. The *LOADCON* instruction places 500 in the accumulator, which is then stored at address 5, the address of the *BRANCH* instruction's operand. Because 500 is not a legal address, execution of the *BRANCH* instruction generates *ADDREXC*. Referring to the Execution-phase Exception Table (Table 5.7), we find that the following conditions are true:

$$i \in op1objectT, \ pc \in [0..MEMSIZ - 2],$$

$$i \neq LOADCON.object, \ op \notin shamaddrT.$$

Here $pc = 4$, $i = mem[pc] = 4$, and $op = mem[pc + 1] = 500$. It is interesting to note that the $BRANCH$ operand was legal at load time, but was overwritten at execution time. This is an instance of code modification, which is generally considered bad programming practice and is prohibited by many operating systems.

Table 5.7   Execution-phase exception table

Let $i = mem[pc]$ and $op = mem[pc + 1]$

Condition	Message
$i \in op0objectT$	Normal case
$i \in op1objectT$	
$\quad pc \in [0..MEMSIZ - 2]$	
$\qquad i = LOADCON.object$	Normal case
$\qquad i \neq LOADCON.object$	
$\qquad\quad op \in shamaddrT$	
$\qquad\qquad i = ADD.object$	
$\qquad\qquad\quad acc + mem[op] \in shamintegerT$	Normal case
$\qquad\qquad\quad acc + mem[op] \notin shamintegerT$	$excmsg(ARITHEXC, pc, "")$
$\qquad\qquad i = SUBTRACT.object$	
$\qquad\qquad\quad acc - mem[op] \in shamintegerT$	Normal case
$\qquad\qquad\quad acc - mem[op] \notin shamintegerT$	$excmsg(ARITHEXC, pc, "")$
$\qquad\qquad true$	Normal case
$\qquad\quad op \notin shamaddrT$	$excmsg(ADDREXC, pc, op)$
$\quad pc = MEMSIZ - 1$	$excmsg(NOOPEXC, pc, "")$
$i \notin objectT$	$excmsg(OBJECTEXC, pc, i)$

Table 5.8   Example: execution-phase exception

Source code	Object code		'After' values		
	Address	Value	pc	acc	$mem[5]$
loadcon 500	0	7	2	500	0
	1	500			
store 5	2	1	4	500	500
	3	5			
br 0	4	4	4	500	500
	5	0			

Input/output format
- Command-line parameters besides *srcfil*.
- Different input format: new tokens, delimiters, and instruction formats.
- Handle overlength lines robustly.

Abstract machine
- Change in word size, number of words in main memory.
- New or extended data types, especially signed integers.
- More registers, e.g., index registers.
- More or different SHAM instructions.
- More addressing modes.
- Symbolic data and branch addresses.

Platform
- Different operating system: other UNIX platforms or MS-DOS.

Exception handling
- Limits on the number of exceptions reported or instructions executed.
- Changes in the conditions defining exceptions and in the message text.

Figure 5.8   BSHAM expected changes

5.3.4   RS section: Expected changes

Figure 5.8 shows the expected changes to the BSHAM system. Changes are frequently requested to input and output formats. Here the command-line format and the *srcfil* format, as well as the handling of overlength lines, are subject to change. The abstract machine is the core of the BSHAM system; the changes listed describe desirable features found in other assemblers. Platform changes are inevitable within a few years of system delivery. We will surely "port" BSHAM to other UNIX platforms and possibly to MS-DOS. Finally, system use will suggest improvements to exception handling.

5.3.5   Summary

The BSHAM system offers a simple service. Nonetheless, developing a complete RS is challenging. While the RS contains many details, the document structure is simple and easy to learn. The document is driven by two FSMs. The load-phase FSM is specified in a half-page (Figure 5.4). This figure is short because most of the details are elsewhere: in the Language Syntax Table (Table 5.2) and the Load-phase Exception Table (Table 5.4). The **Constants**, **Types**, and **Functions** sections are also used. Similarly, the execution-phase FSM (Figure 5.6) is short and depends upon the Language Semantics Table (Table 5.6) and the Execution-phase Exception Table (Table 5.7).

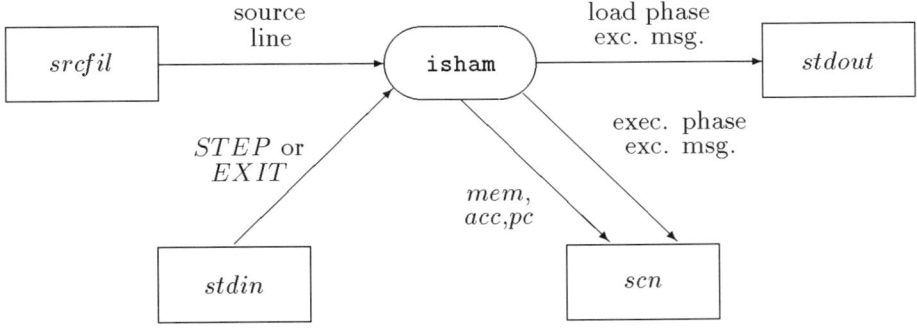

Figure 5.9   ISHAM dataflow diagram

5.4   ISHAM Requirements Specification

The ISHAM RS describes the behavior of the interactive version of the SHAM system. The dataflow diagram in Figure 5.9 sketches the interface between the **isham** program and its environment. As with BSHAM, ISHAM reads source program lines from *srcfil* and writes load-phase exception messages to *stdout*. However, the ISHAM execution phase is different. The user has limited control over execution through *STEP* and *EXIT* commands entered through *stdin*. The values in main memory, the accumulator, and the program counter are displayed on *scn*, the terminal screen. Similarly, the execution-phase exception messages are displayed on *scn*.

The ISHAM RS must specify, in detail, the *scn* contents corresponding to each possible *srcfil* and sequence of commands from *stdin*. The RS focuses on the following areas.

- *Keyboard input.* A new input variable, *stdin*, is introduced to model keyboard input.

- *Formatted screen.* A new output variable, *scn*, is introduced to model screen output. Considerable effort is invested to precisely specify the screen format.

- *Execution phase.* The BSHAM execution-phase FSM is replaced by one that reads commands from *stdin* and updates *scn*.

5.4.1   RS section: Overview

This section specifies the behavior of ISHAM, the interactive version of SHAM. The ISHAM and BSHAM load phases are identical, as are the language syntax and semantics, but the execution phases differ in two ways. In ISHAM:

1. Object code execution is "single-stepped" under user control.

2. Output is through a formatted screen with main memory and the registers displayed and updated after each instruction execution.

Because ISHAM and BSHAM have much in common, this document is written as an addendum to the BSHAM RS, describing only the differences between ISHAM and BSHAM. In summary, these are (1) environment variables to model keyboard input and formatted screen output, (2) a detailed format for precisely describing screen updates, (3) a new execution-phase FSM, and (4) several new expected changes.

5.4.2   RS section: Environment variables

Two new environment variables are needed:

stdin : *string*
   UNIX standard input
scn : *sequence* [24][80] *of char*
   $scn[r][c]$ is the character at screen row r and column c,
   with numbering zero-relative and beginning at the upper-left corner.

As shown in Figure 5.10, we divide *scn* into screen fields that are either *fixed* or *varying*. The fixed fields are written when ISHAM execution begins and remain unchanged while ISHAM is running. The varying fields may change repeatedly during ISHAM execution. Each varying field has an identifier: *MEM*, *ACC*, *PC*, *PRT*, or *MSG*. The extent of each varying field on the screen is the character positions occupied by the field identifier, and the trailing –s if present. When a *MEM*, *ACC*, *PC*, or *PRT* value is shorter than the extent shown, it is right-justified and padded left with blanks; *MSG* values are left-justified and padded right with blanks. The *MEM* field occurs 100 times on the screen, and a particular *MEM* occurrence is indicated by row and column subscripts, numbered zero-relative, top-down, and left-to-right. For example, $MEM[9,0]$ is the leftmost and lowest occurrence.

5.4.3   RS section: State machine

5.4.3.1   Command-line invocation

ISHAM is invoked by typing

```
isham srcfil
```

on the command line. Input is read from *srcfil* and *stdin*, and output is written to *stdout* and *scn*.

```
01234567890123456789012345678901234567890123456789012345678901234567890
************************************************************************
                             SHAM

                 0     1     2     3     4     5     6     7     8     9

Main        0   MEM   MEM   MEM   MEM   MEM   MEM   MEM   MEM   MEM   MEM
memory:    10   MEM   MEM   MEM   MEM   MEM   MEM   MEM   MEM   MEM   MEM
           20   MEM   MEM   MEM   MEM   MEM   MEM   MEM   MEM   MEM   MEM
           30   MEM   MEM   MEM   MEM   MEM   MEM   MEM   MEM   MEM   MEM
           40   MEM   MEM   MEM   MEM   MEM   MEM   MEM   MEM   MEM   MEM
           50   MEM   MEM   MEM   MEM   MEM   MEM   MEM   MEM   MEM   MEM
           60   MEM   MEM   MEM   MEM   MEM   MEM   MEM   MEM   MEM   MEM
           70   MEM   MEM   MEM   MEM   MEM   MEM   MEM   MEM   MEM   MEM
           80   MEM   MEM   MEM   MEM   MEM   MEM   MEM   MEM   MEM   MEM
           90   MEM   MEM   MEM   MEM   MEM   MEM   MEM   MEM   MEM   MEM


                   Program counter:  PC
                      Accumulator:  ACC
              Last value printed:  PRT


Enter command: 's' to single step; 'e' to exit
Message: MSG-----------------------------------------------------------
************************************************************************
```

Figure 5.10   Screen format

If the *srcfil* argument is not present,

$$excmsg(NOFILEXC, 0, "")$$

is written to *stdout*. If *srcfil* is unreadable (or does not exist),

$$excmsg(FILSYSEXC, 0, srcfil)$$

is written to *stdout*. If there are any command-line exceptions, ISHAM execution terminates.

5.4.3.2   Load phase

Unchanged from the BSHAM Requirements Specification.

5.4.3.3   Execution phase

The execution-phase FSM is shown in Figure 5.11. Each input is a keystroke from *stdin*; each output is an update to *scn*. As with BSHAM, the initial state for the execution phase consists of the final values stored in *mem* after the load phase and 0 for *acc* and *pc*.

The **Transitions and outputs** section is more challenging. Briefly, each $STEP$ command causes an update to the state, and a corresponding update to the *scn* fields. Only the $EXIT$ command causes ISHAM to terminate. Examining this section in more detail, we find three cases, based on the value of *c*: (1) $EXIT$, (2) $STEP$, and (3) other. In case (1) we terminate ISHAM, and in case (3) we display an exception message, but do not terminate. Case (2) has three subcases: (a) exception, (b) $HALT$, and (c) other. In cases (a) and (b) we display a message. In case (c), we clear the message field, update the PRT field ($PRINT$ instruction only), and update the FSM state.

The primary effect on the screen is specified separately, by stating a relationship between *scn* and the FSM state that the ISHAM system must maintain. Item (1) requires that the fixed fields be displayed. Item (2) specifies the required correspondence between *mem*, *acc*, and *pc*, and MEM, ACC, and PC. Item (3) requires highlighting of the current instruction. In items (2) and (3), the subscript expressions compute the familiar mapping between linear memory addresses, and row and column indexes in a two-dimensional array overlaying the linear memory.

5.4.4   RS section: Expected changes

The expected changes are shown in Figure 5.12. Screen format changes are common, motivating item (1). With $MEMSIZ = 100$, *mem* is small. However, if it is substantially enlarged, then some form of scrolling will be required, motivating item (2). Finally, single-stepping through a long-running program is tedious; other forms of execution will be requested.

5.4.5   Example

To illustrate the ISHAM execution behavior, Figure 5.13 shows an *scn* value corresponding to the program in Figure 5.3. The *scn* value shown occurs just before the $HALT$ instruction is executed or, equivalently, just after four $STEP$ commands have been executed. During actual execution, the '9' in position $MEM[0, 7]$ would be displayed in inverse video.

5.4.6   Summary

The ISHAM RS has the same structure as the BSHAM RS. The primary differences are the introduction of the *scn* environment variable—to precisely specify screen fields—and the new execution-phase FSM—to specify screen updates.

Inputs

Keystrokes from *stdin*.

Outputs

All outputs are to *scn* and its fields.

States

Same as for the load phase FSM.

Initial state

$mem, acc, pc :=$ (the final value from the load phase FSM), $0, 0$

Transitions and outputs

For each character, c, from *stdin*

if $c = EXIT$ then

clear *scn*

halt ISHAM execution

else if $c = STEP$ then

if the BSHAM Execution-phase Exception Table specifies

an exception for $mem[pc]$ then

$MSG :=$ the specified message

else if $mem[pc] = HALT.object$ then

$MSG := HALTMSG$

else

$MSG :=$ ""

if $mem[pc] = PRINT.object$ then

$PRT := acc$

modify mem, acc, pc, as per the BSHAM Language Semantics Table

else

$MSG := CMDERRMSG$

Notes on screen updating:

- Initially and between transitions, ensure that:
    1. The fixed fields shown in the ISHAM screen format are displayed.
    2. MEM, PC, and ACC are such that
       $$(\forall r, c \in [0..9])(MEM[r, c] = mem[10 \times r + c]) \wedge ACC = acc \wedge PC = pc$$
    3. $MEM[pc/10, pc \bmod 10]$ is displayed in inverse video.
- Initially the MSG and PRT fields are blank

Figure 5.11   ISHAM execution-phase FSM

1. The field positions and the contents of the fixed fields will change.

2. $MEMSIZ$ will exceed 100 and vertical scrolling will be supported.

3. Different forms of stepping through the instructions will be supported, such as executing a specified number of instructions or executing until a specified instruction is reached.

Figure 5.12   ISHAM expected changes

```
0123456789012345678901234567890123456789012345678901234567890123456789012345678901
**********************************************************************************
                                    SHAM


                    0     1     2     3     4     5     6     7     8     9

Main       0        7     2     1     8     2     8     8     9     2     0
memory:   10        0     0     0     0     0     0     0     0     0     0
          20        0     0     0     0     0     0     0     0     0     0
          30        0     0     0     0     0     0     0     0     0     0
          40        0     0     0     0     0     0     0     0     0     0
          50        0     0     0     0     0     0     0     0     0     0
          60        0     0     0     0     0     0     0     0     0     0
          70        0     0     0     0     0     0     0     0     0     0
          80        0     0     0     0     0     0     0     0     0     0
          90        0     0     0     0     0     0     0     0     0     0


                           Program counter:    7
                               Accumulator:    4
                        Last value printed:    4


Enter command: "s" to single step; "e" to exit
Message:
**********************************************************************************
```

Figure 5.13   Example: *scn* contents for $2 + 2$ program

5.5   Verification

5.5.1   Verification procedures

After an RS has been written, it must be verified. As described in Section 2.4, verification can be accomplished using inspection and testing. However, our RSs are not executable and therefore cannot be tested. Figure 5.14 shows the RS inspection criteria. We review the "additional criteria" list from an inspection viewpoint.

1. *Well formed.* The inspectors check for violations of the work product definition, as described in Section 5.2. For example, is the **Expected changes** section present? Is every constant that is used also defined?

2. *Precise and comprehensible.* Here the inspectors serve as representatives of the intended audience. While it is sometimes difficult to inspect for

- **Audience**. System users, system developers.

- **Prerequisites**. A reading knowledge of the RS format and notations.

- **Purpose**. Describe the characteristics of the system required by the user: no more, no less.

- **Additional criteria**.

  1. *Well formed.* The specification is well formed with respect to the format described in Section 5.2.

  2. *Precise and comprehensible.* The specification can be read and understood by the intended audience.

  3. *Complete.* In every situation, either an assumption is violated, an exception is generated, or the normal case is well defined.

  4. *Feasible.* The system can be implemented and tested affordably.

Figure 5.14   Requirements specification criteria

these criteria, disagreement by the inspectors regarding the meaning of the document is strong evidence that it is not precise and comprehensible.

3. *Complete.* The inspection process is well suited for checking adherence to this criterion, especially if the RS has been designed so that the completeness argument is straightforward to construct and comprehend.

4. *Feasible.* Accurately estimating the cost of system development is difficult. However, a good RS can help tremendously. Sketches of the design and implementation may also be required.

5.5.2   Example: completeness of BSHAM execution phase

We illustrate the use of the RS criteria by presenting a completeness argument for the BSHAM execution phase. We make no assumptions about the *mem*, *acc*, and *pc* values passed on from the load phase. The exceptions are defined in the Execution-phase Exception Table (Table 5.7) and the normal case is defined by the Language Semantics Table (Table 5.6). The completeness argument is driven by Table 5.7 and is broken into two steps:

1. *Conditions cover all situations.* Show that the conditions in column one cover every situation.

2. *Actions well defined.* Show that each action in column two is well defined. For the exception entries, we need only show that the *excmsg* call is defined in Table 5.1. For the normal case entries, we must show that the assignment statements in Table 5.6 are well defined.

We begin by noting that $pc \in [0..MEMSIZ - 1]$ is always true, because pc is initially 0 (see Figure 5.6) and is incremented modulo $MEMSIZ$ (see Table 5.6).

5.5.2.1   Conditions cover all situations

We must show that, at each indentation level, every situation is handled.

- From the definitions in Figure 5.7, it is clear that exactly one of $i \in op0objectT$, $i \in op1objectT$, and $i \notin objectT$ must hold.

- Under $i \in op1objectT$: because $pc \in [0..MEMSIZ - 1]$ holds, one of $pc \in [0..MEMSIZ - 2]$ and $pc = MEMSIZ - 1$ must hold as well.

- Under $pc \in [0..MEMSIZ - 2]$: obviously, i is either $LOADCON.object$ or it is not.

- Under $i \neq LOADCON.object$: We know that $pc \in [0..MEMSIZ - 2]$ at this point; therefore, op is defined. Clearly, either $op \in shamaddrT$ or $op \notin shamaddrT$ must hold.

- Under $op \in shamaddrT$: here completeness is immediate because of the *true* entry for the third case.

- Under $i = ADD.object$: obviously, $acc+mem[op]$ is either in $shamintegerT$ or it is not.

- Under $i = SUBTRACT.object$: similarly, $acc - mem[op]$ is either in $shamintegerT$ or it is not.

5.5.2.2   Actions well defined

Examination of Table 5.1 shows that the exception entries are defined. The five **Normal case** entries are more challenging. We discuss them in the order they appear in the table.

1. Because $i \in op0objectT$, i is either a $PRINT$ or a $HALT$ instruction. As Table 5.6 shows, the actions associated with these instructions are always defined.

2. Because acc and op are both of type $shamintegerT$, the $LOADCON$ action is defined.

3. For this case and the next two cases, we know that i is a one-operand instruction other than $LOADCON$ and op is a legal address. Therefore, if $acc + mem[op]$ is in range then the ADD entry in Table 5.6 is defined.

4. Similarly, if $acc - mem[op]$ is in range then the $SUBTRACT$ entry in Table 5.6 is defined.

5. For each of the remaining instructions—*LOAD*, *STORE*, and the branch instructions—the Table 5.6 entry is defined as long as $op \in shamaddrT$ is a legal address.

That concludes the completeness argument for the execution phase. No sophisticated mathematics is required: just careful case analysis of a document designed to support case analysis.

5.6 Summary

The goal of the RS is to specify the required behavior of a software system precisely. The RS provides a written record of the commitment the developers have made to the users. We favor a systematic approach with standardized document sections, notations, and naming conventions. A standardized approach takes extra effort initially, but over time it pays off.

In this chapter, we examine the BSHAM and ISHAM RSs in detail. These documents show how to describe required behavior precisely and compactly long before implementation. While RSs for industrial systems are far larger and more complex, the same techniques apply: FSMs, tables, and functions. An RS is a reference document; frequently less than half the space is occupied by prose paragraphs. There is heavy use of tables and formulas, though no single table or formula is particularly complex. While an RS does not make easy reading, it provides precise answers to important questions about what must be built. Also important, it provides a framework in which to ask precise questions.

The BSHAM and ISHAM RSs are precise and detailed enough to support useful verification for properties such as completeness. It is critical that the RS be developed with verification in mind. Much of the power of a good RS is shown in the chapters that follow; we rely on the RS in every development phase.

5.7 Bibliographic Notes

Our approach to requirements specification has been influenced by the *Software Cost Reduction* approach [56, 57] in which precise specifications are achieved by relying on tables rather than diagrams. Many other approaches have been proposed. Alford describes the Requirements Statement Language [58] and Teichrow presents the Problem Statement Language [10]. DeMarco [23] and Yourdon and Constantine [24] apply Structured Analysis and Structured Design (SA/SD) to requirements specification. Ward and Mellor show how to adapt SA/SD to real-time systems [25]. With *statecharts*, state machine specifications are represented in a graphical, executable form [59]. Dreger uses *function points* to estimate development cost based on a requirements specification [60]. Davis provides a survey of requirements specification methods [61].

Chapter 6

Module Decomposition

Divide et impera.

6.1 Introduction

In multi-version/multi-person programming, the systems are too large and complex to be developed "all at once." Instead, the development task must be divided into modules: programming work assignments. For a given RS, there are a large number of possible module decompositions, some good and some bad. In a good decomposition, the modules are of manageable size and complexity, and are independent. Ideally, each module would be completely independent of the others. However, complete independence is rarely achievable; instead interdependencies are carefully monitored and minimized. A good decomposition should provide the following benefits:

- *Shorter development time.* Programmers working on different modules can work in parallel and with relatively little interpersonal communication. In a decomposition with undisciplined dependencies, such parallel work is infeasible.

- *Improved verification.* Verification is simpler and more reliable because the verification of each module is largely independent of the other modules. Unnecessary dependencies can dramatically increase the difficulty of verification and the likelihood of verification errors.

- *Reduced maintenance cost.* Maintenance costs can be reduced by encapsulating each expected change in a separate module. Careful use of encapsulation can significantly reduce the *ripple effect*: the tendency of a change in module M_1 to cause a change in module M_2, which causes a change in M_3, and so on. When encapsulation is ignored, the ripple effect can be disastrous.

In today's competitive environment, reduced time to market, improved reliability, and lower maintenance costs are all highly desirable.

Below we describe information hiding—the module decomposition technique used in SHAM—and the format of the Module Guide (MG), the module decomposition work product. We review the SHAM decomposition and MG in detail, and close by describing the MG verification procedure. The complete MG may be found in Appendix B.

6.2   Information Hiding

6.2.1   The information-hiding technique

Information hiding is a module decomposition technique well suited to large, complex systems. Information hiding is carried out in three steps.

1. *Identify the expected changes.* Record the characteristics of the system that are likely to change. Consider the behavior seen by the end user, the internal data structures and algorithms, and the underlying hardware and operating system.

2. *Encapsulate each expected change.* Introduce one module for each change. We say that the module *hides* the change, and we call the change the module *secret*.

3. *Design the module interfaces.* For each module, design an interface which will not change even if there is a change in the module secret.

Steps 1 and 2 are the focus of this chapter; step 3 is covered in Chapter 7.

We divide the modules in an information-hiding decomposition into three groups.

- *Behavior-hiding* modules hide the behavior observable to the end user, as described in the RS. Typical secrets include input formats, screen formats, and the text of messages.

- *Software decision–hiding* modules hide the internal data structures and algorithms. For example, a set of strings may be stored in an array, a linked list, or a tree, and may be accessed by linear search or hashing.

- *Machine-hiding* modules hide the characteristics of the underlying machine: the hardware machine or the "virtual machine" provided by the operating system and utilities. Typical secrets are device register formats and the parameter formats for operating system procedure calls.

Grouping modules by secret type is useful in two ways: it provides insight to the designers during module decomposition, and it guides the maintainer when searching for modules affected by a change.

While the information-hiding technique is simple, applying it requires deep thinking. There are limits to what can be hidden; information hiding sometimes conflicts with practicality and must be applied with common sense.

6.2.2 An RS-driven approach to information hiding

In combination, the RS work product and the information-hiding technique support a systematic module decomposition approach. The focus is on the RS variables; for each kind of variable—input, output, and state—a small set of candidate modules is suggested, as follows:

- *Input variables.* For each input variable, two modules are suggested. A machine-hiding module gets input from a hardware device or operating system service and hides the changeable characteristics of that device or service. A behavior-hiding module extracts the relevant information from the input provided by the machine-hiding module and hides the input format. We call this a *behavior-hiding input-format* (or just *input-format*) module.

- *Output variables.* There are three modules corresponding to each output variable: a machine-hiding module, a *behavior-hiding output-format* (or just *output-format*) module, and an additional behavior-hiding module. The machine-hiding module writes output using a hardware device or an operating system service and hides the changeable characteristics of that device or service. The output-format module formats information to be written to the machine-hiding module and hides the output format. The additional behavior-hiding module determines what values should be passed to the output-format module and hides the RS rules that specify those values. We call this a *behavior-hiding output-driver* (or just *output-driver*) module.

- *State variables.* For each state variable, two modules are suggested. A software decision–hiding module provides operations on the state variable and hides the implementation data structures and algorithms. A behavior-hiding module uses the software decision–hiding module to control the state variable value and hides the RS rules that specify state values. We call this a *behavior-hiding state-driver* (or just *state-driver*) module.

While the approach just described provides a useful framework for module decomposition, the designer's judgment is still critical. Sometimes suggested modules will be rejected as unnecessary; at other times additional modules will be needed. Frequently, there will be a single module to handle a group of related variables, instead of one module for each variable. Almost always there will be important considerations other than information hiding.

Module summary
    Long name: descriptive name
    Short name: short mnemonic for file names
    Prefix: short string prepended to exported C identifiers

Module service and secret
    Service: brief description of features provided
    Secret: likely change encapsulated

Figure 6.1   Module guide sections

6.3   Work Product Definition

The module decomposition is described in the *Module Guide* (MG), consisting
of two sections. The **Module summary** section lists the modules, grouped
by secret type. For each module, three names are given. The *long name* is
descriptive and consists of one or more English words. The *short name* is a
mnemonic identifier and is used for file names. The *prefix* is a short string;
it is prepended to every C identifier exported by the module to avoid name
conflicts with other modules. For example, if this naming scheme is applied to
the *stack* module of Figure 2.1, the long name might be "Pushdown Stack,"
the short name *stack*, and the prefix `ps_`. The `stack` directory would contain
most of the files for this module, such as `stack.c`—the Implementation—and
`stack.tplan`—the Test Plan. The initialization access routine would be called
`ps_s_init`; other modules will also have initialization routines, but with different
prefixes.

    The second section, the **Module service and secret** section, contains an
entry for each module, briefly describing the service offered and the likely change
encapsulated by the module. The detailed service specification is contained in
the Interface Specification (see Chapter 7).

    The MG document sections are summarized in Figure 6.1.

6.4   SHAM Module Guide

6.4.1   BSHAM module decomposition

Before applying the procedure of Section 6.2, we make several decomposition
decisions not directly motivated by information hiding. We introduce the Load
(*load*) and Execute (*exec*) modules, which model the RS load and execute phases.
A simple coordinator module, Sham (*sham*), is also introduced to initiate the
load and execution phases. While the BSHAM and ISHAM execution phases
are different, a single *exec* module will handle both versions. This initial decomposition follows the RS closely, simplifying verification. Note that the existence

of the *load* and *exec* modules is not mandated by the RS; the RS constrains the system behavior but *not* its internal structure.

We now continue the decomposition, by considering the candidate modules suggested for each of the RS variables. As described in Section 5.3, there is one input variable (*srcfil*), one output variable (*stdout*), and three state variables (*mem*, *acc*, and *pc*).

- Input variable: *srcfil*. A machine-hiding and an input-format module are suggested. For the machine-hiding module, we use *stdio*, a collection of C functions provided with nearly all C compilers. Following the classical division into lexical and syntactic analysis, we have two input-format modules. The Token (*token*) module extracts tokens from a string and gives access to the token type and string value of each token. The module secret is the set of rules governing token types and separators. The Load (*load*) module performs syntactic analysis on the extracted tokens; *load* hides the values and conditions in the Language Syntax Table and the Load-phase Exception Table.

  We review these modules from the perspective of likely changes. The *stdio* module must change if the underlying file input/output does. While we do not maintain *stdio*, we do rely on its interface being stable. The *token* module changes if, for example, the tab character is accepted in SHAM programs or if signed integers are permitted. Support for symbolic addresses in SHAM source programs will require changes to *load*, though not necessarily to *token*.

- Output variable: *stdout*. For output variables, a machine-hiding, an output-format, and an output-driver module are suggested. Once again, the machine-hiding module is *stdio*. Because the output format is so simple, no output-format module is needed. There are two output-driver modules. The *load* module generates exception messages and hides the exception rules and the exception message formats specified in the Load-phase Exception Table and the RS function *excmsg*. The *exec* module writes normal-case output and exception messages. *exec* hides only the way it uses other modules to implement the execution phase; the language semantics are hidden by a state-driver module, described next.

- State variables: *mem*, *acc*, *pc*. For a state variable, a software decision-hiding and a state-driver module are suggested. The software decision-hiding module Abstract Machine (*absmach*) maintains the values of *mem*, *acc*, and *pc*. In the simplest design, *mem* will be implemented as an integer array, and *acc* and *pc* as integer variables. Because SHAM is a toy language and its main memory is small, this design will probably be used initially and never changed. Thus, the main motivation for encapsulating these variables is not maintainability, but access control; we can detect and signal, for example, an attempt to retrieve the *mem* value at address -10.

There are two state driver modules; *load* provides the initial values for the state variables and *absmach* changes them repeatedly during the execution phase. Considering some likely RS changes and their consequences, we see that *load* will change if object code instructions are always stored on even-word boundaries and *absmach* will change if index registers are added to the SHAM instruction set.

The module services and secrets for the *load, token, exec,* and *absmach* are shown in Figure 6.2.

The *sham* Module

- **Service.** Uses the other modules to provide the load-and-go assembler specified in the SHAM Requirements Specification.
- **Secret.** The way in which the other modules are used and the handling of command-line parameters.

The *load* Module

- **Service.** Performs the load phase. Issues exception messages for incorrect input and, for correct input, stores the resulting object code in the *absmach* module.
- **Secret.** The details of the load-phase user interface, including the source language concrete syntax and the exception messages.

The *token* Module

- **Service.** Extracts tokens from a string supplied by the user. Tokens are retrieved sequentially, in the order they occur in the user's string. The user is given access to the token value (a string) and the token type (integer, identifier, or unknown).
- **Secret.** The rules governing token types and token separators.

The *absmach* Module

- **Service.** Implements the *mem, acc,* and *pc* state variables, as well as the Language Semantics Table from the SHAM Requirements Specification. Following each instruction execution, the user is given a status indicator and access to the state variables.
- **Secret.** The SHAM language semantics, including the execution-phase exceptions.

The *exec* Module

- **Service.** Performs the execution phase, executing the program stored in *absmach* and managing the run-time user interface, batch or interactive.
- **Secret.** The way in which the other modules are used, and the format and content of the exception messages.

Figure 6.2   SHAM module guide—BSHAM module service and secret

We summarize the BSHAM module decomposition from the perspective provided by the dataflow diagram in Figure 6.3. The *load* module reads lines from

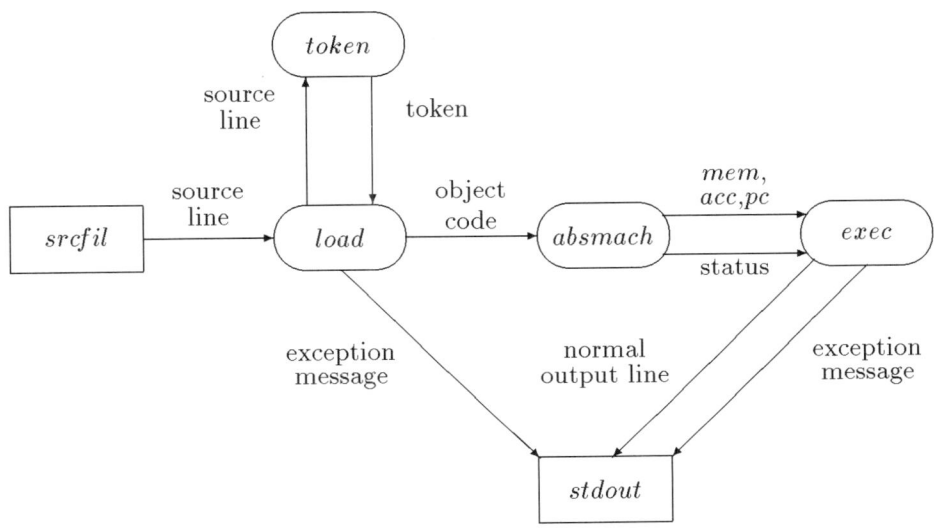

Figure 6.3   BSHAM dataflow diagram

srcfil and passes them to *token* to be split into tokens and classified. For a correct instruction, the object code is loaded into *absmach*; otherwise, an exception
message is written to *stdout*. For a correct source program, instruction execution
is carried out by *absmach* with *exec* monitoring *mem, acc, pc,* and status values.
Output from *PRINT* instructions and exception messages are written to *stdout*
by *exec*.

6.4.2   ISHAM module decomposition

To handle the terminal screen and keyboard, ISHAM adds four modules to the
BSHAM decomposition.

- Input variable: *stdin*. A machine-hiding and an input-format module are
  suggested. The machine-hiding module Keyboard Input (*keybdin*) provides character—not line—oriented input; ISHAM must respond to the
  single-character *STEP* and *EXIT* commands without waiting for a carriage return. No input-format module is required because the input format
  is so simple.

- Output variable: *scn*. A machine-hiding, an output-format, and an output-
  driver module are suggested. The machine-hiding module Screen String
  (*scnstr*) provides access to *scn*, the terminal screen. A string may be written anywhere on *scn* and may be highlighted. To reduce the screen update

The *keybdin* Module

- **Service**. Provides keyboard input, one character at a time, without echoing or waiting for carriage return.

- **Secret**. The UNIX system services used to accomplish this task.

The *scnstr* Module

- **Service**. Provides write access to the terminal screen. A string may be written to any position on the screen, the cursor may be moved to any position on the screen, and any screen position may be highlighted. To allow for efficient screen control, *scnstr* calls are buffered. An "apply changes to screen" access routine is provided; *scnstr* calls have no visible effect on the screen until the apply routine is invoked.

- **Secret**. The UNIX system services used to accomplish this task.

The *scngeom* Module

- **Service**. Provides the length, row, and column position for each screen field, as per the screen format in the SHAM Requirements Specification.

- **Secret**. Hides, until execution time, the length, row, and column values.

The *scndr* Module

- **Service**. Updates the terminal screen, using the values stored by *absmach* and according to the screen format described in the ISHAM Requirements Specification.

- **Secret**. The means used to accomplish screen updates.

Figure 6.4   SHAM module guide—ISHAM module service and secret

time—one place in SHAM where performance is critical—a buffering facility is supported; the effect of several updates may be delayed and applied all at once. *scnstr* hides the system services used for *scn* access, the UNIX *curses* package in this case. The *scn* format shown in Figure 5.10 specifies the row and column position, and the length of each field on *scn*: over 300 values in all. The output-format module Screen Geometry (*scngeom*) provides these values; *scngeom* hides, until run time, the field positions and lengths. The output-driver module Screen Driver (*scndr*) uses *scngeom* and *scnstr* to maintain consistency between *scn* and *absmach*. *scndr* hides the way it uses *scngeom*, *scnstr*, and *absmach*, and even the fact that it uses *scngeom* and *scnstr*.

We consider one likely change for each of the three modules; *scnstr* will change if the relevant *curses* functions do, *scngeom* will change if the *ACC* field is shifted left one column, and *scndr* will change if scrolling of *MEM* is supported. The MG sections for *keybdin*, *scnstr*, *scngeom*, and *scndr* are shown in Figure 6.4.

We summarize the ISHAM decomposition using the dataflow diagram in Figure 6.5. The load phase is unchanged from BSHAM. In the execution phase,

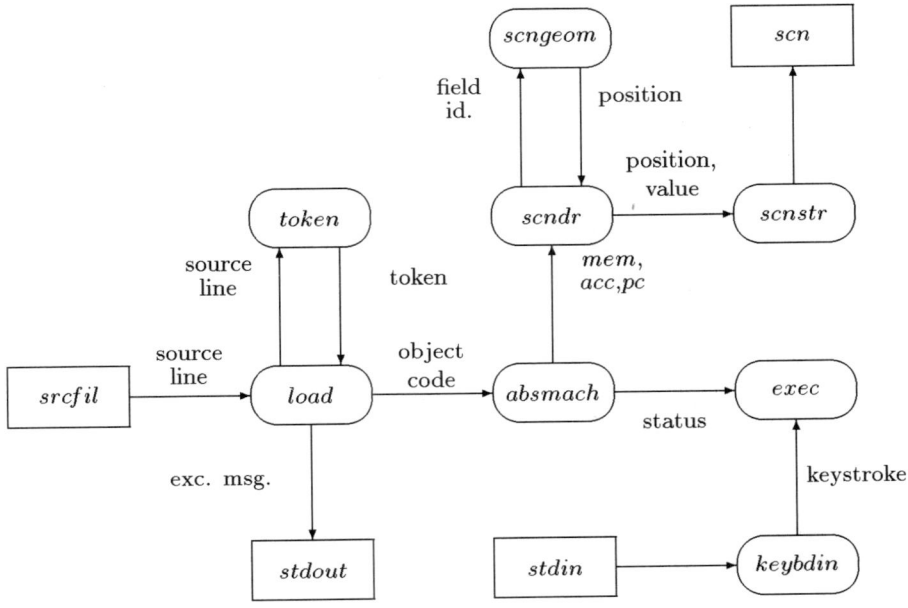

Figure 6.5   ISHAM dataflow diagram

exec uses *keybdin* to retrieve commands from *stdin*. After each *STEP* command, *absmach* modifies *mem*, *acc*, and *pc*, and *scndr* updates *scn*. For each *scn* field, *scndr* passes its identifier to *scngeom*, which supplies the row and column position of the field on *scn*. *scndr* passes this position and the *mem*, *acc*, or *pc* value to *scnstr* to be displayed on *scn*. The unlabeled arrow from *scnstr* to *scn* indicates that information flows from *scnstr* to *scn* but says nothing about its format. The arrow from *stdin* to *keybdin* should be interpreted similarly.

6.4.3   Module summary

The module summary in Figure 6.6 shows the module long name, short name, and prefix for each module, grouped by secret type. The **SHAM MG** consists of the contents of Figures 6.2, 6.4, and 6.6.

6.5   Verification

After an MG has been written, it must be verified. Because the MG is not executable it cannot be tested; verification must be accomplished through inspection. Figure 6.7 shows the inspection criteria for an MG.

format: long name (short name, prefix)

SHAM modules
    Behavior hiding
        Load (*load*, ld_)
        Token (*token*, tk_)
        Abstract Machine (*absmach*, am_)
        Screen Driver (*scndr*, sd_)
        Screen Geometry (*scngeom*, sg_)
    Software decision hiding
        SHAM Coordinator (*sham*)
        Execute (*exec*, ex_)
    Machine hiding
        Keyboard Input (*keybdin*, ki_)
        Screen String (*scnstr*, ss_)

UNIX modules
    ctype, *curses*, *stdio*, *string*, *strtod*

Figure 6.6   SHAM module guide—module summary

We review the "additional criteria" list from an inspection viewpoint.

1. *Well formed.* Violations of this criterion are easily revealed by a line by line review.

2. *Feasible.* It is difficult to inspect for feasibility. In some cases, the only way to clearly establish feasibility is to fully implement the system. Unfortunately, that is a costly approach to revealing decomposition errors. Instead, later development work products can be sketched with just enough detail to judge the feasibility of the decomposition. Module Interface Specification sketches are especially useful, typically including just the access routine names, parameters, and return values.

3. *Flexible.* Again, flexibility is difficult to establish by inspection, and design sketches are often necessary. Not surprisingly, the focus is likely changes. For each module, suppose that the likely change does occur and show that the module encapsulates that change.

We illustrate the use of the flexibility criterion by showing that *scn* field locations can be encapsulated by *scngeom*. A Module Interface Specification sketch is appropriate here. Suppose that *scngeom* provides the access routines g_row and g_col, where g_row(x) and g_col(x) return the *scn* row and column position of field x. Because the code of the *scngeom* user will contain calls to g_row and g_col, rather than hard-coded row and column numbers, *scngeom*

- **Audience**. Software designers and maintainers.
- **Prerequisites**. An understanding of the RS and of information hiding.
- **Purpose**. Describe and motivate the decomposition of the system into modules.
- **Additional criteria**.
  1. *Well formed*. The specification follows the format described in Section 6.3.
  2. *Feasible*. Following this decomposition, a system can be implemented that is correct, and whose cost and performance are acceptable.
  3. *Flexible*. If a likely change is requested, the cost of the resulting modification will be reasonable.

Figure 6.7   Module guide criteria

correctly encapsulates field locations. For example, the RS screen format (see Figure 5.10) specifies that $g\_col(ACC)$ should return 48. Suppose that a change is requested to move ACC two columns to the left; *scngeom* must be modified so that $g\_col(ACC)$ returns 46. However, no changes to other modules are required.

6.6   Summary

Obtaining a good module decomposition is a difficult task. There are many possible decompositions and a poor choice among them can have a profound impact on system quality and cost. To reduce maintenance cost, we must plan for the changes that will occur during maintenance. We cannot make all changes easy so we try to make the likely ones easy. Obviously this approach depends on being able to predict changes. While it is rare that all changes can be predicted, experienced developers and users can predict many changes. Common sense dictates that we plan for those that we can predict. Information hiding guides the planning by suggesting decompositions and providing inspection criteria. The resulting work product, the Module Guide, provides critical guidance for the maintainer.

6.7   Bibliographic Notes

Dijkstra's pioneering work on module decomposition established the basic principles [62] and demonstrated them in practice [63]. The information-hiding technique [64] was developed by Parnas and he demonstrated it in an industrial environment [65]. Stepwise refinement [3, 62, 66] may also be used for module decomposition. Parnas provides a detailed comparison of information hiding and stepwise refinement, as applied to module decomposition [67].

Chapter 7

Module Interface Specification

Hiding representation is the essence of design. [D. L. Parnas]

7.1 Introduction

The previous chapter focused on module decomposition: dividing the development task into modules. This chapter shows how to precisely specify the module interfaces. We view the specification task in terms of the four roles described in Section 2.2. Consider module M. The *designer* decides on M's observable behavior and records it in specification S. The *developer* creates an implementation I to satisfy S. The *verifier* determines whether I does in fact satisfy S. The *user* reads S and writes programs invoking I. Here the user is typically a programmer, not an end user. The purpose of a Module Interface Specification (MIS) is to support the four roles. As a result, the specification must be carefully designed and reviewed. Interfaces that "just happen" result in modules that are difficult to implement and especially difficult to verify and use.

It is common practice to use the module implementation itself as an MIS; users determine a module's behavior by reading its source code. This approach has a number of serious drawbacks. Again consider module M with implementation I.

- During development, opportunities for programmers to work in parallel are limited. Without a specification, developers of modules using M cannot proceed until I is complete.

- There is no record in I of the assumptions that the developer made about how the code will be used. Misunderstandings about these assumptions are a common cause of software failures.

107

- The tester cannot begin work until *I* is complete. Even then, he or she has no basis for correctness and must rely on guesswork in selecting tests and determining expected output.

- If *M*'s implementation is complex, then determining its behavior from the code will be difficult, especially if *M*'s implementation uses other modules that in turn use other modules and so on. Frequently, a module with a complex implementation provides a much simpler service. With an MIS, using the module can be much simpler as well.

- In proprietary systems, the source code is normally not available to the user. Here a specification is essential.

In summary, you will frequently use the source code as a specification; it may be all you have, or it may be simple enough. However, in complex systems, the reliance on code as specification causes serious problems. The techniques of this chapter help to avoid those problems.

Section 7.2 defines the MIS work product, based on the module state machine described in Section 3.8. Section 7.3 explains interface design, discussing the basic issues, presenting a collection of design idioms, and defining heuristics for evaluating design quality. Section 7.4 explains the specification of modules that interact with modules other than their caller or with the environment: for example, the keyboard, screen, and file system. Section 7.5 presents an MIS for each BSHAM module, and Section 7.6 presents an MIS for each additional module used in ISHAM. Section 7.7 shows how to verify an MIS in an inspection meeting. Large portions of the MISs for all nine SHAM modules are presented. The full work products may be found in Appendix C.

7.2   Work Product Definition

The *interface* between two programs is simply the set of assumptions that each makes about the other. A *module interface* is the set of assumptions that (1) a module user is permitted to make about module behavior and (2) the module developer is permitted to make about user behavior. A *Module Interface Specification* (MIS) is a statement of these assumptions. We focus on robust modules: those where the type (1) assumptions dominate and the type (2) assumptions are few. An MIS is divided into two sections: syntax and semantics.

7.2.1   Module interface specification—syntax

The syntax specifies the access routine names, the parameter and return-value types, and the exceptions that are signaled. In addition, any exported types and constants are defined. The access routines are shown in tabular form, and the types and constants are declared using C syntax. For readability, we use the type *boolean*, with constants *true* and *false*, where the actual implementation

Table 7.1 *stack* module interface specification—syntax

```
#define PS_MAXSIZ 100
```

Routine names	Inputs	Outputs	Exceptions
ps_s_init			
ps_s_push	int		ps_full
ps_s_pop			ps_empty
ps_g_top		int	ps_empty
ps_g_depth		int	

will use the C type int, with 0 for *false* and every other value denoting *true*. Table 7.1 shows the interface syntax for the *stack* module. The typewriter font is used for all C identifiers.

Because the interface syntax tables used in the text are not suitable for input to a C compiler, the syntax information is repeated in a C *header file*: a C source file whose name ends in ".h." For example, stack.h is found in Appendix C.

Normally, the inputs are passed as function parameters, and the outputs are passed back to the caller as function return values. For example, the s_push implementation takes a parameter of type int and g_top returns an int. Occasionally, the inputs or outputs are passed differently. For example, some outputs are returned using call by reference: the access routine takes a pointer parameter and places the output values at the address in the pointer. Such special cases are described by comments in the header file.

7.2.2 Module interface specification—semantics

The interface specification semantics are based on the specification trichotomy described in Section 2.2: assumptions, exceptions, and normal case. The assumptions are expressed in prose, and the normal case and exceptions follow the MSM format described in Section 3.8. However, an MIS contains several additional sections: **state invariant**, **local functions**, **local types**, and **local constants**. The *state invariant* is a predicate on the state space that restricts the "legal" states of the module. It is invariant in that, after every access routine call, the state should satisfy the state invariant. For complex specifications, we also make use of *local* functions, types, and constants. These are declared for specification purposes only and are not available to the module user at run time. Occasionally there is information that does not fit anywhere in the format just described; we put this information in a section called "considerations."

Figure 7.1 shows the semantics for the *stack* module. The specification state is the single variable *s*: a sequence of integers holding the stack elements, with the top element in the last position. We assume that s_init will be called before any other access routine. To understand why, consider the alternative: a method would be needed to detect the user's failure to call s_init, and the

state variables
s : *sequence of integer*

state invariant
$|s| \leq$ PS_MAXSIZ

assumptions
ps_s_init is called before any other access routine.

access routine semantics
ps_s_init:
      transition: $s := \langle \rangle$
      exceptions: none
ps_s_push(x):
      transition: $s := s \parallel \langle x \rangle$
      exceptions: $exc := (|s| =$ PS_MAXSIZ $\Rightarrow$ ps_full)
ps_s_pop:
      transition: $s := s[0..|s| - 2]$
      exceptions: $exc := (|s| = 0 \Rightarrow$ ps_empty)
ps_g_top:
      output: $out := s[|s| - 1]$
      exceptions: $exc := (|s| = 0 \Rightarrow$ ps_empty)
ps_g_depth:
      output: $out := |s|$
      exceptions: none

Figure 7.1   *stack* module interface specification—semantics

notinit exception would be added to every access routine except s_init itself. This approach is awkward, and it prompted the simplifying assumption in the specification.

The *stack* transition, output, and exceptions sections are straightforward. s_init sets s to empty and never signals an exception. s_push(i) appends i to s, signaling full if s has PS_MAXSIZ elements. s_pop removes the last element and g_top returns the value of that element; both signal empty if s has no elements. Finally, g_depth returns the number of elements in s.

7.2.3   Exception signaling

The *stack* MIS states precisely *when* exceptions must be signaled, but it does not say *how* the signaling should be done. We briefly describe the available methods for exception signaling and indicate the one used for SHAM modules.

Exception signaling schemes fall into three main categories:

1. *Idiomatic use of data.* Signaling is done using a distinguished return value (e.g., -1), a special status parameter, or a global variable.

2. *Idiomatic use of control flow.* A label or procedure is passed as a parameter to each access routine or established by convention. Exceptions are signaled by branching to the label or invoking the procedure.

3. *Built-in language constructs.* Exceptions are signaled using the special exception constructs available in languages such as PL/I or Ada.

All three methods can be used successfully. However, a systematic and planned approach is important.

In SHAM, we use method 2 above. To signal an exception, a call is made to an exception handler: a C function with the same name as the exception. The module user implements the handler to take whatever action is required. Thus, if s_pop is called on an empty stack, then the **s_pop** implementation must invoke the C function **empty**. Figure 7.2 illustrates how this technique might be used in an s_pop implementation.

There are important differences between RS and MIS exceptions. An RS exception is caused by an end-user error, and it usually produces a text message. An MIS exception is caused by an error made in a call on an access routine and produces a call to an exception handler. Generally speaking, SHAM code is written to ensure that the MIS exceptions are never signaled, except during module testing. For example, a call to s_pop is usually preceded by code such as:

$$\text{if (ps\_g\_depth}() > 0)$$

to ensure that the **s_pop** call will not generate the **empty** exception. Thus, in SHAM code, the occurrence of an MIS exception indicates a fault in the code; the occurrence of an RS exception indicates an error made by the end user.

7.3 Interface Design

Interface design consists of a series of decisions about module behavior. The designer must first see the available alternatives and then record the decisions

```
void ps_s_pop()
{
    if (siz == 0) {
        ps_empty();
        return;
    }
    --siz;
}
```

Figure 7.2 *stack* exceptions—**s_pop** implementation

so that they can be reviewed and communicated to others. The design effort is driven by the module service and secret, as recorded in the MG.

7.3.1   Access routine idioms

Some invention is required in every design. Design from scratch is expensive, however; it is surprising how much trial and error it takes to get it right. Consequently, there is good reason to look for patterns, if they are simple and general enough. We present a collection of *access routine idioms*. Each idiom is a set of routines that provides access to a structure defined with the set, sequence, and tuple type constructors of Section 3.4. Below are simple idioms for each type constructor. These provide the basis for a wide variety of interfaces.

7.3.1.1   Set idioms

Consider a module providing access to a set of at most N elements of type T. One access routine idiom—providing update access—is shown in Table 7.2. s_add(x) adds element x to the set, signaling mem if e is present and full if the set has N elements. s_del(x) deletes x and signals notmem if x is not in the set. g_mem(x) returns *true* if x is present, and g_siz returns the number of elements in the set.

7.3.1.2   Sequence idioms

Consider a sequence of a maximum of N elements of type T. Access is provided by absolute position or sequentially, as shown in Table 7.3. For the absolute position case, s_add(i, x) adds x at position i, shifting right the elements numbered i and higher. s_del(i) deletes the ith element, shifting left the elements numbered $i + 1$ and higher. s_val(i, x) changes the value of the ith element to x, and g_val(i) returns the value of the ith element. g_siz returns the length of the sequence. s_add signals full if the sequence length is N. s_add, s_del, s_val, and g_val signal position if the position parameter is out of range.

Table 7.2   *set* access routine idioms—syntax

Routine names	Inputs	Outputs	Exceptions
s_add	T		mem
			full
s_del	T		notmem
g_mem	T	*boolean*	
g_siz		int	

Table 7.3   *sequence* access routine idioms—syntax

Routine names	Inputs	Outputs	Exceptions
By absolute position			
s_add	int		position
	T		full
s_del	int		position
s_val	int		position
	T		
g_val	int	T	position
g_siz		int	
Sequential			
s_start			
sg_next		T	end
g_end		*boolean*	

Sequential access allows the user to retrieve all of the sequence elements, one at a time. s_start initiates the retrieval process; sg_next returns the next element, signaling **end** if no elements remain; and g_end returns *true* if no elements remain. Note that the sequential access idiom can be applied to any collection of elements, for example, a set or a tree. In the case of a set, the retrieval order is usually unspecified; the elements can be returned in any order as long as each element is returned exactly once.

7.3.1.3   Tuple idioms

Consider a module providing access to a tuple of type

$$T = tuple\ of\ (f_1 : T_1, f_2 : T_2, \ldots, f_N : T_N).$$

Two idioms are presented, as shown in Table 7.4. In the first, one set routine and one get routine are provided for each field in the tuple. This approach is simple, but it is awkward when N is large: with $N = 10$, 20 access routines are required. In the second approach, one set routine and one get routine are used, each passing the entire tuple as a single parameter. This approach works well for larger N: $N > 20$ is common in practice. One disadvantage is that the user must assign and retrieve all fields, even if he or she wants only one.

7.3.2   Quality criteria

The fundamental goal in interface design, and engineering design in general, is achieving the best product at the lowest cost. Under cost, both development and maintenance must be considered. The best product will maximize both run-time

Table 7.4 *tuple* access routine idioms—syntax

Routine names	Inputs	Outputs	Exceptions
One set and one get routine per field			
s_f_1	T_1		
g_f_1		T_1	
s_f_2	T_2		
g_f_2		T_2	
. . .	. . .	. . .	. . .
s_f_N	T_N		
g_f_N		T_N	
One set and one get routine for entire tuple			
s_val	T		
g_val		T	

performance and interface quality. A lot is known about the former but little about the latter: the subject of this section.

We present a set of quality criteria that we have found useful in interface design and review.

- *Consistent*. According to Brooks and Blaauw:

  > A good architecture is *consistent* in the sense that with a partial knowledge of the system the remainder of the system can be predicted. We believe this to underlie all principles of quality [68, page 42].

  While Brooks and Blaauw are referring to CPU interfaces, their advice applies equally well to module interfaces. It is important to consider every aspect of the interface, from naming conventions to exception handling.

- *Essential*. Omit unnecessary features. Do not offer the same service in two ways. Remove an access routine if its service can be provided by a combination of other routines.

- *General*. Realize that users will want to use features in ways never imagined by the designer. Generality includes open-endedness—leaving room for future expansion—and completeness—including all features of a given class.

- *Minimal*. Avoid access routines that offer two different services that might be requested separately by the user. Many set-get routines violate minimality by inappropriately coupling the set and get services.

- *Opaque*. Ensure that the interface obeys the information-hiding principle. In an opaque interface the secrets are hidden: if one of the likely changes does occur, then the interface need not change.

Frequently there is tension among the criteria and between cost and the criteria. For example, minimality and generality increase the number of access routines and hence the cost; implementation considerations force violations of the opaque criteria. It is important to realize that the criteria do not replace the designer's judgment. They do help in improving module interfaces. In our experience, a number of small improvements result that, in sum, often produce a substantial improvement. In summary: be aware of the quality criteria and violate them only with good reason.

We next illustrate the access routine idioms and quality principles on the design of a module interface. We begin the design task by defining the specification state, abstractly modeling the relevant aspects of the past. While the state is often relatively simple, it is important that it be specified precisely. Then access routine design can begin. The access routines are chosen, largely determining how the module service will be offered. Next, the boundaries of the specification trichotomy are established, defining the normal operating range of the module. Finally, the normal-case behavior is specified in detail.

7.3.3 The symbol table (*symtbl*) MIS

Symbol tables are used for a wide variety of purposes, especially in compilers and assemblers. The *symtbl* module specified here was designed to support the use of symbolic addresses in SHAM. *symtbl* stores a set of symbols (strings) and locations (integers). Symbols must be unique; locations need not. The location field may be set and retrieved. *symtbl* is a software decision–hiding module; its secret is the algorithms and data structures used in the implementation.

We represent the module state with the variable *tbl* of type

$$T = set\ of\ tuple\ of\ (sym : string,\ loc : integer)$$

where no two tuples in *tbl* have the same *sym* value. The access routines are based on the set idiom, shown in Table 7.2. The *symtbl* interface syntax is shown in Table 7.5. **s_init** initializes *tbl* to empty, **s_add**(s,x) adds $\langle s,x \rangle$ to *tbl*, and **g_siz** returns the number of pairs in *tbl*. **g_exsym**(s) returns *true* if, for some x, $\langle s,x \rangle \in tbl$. **g_loc**$(s)$ returns the *loc* field in the pair containing s. **s_loc**(s,x) changes the location field in this pair to x. Observe that **s_del** has been omitted, violating generality. We have omitted it to reduce implementation cost; SHAM symbolic addresses will be added but never deleted. While there is no single access routine for checking for set membership, **g_exsym** and **g_loc** can be combined to provide this feature.

It is useful to view *symtbl* from a functional perspective:

$$\text{Let } f(s) = \textbf{g\_loc}(s) \text{ where } dom(f) = \{s \mid \textbf{g\_exsym}(s)\}$$

Table 7.5   *symtbl* module interface specification—syntax

```
#define ST_MAXSYMS 50
#define ST_MAXSYMLEN 20
```

Routine names	Inputs	Outputs	Exceptions
st_s_init			
st_s_add	char* int		st_maxlen st_exsym st_full
st_g_exsym	char*	*boolean*	
st_s_loc	char* int		st_notexsym
st_g_loc	char*	int	st_notexsym
st_g_siz		int	

With f defined, we can see that *symtbl* maintains the function f: s_add and s_loc change f and g_exsym and g_loc compute f. Many modules maintain functions; it pays to recognize such an underlying function early in interface design.

We next discuss the specification trichotomy, defined in the **assumptions** and **exceptions** entries in Figure 7.3. There are two assumptions. They are not specified as exceptions because they are based on conditions that are hard for the *symtbl* developer to check. The exceptions are due to both illegal requests and resource restrictions. To indicate duplicates, s_add signals **exsym**. The module user can "predict" this exception by calling g_exsym. To allow the developer to use static memory allocation, s_add signals **maxlen** and **full**. These exceptions can also be predicted: by **strlen** (from the C library) for **maxlen** and by g_siz for **full**. Both s_loc and g_loc signal **notexsym** to indicate that the request is illegal; **notexsym** can be predicted using g_exsym.

The state invariant expresses (1) the limit on the number of symbols in *tbl*, (2) the limit on the length of each symbol, and (3) the requirement that no two *tbl* entries have the same *sym* value. The restrictions expressed by the state invariant are enforced by the s_add exceptions.

Figure 7.3 contains the normal-case semantics in the **transition** and **output** entries. These sections follow closely the prose semantics given above. The generality criterion applies twice. The empty string is permitted as a symbol, even though we do not expect it to be added. Negative numbers are permitted as locations, though we expect only non-negative values

state variables
$tbl : set\ of\ tuple\ of\ (sym : string, loc : integer)$

state invariant
1. $|tbl| \leq$ ST_MAXSYMS
2. $(\forall t \in tbl)(|t.sym| \leq$ ST_MAXSYMLEN$)$
3. $(\forall t_1, t_2 \in tbl)(t_1 \neq t_2 \rightarrow t_1.sym \neq t_2.sym)$

assumptions
st_s_init is called before any other access routine.
All string parameters are legal C strings.

access routine semantics
st_s_init:
    transition: $tbl := \{\}$
    exceptions: none
st_s_add(sym, loc):
    transition: $tbl := tbl \cup \{\langle sym, loc \rangle\}$
    exceptions: $exc := \quad (|sym| >$ ST_MAXSYMLEN $\Rightarrow$ st_maxlen
                    $| \ (\exists loc_1)(\langle sym, loc_1 \rangle \in tbl) \Rightarrow$ st_exsym
                    $| \ |tbl| =$ ST_MAXSYMS $\Rightarrow$ st_full$)$
st_g_exsym(sym):
    output: $out := (\exists loc)(\langle sym, loc \rangle \in tbl)$
    exceptions: none
st_s_loc(sym, loc):
    transition: $tbl := (tbl - \{\langle sym, loc_1 \rangle\}) \cup \{\langle sym, loc \rangle\}$ where $\langle sym, loc_1 \rangle \in tbl$
    exceptions: $exc := (\neg(\exists loc_1)(\langle sym, loc_1 \rangle \in tbl) \Rightarrow$ st_notexsym$)$
st_g_loc(sym):
    output: $out := loc$, where $\langle sym, loc \rangle \in tbl$
    exceptions: $exc := (\neg(\exists loc)(\langle sym, loc \rangle \in tbl) \Rightarrow$ st_notexsym$)$
st_g_siz:
    output: $out := |tbl|$
    exceptions: none

Figure 7.3   *symtbl* module interface specification—semantics

7.4 Modules with External Interaction

Until now, we have specified modules that are standalone; they are required to interact only with their callers. For example, in the *stack* module, access is provided solely through the access routines: no interaction is required with other modules or with the environment. However, in a number of SHAM modules such "external interactions" are present and must be reflected in the MISs. Four SHAM modules have substantial interaction with the environment: *keybdin*, *scnstr*, *scndr*, and *sham*; three have substantial interaction with other modules: *load*, *exec*, and *sham*.

SHAM modules interact with the environment through the keyboard, the terminal screen, and the file system. Often, the required interaction can be effectively communicated in prose. Occasionally more precision is needed and can be achieved with the same approach used in the RS: model the environment with an *environment variable*. Environment variables are described in a new MIS section: **environment variables**. As with a state variable, an environment variable has a name and type. However, environment variables also have an *interpretation*, which describes the correspondence between the variable's value and the environment. For example, the *scnstr* module provides access routines to modify the contents of the terminal screen. To precisely identify screen locations, we declare an environment variable.

> *scn* : *sequence*[24][80] *of char*
>   *scn*[*r*][*c*] is the character at screen row *r* and column *c*,
>   with numbering zero-relative and beginning at the upper-left corner.

Thus, $scn[23][0] = $ **'x'** is *true* if there is an **'x'** in the lowest, leftmost position of the terminal screen.

SHAM modules also interact with other modules. In some cases the interaction occurs, but it is "hidden": it is present in the implementation but there is no mention of it in the MIS. For example, a *stack* implementation based on a linked list will use the UNIX *malloc* module for dynamic memory allocation. This use is not mentioned in the *stack* MIS. As a result, the choice between array and linked list is hidden from the *stack* user. In other cases, the external interaction should be described in the MIS. Consider the MIS for module M_1, which has required interaction with module M_2. The interaction will be specified in the M_1 specification either by naming calls on M_2 or by naming M_2's state. For example, the *load* module's primary purpose is to store object code in the *absmach* module. Thus, the *load* MIS must describe the effect that *load* access routines have on the state of *absmach*.

7.5   BSHAM Specifications

There are five BSHAM modules, as shown in the SHAM MG.

- *token* extracts tokens from a string.

- *absmach* stores *mem*, *acc*, and *pc* and modifies them by executing instructions.

- *load* drives the load phase, relying on *token* to scan source files and *absmach* to store the resulting object code.

- *exec* performs the execution phase, with most of the work done by *absmach*.

Table 7.6 *token* module interface specification—syntax

```
#define TK_MAXSTRLEN 100
#define TK_MAXIDLEN 10
#define TK_MAXINTLEN 5

typedef enum {TK_ID,TK_INT,TK_BADTOK} tk_toktyp;

typedef struct {
   char val[TK_MAXSTRLEN+1];
   tk_toktyp typ;
} tk_valtyp;
```

Routine names	Inputs	Outputs	Exceptions
tk_s_init			
tk_s_str	char*		tk_maxlen
tk_sg_next		tk_valtyp	tk_end
tk_g_end		*boolean*	

- *sham* serves as coordinator, doing module initialization and invoking *load* and *exec*.

The required service for each of these modules is shown in Figure 6.2. The design and specification of the module interfaces are described in the next five subsections.

7.5.1 The *token* MIS

The *token* MIS illustrates how local functions and types can be used to advantage. We represent the module state with the variable *toklist*, of type

$$T = sequence \ of \ string.$$

Our intention is that, at any time, *toklist* contains the sequence of tokens not yet retrieved by the module user.

The specification syntax, shown in Table 7.6, is based on the sequential access idiom, shown in Table 7.3. We could have provided access by absolute position. We chose the sequential access idiom because it is sufficient for our application and because it is easy to support with the left-to-right scan of the input string often used by developers.

According to the MG, a tuple—a value/type pair—must be returned for each token. We return this tuple using one get routine for the entire tuple, as shown in the lower part of Table 7.4.

Table 7.6 defines the constants, types, and access routines. Three constants establish maximum lengths for the string passed by the user, and for identifier and integer tokens. The type **tk_toktyp** names the token types; **tk_valtyp** is the structure used for returning a value/type pair. The access routine **s_init** initializes the module and **s_str**(s) establishes s as the string to be scanned. **sg_next** returns the value and type of the next token and **g_end** returns *true* if no more tokens remain.

We next present the specification trichotomy and the normal-case semantics, shown in Figure 7.4. The **assumptions** are essentially the same as for *symtbl*. There is one exception due to an illegal request: **sg_next** signals **end** if there are no more tokens. The **end** exception can be predicted by calling **g_end**. There is one exception due to resource limitations: **s_str**(s) signals **maxlen** if s is too long; **maxlen** can be predicted using **strlen**, from the C library.

The normal-case semantics are based on local types and functions. These are used by the **sg_next** entry to specify, for a given string, the tokens, and their types. This information can be conveyed more simply when removed from the **sg_next** entry. As shown in the **local types** section, *idtoksetT* is the set of all identifier tokens and *inttoksetT* is the set of all integer tokens. As shown in the **local functions** section, the function *tokens* defines the scanning rules: a token is a contiguous sequence of non-blanks, beginning at the start of the string or preceded by a blank, and ending at the end of the string or followed by a blank. The function *toktyp*(s) categorizes s as an identifier, integer, or illegal token.

Using the functions and types, the normal-case semantics are straightforward. **s_init** sets *toklist* to empty and **s_str**(s) assigns the tokens in s to *toklist*. **sg_next** returns the value and type of *toklist*[0] and removes it from *toklist*. **g_end** returns *true* when *toklist* is empty .

7.5.2   The *absmach* MIS

The MIS for the *absmach* module is defined in terms of the SHAM RS, demonstrating how precise requirements can be effectively used during design. The *absmach* specification also shows how a variety of access routine idioms can be used in combination. The module state mimics the requirements variables: *acc*, *pc*, and *mem* are declared.

The specification syntax is shown in Table 7.7. We view the state variables as a tuple, with access provided by one set and get routine per field. Using a single set/get pair for the entire tuple would violate minimality: a user who wanted only *acc* would have to retrieve *pc* and the *mem* array as well. While not immediately obvious, execution of SHAM programs is provided using the sequential access idiom (Table 7.2). Access is provided to the sequence of *absmach* states beginning at any given initial state. Because execution may begin from any state, **s_start** is not needed here. The next state is generated by **sg_exec**, which returns status information only. The status value **AM_HALT** makes a **g_end** access routine unnecessary. After **sg_exec** returns, the user may access the state values using **g_acc**, **g_pc**, and **g_mem**.

state variables
toklist : *sequence of string*

state invariant
none

assumptions
tk_s_init is called before any other access routine.
All string parameters are legal C strings.

access routine semantics
tk_s_init:
    transition: $toklist := \langle\rangle$
    exceptions: none
tk_s_str(s):
    transition: $toklist := tokens(s)$
    exceptions: $exc := (|s| > \textbf{TK\_MAXSTRLEN} \Rightarrow \textbf{tk\_maxlen})$
tk_sg_next:
    transition/output: $toklist, out :=$
        $toklist[1..|toklist| - 1],$
        $\langle toklist[0], toktyp(toklist[0])\rangle$
    exceptions: $exc := (toklist = \langle\rangle \Rightarrow \textbf{tk\_end})$
tk_g_end:
    output: $out := (toklist = \langle\rangle)$
    exceptions: none

local types
$idtoksetT = \{s \mid s$ is a string of alphabetic or numeric characters $\wedge$
    $s[0]$ is alphabetic $\wedge \ |s| \in [1..\textbf{TK\_MAXIDLEN}]\}$
$inttoksetT = \{s \mid s$ is a string of numeric characters $\wedge \ |s| \in [1..\textbf{TK\_MAXINTLEN}]\}$

local functions
$tokens : string \rightarrow sequence\ of\ string$
    $tokens(s)$ returns the sequence of tokens in s where
        1. a token is a non-empty subsequence $s[i..j]$ of s
        2. $s[i..j]$ contains no blanks
        3. $(i = 0 \vee s[i-1] = \text{` '}) \wedge (j = |s| - 1 \vee s[j+1] = \text{` '})$
$toktyp : string \rightarrow \textbf{tk\_toktyp}$
    $toktyp(s) :=$
        $(s \in idtoksetT \Rightarrow \textbf{TK\_ID}$
        $| \ s \in inttoksetT \Rightarrow \textbf{TK\_INT}$
        $| \ true \Rightarrow \textbf{TK\_BADTOK})$

Figure 7.4   *token* module interface specification—semantics

Table 7.7   *absmach* module interface specification—syntax

```
#define AM_MEMSIZ 100
#define AM_MAXINT 999

typedef enum {AM_NORMAL,AM_HALT,AM_PRINT,
    AM_ARITHEXC,AM_ADDREXC,
    AM_OBJECTEXC,AM_NOOPEXC
} am_stat;
```

Routine names	Inputs	Outputs	Exceptions
am_s_init			
am_s_acc	int		am_int
am_g_acc		int	
am_s_pc	int		am_addr
am_g_pc		int	
am_s_mem	int		am_addr
	int		am_int
am_g_mem	int	int	am_addr
am_sg_exec		am_stat	

We next discuss the specification trichotomy, based on the **assumptions** and **exceptions** sections in Figure 7.5. We assume that s_init is called first. The exceptions deal with parameters that lie outside fixed ranges. For negative or oversize integers, s_acc and s_mem signal int. For illegal addresses, s_pc, s_mem, and g_mem signal addr.

We conclude with the normal-case semantics. In s_init, there is no compelling reason to prefer one choice of initial state over another. The main virtue of our choice is that it is simple. We could have left the initial state unspecified. The **transition** and **output** sections for the *acc*, *pc*, and *mem* set/get pairs are as expected. The **sg_exec transition-output** section is based directly on sections of the SHAM RS. These sections could be repeated in the MIS, but the duplication would make document maintenance more expensive. The critical point is that, with a detailed RS, a precise *absmach* specification can be developed with relatively little effort.

7.5.3   The *load* MIS

The *load* MIS is shown in Table 7.8 and Figure 7.6. *load* interacts with the environment, but only by writing error messages to *stdout*. There are no state variables because the object code is stored in the *absmach* module. The interface syntax is short and simple: s_init initializes the module and sg_load(*f*) processes the source code in file *f*, loading the object code into *absmach*. The **assumptions** concern module initialization and the file parameter to sg_load.

state variables
$mem : sequence\ [\texttt{AM\_MEMSIZ}]\ of\ [0..\texttt{AM\_MAXINT}]$
$acc : [0..\texttt{AM\_MAXINT}]$
$pc : [0..\texttt{AM\_MEMSIZ} - 1]$

state invariant
none

assumptions
$\texttt{am\_s\_init}$ is called before any other access routine.

access routine semantics
$\texttt{am\_s\_init}$:
  transition: $acc, pc, mem := 0, 0,$ all zeroes
  exceptions: none
$\texttt{am\_s\_acc}(i)$:
  transition: $acc := i$
  exceptions: $exc := (i \notin [0..\texttt{AM\_MAXINT}] \Rightarrow \texttt{am\_int})$
$\texttt{am\_g\_acc}$:
  output: $out := acc$
  exceptions: none
$\texttt{am\_s\_pc}(a)$:
  transition: $pc := a$
  exceptions: $exc := (a \notin [0..\texttt{AM\_MEMSIZ} - 1] \Rightarrow \texttt{am\_addr})$
$\texttt{am\_g\_pc}$:
  output: $out := pc$
  exceptions: none
$\texttt{am\_s\_mem}(a, i)$:
  transition: $mem[a] := i$
  exceptions: $exc := \quad (a \notin [0..\texttt{AM\_MEMSIZ} - 1] \Rightarrow \texttt{am\_addr}$
  $\qquad\qquad\qquad\quad | \; i \notin [0..\texttt{AM\_MAXINT}] \Rightarrow \texttt{am\_int})$
$\texttt{am\_g\_mem}(a)$:
  output: $out := mem[a]$
  exceptions: $exc := (a \notin [0..\texttt{AM\_MEMSIZ} - 1] \Rightarrow \texttt{am\_addr})$
$\texttt{am\_sg\_exec}$:
  transition-output:
      (an error is specified in the Exec. Phase Exception Table $\Rightarrow$
          $out :=$ the error identifier
      $| \; mem[pc] = \texttt{SY\_HALT} \Rightarrow out := \texttt{AM\_HALT}$
      $| \; mem[pc] = \texttt{SY\_PRINT} \Rightarrow out, pc := \texttt{AM\_PRINT}, pc + 1$
      $| \; true \Rightarrow \quad out := \texttt{AM\_NORMAL}$
          $acc, pc, mem :=$ values specified in the RS Lang. Sem. Table)
  exceptions: none

Figure 7.5 *absmach* module interface specification—semantics

Table 7.8 *load* module interface specification—syntax

```
#define typedef enum {LD_NORMAL,LD_ERROR} ld_stat;
```

Routine names	Inputs	Outputs	Exceptions
ld_s_init			
ld_sg_load	FILE*	ld_stat	ld_fil

environment variables
stdout
    UNIX standard output

state variables
none

state invariant
none

assumptions
ld_s_init is called before any other access routine.
The *absmach* and *token* modules have been initialized.
The argument to ld_sg_load points to an open file control block.

access routine semantics
ld_s_init:
    transition: none
    exceptions: none
ld_sg_load(f): defined in terms of the SHAM Requirements Specification.
    transition/output:
        (file f has no load errors $\Rightarrow$
            absmach.mem := the object code version of the program in f
            out := LD_NORMAL
        | *true* $\Rightarrow$
            write the appropriate messages to *stdout*
            out := LD_ERROR)
    exceptions: *exc* := (error reading file $f \Rightarrow$ ld_fil)

considerations
In ld_sg_load(f), if f has load errors or if ld_fil occurs,
the value of *absmach.mem* is "dontcare."

Figure 7.6 *load* module interface specification—semantics

Table 7.9   *exec* module interface specification—syntax

Routine names	Inputs	Outputs	Exceptions
`ex_s_init`			
`ex_s_exec`			

There is one exception: `sg_load` signals `fil` if *f* is unreadable. The normal-case semantics mimic the load section in the SHAM RS. However, here assignments are to *absmach* state variables rather than the requirements state variables. The **considerations** section indicates that in the case where `sg_load` signals an exception, it does not matter what the final value of *mem* is in *absmach*. This violates the assumption discussed in Section 3.8.3, which specifies that calls that signal an exception should not cause a state transition, but it greatly simplifies the implementation of `sg_load`.

7.5.4   The *exec* MIS

The *exec* MIS is shown in Table 7.9 and Figure 7.7. The *exec* module interacts with the environment through the terminal screen and through *stdout*. There are no state variables because the *absmach* module maintains the required state. The interface syntax is simple: `s_init` initializes the module and `s_exec` executes the program stored in *absmach*.

The **assumptions** require the initialization of *exec* and *absmach*, and also require the setting of a compile-time flag. With this flag, and the C preprocessor's conditional compilation features, batch and interactive execution can be supported by a single *exec* implementation. There are no exceptions signaled to callers of *exec* routines. If the program stored in *absmach* aborts, the end user will be informed through a message.

In the normal-case semantics there are separate cases for BSHAM and ISHAM. These merely refer to the execution-phase FSMs from the BSHAM and ISHAM RSs. The alternative is to repeat these FSMs in the *exec* MIS, modified slightly to reference the *absmach* MIS state variables rather than the RS state variables. However, this approach provides little benefit to the reader of the *exec* MIS and generates a significant maintenance problem: it is hard to keep the RS and MIS FSMs consistent.

7.5.5   The *sham* MIS

The interface to *sham*, the SHAM Coordinator module, is significantly different from the other SHAM module interfaces. *sham* has no access routines, interacting solely through the keyboard, screen, and file system. As a result, its interface does not fit the module state machine scheme used for the other modules. The *sham* interface is specified in the SHAM RS. Also, while *sham* uses

environment variables
scn
        the terminal screen
stdout
        UNIX standard output

state variables
none

state invariant
none

assumptions
Before `ex_s_exec` is called, `ex_s_init` has been called and
        the *absmach* module has been initialized.
At compile time, exactly one of these preprocessor flags is defined:
`BSHAM, ISHAM`

access routine semantics
`ex_s_init`:
        transition:
                if flag `ISHAM` is set then
                        initialize the screen
        exceptions: none
`ex_s_exec`:
        transition:
                if flag `BSHAM` is set then
                        perform the execution phase as described in the BSHAM RS
                else if flag `ISHAM` is set then
                        perform the execution phase as described in the ISHAM RS
                In either case:
                                • Use the *mem*, *acc*, and *pc* values stored in the *absmach* module
                                • Invoke `am_sg_exec` to execute the next instruction
                                • Use the `am_sg_exec` return value to determine whether
                                        a normal case or exception output is needed
        exceptions: none

Figure 7.7 *exec* module interface specification—semantics

Table 7.10 *keybdin* module interface specification—syntax

Routine names	Inputs	Outputs	Exceptions
ki_s_init			
ki_sg_next		char	
ki_s_end			

other modules, that use is hidden. In summary, for *sham*, there is no MIS; the RS provides the information normally found in an MIS. This approach is typical for coordinator modules.

7.6 ISHAM Specifications

There are nine ISHAM modules. Five of these are shared with BSHAM; the other four are introduced to handle interaction with the keyboard and screen:

- *keybdin* provides character-at-a-time keyboard access.

- *scngeom* stores the position, length, and initial value of each screen field.

- *scnstr* provides write access to the screen.

- *scndr* keeps the screen image up to date, relying on *scngeom* and *scnstr* to help do so.

The required service for each of these modules is shown in Figure 6.4.

7.6.1 The *keybdin* MIS

The *keybdin* MIS is shown in Table 7.10 and Figure 7.8.

The specification syntax is based on the sequential access idiom, shown in Table 7.3: **s_init** begins the scan and **sg_next** returns the next character. Here, there is no **end** exception or **g_end** access routine.

The **assumptions** say that *keybdin* users must call the terminating access routine, **s_end**, if they wish to reinitialize. The normal-case semantics are short. **s_init** turns echoing off, **sg_next** returns the next available character, and **s_end** sets character echoing back to normal. The note under **considerations** addresses the common situation where the next character has not yet been typed. Here **sg_next** blocks, not returning to its caller until a key is pressed.

7.6.2 The *scngeom* MIS

The *scngeom* module provides an example of a module with no state: current access routine behavior does not depend on previous calls. The lack of state causes no difficulties. Indeed, the *scngeom* MIS is simple. Because *scngeom* provides access to a collection of constants, no state is needed.

environment variables
stdin : string
    UNIX standard input

state variables
none

state invariant
none

assumptions
The *curses* module has been initialized.

Calls to *keybdin* obey the following pattern:
(ki_s_init.ki_sg_next ∗ .ki_s_end)∗, where $X*$ indicates zero or more occurrences of X

access routine semantics
ki_s_init:
    transition: turn off keystroke echoing
    exceptions: none
ki_sg_next:
    transition-output: *out* := the next available character
    exceptions: none
ki_s_end:
    transition: turn on keystroke echoing
    exceptions: none

considerations

- Keystrokes are returned by ki_sg_next in first-in–first-out order.

- Characters are returned immediately, without waiting for a newline.

- If, on entry, there is no new keystroke available, ki_sg_next will not return until another keystroke occurs.

Figure 7.8   *keybdin* module interface specification—semantics

The interface syntax is shown in Table 7.11. We view *scngeom* as computing the function f, mapping a screen field identifier to a row/column/length/initial–value tuple. One get routine is provided for each field in this tuple. Thus, g_legfld defines the domain of f and g_row, g_col, g_len, and g_val together compute f.

A portion of the interface semantics is shown in Figure 7.9 (see the full version in Appendix C). For each field identifier, the table in this figure defines the legal row and column positions, and the associated field in the screen format from the RS. The specification trichotomy is straightforward; s_init must be called first. The last four get calls reject invalid screen field identifiers, signaling badfld.

Table 7.11   *scngeom* module interface specification—syntax

```
#define SG_NUMROW 24
#define SG_NUMCOL 80

typedef enum {
    SG_MEM,SG_PC,SG_ACC,SG_PRT,SG_MSG,
    SG_SCNTTL,SG_MEMTTL1,SG_MEMTTL2,SG_MEMCOLHDR,SG_MEMROWHDR,
    SG_PCTTL,SG_ACCTTL,SG_PRTTTL,SG_PROMPTTTL,SG_MSGTTL
} sg_fldnam;

typedef struct {
    sg_fldnam nam;
    int row;
    int col;
} sg_fld;
```

Routine names	Inputs	Outputs	Exceptions
sg_s_init			
sg_g_legfld	sg_fld	*boolean*	
sg_g_row	sg_fld	int	sg_badfld
sg_g_col	sg_fld	int	sg_badfld
sg_g_len	sg_fld	int	sg_badfld
sg_g_val	sg_fld	char*	sg_badfld

7.6.3   The *scnstr* MIS

The *scnstr* MIS is shown in Table 7.12 and Figures 7.10 and 7.11. The specification syntax is based on the *by absolute position* idiom shown in Table 7.3. Because the screen size is fixed, **s_add** and **s_del** are not provided, and the array height and width are supplied as constants. **s_init** initializes the module and **s_clrscn** clears the screen. **s_str**(r, c, s) writes the string s, beginning at screen row r and column c. **s_hlt**(r, c, l, f) modifies the highlighting of the screen, beginning at row r and column c for l positions; highlighting is turned on if f is *true* and off otherwise. Calls to **s_clrscn**, **s_str**, **s_hlt**, and **s_cur** have no visible effect until **s_ref** ("refresh") is called. At that point, all the changes since the last **s_ref** call are applied.

Three environment variables are used to model the terminal screen: *scn* contains the characters displayed at each screen position, *hlt* indicates whether each screen position is highlighted, and *cur* indicates the position of the terminal cursor. The state variables *scnbuf*, *hltbuf*, and *curbuf* have the same type as their environment variable counterparts, and they are used to specify the buffered-write scheme described in the MG.

Identifier	Legal row values	Legal column values	Associated field in ISHAM RS
Variable fields			
SG_MEM	[0..9]	[0..9]	*MEM*
SG_PC	0	0	*PC*
SG_ACC	0	0	*ACC*
SG_PRT	0	0	*PRT*
SG_MSG	0	0	*MSG*
Fixed fields			
SG_SCNTTL	0	0	Screen title
SG_MEMTTL1	0	0	*MEM* title line 1
SG_MEMTTL2	0	0	*MEM* title line 2
...			
SG_MSGTTL	0	0	Error message title

state variables
none

state invariant
none

assumptions
sg_s_init is called before any other access routine

access routine semantics
sg_s_init:
      transition: none
      exceptions: none
sg_g_legfld(fld):
      output: out := (fld is a legal field identifier)
      exceptions: none
sg_g_row(fld):
      output: out := starting screen row for fld, zero-relative
      exceptions: exc := (fld is not a legal field identifier $\Rightarrow$ sg_badfld)
sg_g_col(fld):
      ...
sg_g_len(fld):
      ...
sg_g_val(fld):
      output: out :=
            (fld is a fixed screen field $\Rightarrow$ as shown in the ISHAM RS
            | fld is a variable screen field $\Rightarrow$ "")
      exceptions: exc := (fld is not a legal field identifier $\Rightarrow$ sg_badfld)

Figure 7.9   *scngeom* module interface specification—semantics

Table 7.12   *scnstr* module interface specification—syntax

```
#define SS_NUMROW 24
#define SS_NUMCOL 80
```

Routine names	Inputs	Outputs	Exceptions
ss_s_init			
ss_s_clrscn			
ss_s_str	int		ss_row
	int		ss_col
	char*		ss_len
ss_s_hlt	int		ss_row
	int		ss_col
	int		ss_len
	boolean		
ss_s_cur	int		ss_row
	int		ss_col
ss_s_ref			
ss_s_end			

The **assumptions** state that the **s_init/s_end** bracketing convention used in *keybdin* is also required in *scnstr*. The legality of string parameters is also assumed. There are three exceptions, all due to inherently illegal requests; **row**, **col**, and **len** are signaled when the indicated position(s) does not lie on the screen.

In the normal-case semantics, **s_clrscn**, **s_str**, **s_hlt**, and **s_cur** affect only the state variables; **s_ref** specifies the effect on the environment simply by assigning each state variable to the corresponding environment variable.

We note two violations of the quality heuristics.

1. **s_clrscn** violates minimality by homing the cursor: the user may want it left where it was. However, the current design is sufficient for our needs and is simpler to implement.

2. The lack of get calls violates generality. For example, **s_str** writes a string to the screen, and no access routine reads from the screen. Again, the current design is sufficient for SHAM and is simpler.

However, note that **s_str** and **s_hlt** accept "zero-length requests" to avoid violating generality. Finally, we note that *scnstr* will interact with another module: the system module providing screen access. The nature of this interaction is hidden—it is *scnstr*'s secret—and so is not mentioned in the MIS.

environment variables

scn : sequence [SS_NUMROW][SS_NUMCOL] *of char*

    $scn[r][c]$ is the character at screen row r and column c,

    with numbering zero-relative and beginning at the upper-left corner

hlt : sequence [SS_NUMROW][SS_NUMCOL] *of boolean*

    $hlt[r][c]$ is true if the position at screen row r and column c is highlighted,

    with numbering zero-relative and beginning at the upper-left corner

cur : tuple of $(row : [0..SS\_NUMROW - 1], col : [0..SS\_NUMCOL - 1])$

    the terminal cursor is at screen row *cur.row* and column *cur.col*

    with numbering zero-relative and beginning at the upper-left corner

state variables

scnbuf : sequence [SS_NUMROW][SS_NUMCOL] *of char*

hltbuf : sequence [SS_NUMROW][SS_NUMCOL] *of boolean*

curbuf : tuple of $(row : [0..SS\_NUMROW - 1], col : [0..SS\_NUMCOL - 1])$

state invariant

assumptions

The *curses* module has been initialized.

Calls to *scnstr* obey the following pattern:

    $(ss\_s\_init.T * .ss\_s\_end)*$, where

        T is any call other than ss_s_init or ss_s_end

        $X*$ indicates zero or more occurrences of X

String parameters are legal C strings.

Figure 7.10   *scnstr* module interface specification—semantics part 1

access routine semantics
ss_s_init:
    transition: none
    exceptions: none
ss_s_clrscn:
    transition: $scnbuf, hltbuf, curbuf :=$ all ' ', all $false, \langle 0, 0 \rangle$
    exceptions: none
ss_s_str(row, col, s):
    transition: $(|s| > 0 \Rightarrow scnbuf[row][col..col + |s| - 1] := s)$
    exceptions: $exc :=$
        $(row \notin [0..\text{SS\_NUMROW} - 1] \Rightarrow$ ss_row
        $| col \notin [0..\text{SS\_NUMCOL} - 1] \Rightarrow$ ss_col
        $| |s| \notin [0..\text{SS\_NUMCOL} - col] \Rightarrow$ ss_len)
ss_s_hlt(row, col, l, f):
    transition: $(l > 0 \Rightarrow hltbuf[row][col..col + l - 1] := f)$
    exceptions: $exc :=$
        $(row \notin [0..\text{SS\_NUMROW} - 1] \Rightarrow$ ss_row
        $| col \notin [0..\text{SS\_NUMCOL} - 1] \Rightarrow$ ss_col
        $| l \notin [0..\text{SS\_NUMCOL} - col] \Rightarrow$ ss_len)
ss_s_cur(row, col):
    transition: $curbuf := \langle row, col \rangle$
    exceptions: $exc :=$
        $(row \notin [0..\text{SS\_NUMROW} - 1] \Rightarrow$ ss_row
        $| col \notin [0..\text{SS\_NUMCOL} - 1] \Rightarrow$ ss_col)
ss_s_ref:
    transition: $scn, hlt, cur := scnbuf, hltbuf, curbuf$
    exceptions: none
ss_s_end:
    transition: none
    exceptions: none

considerations
ss_s_str and ss_s_hlt may alter the value of *curbuf*.

Figure 7.11   *scnstr* module interface specification—semantics part 2

Table 7.13   *scndr* module interface specification—syntax

Routine names	Inputs	Outputs	Exceptions
sd_s_init			
sd_s_clrscn			
sd_s_con			
sd_s_mem			
sd_s_pc			
sd_s_acc			
sd_s_prt	int		
sd_s_msg	char*		
sd_s_hlt	int *boolean*		

7.6.4   The *scndr* MIS

The *scndr* MIS is shown in Table 7.13 and Figure 7.12. The *scndr* syntax includes one call per screen field, plus a few utility calls. s_init initializes the module, s_clrscn clears the screen, and s_con displays all of the constant screen fields. s_mem, s_pc, and s_acc copy the corresponding *absmach* values to the appropriate screen locations. s_hlt(a, f) turns highlighting on or off in the *MEM* field with address a. s_prt(i) displays i in the *PRT* field; s_msg(s) displays s in the *MSG* field.

The environment variable *scn* is used to specify the effects of calls on the terminal screen. No state variables are declared because *scndr* displays the values stored by *absmach*. The **assumptions** concern initialization of *scndr* and of the three other modules on which it depends. Note that there are no assumptions regarding the *absmach* module state: whatever is there is displayed.

The normal-case semantics are straightforward, based on assignments to screen fields. While we have focused on *scndr*'s interaction with the environment, it does of course interact with the *absmach* module as well. Here the interaction is specified because the *scndr* user needs to know where the displayed values come from.

7.7   Verification

After an MIS has been written, it must be verified. As described in Section 2.4, verification can be accomplished using inspection and testing. However, our MISs are not executable and therefore cannot be tested. Figure 7.13 shows the MIS inspection criteria. We review the "additional criteria" list from an inspection viewpoint. Note that items 1–3 describe characteristics of the specification document, while items 4–6 describe characteristics of the interface specified.

environment variables
scn
    the terminal screen

state variables
none

state invariant
none

assumptions
sd_s_init is called before any other access routine.
The *absmach*, *scnstr*, and *scngeom* modules have been initialized.
The address passed to sd_s_hlt is a legal address.

access routine semantics
Note: *MEM*, *PC*, *ACC*, *PRT*, and *MSG* are screen fields from the ISHAM RS.

sd_s_init:
    transition: none
    exceptions: none
sd_s_clrscn:
    transition: clear terminal screen
    exceptions: none
sd_s_con:
    transition: display the fixed screen fields
    exceptions: none
sd_s_mem:
    transition:
$$(\forall r, c \in [0..9]) MEM[r,c] := am\_g\_mem(10 \times r + c),$$
        converted to ASCII, right justified and padded left with blanks
    exceptions: none
sd_s_pc: ...
sd_s_acc: ...
sd_s_prt(x): ...
sd_s_msg(s): ...
sd_s_hlt(a, f):
    transition:
        ($f = true \Rightarrow$ display MEM[$a/10, a\%10$] in inverse video
        $| \ f = false \Rightarrow$ display MEM[$a/10, a\%10$] normally)
    exceptions: none

considerations
For each field displayed by *scndr*, the value is truncated to the field
length returned by *scngeom*.

Figure 7.12 *scndr* module interface specification—semantics

1. *Well formed.* The inspectors check for misuses of the MSM language. For example, does every set call have a **transition** entry and an **exceptions** entry? Do calls in the semantics have the number and type of arguments shown in the syntax?

2. *Comprehensible.* Can the inspection team understand the document? Here the team members serve as representatives of the intended audience.

3. *Complete.* Completeness is an ideal target for inspections: it is well suited to the inspection framework and lack of completeness is a common cause of failures. The key questions are

   - Are the assumptions reasonable?
   - Are the exceptions detectable?
   - On the normal-case domain—no assumption is violated and no exception is generated—are the **transition, output,** and **transition-output** entries well defined?

4. *State invariant holds.* Is the state invariant always true on access routine exit? Typically, the reader argues that (1) when s_init returns, the state invariant is true and (2) for any other access routine, if the state invariant holds when the routine is invoked, then it also holds when the routine returns.

5. *Sufficient.* It is often difficult to demonstrate sufficiency because the only precise specification of the service is the MIS itself; the MG entry provides only a sketch. In some cases, hypothetical user code (or pseudocode) is helpful. For example, Figure 7.14 shows that the token interface can extract the token values and types from a string containing a variable number of tokens. In other cases, the RS can be exploited. For example, the *scnstr* interface is sufficient because it can display and update the screen shown in the ISHAM RS.

6. *Feasible.* While an MIS makes no mention of the underlying implementation, it is important that the interface be implementable and that the implementation be testable through the interface. Where feasibility is in question, it can be demonstrated with solution sketches, e.g., pseudocode implementations or partial test plans.

7. *High quality.* The quality heuristics can be applied in a checklist fashion. Where the heuristics are violated, justification must be provided.

We illustrate criterion 4 by showing that the *stack* state invariant shown in Figure 7.1 is established by s_init and maintained by the other access routines. Immediately following s_init, $s = \langle \rangle$ and so $|s| = 0$. Thus, calling s_init establishes the state invariant. Scanning the *stack* MIS, we see that only s_push and s_pop change s. s_pop decreases $|s|$ and so cannot cause $|s|$ to exceed MAXSIZ.

- **Audience**. Module designer, implementor, tester, and user.

- **Prerequisites**. A reading knowledge of the Module Interface Specification language.

- **Purpose**. Describe the assumptions that users are permitted to make about module behavior, independent of the underlying implementation. Also describe the assumptions the module implementor is permitted to make.

- **Additional criteria**.

  1. *Well formed*. The specification is well formed with respect to the format described in Section 3.8.

  2. *Comprehensible*. The specification can be read and understood by the intended audience.

  3. *Complete*. Every call in every state violates an assumption, generates an exception, or is handled by the normal-case semantics.

  4. *State invariant holds*. The state invariant is true after every access routine call.

  5. *Sufficient*. The specified interface provides the required service.

  6. *Feasible*. The module can be implemented and tested affordably.

  7. *High quality*. Where practical, the interface satisfies the quality heuristics described in Section 7.3.

Figure 7.13   Module interface specification criteria

```
char s[TK_MAXSTRLEN+1];
tk_valtyp valtyp;

tk_s_init();
...
tk_s_str(s);
while (!tk_g_end()) {
    tk_sg_next(&valtyp);
    printf("val=%s typ=%d\n", valtyp.val,valtyp.typ);
}
```

Figure 7.14   Sufficiency: *token* module interface specification

s_push does increase $|s|$ by 1, but, due to the exception entry, does so only if $|s| <$ MAXSIZ. Thus, s_push maintains the state invariant.

7.8   Summary

Module Interface Specifications (MISs) play a vital role in controlling large software systems. While much of this chapter is concerned with notational details, the notations themselves are secondary. The primary concern is support for the four key roles in modular software development: designer, developer, verifier, and user. An MIS gives the designer a medium for design and review, provides the developer with a clear statement of the required task, supplies the verifier with a basis for correctness, and frees the user from having to know about module internals. Without an MIS, the effectiveness of information hiding is severely limited. Throughout, the goal is precise, written communication.

Our MISs are based directly on the MSMs presented in Section 3.8. To produce better interfaces with less effort, we package past experience in the form of design idioms and quality heuristics. Special consideration is given to modules with external interaction with other modules or with the environment.

The SHAM MISs show how precise, practical MISs can be written for a variety of behavior-hiding, machine-hiding, and software decision–hiding modules.

Interface errors are a significant problem in large systems. By relying on the criteria presented in Section 7.7, MIS faults can be detected before coding begins.

7.9   Bibliographic Notes

Parnas's pioneering work established the key concepts and demonstrated the feasibility of precise Module Interface Specifications [69]. Later work by Parnas et al. shows the tradeoffs required when designing interfaces for performance-critical applications [70]. The industrial case study by Jackson and Hoffman shows how to verify Module Interface Specifications in inspection meetings [39]. Considerable effort has been invested in highly formal approaches to interface specification using VDM [12], Z [11], algebraic methods [17, 71], and the trace method [18, 72]. Object-oriented methods often employ Module Interface Specifications in some form, as shown by Meyer's *design by contract* [73] and in the documentation for *The C++ Booch Components* [74].

Chapter 8

Module Internal Design

Representation is the essence of programming. [F. P. Brooks]

8.1 Introduction

After an MIS is written for a module M, the first step towards implementing M is to design the internal data structures for M. The choice of data structures is recorded in the Module Internal Design (MID).

The MIS and the Module Implementation for M differ in two fundamental ways.

1. They differ in their use of state: the MIS uses abstract state variables, whereas the Module Implementation uses variables of the implementation language.

2. They differ in their expression language: the MIS expresses the behavior of the access programs in terms of mathematical expressions and prose, whereas the Module Implementation uses statements of the implementation language.

When the abstract and the concrete state differ significantly, it pays to overcome the above two differences in two steps. The MID deals with the first difference: it specifies the concrete state of the module, and the effect of each access routine in terms of this concrete state.

The abstract state is chosen for the clarity of the MIS. There are two reasons for introducing a concrete state that is different from an abstract state.

1. The types of the abstract state variables are unavailable in the implementation language. For example, while sequences and tuples have direct counterparts in C (arrays and structures), there is no counterpart for sets.

2. An implementation using the abstract state is inefficient. For example, while look-up in an unordered sequence takes linear time, it can be done in logarithmic time in an ordered sequence. Here, there is no advantage in ordering the elements in the MIS, but it might be important for the Module Implementation.

Since the only difference between an MIS and an MID is the state space, the benefits from an MID are greatest when there are major differences between the abstract and concrete states. In fact, there are no benefits to an MID when the two state spaces are identical or when there is no concrete state. For such modules, we omit the MID.

Section 8.2 introduces the MID work product, based on the module state machine described in Section 3.8. In addition, the MID defines a *state invariant* and an *abstraction function*, whose roles are discussed in Section 8.3. Section 8.4 discusses the MID of modules with external interaction and Sections 8.5 and 8.6 discuss the MIDs of the BSHAM and ISHAM modules. Section 8.7 shows how to verify an MID in an inspection meeting. The MIDs for all SHAM modules that have an MID are presented in detail. The full work products may be found in Appendix D.

8.2 Work Product Definition

The format of an MID closely follows that of an MIS. Since the interface syntax is the same as in the MIS, it is not repeated in the MID. The semantics of the MID follow the MSM format described in Section 3.8. In this case, the state variables are defined in the implementation language. In addition to the **state variables** and **access routine semantics** sections, the MID contains two more sections: **state invariant** and **abstraction function**. The *state invariant* is similar to the state invariant of the MIS and defines a predicate on the concrete state space that restricts the "legal" states of the module. Thus, after every access routine call, the concrete state satisfies the state invariant. The *abstraction function* associates an abstract state with each concrete state. Specifically, it is a function from the legal concrete states to the abstract states. Just as for MISs, complex MIDs sometimes make use of *local* functions, types, and constants. These are declared for specification purposes only and need not be implemented. Information that does not fit anywhere in this format is placed in a section called **considerations**.

8.2.1 The *stack* MID

Figure 8.1 shows the MID for the *stack* module. Recall that the abstract state for *stack* is the single variable s representing the sequence of integers in the stack (Figure 7.1). Similarly, the concrete state contains an array of integers, `stack`, to store the elements in the stack. Since there is no way of obtaining the depth

state variables
int stack[PS_MAXSIZ];
int siz;

state invariant
$siz \in [0..PS\_MAXSIZ]$

abstraction function
$|s| = siz \wedge (\forall i \in [0..siz - 1])(s[i] = stack[i])$

access routine semantics
ps_s_init:
    transition: $siz := 0$
    exceptions: none
ps_s_push(x):
    transition: $stack[siz], siz := x, siz + 1$
    exceptions: $exc := (siz = PS\_MAXSIZ \Rightarrow ps\_full)$
ps_s_pop:
    transition: $siz := siz - 1$
    exceptions: $exc := (siz = 0 \Rightarrow ps\_empty)$
ps_g_top:
    output: $out := stack[siz - 1]$
    exceptions: $exc := (siz = 0 \Rightarrow ps\_empty)$
ps_g_depth:
    output: $out := siz$
    exceptions: none

Figure 8.1 *stack* module internal design

of the stack from this array, the concrete state also contains the integer siz, representing the depth of the stack.

The state invariant specifies that the value of siz must range between 0 and PS_MAXSIZ: when it is 0 the stack is empty, and when it is PS_MAXSIZ the stack is full. Note that the state invariant must not restrict the contents of the array stack: for any stack value, there is a trace that generates that value.

For each concrete state, the abstraction function defines the corresponding abstract state. For *stack*, the length of s corresponds to the value of siz, and the contents of s correspond to the contents of the first siz elements of stack. Note that the expression

$$(\forall i \in [0..siz - 1])(s[i] = stack[i])$$

is not defined for values of siz > PS_MAXSIZ, because stack contains only PS_MAXSIZ elements. However, the state invariant guarantees that this situation will not occur; the abstraction function is defined for all legal states.

Table 8.1   *stack* module internal design—execution tables ($\text{PS\_MAXSIZ} = 3$)

(a) s_init.s_push(1).s_push(2).g_top

	Call	Abstract state	Concrete state	Output	Exception
(1)	s_init	$\langle\rangle$	$\langle\langle ?,?,? \rangle, 0\rangle$	—	—
(2)	s_push(1)	$\langle 1 \rangle$	$\langle\langle 1,?,? \rangle, 1\rangle$	—	—
(3)	s_push(2)	$\langle 1,2 \rangle$	$\langle\langle 1,2,? \rangle, 2\rangle$	—	—
(4)	g_top	$\langle 1,2 \rangle$	$\langle\langle 1,2,? \rangle, 2\rangle$	2	—

(b) s_init.s_push(1).s_pop.g_top

	Call	Abstract state	Concrete state	Output	Exception
(1)	s_init	$\langle\rangle$	$\langle\langle ?,?,? \rangle, 0\rangle$	—	—
(2)	s_push(1)	$\langle 1 \rangle$	$\langle\langle 1,?,? \rangle, 1\rangle$	—	—
(3)	s_pop	$\langle\rangle$	$\langle\langle 1,?,? \rangle, 0\rangle$	—	—
(4)	g_top	$\langle\rangle$	$\langle\langle 1,?,? \rangle, 0\rangle$	?	empty

The *stack* access routine semantics are straightforward. s_init sets siz to 0 and never signals an exception. s_push(x) places x in stack[siz] and increments siz, signaling full if siz is PS_MAXSIZ. s_pop decrements siz, and g_top returns the value of stack[siz -1]; both signal empty if siz is 0. Finally, g_depth returns siz.

8.3   State Invariants and Abstraction Functions

The state invariant and the abstraction function are important aids in understanding the choice of concrete state. They serve as useful documentation expressing the designer's intentions. The state invariant restricts the concrete state space by eliminating values that are unreachable. The abstraction function provides an interpretation of the legal concrete states by defining how each legal concrete state corresponds to an abstract state. The state invariant and the abstraction function also play an important role in the verification of an MID, as described in Section 8.7.

Let us look at some examples for *stack*.   Table 8.1(a) shows the execution table for the abstract and concrete states of *stack* for the trace

s_init.s_push(1).s_push(2).g_top

For brevity, we assume that PS_MAXSIZ = 3. To represent the concrete state, we use terms of the form $\langle\langle s[0], s[1], s[2] \rangle, n\rangle$, where $\langle s[0], s[1], s[2] \rangle$ represents the contents of the array stack and n represents the value of siz. For state and output values, the symbol ? is used where no particular value is specified by the MID.

Note that in Table 8.1(a), after every call (1) the state invariant is satisfied by the concrete state, and (2) applying the abstraction function to the concrete state produces the abstract state. It is straightforward to see that the state invariant ($\mathtt{siz} \in [0..3]$ since $\mathtt{PS\_MAXSIZ} = 3$) is satisfied by each concrete state. Since $\mathtt{siz} = 0$ in the initial concrete state, applying the abstraction function to this state results in the abstract state $\langle\rangle$, which is the initial abstract state. Similarly, if we apply the abstraction function to the concrete state after $\mathtt{s\_push}(1)$, namely $\langle\langle 1, ?, ?\rangle, 1\rangle$, then we obtain $\langle 1\rangle$, the abstract state after the same call. Finally, after $\mathtt{s\_push}(2)$ the concrete state is $\langle\langle 1, 2, ?\rangle, 2\rangle$, which corresponds to the abstract state $\langle 1, 2\rangle$. In addition, $\mathtt{g\_top}$ returns 2 for both the concrete state and the corresponding abstract state.

As a second example, the execution table for the trace

$$\mathtt{s\_init.s\_push}(1).\mathtt{s\_pop.g\_top}$$

is shown in Table 8.1(b). Again, it is straightforward to see that the state invariant is satisfied and that the initial concrete state corresponds to the initial abstract state. Moreover, the next call—$\mathtt{s\_push}(1)$—is the same as in the previous example. After $\mathtt{s\_pop}$ the concrete state is $\langle\langle 1, ?, ?\rangle, 0\rangle$, and if we apply the abstraction function to this state, we obtain the abstract state $\langle\rangle$. Finally, the operation of $\mathtt{g\_top}$ signals the exception $\mathtt{empty}$ for both the concrete state and the corresponding abstract state. Note the output ? shown for $\mathtt{g\_top}$; because of the exception, any integer value is correct.

8.3.1 The *symtbl* MID

The *stack* state invariant and abstraction function are both simple. Figure 8.2 shows the MID for *symtbl*, which has a more interesting state invariant and abstraction function. The abstract state for *symtbl* is the set *tbl* of symbol/location pairs (Figure 7.3). Similarly, the concrete state consists of the array $\mathtt{tbl}$ of symbol/location pairs and the integer $\mathtt{tblcnt}$ that represents the number of elements in the table. The symbols are stored in $\mathtt{tbl}[0..\mathtt{tblcnt} - 1]$ and each symbol is stored in an array of $\mathtt{ST\_MAXSYMLEN} + 1$ characters: the symbol is at most $\mathtt{ST\_MAXSYMLEN}$ characters long, and the extra character is needed to store the null character that terminates the string. For simplicity, we have chosen to implement the symbol table as an array because for this application it is not worth allocating the memory dynamically.

The state invariant is defined in three parts.

1. Every symbol in $\mathtt{tbl}[0..\mathtt{tblcnt}-1]$ contains a null character and is therefore a valid C string. This could be expressed more formally as

$$(\forall i \in [0..\mathtt{tblcnt} - 1])(\exists j \in [0..\mathtt{ST\_MAXSYMLEN}])$$
$$(\mathtt{tbl}[i].\mathtt{sym}[j] \text{ is the null character})$$

but we prefer the informal version because it is unambiguous and easier to understand.

state variables
```
struct {
    char sym[ST_MAXSYMLEN+1];
    int loc;
} tbl[ST_MAXSYMS];
int tbl_cnt;
```

state invariant
1. Every symbol in tbl[0..tblcnt − 1] contains a null.
2. There are no duplicate symbols in tbl[0..tblcnt − 1].
3. tblcnt ∈ [0..ST_MAXSYMS]

abstraction function
$tbl = \{\langle sym, loc \rangle \mid (\exists i \in [0..\texttt{tblcnt} - 1])(sym = \texttt{tbl}[i].\texttt{sym} \wedge loc = \texttt{tbl}[i].\texttt{loc})\}$

access routine semantics
st_s_init:
    transition: tblcnt := 0
    exceptions: none
st_s_add(sym, loc):
    transition: $\texttt{tblcnt}, \texttt{tbl}[\texttt{tblcnt}] := \texttt{tblcnt} + 1, \langle sym, loc \rangle$
    exceptions: $exc :=$ $(|sym| > \texttt{ST\_MAXSYMLEN} \Rightarrow \texttt{st\_maxlen}$
                  $\mid findsym(sym) \neq \texttt{NOTFOUND} \Rightarrow \texttt{st\_exsym}$
                  $\mid \texttt{tblcnt} = \texttt{ST\_MAXSYMS} \Rightarrow \texttt{st\_full})$
st_g_exsym(sym):
    output: $out := (findsym(sym) \neq \texttt{NOTFOUND})$
    exceptions: none
st_s_loc(sym, loc):
    transition: $\texttt{tbl}[findsym(sym)].\texttt{loc} := loc$
    exceptions: $exc := (findsym(sym) = \texttt{NOTFOUND} \Rightarrow \texttt{st\_notexsym})$
st_g_loc(sym):
    output: $out := \texttt{tbl}[findsym(sym)].\texttt{loc}$
    exceptions: $exc := (findsym(sym) = \texttt{NOTFOUND} \Rightarrow \texttt{st\_notexsym})$
st_g_siz:
    output: $out := \texttt{tblcnt}$
    exceptions: none

local constants
```
#define NOTFOUND -1
```

local functions
$findsym : string \rightarrow integer$
    $findsym(s) = \quad ((\exists i \in [0..\texttt{tblcnt} - 1])(s = \texttt{tbl}[i].\texttt{sym}) \Rightarrow i$
                    $\mid true \Rightarrow \texttt{NOTFOUND})$

Figure 8.2 *symtbl* module internal design

2. There are no duplicate symbols in $\texttt{tbl}[0..\texttt{tblcnt} - 1]$. Again, we could express this more formally as

$$(\forall i, j \in [0..\texttt{tblcnt} - 1])(i \neq j \rightarrow \texttt{tbl}[i].\texttt{sym} \neq \texttt{tbl}[j].\texttt{sym})$$

but we prefer the informal version.

3. $\texttt{tblcnt}$ is restricted to $[0..\textbf{ST\_MAXSYMS}]$. In this case, the formal expression is shorter and clearer.

According to the abstraction function, the abstract state consists of the first $\texttt{tblcnt}$ symbol/identifier pairs of the array $\texttt{tbl}$. Note that the first and third part of the state invariant are sufficient to ensure that the abstraction function is defined for all legal states. Although we could have weakened the state invariant by omitting the second part, it provides valuable information about the concrete state space. In general, the state invariant defines a superset of the concrete states that can be reached by a sequence of calls. Where feasible, we want the state invariant to define exactly which concrete states are reachable.

To define the access routine semantics, we use the local function $findsym$. If s is one of the the first $\texttt{tblcnt}$ elements of $\texttt{tbl}$, $findsym(s)$ returns the index of s in $\texttt{tbl}$; otherwise, it returns the local constant $\textbf{NOTFOUND}$. The definition of $findsym$ contains a slight abuse of notation. Strictly speaking, the last occurrence of i in the expression

$$(\exists i \in [0..\texttt{tblcnt} - 1])(s = \texttt{tbl}[i].\texttt{sym}) \Rightarrow i$$

is free (it appears outside the scope of the existential quantifier) and its value is therefore undefined. We have taken this liberty, because we feel that the above expression is clear enough, and the alternative expression

$$(\exists i \in [0..\texttt{tblcnt} - 1])(s = \texttt{tbl}[i].\texttt{sym}) \Rightarrow i, \text{ such that}$$
$$i \in [0..\texttt{tblcnt} - 1] \wedge s = \texttt{tbl}[i].\texttt{sym}$$

is clumsy and hard to understand.

A second liberty we have taken with the definition of $findsym$ is that, as it is defined above, $findsym$ is not really a function: its return value depends on the values of $\texttt{tblcnt}$ and $\texttt{tbl}$. To remedy the situation, $\texttt{tblcnt}$ and $\texttt{tbl}$ would have to be added as arguments to $findsym$. Since it occurs regularly that state variables are used in local functions, we assume that the state variables are implicit arguments to every local function.

With the definition of $findsym$, the access routine semantics are straightforward.

8.4 Modules with External Interaction

Just as for MISs, MIDs for modules with external interaction can be quite different from MIDs for standalone modules. We first discuss interaction with the environment and then interaction with other modules.

Interaction with the environment is typically modeled in an MIS by introducing environment variables. These differ from state variables in that they not only have a name and type, but also an interpretation. For example, the *scnstr* MIS (Figure 7.10) defines the *scn* environment variable, representing the characters displayed on the screen. The Module Implementation cannot use such variables, and often interaction with the environment is accomplished through the use of system libraries. For example, in *scnstr*, we use the UNIX *curses* library to obtain access to the screen.

For such modules, there need not be a direct relationship between the abstract and the concrete state and we cannot define an abstraction function. This in turn means that there is little or no relationship between the operations of the access routines on the abstract and on the concrete state. Three possible ways of dealing with this situation are:

1. Just as for an MIS, introduce environment variables in the MID. Thus, the state space of an MID would consist of both the concrete state and the environment variables.

2. Invent a state space for the libraries that are used in the Module Implementation, and express the effect of the access routines in terms of this hypothetical state.

3. Omit the MID.

We prefer option 3. By introducing environment variables, the MIS and the MID become identical, and the MID does not contribute anything at all. Similarly, inventing a new state space is a considerable amount of work that contributes little to the primary purpose of an MID: to facilitate the construction and verification of the Module Implementation.

For modules that interact with other modules, the MIS typically references access routines or the abstract state of the other modules. For example, in the *load* MIS (Figure 7.6), the effect of `ld_sg_load` is expressed in terms of the state variable *mem* of the *absmach* MIS. In the Module Implementation, this effect is accomplished by calling access routines of the other module and often no concrete state is needed. To express this effect in an MID, we would again refer to the access routines or the abstract state of the other module, since we definitely do not want to refer to the concrete state of the other module. This means that the MIS and the MID would be the same, and we therefore omit the MID.

In the discussion above we have assumed idealized modules whose only purpose is either to interact with the environment or with other modules. In general, we do not omit the MID simply because the module interacts with the environment or other modules. We consider each module separately, taking into account both how the interaction is modeled in the MIS, and how the interaction can be accomplished in the Module Implementation. For example, even if a module has external interactions, part of the abstract state space might have a corresponding part in the concrete state space. In such a case, we would define an MID for that part of the state space. In the following sections, we discuss each of the SHAM modules and consider the above issues for the modules that have external interactions.

8.5 BSHAM Module Internal Designs

In this section, we discuss the MIDs of the BSHAM modules. Since we assume that the reader already knows how to program, we do not explain how to choose an appropriate concrete state. Instead, we focus on how to record the choice of concrete state in an MID.

8.5.1 The *token* MID

The abstract state for *token* is the sequence of tokens that have not yet been returned by sg_next (Figure 7.4). A possible concrete state would consist of an array to store the string passed by s_str and an index to keep track of the last character to be scanned. However, with such a concrete state there are many special cases that must be considered for sg_next: a string with only blanks, blanks (or not) before the first token in the string, and blanks (or not) after the last token. We reduce the number of special cases by using two simple techniques.

1. Use a *sentinel* character. By placing a blank after the last character in the string, we are guaranteed that every token in the string is immediately followed by a blank.

2. Always advance to the next token. By skipping over leading blanks, we are guaranteed that if there is a token remaining, then we are always placed at the start of that token.

An MID for *token* incorporating these decisions is shown in Figure 8.3. The concrete state consists of the array of characters buf to store the string, and the index cur to indicate the current character in the array. Note the two extra characters in buf; one for the sentinel, and one for the null terminator.

The state invariant contains three parts. The first part states that buf contains a valid C string. The second part restricts cur to [0..*leftnull*(buf)]; where *leftnull* is a local function that returns the index of the leftmost null character in an array of characters. Note that *leftnull* is undefined when there is no null character in the array and must therefore be applied with care. The third part states that if there is a token remaining in buf, then (1) there is no leading blank before the next token and (2) the character before the leftmost null character is a blank: the sentinel.

The abstraction function states that *toklist*, the sequence of remaining tokens, is the sequence of tokens in buf, starting from buf[cur]. Since the MIS

state variables
char buf[TK_MAXSTRLEN+2] ;
int cur;

state invariant
1. buf[0..TK_MAXSTRLEN + 1] contains a null.
2. cur $\in [0..leftnull(\mathrm{buf})]$
3. cur $< leftnull(\mathrm{buf}) \rightarrow (\mathrm{buf}[\mathrm{cur}] \neq$ ' ' $\land \mathrm{buf}[leftnull(\mathrm{buf}) - 1] =$ ' ')

abstraction function
toklist = the sequence of tokens in buf[cur..*leftnull*(buf) − 1]

access routine semantics
tk_s_init:
      transition: buf, cur := "", 0
      exceptions: none
tk_s_str(s):
      transition:
          buf := (there is a token in $s[0..leftnull(s) - 1] \Rightarrow rmblanks(s) \parallel$ " "
                | *true* $\Rightarrow$ "")
          cur := 0
      exceptions: $exc := (|s| > \mathrm{TK\_MAXSTRLEN} \Rightarrow \mathrm{tk\_maxlen})$
tk_sg_next:
      transition/output:
          Let   *curtok* be the token beginning at buf[cur]
                    curtoktyp be the token type of *curtok*
          out := $\langle curtok, curtoktyp \rangle$
          cur := (there is a token, beginning at position i,
                in buf[cur + $|curtok|$ + 1..*leftnull*(buf) − 1]
                    $\Rightarrow i$
                | *true* $\Rightarrow leftnull(\mathrm{buf}))$
      exceptions: $exc := (\mathrm{buf}[\mathrm{cur}] = null \Rightarrow \mathrm{tk\_end})$
tk_g_end:
      output: $out := (\mathrm{buf}[\mathrm{cur}] = \mathrm{null})$
      exceptions: none

local functions
leftnull : *string* → *integer*
      leftnull(s) := (there is a null in $s \Rightarrow$ the index of the leftmost one)
rmblanks : *string* → *string*
      rmblanks(s) := s, with leading blanks removed

Figure 8.3   *token* module internal design

state variables
int acc,pc;
int mem[AM_MEMSIZ];

state invariant
1. acc $\in [0..\text{AM\_MAXINT}]$
2. pc $\in [0..\text{AM\_MEMSIZ} - 1]$
3. $(\forall i \in [0..\text{AM\_MEMSIZ} - 1])(\text{mem}[i] \in [0..\text{AM\_MAXINT}])$

considerations
Since the abstract and concrete states are identical, the abstraction function and the access routine semantics are omitted.

Figure 8.4   *absmach* module internal design

already defines what constitutes a token, there is no need to repeat that information here.

The interesting access routines are **s_str** and **sg_next**, where we rely on the state invariant for guidance on (1) what to depend on at call invocation and (2) how to "clean up" just before call return. In **s_str**(s), to satisfy the state invariant, we remove the leading blanks from s and append the sentinel to the end of s. In **sg_next**, we return the current token and its type, where we rely on the fact that there are no leading blanks. Again we use the fact that the MIS already defines what constitutes a token and the type of a token. We also advance **cur** to the next token in **buf**, if there is one; otherwise, we advance to the leftmost null in **buf**.

8.5.2   The *absmach* MID

The abstract state for *absmach* consists of the integer variables *acc* and *pc*, and the sequence *mem*. Similarly, the concrete state consists of the integer variables **acc** and **pc**, and the integer array **mem**. The MID is shown in Figure 8.4. The state invariant restricts the range of **acc**, **pc**, and the values in **mem**. Because the abstract and concrete states are nearly identical and the mapping between the two is obvious, the other sections of the MID are omitted. For example, if we would have added the access routine semantics, the entries would be identical to those of the MIS. Such redundant entries are not worth maintaining, and we therefore omit them.

8.5.3   The *load* MID

The *load* MIS (Figure 7.6) references the *stdout* environment variable, representing the UNIX standard output, and the *absmach* abstract state variable *mem*. In the Module Implementation, the UNIX standard output is affected by a call to **printf** and the *absmach* concrete state is updated by calls to **am_s_mem**. Therefore, there is no concrete state for *load* and the MID is omitted.

8.5.4   The *exec* MID

The *exec* MIS (Figure 7.7) references the environment variables *scn*, representing the terminal screen, and *stdout*, representing the UNIX standard output. It also makes references to calls from *absmach*. The *exec* Module Implementation affects the terminal screen by calls to *scndr* access routines, and the UNIX standard output by calls to **printf**. It also calls access routines from *absmach*. Therefore there is no concrete state for *exec* and the MID is omitted.

8.5.5   The *sham* MID

sham is the SHAM Coordinator module. It has no access routines and its interface is specified in the SHAM RS. It therefore has neither an MIS, nor an MID.

8.6   ISHAM Module Internal Designs

8.6.1   The *keybdin* MID

The *keybdin* module reads input from the keyboard. There is no concrete state for *keybdin* and it obtains access to the sequence of characters entered through the UNIX *curses* library. Therefore, there is no *keybdin* MID.

8.6.2   The *scngeom* MID

Because the *scngeom* module does not have an abstract state (Figure 7.9), no concrete state is required. This is a special case of a module whose abstract and concrete state are the same. Since there are no state variables, there is no state invariant. That is, for *scngeom*, the MID is omitted because it is identical to the MIS.

8.6.3   The *scnstr* MID

The *scnstr* module provides write access to the terminal screen. The MIS (Figure 7.10) defines three environment variables: *scn* represents the characters on the screen, *hlt* indicates which characters on the screen are highlighted, and *cur* represents the cursor position. There are also three state variables that serve as buffers for these environment variables. Since the *curses* library provides all the services required to implement *scnstr*, there is no concrete state in the Module Implementation. As a consequence, we omit the MID.

- **Audience**. Module designer and implementor.
- **Prerequisites**. An understanding of the MIS and of the C constructs for variable declaration.
- **Purpose**. Describe the behavior of each access routine in terms of the concrete state.
- **Additional criteria**.

    1. *Well formed*. The MID is well formed with respect to the format described in Section 8.2. The state variables are defined in the C language and the MID defines a state invariant and an abstraction function.
    2. *Comprehensible*. The MID can be read and understood by the intended audience.
    3. *Correct*. The MID is correct with respect to the MIS.
    4. *Feasible*. The module can be implemented affordably.

Figure 8.5   Module internal design criteria

8.6.4   The *scndr* **MID**

The *scndr* MIS defines the environment variable *scn*, representing the terminal screen. In the Module Implementation, it can use the access routines of *absmach* to access the screen data, those of *scngeom* to obtain the screen positions, and those of *scnstr* to apply the changes to the screen. Therefore, no concrete state is needed, and we omit the MID.

8.7   Verification

8.7.1   Work product criteria

The criteria for an MID are shown in Figure 8.5. Note that the intended audience does *not* include the module user; thus, the MID audience is usually much smaller than the MIS audience. Since the MID is not executable, we can verify it only by inspection. Except for correctness, the "additional criteria" for an MID are similar to the ones for the MIS (see Section 7.7) and can be inspected in the same way.

With an MID, we can verify the correctness of a Module Implementation in two steps. We verify first that the MID is correct with respect to the MIS and second that the Module Implementation is correct with respect to the MID. In this section, we discuss the first of these two steps.

To verify that an MID is correct with respect to an MIS, the state invariant and abstraction function play important roles. We first verify that the state invariant holds in the same way that we verify that the state invariant holds for an MIS. Second, we verify that if we apply the abstraction function to the initial concrete state, we get the initial abstract state. Third, we verify that for each concrete state satisfying the state invariant, the operations of the access routines on the concrete state correspond to the same operations on the corresponding abstract state. After reviewing these steps in detail, we illustrate the techniques on the *stack* MID.

8.7.2   Maintaining the state invariant

To verify that the concrete state satisfies the state invariant after every call, we first verify that it is established by **s_init**. Second, we verify that every other access routine maintains the state invariant. That is, we assume that the state invariant holds before a call to an access routine, and we verify that it must also hold after the call.

8.7.3   Correctness of initial state

In the following, we use $\mathcal{A}$ to denote the abstraction function. For simplicity, we assume that all the access routines are deterministic, but the following verification procedures can be extended to deal with non-deterministic MISs and MIDs [53]. To verify the correctness of the initial state, we must show that $\mathcal{A}$ applied to the initial concrete state produces the initial abstract state.

8.7.4   Access routine correctness

The verification procedures are specified for set, get, and set-get routines.

8.7.4.1   Set access routines

To verify the correctness of a set access routine, we must verify the correctness of the exceptions and the transition. For the exception behavior, we must verify that, for every concrete state s that satisfies the state invariant, the MID specifies an exception e for s if and only if the MIS specifies the exception e for $\mathcal{A}(s)$.

For the transition correctness of a set access routine call c, we must verify that, for every concrete state s_1, applying c to $\mathcal{A}(s_1)$ yields the same abstract state as first applying c to s_1 and then applying $\mathcal{A}$. More intuitively, what we must verify is that first abstracting and then applying the transition operation is the same as first applying the transition and then abstracting. This intuition is captured by the *commuting diagram* in Figure 8.6(a). In the diagram, we use $A.c$ to denote the transition for c in the MIS and $C.c$ for the corresponding transition in the MID. We must verify that this diagram commutes along the two paths beginning in the lower left and terminating in the upper right. That is, if we let s_2 denote the state resulting from applying c to s_1 and s_3 the state resulting from applying c to $\mathcal{A}(s_1)$, then we must show that $s_3 = \mathcal{A}(s_2)$.

In showing that the diagram commutes, we may make two assumptions. First, we may assume that the concrete state s satisfies the state invariant.

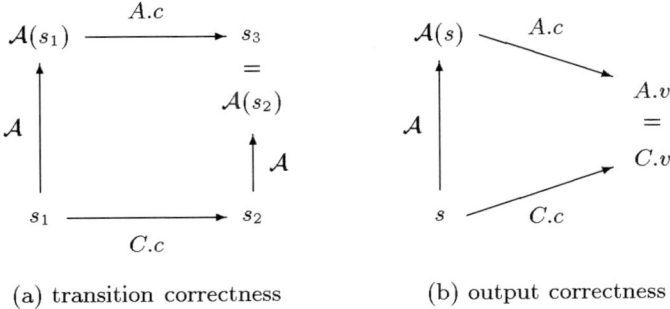

(a) transition correctness   (b) output correctness

Figure 8.6   Transition and output commuting diagrams

Second, since there is no transition when c signals an exception for state s, we may also assume that c does not signal an exception.

8.7.4.2   Get access routines

For a get access routine, we must verify the correctness of the exceptions and the output. The verification of the exceptions is the same as for a set access routine. The commuting diagram for output correctness of a get access routine c is shown in Figure 8.6(b). Here the intuition is that first abstracting and then applying the output operation must yield the same output as applying the output operation directly. Thus we must verify that, for every concrete state s, the output value $C.v$ specified by the MID is the same as the output value $A.v$ specified by the MIS for $A(s)$. Again, in verifying the output correctness, we may assume that s satisfies the state invariant and that c does not signal an exception.

8.7.4.3   Set-get access routines

For a set-get access routine, we must verify the correctness of the exceptions, the transition, and the output. The verification of the exceptions and the transition are the same as for a set access routine, and the verification of the output is the same as for a get access routine.

8.7.5   Verification of *stack*

The semantics of the *stack* MIS is shown in Figure 7.1, and the *stack* MID is shown in Figure 8.1.

8.7.5.1   Maintaining the state invariant

We first verify that the state invariant is maintained by showing that s_init establishes it, and that the other access routines maintain it. The state invariant is `siz` ∈ [0..PS_MAXSIZ] and the transition for `s_init` is `siz` := 0. So clearly, `s_init` establishes the state invariant.

For `s_push`, the state transition for `siz` is `siz` := `siz` + 1. If we assume that the state invariant, `siz` ∈ [0..PS_MAXSIZ], holds before the call, then the state invariant is satisfied unless `siz` = PS_MAXSIZ. But in that case `s_push` signals the exception **full**, and there is no state transition. This shows that if the state invariant is satisfied before a call to `s_push`, then it is also satisfied afterwards.

For `s_pop`, the state transition is `siz` := `siz` − 1. In this case, assuming that the state invariant holds before the call, the state invariant is satisfied after the call unless `siz` = 0. But this is exactly when `s_pop` signals **empty**, in which case there is no state transition.

The other two access routines, `g_top` and `g_siz`, are get access routines and have no state transitions. Therefore, if the state invariant is satisfied before a call to these access routines, then it is also satisfied after the call.

8.7.5.2   Correctness of initial state

In the initial concrete state, the value of `siz` is 0 and the value of `stack` is unrestricted. Since `siz` = 0, applying the abstraction function to this state yields $\langle\rangle$, the initial abstract state, as required.

8.7.5.3   Access routine correctness

The exception behavior for `s_push` in the MIS is

$$\textbf{exceptions}: exc := (|s| = \text{PS\_MAXSIZ} \Rightarrow \text{ps\_full})$$

and the exception behavior in the MID is

$$\textbf{exceptions}: exc := (\text{siz} = \text{PS\_MAXSIZ} \Rightarrow \text{ps\_full})$$

Since the abstraction function specifies that $|s|$ = `siz`, the expression `siz` = PS_MAXSIZ in the MID is equivalent to the expression $|s|$ = PS_MAXSIZ in the MIS. Therefore the exception behavior for `s_push` is correct. For most access routines, as is the case here, the MIS and the MID exception sections have a conditional rule with the same number of components and the same right-hand sides. This greatly simplifies the proof of correctness, because all we need to show is the equivalence of the corresponding left-hand sides (the conditions of the conditional rule), assuming the state invariant and the abstraction function.

The commuting diagram for the transition correctness of `s_push` is shown in Figure 8.7. We show the concrete state as a term of the form $\langle\langle s_0, \ldots, s_{M-1}\rangle, n\rangle$, where $\langle s_0, \ldots, s_{M-1}\rangle$ represents the contents of the array `stack`, n represents the value of `siz`, and M is a shorthand for PS_MAXSIZ.

Recall that to verify the transition correctness, we must show that first abstracting and then applying the transition is the same as first applying the transition and then abstracting. Since n is the value of `siz`, abstracting the concrete

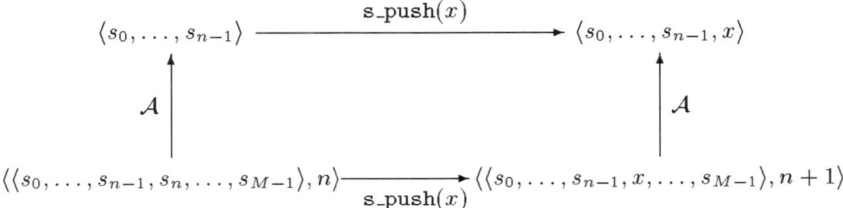

Figure 8.7 *stack* module internal design—**s_push** transition correctness

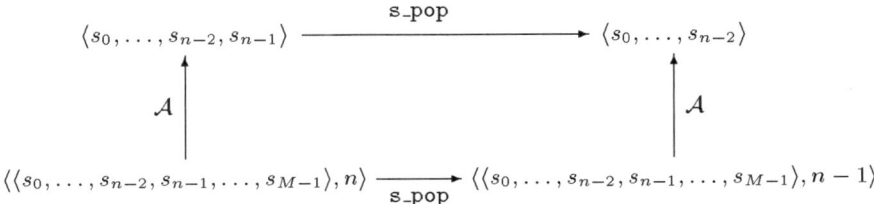

Figure 8.8 *stack* module internal design—**s_pop** transition correctness

state first yields the abstract state $\langle s_0, \ldots, s_{n-1} \rangle$ and applying the transition for **s_push** produces $\langle s_0, \ldots, s_{n-1}, x \rangle$. Note that we rely on the state invariant here, because if n does not fall in the range $[0..\textbf{PS\_MAXSIZ}]$ then the abstraction function is undefined.

Going the other way, we first apply the state transition and then abstract. Applying the MID transition first produces the concrete state

$$\langle \langle s_0, \ldots, s_{n-1}, x, s_{n+1}, \ldots, s_{M-1} \rangle, n+1 \rangle$$

Here we use the state invariant and the fact that **s_push** does not signal an exception, so we know that $n \in [0..\textbf{PS\_MAXSIZ}-1]$ before the call to **s_push**. Abstracting the above concrete state also produces the abstract state $\langle s_0, \ldots, s_{n-1}, x \rangle$, and thus the transition for **s_push** is correct.

The exception correctness of **s_pop** follows from the fact that **siz** $= 0$ in the MID if and only if $|s| = 0$ in the MIS. Figure 8.8 shows the commuting diagram for the transition correctness of **s_pop**. Abstracting first and then applying the transition produces the abstract state $\langle s_0, \ldots, s_{n-2} \rangle$. Applying the MID transition first produces $\langle \langle s_0, \ldots, s_{n-2}, s_{n-1}, \ldots, s_{M-1} \rangle, n-1 \rangle$; here $n > 0$ because we are assuming that **s_pop** does not signal an exception. Since abstracting this concrete state also produces $\langle s_0, \ldots, s_{n-2} \rangle$, the transition for **s_pop** is correct.

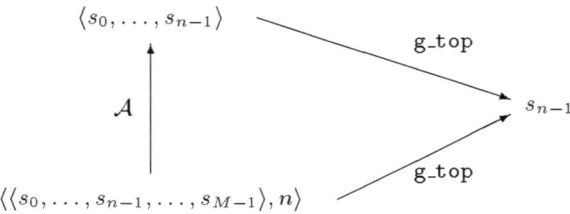

Figure 8.9   *stack* module internal design—**g_top** output correctness

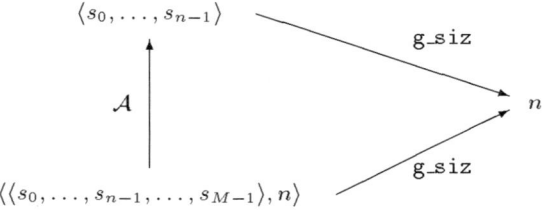

Figure 8.10   *stack* module internal design—**g_siz** output correctness

The exception behavior for **g_top** is identical to **s_pop**, and is therefore also correct. The commuting diagram for the output correctness of **g_top** is shown in Figure 8.9. Abstracting first yields the abstract state $\langle s_0, \ldots, s_{n-1} \rangle$, and applying the output function to this abstract state produces s_{n-1}. Since s_{n-1} is also the result of applying the output function directly to the concrete state, the output for **g_top** is correct.

The exception behavior for **g_siz** is correct, since both the MID and the MIS specify that no exception is ever signaled. Figure 8.10 shows the commuting diagram for the output correctness of **g_siz**. Abstracting first yields $\langle s_0, \ldots, s_{n-1} \rangle$ and applying the output function produces n, which is also the result of applying the output function directly to the concrete state.

8.7.5.4   Discussion

Note that even for a simple module such as *stack*, it takes quite a bit of work to rigorously verify the correctness of the MID. In practice, we must verify at rates that are far higher than can be attained during a rigorous proof such as the one above. Therefore, such a detailed verification is only performed if there are serious doubts about the correctness of the MID. For example, it may be warranted if several faults have been discovered in the MID.

However, it is important to have a good understanding of the full verification procedures. Although the actual verifications are substantially abbreviated, they must, in principle, be extensible to a rigorous proof.

8.8 Summary

The MID serves as an intermediate work product between the MIS and the Module Implementation. It specifies the concrete state of the Module Implementation and the effect of each access routine in terms of this concrete state.

Since the interface syntax of the MID is the same as in the MIS, it is not repeated in the MID. The semantics of the MID follow the MSM format described in Section 3.8. In addition, the MID defines a *state invariant* and an *abstraction function* to clarify the choice of concrete state. The state invariant is a logical expression on the concrete state space that restricts the legal states of the module. The abstraction function provides an interpretation of the legal concrete states by defining how each legal concrete state corresponds to an abstract state. The state invariant and the abstraction function also play an important role in verifying that an MID is correct with respect to an MIS.

Since the only difference between an MIS and an MID is the state space, the benefits from an MID are greatest when there are major differences between the abstract and concrete states. When the abstract and concrete states are very similar or when there is no concrete state, it may not be cost-effective to develop and maintain the MID.

8.9 Bibliographic Notes

Our notion of MID is based on the module design document proposed by Parnas [1]. Hoare [75] is usually given credit for the key ideas of data refinement, which is the replacement of an abstract state by a concrete one. More recently, this idea has been used extensively in the work on VDM [12] and Z [11]. The verification procedures for MIDs are based on the theory of modules developed by Gannon, Hamlet, and Mills [76]. Hoffman and Jones [53] adapted these ideas to the MIS and MID work products discussed in this text and extended the method to handle non-determinism and exceptions. Similar verification procedures also exist for VDM [12] and Z [77].

Chapter 9

Module Implementation

Executability is the essence of programming.

9.1 Introduction

While the Module Implementation (MI) is perhaps the most important work product, it is also the one that is easiest to produce. The MI is important because it is the work product that makes up the executable version of the system. Since the MI must be executable, machine readability is essential. For the other work products, human readability is the essential quality. However, with the other work products in place, it should be straightforward to construct an MI. The important design decisions have already been made in the RS, the MG, the MIS, and the MID.

Programming is commonly considered as a trial and error process. However, first writing a program and then trying to remove its errors leaves us with the difficult task of deciding when we have removed the last error. As Linger et al. point out:

> Since there is no way to be certain that you have found the *last* error, your real opportunity to gain confidence in a program is to never find the *first* error. [3]

Thus, it is the programmer's responsibility not to introduce any errors in the first place. It is *not* the tester's responsibility to remove all the errors that were made by the programmer; testing is effective only as an independent check.

Clearly, it is not reasonable to ask a programmer to write a program of several hundred lines of code without any errors. However, by carefully decomposing the system into modules, each access routine will typically consist of less than a page of code. In addition, we can implement an access routine without errors only if we know precisely what the access routine is supposed to do. This is

```
void ps_s_push(x)
int x;
{
    if (siz == PS_MAXSIZ)
        ps_full();
        return;
    }
    stack[siz++] = x;
}
```

Figure 9.1   *stack* module implementation—s_push

exactly what the MID (or the MIS if the MID is omitted) tells us: it allows us to *code to specification*.

Section 9.2 defines the MI work product. The technique of *stepwise refinement*, which is the subject of Section 9.3, can be used to develop an MI from an MID in a series of refinement steps. Examples from *stack* and *symtbl* are shown. The next two sections discuss the MIs of the BSHAM and ISHAM modules. Section 9.6 shows how to verify an MI in an inspection meeting; the testing of MIs is the subject of the next chapter. While we discuss the MI of every SHAM module, we do not present every MI in full detail. The complete work products may be found in Appendix E.

9.2   Work Product Definition

9.2.1   Format

The format of the MI is dictated by the rules of the implementation language—the C language in our case. Thus, although the MI is also an MSM, we cannot follow the MSM format described in Section 3.8. In addition, the state of the MI is already defined in the MID. Just as for the MIS and the MID, an MI sometimes makes use of *local* functions, types, and constants. In the MID, the local functions, types, and constants are used only for specification purposes, so that they need not appear in the MI. However, the same functions, types, and constants might also simplify the MI, and as such they are often included in the MI.

The concrete state for the *stack* module (see Figure 8.1) consists of an array of integers, stack, and the integer siz. Given this state, an implementation for s_push is shown in Figure 9.1. Recall that we signal an exception by calling a C function with the same name as the exception (Section 7.2.3). Thus, s_push calls ps_full when siz = PS_MAXSIZ.

In addition to the access routines, an MI often defines the function g_dump, implemented for debugging purposes. This function prints the concrete state of

```
void ps_g_dump()
{
    int i;

    printf("siz=%d\n",siz);
    for (i = 0; i < siz; i++)
        printf("stack[%d]=%d\n",i,stack[i]);
}
```

Figure 9.2   *stack* module implementation—**g_dump**

the module in a suitable format. Figure 9.2 shows the implementation of **g_dump** for *stack*. It prints the value of **siz**, and the first **siz** elements of the array **stack**.

9.2.2   Modules in C

To support modules in C, *header files* declare the exported identifiers of a module: the access routines, the exported constants and types, and the exception handlers for the module. Note that the local functions, constants, and types are defined in the MI, and not in the header file. We follow the convention that header files have the suffix .h; the header files for all the SHAM modules are contained in Appendix C.

Every MI that uses an identifier exported from module *M* must import the header file for *M* with the **#include** preprocessor command. This includes the MI of *M* itself. In addition, every MI also imports the header file **system.h**, which defines the system-wide constants and types for SHAM. For example, the first two lines of the *stack* MI are:

```
#include "system.h"
#include "stack.h"
```

9.2.3   Code format rules

Each programmer typically has his or her own unique approach to spacing, commenting, indenting, etc. If we allow each programmer to use his or her own style, then the format of the MIs will vary widely between different parts of the system, making them harder to read and maintain. In addition, programmers will likely spend hours converting code to their style and arguing about what the "best" format is. Therefore, each software project should have a set of clearly defined rules regarding programming style.

The Code Format Rules for SHAM are shown in Appendix G. Since there clearly is no "best" set of rules, these rules were chosen somewhat arbitrarily. It

```
void ps_empty()
{
    fprintf(sy_excfilp,"Exception ps_empty occurred\n");
}

void ps_full()
{
    fprintf(sy_excfilp,"Exception ps_full occurred\n");
}
```

Figure 9.3   *stack*—default exception handlers

is not the rules themselves that are important; what is important is that they are applied consistently.

9.2.4   Default exception handlers

In SHAM, it is the responsibility of the user of module M to implement the exception handlers for M (see Section 7.2.3). Since for many applications simple exception handlers suffice, we provide default exception handlers for each module. This has the added advantage that, if a module is used in more than one application, the same exception handlers can be used in every application.

Figure 9.3 shows the default exception handlers for the two *stack* exceptions: **empty** and **full**. The default exception handlers write an appropriate message to the globally defined file **sy_excfilp**. These default exception handlers are used in both BSHAM and ISHAM. In BSHAM, the file pointer is set to *stdout*, the UNIX standard output. Using *stdout* does not work very well for ISHAM, since it repeatedly redraws the terminal screen. This means that if an exception message were printed to *stdout*, it could easily be "lost" between screen updates. Therefore, for ISHAM, **sy_excfilp** directs the output to a file: the one whose name is defined by the constant **SY_EXCFIL**.

9.3   Stepwise Refinement

The technique of *stepwise refinement* provides a systematic way for developing an MI from an MID [66]. With this technique, we gradually develop the MI through a sequence of refinement steps. At each stage in the refinement process, we have a complete description of the program, with a mix of notation from the specification and the implementation language. Each refinement step decomposes one or several specification "statements" into more detailed statements in either the specification or the implementation language. We start this process with the MID, which is defined in terms of the specification language. We end

ps_s_push(x):
    transition: $\text{stack[siz]}, \text{siz} := x, \text{siz} + 1$
    exceptions: $exc := (\text{siz} = \text{PS\_MAXSIZ} \Rightarrow \text{ps\_full})$

Figure 9.4   *stack* module internal design—**s_push**

```
void ps_s_push(x)
int x;
{
    if (/*siz = PS_MAXSIZ*/) {
        ps_full();
        return;
    }
    /*stack[siz], siz := x, siz + 1*/
}
```

Figure 9.5   *stack*—first refinement of **s_push**

up with the MI, which is executable because it contains only statements from the implementation language.

9.3.1   Example: *stack*

As an example, we show how we can obtain the implementation of **s_push**, shown in Figure 9.1, by a stepwise refinement of its specification in the MID, shown in Figure 9.4. In the first refinement step, we choose a control structure that will first check for an exception and then change the state only if no exception occurs. Recall that the **transition** section applies only if the **exceptions** section does not specify an exception. In C, we can implement this with an if-statement, and the resulting "program" is shown in Figure 9.5. The parts of the "program" that are not executable and that are still expressed in the specification language are shown in comments. Figure 9.5 does not represent the only way in which we can refine the exception semantics. For example, Figure 9.6 shows another possible refinement. In this way, stepwise refinement allows us to choose between various implementations, by making a design decision during each refinement step.

    The program in Figure 9.5 still contains two statements in the specification language (as comments) and must be refined further. The expression

`/*siz = PS_MAXSIZ*/`

is further refined to

`siz == PS_MAXSIZ`

```
void ps_s_push(x)
int x;
{
    if (/*siz = PS_MAXSIZ*/)
        ps_full();
    else
        /*stack[siz], siz := x, siz + 1*/
}
```

Figure 9.6   *stack*—alternative first refinement of **s_push**

Finally, the statement

/*stack[siz], siz := x, siz + 1*/

is refined into the single C statement

```
stack[siz++] = x;
```

resulting in the implementation shown in Figure 9.1.

The implementation of the other access routines for *stack* is straightforward, and can be derived in a similar way. The *stack* MI is so simple that the power of stepwise refinement is not apparent; with *symtbl*, the advantages are clearer.

9.3.2   Example: *symtbl*

Figure 9.7 shows the concrete state, the local constants, and the local functions of the *symtbl* MID, as well as the specification of the access routine **s_add**. The concrete state consists of an array **tbl** of symbol/location pairs, and the integer **tblcnt** that represents the number of symbols currently stored. The local function *findsym* searches for a symbol in the table; *findsym(s)* returns the index of s in the table, or **NOTFOUND** if s is not in the table.

We now use stepwise refinement to implement **s_add**. As a first step, we refine the exception semantics, which produces the program shown in Figure 9.8. The further refinement of

/*strlen(sym) > ST_MAXSYMLEN*/

and

/*tblcnt = ST_MAXSYMS*/

into C is straightforward.

To refine the expression

/*$findsym$(sym) $\neq$ NOTFOUND*/

state variables
```
struct {
    char sym[ST_MAXSYMLEN+1];
    int loc;
} tbl[ST_MAXSYMS];
int tblcnt;
```

access routine semantics

...

$st\_s\_add(sym, loc)$:

transition: $\text{tblcnt}, \text{tbl}[\text{tblcnt}] := \text{tblcnt} + 1, \langle sym, loc \rangle$ '

exceptions: $exc :=$ $(|sym| > \text{ST\_MAXSYMLEN} \Rightarrow \text{st\_maxlen}$

$| findsym(sym) \neq \text{NOTFOUND} \Rightarrow \text{st\_exsym}$

$| \text{tblcnt} = \text{ST\_MAXSYMS} \Rightarrow \text{st\_full})$

...

local constants
```
#define NOTFOUND -1
```

local functions

$findsym : string \rightarrow integer$

$findsym(s) =$ $((\exists i \in [0..\text{tblcnt} - 1])(s = \text{tbl}[i].\text{sym}) \Rightarrow i$

$| true \Rightarrow \text{NOTFOUND})$

Figure 9.7   *symtbl* module internal design—**s_add**

```
void ps_s_add(sym,loc)
char *sym;
int loc;
{
    if (/*strlen(sym) > ST_MAXSYMLEN*/) {
        st_maxlen();
        return;
    } else if (/*findsym(sym) ≠ NOTFOUND*/) {
        st_exsym();
        return;
    } else if (/*tblcnt = ST_MAXSYMS*/) {
        st_full();
        return;
    }
    /*tblcnt, tbl[tblcnt] := tblcnt + 1, ⟨sym, loc⟩*/
}
```

Figure 9.8   *symtbl*—refinement of **s_add**

we have, as usual, several options. The first of these is to implement the function *findsym* as a local function in the MI. Recall, however, that local functions in the MID are there only to simplify the specification, and as such they do not have to be implemented. A second option is therefore to refine *findsym*, and to incorporate its implementation in s_add. We prefer the first option, because *findsym* is also useful in the access routines g_exsym, s_loc, and g_loc. Recognizing "shared operations" like *findsym* is an important part of stepwise refinement, since it can greatly simplify the resulting MI. Implementing *findsym* in this case has the additional advantage that the implementation of s_add closely follows its specification in the MID, making it easy to verify the correctness of s_add. We therefore implement the local function findsym and the local constant NOTFOUND. The above statement is then simply refined to

```
findsym(sym) != NOTFOUND
```

The last statement in s_add that we must refine is

/*tblcnt, tbl[tblcnt] := tblcnt + 1, ⟨sym, loc⟩*/

We first replace it by the three assignment statements

/*tbl[tblcnt].sym := sym*/
/*tbl[tblcnt].loc := loc*/
/*tblcnt := tblcnt + 1*/

which can then be further refined to

```
strcpy(tbl[tblcnt].sym,sym);
tbl[tblcnt].loc = loc;
tblcnt++;
```

Note that when refining a multiple assignment statement into more than one single assignment statement, the ordering of these statements must preserve the meaning of the multiple assignment statement.

Figure 9.9 shows the complete implementation of s_add that results from this refinement. Note that the correctness of this implementation depends upon the specification of *findsym* and is independent of the implementation for findsym.

What remains is to implement findsym, whose specification is given in the MID (Figure 9.7). The predicate $(\exists i \in [0..\text{tblcnt} - 1])(s = \text{tbl}[i].\text{sym})$ in the specification suggests that we search through the array tbl. One way to implement such a search is with a **for** loop, which leads to the refinement shown in Figure 9.10. The only remaining non-executable statement

/*sym = tbl[i].sym*/

can then be refined to

```
!strcmp(sym,tbl[i].sym)
```

The refinement of the other *symtbl* access routines is straightforward, and some of them also use the local function findsym. Note that with findsym, the *symtbl* MI is quite straightforward; only a *single* loop is needed.

```
void st_s_add(sym,loc)
char *sym;
int loc;
{
    if (strlen(sym) > ST_MAXSYMLEN) {
        st_maxlen();
        return;
    } else if (findsym(sym) != NOTFOUND) {
        st_exsym();
        return;
    } else if (tblcnt == ST_MAXSYMS) {
        st_full();
        return;
    }
    strcpy(tbl[tblcnt].sym,sym);
    tbl[tblcnt].loc = loc;
    tblcnt++;
}
```

Figure 9.9 *symtbl* module implementation—**s_add**

9.3.3 Discussion

In the preceding examples, we went through a lot of steps and trouble to come up with fairly straightforward implementations. In practice, and in the following sections, many of the intermediate refinement steps are skipped. However, it is important to know that, when things get complicated, we can fall back on stepwise refinement to obtain—and explain—our implementation through a sequence of refinements.

In the definition and the use of local functions, we use the idea of stepwise refinement in a disciplined and consistent way. Every local function in an MI must have an explicit specification. This holds for local functions that appear in the MID, such as *findsym*, and also for local functions that are not defined in the MID. This means that when we call a local function from an access routine, we determine the function's behavior from its specification, not its implementation. As a separate step, the local function is then implemented according to its specification. This separation of specification and implementation of local functions is a key application of separation of concerns, and it is the reason why stepwise refinement scales up to larger programs.

```
void findsym(sym)
char *sym;
{
    int i;

    for (i = 0; i < tblcnt; i++) {
        if (/*sym = tbl[i].sym*/)
            return(i);
    }
    return(NOTFOUND);
}
```

Figure 9.10   *symtbl*—refinement of `findsym`

9.4   BSHAM Module Implementations

9.4.1   The *token* MI

Figure 9.11 shows the **state variables** and the **state invariant** sections of the *token* MID. The state consists of the array of characters `buf` to store the string and the index `cur` to indicate the current character in the array. Recall that the *token* MID requires that (1) a sentinel blank character is stored after the last character in the string and (2) we skip over leading blanks so that we are always placed at the beginning of the next token (see Section 8.5.1). These decisions are enforced by the third condition of the state invariant.

As we noted for the MID, the state invariant guides the processing that has to be performed by each access routine. This carries over to the MI. For example, the transition for `s_str` is shown in Figure 9.11. This transition is implemented in `s_str` by the code shown in Figure 9.12. Following the exception check, a two-line while loop implements *rmblanks*. Then, if *s* has any non-blanks, the sentinel is added.

The implementation of **sg_next** is the most complicated part of the *token* MI. The purpose of **sg_next** is to return the value and the type of the current token and to advance `cur` to the next token. To recognize the type of token, we use a simple FSM (see Section 3.7) with five states: **START**, **ID**, **INT**, **ERR**, and **END**. The initial state is **START**. The state **ID** indicates that the token recognized so far is an identifier, **INT** that it is an integer, and **ERR** that it is neither an identifier nor an integer. The inputs to the state machine are the characters in the array `buf`, starting with `buf[cur]`. Table 9.1 shows the state transitions, based on the type of the current character, `buf[cur]`. We distinguish four types of characters: blank, numeric, alphabetic, and other. Note that for **START** there is no transition defined for a blank character, because the state invariant guarantees that this will not happen.

state variables
```
char buf[TK_MAXSTRLEN+2];
int cur;
```

state invariant
1. buf[0..TK_MAXSTRLEN + 1] contains a null.
2. cur ∈ [0..*leftnull*(buf)]
3. cur < *leftnull*(buf) → (buf[cur] ≠ ' ' ∧ buf[*leftnull*(buf) − 1] = ' ')

access routine semantics

...

tk_s_str(s):
>   **transition:**
>> buf := (there is a token in $s[0..leftnull(s) - 1] \Rightarrow rmblanks(s) \parallel$ " "
>> | $true \Rightarrow$ "")
>> cur := 0
> **exceptions:** $exc := (|s| >$ TK_MAXSTRLEN $\Rightarrow$ tk_maxlen)

...

Figure 9.11 *token* module internal design

```
void tk_s_str(s)
char *s;
{
    if (strlen(s) > TK_MAXSTRLEN) {
        tk_maxlen();
        return;
    }
    while (*s == ' ') /*skip over leading blanks*/
        s++;
    strcpy(buf,s); /*copy in what remains*/
    if (*s != '\0')
        strcat(buf," "); /*add trailing blank as sentinel*/
    cur = 0;
}
```

Figure 9.12 *token* module implementation—s_str

Table 9.1   *token* module implementation—state machine

Old state	buf[cur]	New state
START	alphabetic	ID
	numeric	INT
	other	ERR
ID	blank	END
	alphabetic or numeric	ID
	other	ERR
INT	blank	END
	numeric	INT
	alphabetic or other	ERR
ERR	blank	END
	alphabetic, numeric, or other	ERR

Part of the code that implements this state machine is shown in Figure 9.13. The state machine is implemented as a loop over a case statement; each iteration of the loop performs one state transition, and the loop terminates when the state END is reached. The case statement performs the state transition based on the current state and the next input character. In sg_next, the states are defined through an enumerated type, and the local variable state is used to maintain the current state. After the state is initialized to START, the appropriate state transitions are performed by the case statement inside the loop. For example, for the current state ID, the next input character is tested. If it is a blank, a transition to END is performed, the end of the token is marked, and the value of the token type is set in the typ field of the parameter valtyp. If the character is either alphabetic or numeric (tested with the C library function isalnum), then there is no state transition. For other characters, the token is not a valid identifier, and there is a transition to ERR.

The above code recognizes the type of characters of the current token, but it does not check the length of the token. This is one of the things that is done after the loop; Figure 9.14 shows all the post-processing that is done after the loop in sg_next. For tokens that are too long, the token type is set to TK_BADTOK. There is also code to copy the value of the token to the val field of the parameter valtyp. Finally, there is code to restore the state invariant, by skipping over intermediate blanks and advancing to the next token, if there is one.

```
enum {START,INT,ID,ERR,END} state; /*lexical analyzer state*/
int tokstart,tokend,toklen;
int i;
...
tokstart = cur; /*needed later to save value of token*/
state = START;
while (state != END) {
    switch (state) {
    case START:
        ...
    case ID:
        if (buf[cur] == ' ') {
            state = END;
            tokend = cur-1;
            valtyp->typ = TK_ID;
        } else if (isalnum(buf[cur]))
            cur++;
        else {
            state = ERR;
            cur++;
        }
        break;
    case INT:
        ...
    case ERR:
        ...
    }
}
```

Figure 9.13 *token* module implementation—**sg_next**

9.4.2 The *absmach* MI

In the introduction to this chapter, we mention that it is the responsibility of the programmer to show that the MI is correct with respect to the MID. This task is greatly simplified if the MI closely resembles the MID. It therefore pays to follow the MID as closely as possible, unless there are clear reasons not to do so (efficiency might be one such reason). For example, by implementing the local function **findsym**, we were able to follow the *symtbl* MID quite closely in the MI. The *absmach* MI provides a more striking example.

The concrete state for *absmach* consists of the integers **acc** and **pc**, and the array **mem** (see Figure 8.4). With this concrete state, the implementation of all access routines, except for **sg_exec**, is trivial. The MIS for **sg_exec** is shown in Figure 9.15. Since the abstract and concrete state for *absmach* are so similar, the specifications for the access routines from the MIS are not duplicated in the

```
/*check maximum lengths*/
switch (valtyp->typ) {
case TK_ID:
    if (tokend-tokstart+1 > TK_MAXIDLEN)
        valtyp->typ = TK_BADTOK;
    break;
case TK_INT:
    if (tokend-tokstart+1 > TK_MAXINTLEN)
        valtyp->typ = TK_BADTOK;
    break;
}

/*copy token to valtyp*/
toklen = tokend-tokstart+1;
for (i = 0; i < toklen; i++)
    valtyp->val[i] = buf[tokstart+i];
valtyp->val[toklen] = '\0';

/*skip over blanks preceding next token*/
while (buf[cur] == ' ')
    cur++;
```

Figure 9.14 *token* module implementation—after the loop in **sg_next**

MID. That is why we use the **sg_exec** specification from the MIS instead of the MID. Since the Execution-phase Exception Table (Table 5.7) is non-trivial, it is implemented as the local function **execexc**, which returns the exception identifier specified in the table, or **AM_NORMAL** if no exception is specified. Figure 9.16 shows the **execexc** specification and implementation. Since **execexc** is a local function in the MI but not in the MID, we include its specification as a C comment in front of the implementation. For consistency, we do the same for all local functions, even if their specification appears in the MI. This implementation closely follows Table 5.7, the SHAM Execution-phase Exception Table. To increase the resemblance, the macros **SY_OP0** and **SY_OP0**, defined in **system.h**, are used to mimic the types *op0objectT* and *op1objectT* from the RS. With the Execution-phase Exception Table, the implementation of **execexc** is straightforward, which illustrates the value of a precise RS.

The remainder of **sg_exec** is also straightforward, and consists mainly of a case statement implementing the SHAM Language Semantics Table (Table 5.6). As in the RS, the *HALT* and *PRINT* instructions are dealt with separately.

```
am_sg_exec:
    transition-output:
        (an error is specified in the Exec. Phase Exception Table ⇒
                        out := the error identifier
        | mem[pc] = SY_HALT ⇒ out := AM_HALT
        | mem[pc] = SY_PRINT ⇒ out, pc := AM_PRINT, pc + 1
        | true ⇒         out := AM_NORMAL
                        acc, pc, mem := values specified in the RS Language
                                Semantics Table)
    exceptions: none
```

Figure 9.15   *absmach* module interface specification—**sg_exec**

9.4.3   The *load* MI

For modules with external interaction, such as *load*, the decisions on how this interaction is accomplished are often already made in the MID. For *load*, load-time exception messages are printed to *stdout* with the C function `printf`, and the concrete state of *absmach* is updated by calls to `am_s_mem` (Section 8.5.3). In addition, *load* calls access routines from *token* to parse the lines of input.

To simplify the MI, *load* contains three local functions. The first function, `getinstr`, returns the SHAM instruction represented by a character string. Specifically, the call `getinstr`(s, i) returns *true* and sets i to the instruction name represented by the string s if s represents a valid instruction, and it returns *false* otherwise. The function `excmsg` prints the load-time exception message specified by Table 5.4 when an exception has occurred. Finally, `parse` parses an input line using calls on *token*. If Table 5.4 specifies a load-time exception for the current line, `parse` prints the appropriate exception message by calling `excmsg`. Otherwise, `parse` returns the instruction name and its operand value, if there is an operand.

With these three local functions, the implementation for **sg_load** is straight-forward, and it closely follows the pseudocode shown in Figure 5.4.

9.4.4   Version control through conditional compilation

In the MIS for *exec* we decided that there was going to be a single *exec* MI, supporting both the batch and interactive version of SHAM (Section 7.5.4). We could have created two versions, but this would mean maintaining two versions with only small differences between them. By using the C preprocessor's conditional compilation features, we can maintain the two versions in a single file, and, more importantly, the two versions can share much of the code. Similarly, there is only a single MI of the Coordinator module *sham*. We briefly present an overview of the conditional compilation features of C that we use in SHAM; these features are explained in detail in [78].

```
/*out := (state invariant holds =>
*     (an exception is specified in Execution-phase Exception Table of RS
*          => the associated exception identifier
*     | true => AM_NORMAL))
*/
static am_stat execexc()
{
    sy_instr cmd;
    int op;

    if (SY_OP0(mem[pc]))
            return(AM_NORMAL);
    if (SY_OP1(mem[pc])) {
        cmd = (sy_instr)mem[pc];
        if (pc < AM_MEMSIZ-1) {
            op = mem[pc+1];
            if (cmd == SY_LOADCON)
                return(AM_NORMAL);
            /*we know that cmd != SY_LOADCON*/
            if (op >= 0 && op <= AM_MEMSIZ-1) {
                if (cmd == SY_ADD) {
                    if (acc+mem[op] <= AM_MAXINT)
                        return(AM_NORMAL);
                    else
                        return(AM_ARITHEXC);
                } else if (cmd == SY_SUBTRACT) {
                    if (acc-mem[op] >= 0)
                        return(AM_NORMAL);
                    else
                        return(AM_ARITHEXC);
                } else
                    return(AM_NORMAL);
            }
            /*we know that op not in shamaddrT*/
            return(AM_ADDREXC);
        }
        /*we know that pc == AM_MEMSIZ-1*/
        return(AM_NOOPEXC);
    }
    /*we know that mem[pc] not in objectT*/
    return(AM_OBJECTEXC);
}
```

Figure 9.16 *absmach* module implementation—**execexc**

To compile either *exec* or *sham*, one of the two compile-time flags `ISHAM` or `BSHAM` must be defined. Depending upon whether a compile-time flag is set or not, the C preprocessor can conditionally include or exclude code fragments for compilation. For example, the code fragment

```
#ifdef BSHAM
    stat = am_sg_exec();
#endif
```

contains the preprocessor commands `#ifdef BSHAM` and `#endif`, and one C statement. The C statement is included in the code that is compiled if the compile-time flag `BSHAM` is defined, and it is excluded otherwise. The other C preprocessor command we use in SHAM is

```
#ifdef FLAG
    ...
#else
    ...
#endif
```

where the statements between `#else` and `#endif` are compiled when the compile-time flag `FLAG` is not defined.

9.4.5 The *exec* MI

The BSHAM version of *exec* interacts with the environment, by printing run-time exception messages to *stdout*, and with another module, *absmach*. The local function `excmsg` returns, as a C string, the run-time exception messages corresponding to an exception identifier. This is similar to the `excmsg` local function in *load*, except that it returns the message as a string rather than printing it. With this design, the BSHAM and ISHAM versions of *exec* can use the same `excmsg` function. Figure 9.17 shows the implementation of the BSHAM version of `s_exec`. After initializing the *absmach* accumulator and program counter, it repeatedly calls `am_sg_next` to execute the next command, until either a run-time exception occurs or the *HALT* instruction is reached. If a run-time exception occurs, it prints the message returned by `excmsg` as its last argument using the C function `printf`.

9.4.6 The *sham* MI

There are also two versions of the *sham* MI. Since *sham* is the Coordinator module, it defines the function `main`, where execution begins when BSHAM is invoked. The BSHAM version of `main` first checks the command-line argument, which should be the name of the file with the SHAM source code. It attempts to open this file using the C function `fopen`; if `fopen` fails, *sham* prints an error message and exits. Otherwise, it initializes *absmach*, *token*, *exec*, and *load*,

```
void ex_s_exec()
{
    am_stat stat;
    char buf[80];

    am_s_acc(0);
    am_s_pc(0);
    stat = am_sg_exec();
    while (stat == AM_NORMAL || stat == AM_PRINT) {
        if (stat == AM_PRINT)
            printf("%d\n",am_g_acc());
        stat = am_sg_exec();
    }
    if (stat != AM_HALT) {
        errmsg(stat,am_g_pc(),buf);
        printf("%s\n",buf);
    }
}
```

Figure 9.17   *exec* module implementation—**s_exec**

and loads the program by calling **ld_sg_load**. Finally, if there are no load-time exceptions it executes the program by calling **ex_s_exec**. Note that most of the work is done by the other modules, and that the *sham* MI is straightforward.

9.5   ISHAM Module Implementations

The ISHAM modules interact with the environment by reading characters from the keyboard and by providing formatted screen output. Both these tasks are performed using the UNIX *curses* library.

9.5.1   The *keybdin* MI

The *keybdin* module provides access to the keyboard, one character at a time, and also controls the echoing of these characters (Figure 7.8). The MI uses the following functions from the *curses* library.

- **noecho**: turns off keyboard echoing.

- **cbreak**: makes characters that are typed immediately available to the program. Normally, no output is available until the return key is pressed.

- **getch**: reads a character from the keyboard.

- **echo**: turns keyboard echoing on.

- `nocbreak`: buffers characters and makes them available to the program after a *NEWLINE* or *RETURN* is typed.

With these functions, the *keybdin* MI is straightforward.

9.5.2 The *scngeom* MI

scngeom provides run-time access to the screen geometry of ISHAM and has no state (Figure 7.9). The MI defines the local function `legfld`; `legfld(f)` returns *true* if f is a legal field identifier and *false* otherwise. The MI also defines the array `fldtbl`, which contains the row, column, and length for each screen field. With `legfld` and `fldtbl`, the implementations of the access routines for *scngeom* are straightforward.

9.5.3 The *scnstr* MI

scnstr provides buffered write access to the terminal screen. Fortunately, *curses* automatically buffers all the updates to the screen until the *curses* function `refresh` is called. This greatly simplifies the *scnstr* MI. The only remaining challenge is the code dealing with the highlighting of strings in `s_hlt`. With *curses*, a string is highlighted by turning highlight mode on, writing the string, and turning highlight mode off. Thus, to highlight a string currently displayed, that string's value must first be retrieved. Figure 9.18 shows the implementation of `s_hlt`, where we have omitted the code that detects and signals exceptions. The local function `instr` returns, as a C string, the sequence of `l` characters that is currently displayed starting at row `r` and column `c`. To highlight this string (when `f` is *true*), we turn on the *curses* highlighting by calling `standout`, move the cursor to the appropriate position on the screen with `move`, display the string using `addstr`, and turn off the highlighting with `standend`. To display the string without highlighting (`f` is *false*), we first move the cursor, and then copy the string while the *curses* highlighting is turned off (the default).

9.5.4 The *scndr* MI

The *scndr* module updates the terminal screen so that the values on the screen correspond to the ones stored by *absmach*. Although the MI has to deal with some technical details, the underlying idea behind it is quite simple:

1. For a field f, use *scngeom* to get the position on the screen of f.

2. For a fixed field, use *scngeom* to obtain its value; for a varying field, use *absmach* to obtain its current value.

3. Use *scnstr* to display the value in the correct position.

```
void ss_s_hlt(r,c,l,f)
int r,c,l,f;
{
    char s[SS_NUMCOL+1];

    ...
    if (l > 0) {
        instr(r,c,l,s);
        if (f) {
            standout();
            move(r,c);
            addstr(s);
            standend();
        } else {
            move(r,c);
            addstr(s);
        }
    }
}
```

Figure 9.18   *scnstr* module implementation—**s_hlt**

To handle the details, the local function **prtcon** prints out the initial value for a fixed screen field, **ljust** left-justifies a string field by padding it to the right with blanks, and **rjust** right-justifies a string. Finally, the **FLD** macro, defined by

```
#define FLD(f,t,r,c) (f.nam = t, f.row = r, f.col = c)
```

simplifies the assignment of values to a screen field.

9.5.5   The *exec* MI

There are two versions of the *exec* MI; the BSHAM version was discussed in Section 9.4.5. The major difference between the two versions is the loop that controls the execution in **s_exec**. Figure 9.19 shows this loop for the ISHAM version. This code closely follows the pseudocode in the execution FSM in the ISHAM RS (Figure 5.11). Characters are read from the keyboard by calling **ki_sg_next**, a single SHAM instruction is executed by calling **am_sg_next**, and screen fields are updated by calling access routines from *scndr*. To control the highlighting of the current instruction, the memory location of the old instruction is saved in the variable **oldpc** before **am_sg_next** is called. After the successful execution of an instruction, **sd_s_hlt** is used to turn off the highlighting of the old instruction and to turn on the highlighting for the new instruction.

```
ch = ki_sg_next();
while (ch != EXIT) {
    if (ch == STEP) {
        oldpc = am_g_pc();
        stat = am_sg_exec();
        if (stat != AM_PRINT && stat != AM_NORMAL &&
            stat != AM_HALT) {
            excmsg(stat,am_g_pc(),buf);
            sd_s_msg(buf);
        } else if (stat == AM_HALT) {
            sd_s_msg("HALT instruction reached");
        } else {
            /*update screen*/
            sd_s_msg("");
            if (stat == AM_PRINT)
                sd_s_prt(am_g_acc());
            sd_s_mem();
            sd_s_acc();
            sd_s_pc();
            /*update highlighting of cursor*/
            sd_s_hlt(oldpc,0);
            sd_s_hlt(am_g_pc(),1);
        }
    } else
        sd_s_msg("Illegal keyboard entry: type 's' or 'e'.");
    ch = ki_sg_next();
}
```

Figure 9.19 *exec* module implementation—loop for **s_exec**

9.5.6 The *sham* MI

There are also two versions of the MI of *sham*, the SHAM Coordinator module. The two versions are very similar, except that the ISHAM version contains additional code to initialize and terminate *curses* and the keyboard and screen handling modules. The only other difference is that the BSHAM version sets the file pointer for exception messages to *stdout*, and the ISHAM version sets it to SY_EXCFIL, as discussed in Section 9.2.4.

9.6 Verification

9.6.1 Work product criteria

Figure 9.20 shows the inspection criteria for an MI. In Figure 9.20 and in the remainder of this section, we assume that every module has an MID. If the MID

- **Audience**. Module implementor and tester.
- **Prerequisites**. An understanding of the MID and the implementation programming language.
- **Purpose**. Implement the module so that it satisfies the MID.
- **Additional criteria**.

    1. *Well formed.* Satisfies the Code Format Rules shown in Appendix G. The MI includes a set of default exception handlers, providing trivial exception reporting.

    2. *Comprehensible.* The MI can be read and understood by the intended audience.

    3. *Reliable.* No fatal errors will occur at run time.

    4. *Testable.* The module can be tested affordably—there are no unjustifiable controllability or observability problems.

Figure 9.20   Module implementation criteria

is omitted, then we assume that the MIS plays the role of the MID. Since the testing of an MI is the subject of the next chapter, we discuss only the verification of an MI by inspection here. In Section 9.2, we discussed the Code Format Rules and the default exception handlers. In this section, we focus on the correctness of the MI: how we verify that an MI satisfies an MID and how we inspect for the absence of fatal run-time errors.

9.6.2   MI satisfies module internal design

Verifying that an MI satisfies an MID is often simpler than verifying that an MID satisfies an MIS, because the MI and the MID share the same concrete state.

To verify the correctness of an MI, we separate the verification of local functions from the verification of access routines. As explained in Section 9.3, each local function has a specification. This specification is used in the verification of the access routines, without reference to the implementation of the local function. The correctness of the implementation of the local function with respect to its specification is then verified separately. In Section 9.3.2, we illustrated this verification method with the local function **findsym** and the access routine s_add of *symtbl*.

To verify the access routines, there are different procedures for set, get, and set-get access routines.

(a) Module Internal Design

ps_s_push(x):
    transition: stack[siz], siz := x, siz + 1
    exceptions: exc := (siz = PS_MAXSIZ $\Rightarrow$ ps_full)

(b) Module Implementation

```
void ps_s_push(x)
int x;
{
    if (siz == PS_MAXSIZ)
        ps_full();
        return;
    }
    stack[siz++] = x;
}
```

Figure 9.21   *stack*—**s_push** internal design and implementation

9.6.2.1   Set access routines

To verify the correctness of a set access routine, we must verify the correctness of the exceptions and the transition. For the exceptions, we verify that the MI signals an exception e if and only if the MID specifies the exception e. In addition, we check that when an exception is signaled there is no change in state. For the transition, we verify that, if no exception is signaled, the MI changes the state according to the MID.

As an example, Figure 9.21 shows the MID and the MI of the *stack* access routine **s_push**. Clearly the MI signals **full** if and only if the MID does. Also, the **return** immediately after the call to the exception handler ensures that there is no change of state when **full** is signaled. The correctness argument for the transition is also straightforward.

9.6.2.2   Get access routines

For a get access routine, we must verify the correctness of the exceptions and the output. For the exceptions, we verify that the MI signals an exception e if and only if the MID specifies the exception e. We also verify that the MI returns a value of the correct type when an exception is signaled. For the output, we verify that the MI returns the value that is specified in the MID.

Figure 9.22 shows the MID and the MI of the *stack* access routine **g_top**. It is easy to verify that the exception behavior is correct and that when the MI signals **empty**, it returns 0, a value of type **int**. The output specified in the MID and the value returned in the MI are identical and so the output is also correct.

(a) Module Internal Design

```
ps_g_top:
     output: out := stack[siz − 1]
     exceptions: exc := (siz = 0 ⇒ ps_empty)
```

(b) Module Implementation

```
int ps_g_top()
{
    if (siz == 0)
        ps_empty();
        return(0);
    }
    return(stack[siz-1]);
}
```

Figure 9.22   *stack*—**g_top** internal design and implementation

9.6.2.3   Set-get access routines

For a set-get access routine, we must verify the correctness of the exceptions, the transition, and the output. For the exceptions, we verify that the MI signals the exceptions specified by the MID, that the MI does not change the concrete state when an exception is signaled, and that it returns a value of the correct type. The verification of the transition is the same as for a set access routine, and the verification of the output is the same as for a get access routine.

9.6.3   Absence of fatal errors

There are several types of run-time errors that occur regularly and that have fatal consequences on the execution of an MI. A well-known example is the *divide-by-zero* error, which occurs when the divisor in a division is zero. The regular occurrence and the severe consequences of such errors warrant that we verify, on a line by line basis, that these errors cannot occur. It is easy to verify that there is no division by zero in SHAM, since there is no division at all. We discuss the type of errors that do need to be checked in SHAM, together with some examples.

Subscript out of range. For an array of size n, every time the array is accessed, we verify that its subscript falls between 0 and $n − 1$. For example, the array *stack* is accessed in the statement

```
stack[siz++] = x;
```

in the implementation of **s_push** of *stack* (Figure 9.1). We must verify that **siz** lies between 0 and **PS_MAXSIZ** − 1. The state invariant for *stack*,

$$\texttt{siz} \in [0..\texttt{PS\_MAXSIZ}]$$

guarantees that **siz** falls between 0 and **PS_MAXSIZ**. Moreover, **s_push** signals an exception when **siz** = **PS_MAXSIZ**, and the above statement is only executed when **s_push** does not signal an exception. Therefore **siz** lies between 0 and **PS_MAXSIZ** − 1 when the above statement is executed.

It is quite common that the state invariant plays a key role in showing the absence of run-time errors. This is another reason why it pays to make the state invariant as strong as possible.

Illegal pointer use. Another common source of problems is when a pointer has gone astray (sometimes referred to as a *dangling* pointer). An example of pointer use in SHAM is in the access routine **sg_next** in *token*. In this case, the pointer **valtyp** is passed as a parameter to **sg_next** and used to return the output. In **sg_next**, we assume that space is allocated and that the pointer is set by the caller. That this is the case must then be verified whenever **sg_next** is called. In SHAM, **sg_next** is called twice from the local function **parse** in *load*. Both times the address of a local variable is passed as a parameter; thus, the space is allocated and the pointer is set correctly.

Variable used before it is defined. It is typically straightforward to verify that every variable is defined before it is used. For example, the variable i in the local function **findsym** in *symtbl* is set in the first part of the for-statement, before it is used in the body.

Endless loop. Although it can be quite complicated in general to show that a loop terminates, the loops in SHAM are so simple that they do not pose any problems. Consider the for-statement

```
for (i = 0; i < tblcnt; i++) {
    if (!strcmp(sym,tbl[i].sym))
        return(i);
}
```

in the local function **findsym** in *symtbl*. The value of i is incremented at the end of each iteration of the loop, and neither the value of i nor the value of **tblcnt** is changed in the body of the loop. The state invariant for *symtbl* (Figure 8.2) implies that $\texttt{tblcnt} \in [0..\texttt{ST\_MAXSYMS}]$. Since i starts out at 0, it must eventually equal **tblcnt**, at which time i < **tblcnt** becomes *false* and the loop terminates.

9.7 Summary

The MI is a critically important work product because it is, after compilation, the primary product delivered to the customer. However, the other work products greatly simplify the MI development. If the system is carefully decomposed into modules, each of which is then precisely specified in an MIS and an MID, then we can code *to specification* in the MI.

Although the MI is an MSM, the format of the MI is restricted by the implementation language chosen and we cannot follow the MSM format described in Section 3.8. However, a set of Code Format Rules is used to ensure that a uniform coding style is followed throughout the system.

In some cases, it is straightforward to write a correct MI from the MID, by closely mimicking the specification in our implementation. When it is not straightforward to implement a module, *stepwise refinement* can be used to develop the MI through a sequence of refinement steps. Each refinement in the sequence represents a (partially) completed implementation in which specification fragments are gradually replaced by implementation fragments. The process terminates when the entire program is expressed in the implementation language.

To verify the correctness of an MI by inspection, we verify that an MI satisfies an MID and we inspect for the absence of fatal run-time errors. To facilitate the verification and to support stepwise refinement, every local function in the MI has an explicit specification. In the verification of an access routine that uses a local function, the specification of the local function is used to determine its behavior. As a separate step, we verify that the local function is implemented according to its specification.

9.8   Bibliographic Notes

The technique of stepwise refinement was first proposed by Wirth [66]; since then it has received considerable attention in the literature [3, 62]. Parnas [67] provides a comparison between stepwise refinement and information hiding. Fagan [41] introduced inspections as a method for verifying software. Our use of inspection for the absence of fatal errors is inspired by Fagan's inspection checklists. Russell [35] reports on the industrial application of inspections. More formal approaches for showing the correctness of implementations have been proposed by Hoare [79], Dijkstra [9], Gries [80], and, more recently, Morgan [81] and many others.

Chapter 10

Testing

Redundancy is the essence of testing.

10.1 Introduction

At this point, we encourage the reader to review Section 2.4.

10.1.1 Systematic testing

It is common practice to ignore testing until after implementation, and to discard the tests shortly after acceptance of the software. This ad hoc approach to testing is ineffective: because the testing is developed too late to influence design decisions, the resulting software is often hard to test. This approach to testing is also expensive, because the testing is not reused during maintenance.

A systematic approach to testing requires that the testing be

- *planned*: to permit design for testability,

- *documented*: so that the test cases can easily be understood and the adequacy of the test cases can be evaluated, and

- *maintained*: so that the test cases can be executed after every change to the software.

To perform systematic testing, we maintain two work products for each module in SHAM: the *Test Plan* (TP) describes the strategy for selecting and executing the tests, and the *Test Implementation* (TI) implements the TP.

When designing test cases, it is important to keep in mind Dijkstra's Law of testing (see Section 2.4): "program testing can be used to show the presence of bugs, but never their absence" [36]. This means that the focus of testing should be to detect program errors, *not* to show that the program is free of errors. Although this difference is a subtle and mostly psychological one, its

185

consequencès are important. It means we should design test cases so that they are likely to expose errors.

Despite the limitations of testing, it is important as an independent check on code that has been carefully designed and inspected.

10.1.2   Testing tasks

We distinguish six testing tasks.

1. Build the test harness.

2. Generate the test inputs.

3. Determine the expected outputs for each of the test inputs.

4. Execute the test cases, monitoring the behavior of the program.

5. Compare the actual outputs to the expected outputs.

6. Evaluate the test results and decide whether the program is ready to be put into production.

Note that the last three steps incur costs every test run. As a result, to reduce the overall cost of testing, it is advantageous to automate these steps as much as possible.

10.1.3   Overview

In Section 10.2, we discuss the purpose and contents of a TP and a TI. This is followed by a discussion of the distinction between system and module testing, and an explanation of why module testing is important. In the next section, we describe our method for selecting test inputs, based on functional testing. Section 10.5 describes the PGMGEN testing tool and illustrates it with the TIs of *stack* and *symtbl*. The design of a system has a major influence on the ease with which the modules in the system can be tested, and design for testability is the subject of Section 10.6. Sections 10.7 and 10.8 discuss the testing of the BSHAM and the ISHAM modules. Although module testing is important, we cannot ignore system testing; the SHAM system testing is discussed in Section 10.9. In Section 10.10, we review the work product criteria and the verification procedures for a TP and a TI. While we discuss the testing of every SHAM module, we do not present every TP and TI in full detail. The complete work products may be found in Appendix F.

10.2   Work Product Definition

10.2.1   Test plan

The TP for module M is intended for those considering running or modifying the testing of M. It serves as a specification for the TI for M: it describes the strategy used for selecting test cases and for executing these test cases.

A TP contains four required sections.

- **assumptions**: defines any assumptions, not contained in the MIS, on which the testing depends.

- **test environment**: describes the environment, such as test scaffolding, in which the testing is performed.

- **test case selection strategy**: describes how test cases are selected.

- **test implementation strategy**: describes the key aspects of the TI.

In addition, the **considerations** section is sometimes used for information that does not fit in any of the required sections.

10.2.2   Test implementation

The TI for module M implements the TP for M as simply and inexpensively as possible. The TI includes the test scaffolding, such as drivers and stubs, the test data files, and the procedures, both manual and automated, required to execute the tests. The SHAM modules with a call-based interface contain at least an interactive or a batch driver, and these modules often contain both. Typically, the interactive driver prompts the user for an access routine name and parameter values, invokes the access routine and, for a get call, displays the return value. The batch driver, on the other hand, typically contains a large number of test cases, and it is automated so that it can easily be run after every change to the module.

Part of the interactive test driver for the *stack* module is shown in Figure 10.1. A constant is defined for each access routine, and **main** contains a loop that repeatedly prompts the user to select an access routine using the function **nextcall**. The case statement inside the loop prompts the user for the parameters, if any, of the access routine, and invokes the access routine. For example, the function **readint** prompts the user for an integer parameter. For a get call, the value returned by the call is printed. The interactive driver also provides access to the routine **g_dump**, which is implemented for debugging purposes and displays the concrete module state (see Section 9.2).

The interactive test drivers are convenient for executing small numbers of test cases and for debugging, where the behavior of one test case determines what other test cases are interesting. However, thorough and systematic module testing requires that large numbers of test cases are executed after every change

```
#define QUIT 0
#define S_INIT 1
#define S_PUSH 2
#define S_POP 3
#define G_TOP 4
#define G_DEPTH 5
#define G_DUMP 6

...

main()
{
    int reply,i;

    while ((reply=nextcall()) != QUIT) {
        switch(reply) {
        case S_INIT:
            ps_s_init();
            break;
        case S_PUSH:
            i = readint("Enter element:");
            ps_s_push(i);
            break;
        case S_POP:
            ps_s_pop();
            break;
        case G_TOP:
            i = ps_g_top();
            printf("returns %d\n",i);
            break;
        case G_DEPTH:
            i = ps_g_depth();
            printf("returns %d\n",i);
            break;
        case G_DUMP:
            ps_g_dump();
            break;
        }
    }
    return(0);
}
```

Figure 10.1 *stack* interactive driver—**main**

to the module. Executing these with the interactive drivers would be a tedious and error-prone task, and automation is desirable. We automate those aspects of testing that are most tedious and repetitive: the tedious aspects because they are typically easiest to automate, and the repetitive tasks because the payoff of automation will be highest for those tasks. We do not attempt to automate those steps where manual approaches are cost-effective, or steps where it is unclear how we can automate. In particular, we do not automate the selection of test inputs, but we do automate the execution of the test cases, and the comparison of actual with expected behavior.

To automate the testing, most of the modules in SHAM contain a batch driver. For many of the modules, we use the PGMGEN test-driver generation tool to generate the batch driver. For the other modules, we use customized batch drivers.

10.3 Module and System Testing

Due to a lack of controllability and observability, it is hard to test a module M when it is installed in a production system. M's access routines are often not directly accessible. If M is a general-purpose module, some of its access routines may not be called at all in a particular production system. For example, if SHAM works as intended, none of the exception handlers will ever be called. Thus it is impossible to test the exception handlers using the production code of SHAM. To test a module thoroughly, we need to test it in isolation from its production environment.

While it is important to test each module in isolation, we also need to perform *integration* and *system testing*. With integration testing, we test combinations of modules that can be tested as single subsystems. Finally, we need to test the entire system. The extent of integration and system testing depends on the size of the system, the reliability requirements, and the amount of module testing that has been performed.

10.3.1 Top-down testing

Integration testing can be performed *top-down* or *bottom-up*. In *top-down* testing, we start by testing a top-level module using stubs, and gradually replace the stubs by production code. Although we can use stubs for some access routines of a module and production code for others, typically we use stubs for all or none of the access routines of a module. Therefore, in the following, when we refer to stubs for a module M, we mean stubs for all the access routines of M.

An example of top-down testing of BSHAM is shown in Table 10.1, where the *t*s represent various stages in the progression of testing. We start by testing the *sham* coordinator using stubs for the other modules. After this we can proceed in several ways. In this case, we replace the stubs for *load* and *token* by their MIs. We could have replaced only *load* by its MI, but it is hard to test *load*

Table 10.1   Top-down testing of BSHAM

module	t_1	t_2	t_3	t_4
sham	MI	MI	MI	MI
load	stubs	MI	MI	MI
exec	stubs	stubs	stubs	MI
token	stubs	MI	MI	MI
absmach	stubs	stubs	MI	MI

Table 10.2   Bottom-up testing of BSHAM

module	t_1	t_2	t_3
sham	not used	not used	MI
load	not used	MI	MI
exec	not used	MI	MI
token	MI	MI	MI
absmach	MI	MI	MI

thoroughly using stubs for *token*. At the next stage, we use the MI for *absmach*, and finally we replace the stubs for *exec* by the MI.

10.3.2   Bottom-up testing

In *bottom-up* testing, we first test low-level modules using test drivers, and gradually we replace the drivers by higher-level modules. An example of how we could test BSHAM with bottom-up testing is shown in Table 10.2. In *bottom-up* testing, we first test low-level modules. We test *token* and *absmach* using drivers. Note that we can test these in either order, or even in parallel. We then test *load* and *exec* using drivers and the MIs for *token* and *absmach*. Again, *load* and *exec* can be tested in either order or in parallel. Finally, we test the *sham* Coordinator module using the MIs for all other modules.

10.3.3   Top-down versus bottom-up testing

One advantage of top-down testing is the early availability of an executable program for the end user, so that he or she can give feedback as soon as testing is started. Another advantage is that integration testing occurs early in the testing, so that flaws in the interface design can be detected as early as possible. The major disadvantages of top-down testing are (1) that observability and controllability are typically poor when testing the lower-level modules and (2) that the cost of developing and maintaining the stubs is high. Although simple stubs are easy to generate, they provide very little support for thorough testing. More sophisticated stubs are expensive to develop.

The advantage of bottom-up testing is that it provides better controllability and observability than top-down testing. A disadvantage of bottom-up testing is the cost of developing and maintaining the test drivers. Another disadvantage is that we cannot demonstrate an executable to the end user until we have implemented all the lower-level modules.

In testing SHAM, we use a mixture of top-down and bottom-up testing. To improve controllability and observability we test the standalone modules using test drivers. For the other modules, we use a mixture of test scaffolding and production code, where the critical tradeoff is between the benefits realized through isolation, and the cost of developing and maintaining the test scaffolding.

10.4   Test Case Selection

We describe two methods for selecting test cases: *functional testing* and *structural testing*. With functional testing we base our tests primarily on the specification of the module. With structural testing we base our tests on the internal structure of the code implementing the module. Finally, we describe our approach for selecting test cases, which uses functional testing to select test cases and structural analysis as a cross-check on their adequacy.

10.4.1   Functional testing

Functional testing provides us with a systematic approach for choosing special values for test cases. Consider an access routine $f(p_1, ..., p_n)$. For each p_i, we choose a set S_i of special values and test f on every tuple in $S_1 \times ... \times S_n$. The choice of special values is determined by the parameter types and, in some cases, the implementation of the access routine. The special values include both normal-case and exceptional values for each parameter. In some cases, there are dependencies between the sets. For example, a value for p_1 may be special only for certain p_2 values.

In addition to choosing special values for each parameter of each access routine, we also choose special values for the internal module state. However, we need to consider only normal-case values for the module state, because the exception-detection code should prevent exceptional values.

To illustrate the choice of special values, we present two heuristics. The *interval rule* applies to an integer parameter restricted to an interval $[L..U]$. For normal-case testing, at least three special values are chosen: the boundary points L and U, and at least one value interior to $[L..U]$. For exception testing, special values are chosen on the boundary and interior points of $(-\infty..L-1]$ and $[U+1..\infty)$. Thus, for an integer parameter restricted to $[1..100]$, we might choose the following special values: $\{-1000, 0, 1, 50, 100, 101, 1000\}$. Sometimes we can apply the interval rule indirectly. For example, for the *stack* module, the stack size is restricted to the interval [0..PS_MAXSIZ], and thus we test it for an empty stack, a stack of size PS_MAXSIZ, and a stack with some, but less than PS_MAXSIZ, integers.

The second heuristic applies to a parameter with an enumerated type. If the number of elements in the enumerated type is small, we test the parameter for every value in the enumerated type. For example, for the *token* module, since there are only three types of tokens, we include test cases for all of these. If exhaustive testing is too costly, we divide the elements into classes of "similar" ones and select at least one value from each class. For example, for an ASCII-character parameter we might include one alphabetic character, one digit, one punctuation mark, and one non-printable character. Similar heuristics can be applied to choose special values for other parameter types.

Now that we know how to choose special values for individual parameters, let us see how to combine these to come up with a set of test cases for access routines. Consider an access routine $f(p_1, p_2)$ with two parameters. Let us assume that p_1 is an integer restricted to the interval [1..100], and that p_2 belongs to the enumerated type $\{red, green, blue\}$. A suitable set of normal-case values for p_1 is $\{1, 50, 100\}$, and a suitable set of exceptional values is $\{-1000, 0, 101, 1000\}$. Since the enumerated type for p_2 contains only three values, we include all of these. There are no exceptional values for p_2, since we can use the compiler to ensure that f is always called with a value belonging to the enumerated type. To test f, we use all combinations of special values for both p_1 and p_2. Since p_1 has $3 + 4 = 7$ special values and p_2 has 3 special values, we should test f for all 21 combinations of these.

Thus, ignoring special values for the module state, a simple access routine such as the one above requires 21 test cases. This is a characteristic of our approach to functional testing: it leads to a large number of test cases. It thus appears that automated support is essential to perform this style of functional testing. Fortunately, automation is feasible because the large number of test cases result from simple combinations.

10.4.2   Structural testing

With structural testing we select test cases based on the internal structure of the program. The motivation for structural testing is that we want to exercise or "cover" as many parts of the program as possible. We select our test cases so that a certain aspect of the source code is covered. We consider three types of coverage for structural testing: *statement*, *branch*, and *path coverage*.

The simplest form of coverage is *statement coverage*, where we select test cases so that every statement in the program is executed at least once. Consider the C function tst shown in Figure 10.2. To achieve statement coverage for tst a single test case suffices; for example, tst(2) will do. In the following, we abbreviate a set of test cases for tst by the set of parameter values. For example, the above test set is represented by the set {2}.

```
void tst(x)
int x;
{
    if (x > 0)
        pos = pos+1;
    if (x % 2 == 0)
        even = even+1;
    return;
}
```

Figure 10.2   Implementation of **tst**

With *branch coverage*, we require that the set of test cases execute every branch in the program at least once. That is, every decision in the program has to evaluate to *true* and *false* at least once. For **tst**, we need at least two test cases to achieve branch coverage, for example, $\{-1, 2\}$. For -1 both decisions in **tst** evaluate to *false*, and for 2 both evaluate to *true*.

A path of control flow through a program is *feasible* if there exist values for the parameters of the program that exercise that path. With *path coverage*, we require that the set of test cases execute every feasible path through a program at least once. Since there are two decisions in **tst**, there are four paths of control flow through it, all of which are feasible. The test set $\{-2, -1, 1, 2\}$ achieves path coverage.

Unfortunately, path coverage is rarely practical. In programs with loops, the number of feasible paths is often infinite, and even when it is not, typically the number is so large that path coverage is impractical. Moreover, it is in general undecidable whether or not a path through a program is feasible. In practice, most programs contain many infeasible paths. To address these shortcomings, variations on path coverage have been proposed. However, all forms of structural coverage, including these proposals, suffer from the following weaknesses:

- *Structural coverage is not sufficient.* Many simple faults are not detected even by path testing, the most demanding coverage measure. For example, consider the faulty implementation of **tst** in Figure 10.3. There are two faults in this program: the first condition should be **x > 0**, and the second if-statement is omitted. Yet, the test set $\{-1, 1\}$ achieves path coverage, and the program behaves correctly for this test set. This indicates two reasons why structural coverage alone is not sufficient: it is not suited for detecting missing functionality such as the second if-statement, and it does not select special values that should be tested, such as 0 in the case of **tst**.

- *Insufficient automated support.* Although tools exist for measuring structural coverage, typically they can measure only statement and branch coverage. For example, the UNIX utility *tcov* measures statement coverage.

```
void tst(x)
int x;
{
    if (x >= 0)
        pos = pos+1;
    return;
}
```

Figure 10.3   Faulty implementation of `tst`

Building a tool for measuring path presents considerable problems. First, since the number of paths is typically infinite or very large, there is the problem of presenting large volumes of data to the tester. Second, since there is no general way of detecting which paths are feasible, many of the paths will never be executed. Discovering which ones are feasible would have to be left to the tester. Third, there is the problem of displaying, in an understandable manner, an arbitrary path through a program.

10.4.3   Our approach

In the preceding sections we explained that

1. functional testing provides a systematic approach to test case selection that can be partially automated, and

2. structural testing provides little or no guidance with the selection of test cases, but statement coverage can be measured easily for a given set of test cases.

Therefore, our approach to testing uses functional testing for the selection of test cases and statement coverage analysis as a cross-check on their adequacy.

In particular, to select test cases for module M, we first consider M's MIS. Based on the MIS, we use functional testing to select special values for the access routine parameters and the module state. For the access routine parameters, we select normal-case and exceptional values; for the module state we select only normal-case values. We then consider M's MID and MI to see if there are any other special values, not suggested by the MIS, that we should test for. Finally, when executing the test cases, we use the UNIX utility *tcov* to measure the statement coverage achieved by our test cases. The details of *tcov* are discussed in Section 10.10. We require that our test cases achieve 100 percent statement coverage. We view this 100 percent statement coverage as a necessary, but not a sufficient, condition for a test set. It is used as a simple check on the test case selection strategy, not as a goal in itself.

test case selection strategy
  special values
    module state
      interval rule on size of stack: [0..PS_MAXSIZ]
    access routine parameters
      none
  test cases
    For each of the special module state values,
      call ps_s_push, ps_s_pop, ps_g_top, ps_g_depth
      check exception behavior
      after set calls, check get call values

Figure 10.4　*stack* test plan—**test case selection strategy**

To illustrate our approach to test case selection, consider the test case selection strategy for the *stack* module, shown in Figure 10.4. Recall the *stack* MIS semantics from Figure 7.1. The contents of the stack are maintained as a sequence of integers. Since there is no reason to believe any value will be treated differently from any other value, there are no special values for the stack elements. We do apply the interval rule to the size of the stack; we test the module for an empty, a partially full, and a full stack. The only access routine parameter is to **s_push**, which is an integer. Again, it is reasonable to believe that all values will be treated the same, so there are no special values for this parameter. For each special module state, we check both the exception behavior and, using get calls, the normal-case behavior.

10.5　Test Driver Generation

Although implementing test drivers manually is straightforward, it is also time-consuming, repetitive, and error-prone, and it produces code that is costly to maintain. As a result, test driver generation is a good candidate for automated support. For most modules with a call-based interface, we use the testing tool PGMGEN to generate batch test drivers from test scripts.

10.5.1　Test script language

A test case is described by providing a trace on a module and associating it with some aspect of the required behavior of the module in response to that trace. We represent a test case as a five-tuple

$$\langle trace, expexc, actval, expval, type \rangle$$

with the following interpretation.

```
module
    ps_

accprogs
    <s_init,s_push,s_pop,g_top,g_depth>

exceptions
    <empty,full>

globcod
{%
#include "system.h"
#include "stack.h"
%}

cases
<s_init().g_top(), empty, dc, dc, dc>
<s_init().s_push(10), noexc, g_top(), 10, int>
```

Figure 10.5   *stack*—small test script

trace: a trace used to exercise the module.

expexc: the name of the exception that *trace* is expected to generate (or **noexc** if no exception is expected).

actval: an expression (typically a get call) to be evaluated after *trace* and whose value is taken to be the "actual value" of the trace.

expval: the value that *actval* is expected to have.

type: the data type of *actval* and *expval*.

Below are two test cases for the *stack* module.

```
<s_init().g_top(), empty, dc, dc, dc>
<s_init().s_push(10), noexc, g_top(), 10, int>
```

In test cases developed solely to do exception checking, the *actval*, *expval*, and *type* fields contain **dc**, for "don't care." The first trace initializes the module and calls **g_top**, which should signal the exception **empty**. The second trace pushes 10 onto the stack, and checks that **g_top** returns the correct value.

A complete test script for *stack* containing the above two test cases is shown in Figure 10.5.   The **module** section defines the module prefix, which PGMGEN places in front of every access routine and exception name. The **accprogs** and **exceptions** sections define the list of access routines and the exceptions of the

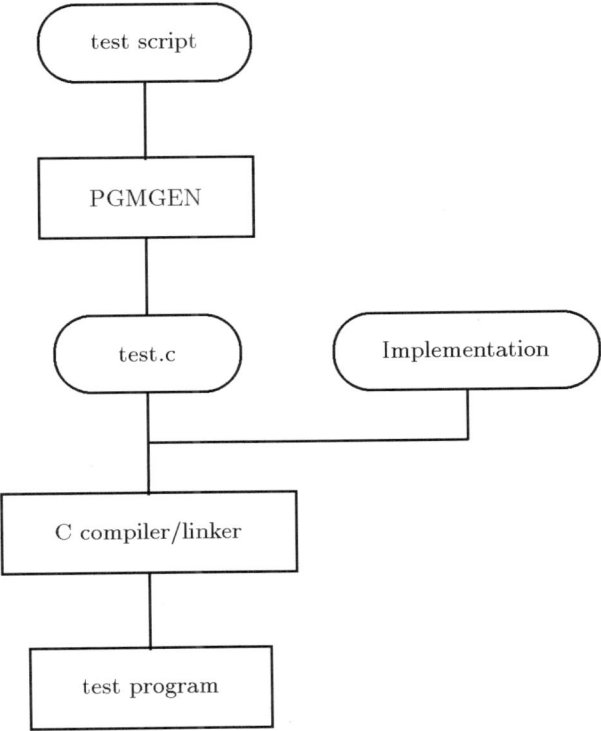

Figure 10.6 PGMGEN system flowchart

module. The `globcod` section contains global C code, delimited by the symbols {% and %}. PGMGEN places this global code at the top of the generated test driver. The test programmer can use the global code to define include files, stubs, and other functions that are called from the test cases. Finally, the `cases` section contains the test cases.

A test script may be viewed as a partial specification for a module, expressing its required behavior under specific circumstances. The purpose of PGMGEN is to generate a driver that will automatically determine whether an MI satisfies this partial specification.

10.5.2 Test program generation

The system flow for PGMGEN is shown in Figure 10.6—ovals indicate human-readable files and boxes indicate executable programs. The test programmer prepares the script using a text editor. PGMGEN reads that script and generates the C driver `test.c`, which is compiled and linked with the MI. For example, for

invoke $c_1, \cdots, c_n$, monitoring exception occurrences
compare the actual occurrences to *expexc*
if there are any differences
    print a message
else
    if *actval* $\neq$ *expval*
        print a message
    if any exceptions have occurred since c_n was invoked
        print a message
update summary statistics

Figure 10.7   Steps performed for a PGMGEN test case

stack, the test script is stored in the file `stack.script`, the MI in `stack.c`, and the executable test program that is generated is called `stack_b`. When `stack_b` is executed, it runs the test cases from `stack.script` and reports any errors.

To generate the test driver, PGMGEN first generates code to record exception occurrences. Then, for each test case of the form

$$\langle c_1. \cdots . c_n, expexc, actval, expval, type \rangle$$

PGMGEN generates code that performs the steps outlined in Figure 10.7. Following the last case, code is generated to print summary statistics.

10.5.3   The *stack* TP and TI

The production TP for the *stack* module is shown in Figure 10.8. The test environment section describes the test scaffolding used for testing *stack*. The test case selection strategy is explained in Section 10.4. The test implementation strategy section defines the key aspects of the TI: the C function `load(n)` is used to load the stack with the values $10, 20, \ldots, 10 \times n$, and *tcov* (discussed in Section 10.10) is used to measure statement coverage. Note that for the function `load` the values themselves are not important, but they should be unique and easy to generate.

The `globcod` and `cases` sections of the test script are shown in Figure 10.9; the `module`, `accprogs`, and `exceptions` sections are the same as in Figure 10.5. The `globcod` section defines the function `load`. Note that the `globcod` section is copied unchanged to the test driver by PGMGEN. This means that explicit module prefixes are required for the access routine calls in this section, such as `s_init` and `s_push` in Figure 10.9. In the `cases` section, we separate the cases for the three special module states. For each special module state, we check the return values of `g_top` and `g_depth` in that state, and after calls to `s_push` and `s_pop`. However, `s_pop` signals an exception for the empty stack, and `s_push` signals an exception for the full stack, and thus we do not check the return values

assumptions
    PS_MAXSIZ > 2

test environment
    PGMGEN driver
    no stubs

test case selection strategy
    special values
        module state
            interval rule on size of stack: $[0, \texttt{PS\_MAXSIZ}]$
        access routine parameters
            none
    test cases
        for each of the special module state values,
            call `ps_s_push, ps_s_pop, ps_g_top, ps_g_depth`
            check exception behavior
            after set calls, check get call values

test implementation strategy
    `load`(n)
        loads stack with $10, 20, \ldots, 10 \times n$
    statement coverage measured using the UNIX utility *tcov*

Figure 10.8   *stack* test plan

of the get calls for these cases. For the partially full stack, there are test cases with a stack size of 3, and the expected behavior for these cases indicates that no exception should be signaled. This happens only if **PS_MAXSIZ** > 2, and hence the assumption in the TP.

The entire script for stack is 48 lines long and contains 16 test cases. The test driver generated by PGMGEN from this script is 453 lines: almost 10 times the size of the script. When the driver is compiled and linked with a correct MI, it produces the output shown in Figure 10.10.

10.5.4   Embedded C code

In developing PGMGEN, our goal was to provide a test language powerful enough to describe the test cases we encountered in practice, but which was as cost-effective as possible. In particular, we wanted to minimize the training time for the test programmer, the cost of implementing and maintaining PGMGEN, and the cost of changing its target language and operating system. Therefore, we have allowed code written in C to be embedded freely in test scripts. As a result, there is no need in the script language for functions, macros, or iteration

```
globcod
{%
#include "system.h"
#include "stack.h"

static void load(n)
int n;
{
    int i;

    ps_s_init();
    for (i = 0; i < n; i++)
        ps_s_push((i+1)*10);
}
%}

cases

/*empty stack*/
<load(0).s_push(10), noexc, g_top(), 10, int>
<load(0).s_push(10), noexc, g_depth(), 1, int>
<load(0).s_pop(), empty, dc, dc, dc>
<load(0).g_top(), empty, dc, dc, dc>
<load(0), noexc, g_depth(), 0, int>

/*partially full stack*/
<load(2).s_push(30), noexc, g_top(), 30, int>
<load(2).s_push(30), noexc, g_depth(), 3, int>
<load(2).s_pop(), noexc, g_top(), 10, int>
<load(2).s_pop(), noexc, g_depth(), 1, int>
<load(2), noexc, g_top(), 20, int>
<load(2), noexc, g_depth(), 2, int>

/*full stack*/
<load(PS_MAXSIZ).s_push(0), full, dc, dc, dc>
<load(PS_MAXSIZ).s_pop(), noexc, g_top(), (PS_MAXSIZ-1)*10, int>
<load(PS_MAXSIZ).s_pop(), noexc, g_depth(), PS_MAXSIZ-1, int>
<load(PS_MAXSIZ), noexc, g_top(), PS_MAXSIZ*10, int>
<load(PS_MAXSIZ), noexc, g_depth(), PS_MAXSIZ, int>
```

Figure 10.9   *stack* test implementation

```
Statistics:
        Number of test cases: 16
        Number correct: 16
        Percentage correct: 100.00
        Number of exception errors: 0
        Number of value errors: 0
```

Figure 10.10   *stack*—output produced by test script

constructs—these are available in C and are presumably understood by the test programmer.

Besides the global C code in the **globcod** section, C code delimited by {% and %} may also be inserted in the following places in the **cases** section: between test cases, as a call in the trace of a test case, as the *actval* or *expval* field of a test case, and as a parameter of any call. As for the global C code, this code is copied unchanged to the test driver by PGMGEN.

Consider the *stack* test case

```
<s_init().s_push(10), noexc, g_top(), 10, int>
```

Suppose we want to test **s_push** and **g_top** not only for 10, but for all values in $\{10, 20, \ldots, 100\}$. We can write 10 test cases, but we can also embed the test case inside a for-loop, as in

```
{% for (i = 1; i <= 10; i++) %}
    <s_init().s_push(10*i), noexc, g_top(), 10*i, int>
```

The variable i is used both in the parameter to **s_push** and in the *expval* field of the test case. For this, i needs to be declared somewhere in the test script, for example, in the **globcod** section. The code generated by a test case is a single C statement. Thus, to include two test cases inside a for-loop, we need to enclose them by { and }, as in

```
{% for (i = 1; i <= 10; i++) { %}
    <s_init().s_push(10*i), noexc, g_top(), 10*i, int>
    <s_init().s_push(10*i), noexc, g_depth(), 1, int>
{% } %}
```

10.5.5   The *symtbl* TP and TI

To illustrate the use of embedded code, we consider the testing for *symtbl*. Part of the *symtbl* TP is shown in Figure 10.11. The MIS semantics for *symtbl* are shown in Figure 7.3. The abstract state is a set of symbol/location pairs. There are two characteristics of this state for which we choose special values: the size of

assumptions

ST_MAXSYMLEN $\geq$ length of ST_MAXSYMS $- 1$ in string form

ST_MAXSYMS > 0

. . .

test case selection strategy

special values

module state

number of symbols in table: $\{0, 1, \text{ST\_MAXSYMS}/2, \text{ST\_MAXSYMS}\}$

symbol length: short, ST_MAXSYMLEN

access routine parameters

st_s_add: strings of length $\{0, \text{ST\_MAXSYMLEN} + 1, 2 * \text{ST\_MAXSYMLEN}\}$

st_s_add, st_s_loc, st_g_loc, st_g_exsym: empty string

test cases

exceptions

. . .

normal

check st_g_exsym for empty string in empty table

add the empty string, check and change its location

for each special module state

check table length

check that a very long symbol is not in table

for each i in $[0..\text{ST\_MAXSYMS} - 1]$

if i in $[0..\text{t\_siz} - 1]$

check t_sym(i) in table with correct location

check st_s_loc resets location

else

check t_sym(i) not in table

test implementation strategy

C functions to support iterating over the special module states, viewed as a sequence:

void t_init: initialize to the first state

void t_next: load next state

int t_end: return *true* if no states remain

C functions to generate and check symbols in current state:

int t_siz: number of symbols in current state

char *t_sym(i): i-th symbol in current state

int t_loc(i): location of i-th symbol in current state

char *t_mksym(i, l): string consisting of i converted to ASCII, padded right with *'s to length l

statement coverage measured using the UNIX utility *tcov*

Figure 10.11   *symtbl* test plan—normal case test cases

the table, and the length of the symbols in the table. For the table size, we apply the interval rule to [0..ST_MAXSYMS]. In this case, we select two interior points, 1 and ST_MAXSYMS/2, because we feel that a table size of 1 is different enough from the other table sizes to include it as a special case. Note that this does not violate the interval rule, which states that *at least* one point from the interior of an interval should be selected. For the length of the symbols in the table, we apply the interval rule to [0..ST_MAXSYMLEN]. Since there is only one symbol of length 0, we test it separately; for the special module states we choose tables with short symbols and symbols of length ST_MAXSYMLEN. The special values for access routine parameters are overlength symbols for s_add, and the empty string for the access routines that take a symbol as parameter. The test cases that are executed for each module state have been divided into those test cases that should signal an exception and the normal-case test cases. For simplicity, we have shown only the normal-case test cases in Figure 10.11.

To loop over the special module states, we define C functions that iterate over the sequence of special module states using one of the sequence idioms discussed in Section 7.3. Although we are not designing a module interface, the idioms are still helpful. In this case, the function t_init initializes the sequence, t_next advances to the next special module state, and t_end indicates if the end of the sequence has been reached. Each special module state is characterized by n, the table size, and l, the length of the symbols in the table. There are also several functions that return information about the current state in the sequence: t_siz returns n, t_sym(i) the i-th symbol in the table, and t_loc(i) the location value of the i-th symbol.

Symbol values and their locations are unimportant, as long as they are unique and easy to generate. To define the symbol values, we use the function t_mksym(i, l), whose value is i in string form padded right with '*' characters to length l (or zero '*' characters if i has l or more digits). For a given n and l, the special module state is a table with the symbols t_mksym(i, l), for $i \in [0..n-1]$. For the location in position i, we use the value $10 \times i$.

We can now explain the assumption:

ST_MAXSYMLEN $\geq$ length of ST_MAXSYMS -1 in string form

The maximum number of elements stored in the table is ST_MAXSYMS, and therefore the longest string stored in the table will be ST_MAXSYMS -1 in string form, possibly padded with '*' characters. Thus, if the assumption was violated, one of the special module states would contain a string with more than ST_MAXSYMLEN characters. However, this string could not be added to the module state, because s_add would signal the exception maxlen for it.

The normal-case test cases from the *symtbl* test script are shown in Figure 10.12. We have used indenting and comments taken from the TP to make the test script more readable. The embedded code reduces the size of the test script considerably: although the entire test script contains only 18 test cases, it produces a driver that executes 868 test cases.

```
/*check g_exsym for empty string in empty table*/
<s_init(), noexc, g_exsym(""), 0, bool>
/*add the empty string, check and change its location*/
<s_init().s_add("",10), noexc, g_exsym(""), 1, bool>
< , noexc, g_loc(""), 10, int>
<s_loc("",20), noexc, g_loc(""), 20, int>

{%
t_init();
t_next();
while (!t_end()) {
%}
    /*check table length*/
    < , noexc, g_siz(), t_siz(), int>
    /*check that a very long symbol is not in table*/
    < , noexc, g_exsym(t_mksym(0,2*ST_MAXSYMLEN)), 0, bool>
{%
    for (i = 0; i < ST_MAXSYMS; i++) {
        if (i < t_siz()) {
%}
            /*check t_sym(i) in table with correct location*/
            < , noexc, g_exsym(t_sym(i)), 1, bool>
            < , noexc, g_loc(t_sym(i)), t_loc(i), int>
            /*check s_loc resets location*/
            <s_loc(t_sym(i),t_loc(-i)), noexc,
                    g_loc(t_sym(i)), t_loc(-i), int>
{%
        } else {
%}
            /*check t_sym(i) not in table*/
            < , noexc, g_exsym(t_sym(i)), 0, bool>
{%
        }
    }
    t_next();
}
%}
```

Figure 10.12   *symtbl* test implementation—normal case test cases

```
int cmp_bool(aval,eval)
int aval,eval;
{
     if ((eval == 0) && (aval == 0)) return(1);
     else if ((eval != 0) && (aval != 0)) return(1);
     else return(0);
}

int prt_bool(aval,eval)
int aval,eval;
{
     printf("\tExpected value:%d.  Actual value:%d\n",eval,aval);
}
```

Figure 10.13   cmp_bool and prt_bool

10.5.6   Comparing actual and expected value

Consider the test case

$$\langle trace, expexc, actval, expval, type \rangle.$$

As Figure 10.7 shows, after the calls in *trace* are executed, *actval* and *expval* are compared. To compare them, PGMGEN generates a call to the boolean C function whose name is cmp_ followed by *type*. The arguments to this function are *actval* and *expval*. For example, for the *stack* test case

```
<s_init().s_push(10), noexc, g_top(), 10, int>
```

PGMGEN generates the call cmp_int(ps_g_top(), 10) (note that PGMGEN places the prefix ps_ in front of the call to g_top). This C function should return *true* when *actval* = *expval*, and *false* otherwise.

When the above function returns *false*, PGMGEN generates a call to the C function whose name is prt_ followed by *type*, again with *actval* and *expval* as its arguments. The purpose of this function is to print a message indicating that *actval* $\neq$ *expval* and displaying both values.

PGMGEN provides the cmp_ and prt_ functions for the data types bool (*boolean*), char, float, int, and string. For example, the implementation of cmp_bool and prt_bool are shown in Figure 10.13.

For other data types, the tester must define these functions, typically in the globcod section of the test script. These functions can also be used to define customized comparison and printing functions for standard data types. For example, the function cmp_float provided by PGMGEN uses an exact comparison to compare two floating-point numbers. For certain applications, it is impossible to define the actual value of a floating-point number with such accuracy.

```
float epsilon = 0.00001;

int cmp_fuzz(aval,eval)
float aval,eval;
{
    float diff;

    diff = eval-aval;
    if (diff > epsilon || diff < -epsilon) return(0);
    else return(1);
}

int prt_fuzz(aval,eval)
float aval,eval;
{
    printf("\texpval:%f.  actval:%f.  epsilon:%f\n",eval,aval,epsilon);
}
```

Figure 10.14   cmp_fuzz and prt_fuzz

For these cases the tester could define the functions cmp_fuzz and prt_fuzz as shown in Figure 10.14. cmp_fuzz considers two floating-point numbers equal if they are within epsilon of each other. Note that prt_fuzz also prints out the value of epsilon. To use these functions in a test case, the *type* field of the test case should be defined as fuzz.

10.6   Design for Testability

Both the module decomposition and the module interface design influence the testability of a module. To make testing affordable and effective, we need to consider testability of a module at design time, before the implementation is started. In this section, we review the key principles in design for testability: *controllability* and *observability*. While controllability and observability are known to be important in hardware testing, they are often ignored in software testing. Controllability and observability are critical when software interacts with the environment, however, as is the case with most software systems. Poor controllability and observability also make it difficult to automate the testing, which is necessary to make testing affordable.

A common example of poor controllability in software is the lack of explicit initialization. Consider the three test cases

```
<s_init().s_push(10).s_push(20), noexc, g_top(), 20, int>
<s_init().s_push(10).s_push(20), noexc, g_depth(), 2, int>
<s_init().s_push(10).s_pop, noexc, g_depth(), 0, int>
```

for the *stack* module. Without the access routine `s_init`, these would have to be changed to

```
<s_push(10).s_push(20), noexc, g_top(), 20, int>
< , noexc, g_depth(), 2, int>
<s_pop.s_pop, noexc, g_depth(), 0, int>
```

where we rely on the fact that the stack is empty when the first test case is reached. Without `s_init`, a large number of changes would have to be made to the *stack* test script shown in Figure 10.9. The need for explicit initialization is recognized in hardware testing, where integrated circuits frequently contain reset circuitry.

A common example of poor observability in software is the undisciplined use of print statements. Exceptions are often signaled by printing a message, which makes it hard to automate the testing of exceptions. For example, it is not clear how we could use PGMGEN to test the *stack* module if exceptions were signaled by a call to **printf** rather than a call to an exception handler.

Another cause for poor controllability or observability is external interaction. While the lack of explicit initialization and the uncontrolled use of print statements can be avoided, external interaction cannot be completely eliminated. Every system will have modules that interact with other modules. To improve the testability of such a module, we isolate it where possible and affordable, and we limit the amount of interaction by careful interface design. Most systems also interact with the environment, for example, by reading input from the keyboard or by printing output to the screen. To improve the testability of SHAM modules, we have isolated the interaction with the environment in a small number of modules, so that the other modules can be tested without controllability and observability problems. Examples are discussed in the next two sections.

10.7 BSHAM Test Plans and Implementations

10.7.1 The *token* TP and TI

Since *token* does not have any controllability and observability problems we test it with PGMGEN. Recall that the abstract state for *token* (Figure 7.4) is a sequence of tokens. In this case, the special module state values we select are determined by the number of tokens in the sequence and their types. There is a minimum but no maximum number of tokens defined, and we apply the interval rule to $[0..\infty)$: we test for states with 0, 1, and 3 tokens. Since there are only three token types, we include test cases for all of these. Every token type, except for **TK_BADTOK**, has a maximum length associated with it, and we apply the interval rule to the length of the tokens. For **TK_BADTOK**, we include test cases for tokens that are "almost" of some other type. For example, we include a token consisting of **TK_MAXINTLEN** + 1 digits, which would be an integer, except that it is too long. The only access routine for which we include special parameter

```
int cmp_valtyp(actvtp,expvtp)
tk_valtyp *actvtp,*expvtp;
{
    if (!strcmp(actvtp->val,expvtp->val))
        return(actvtp->typ == expvtp->typ);
    else
        return(0);
}


void prt_valtyp(actvtp,expvtp)
tk_valtyp *actvtp,*expvtp;
{
    printf("Expected value:<%s,%d>. Actual value:<%s,%d>\n",
        expvtp->val,expvtp->typ,actvtp->val,actvtp->typ);
}
```

Figure 10.15 *token* test implementation—**cmp_valtyp** and **prt_valtyp**

values is **s_str**; we apply the interval rule to the length of the string and vary the number of blanks before and after tokens in the string.

The access routine **sg_next** returns a value of type **tk_valtyp**, a structure containing the value of the token and its type. To compare expected and actual values of this type, we must define **cmp_** and **prt_** functions as discussed in Section 10.5.6. We define the functions **cmp_valtyp** and **prt_valtyp** shown in Figure 10.15 in the **globcod** section of the test script. Both functions take two pointers to **tk_valtyp** as their arguments. To compare the two values, **cmp_valtyp** compares both the value of the token and its type. Similarly, **prt_valtyp** prints out the values and types of both its parameters.

10.7.2 The *absmach* TP and TI

absmach is also tested using PGMGEN. The abstract state for *absmach* (Figure 7.5) consists of the accumulator, the program counter, and the memory. The special module state values that we select are determined by the effect of these three on the behavior of **sg_exec**. In particular, we include state values so that every SHAM run-time exception occurs at least once and every SHAM instruction is executed at least once. For each instruction, we check the effect it has on the accumulator and the program counter. For instructions that also alter memory contents, we check that the change is made correctly. For the access routine parameters, we apply the interval rule to the parameters of **s_acc**, **s_pc**, **s_mem**, and **g_mem**.

test environment

> *sham* Coordinator used as driver
> stubs for *absmach* and *exec*, production code for *sham* and *token*
> input stored in files
> output saved in files, checked with delta testing
> directory structure:
>> `load/`
>>> `input/` - test cases stored one per file
>>> `exp/` - expected results of test case (same file name)
>>> `act/` - actual results of test case (same file name)

Figure 10.16 *load* test plan—**test environment**

10.7.3 The *load* TP and TI

The *load* MIS semantics are shown in Figure 7.6. *load* interacts with both the environment and other modules. It reads input, produces output, and calls access routines from *token* and *absmach*. Before we select test cases, we must decide on the test environment we are going to use: how to provide input, how to check the output, and whether to use stubs or production code for *token* and *absmach*.

The test environment section of the *load* TP is shown in Figure 10.16. Since *load* reads input from a file, it is hard to test it with PGMGEN, which has no facility to deal with access routines that read input. Therefore we must either build a customized driver to test *load*, or use the *sham* Coordinator. We use the *sham* Coordinator, because it is simple, it provides good controllability, and it saves us implementing a customized driver. Note that although we use the *sham* Coordinator, we are not interested in testing it at this point.

load uses *token* to retrieve the tokens from the input. To test *load* thoroughly with stubs for *token* would require stubs almost as complicated as the production code for *token*. In such a case, the production code is the clear choice, since it avoids the need to maintain the complicated stubs. On the other hand, *load* uses *absmach* to load the memory only, and the production code for *absmach* is non-trivial. We therefore use stubs for *absmach*. Finally, because we use the production *sham* Coordinator, we must decide whether or not to use stubs for *exec*. In this case the choice is easy: simple stubs suffice and the production code is complicated. In summary, we use stubs for *absmach* and *exec*, and production code for *sham* and *token*.

Since we use the *sham* Coordinator as a test driver, we can store the test inputs in several files. For each input file, we maintain a file that contains the expected output for that input. To organize the files, we use three directories:

- `input` contains the input files.

test case selection strategy
    special values
        module state
            none
        access routine parameters
            input file for `ld_sg_load`:
                every load-time exception for every instruction
                every SHAM instruction at least once
                    interval rule for instructions with an operand
                completely fill up memory
    test cases
        load-time exceptions
            `ldexc1`: all load-time exceptions except *NOMEMEXC*
            `ldexc2`: *NOMEMEXC*
        normal case
            `instr`: every SHAM instruction
            `fill`: completely fill up memory

Figure 10.17   *load* test plan—**test case selection strategy**

- **exp** contains the expected output files, one for each input file.

- **act** is used to store the actual output files for a test run, again one for each input file.

The output produced by *load* is non-trivial to check. We automate the checking using *delta testing*, where the expected output for a test run is the output from an earlier test run. If there are any differences between the actual and the expected output, the tester must verify which of the two is the correct output, and modify either the expected output or the program. A critical part of delta testing is the creation of the initial expected output. This can be done manually or using the initial version of the production code. In the latter case, the output should be checked carefully, because if it contains erroneous data, this may mask program errors in future test runs.

The test case selection strategy of the TP for *load* is shown in Figure 10.17. Note that *load* has no internal state, and the only access routine parameter is the file pointer passed to **sg_load**. The special values for this parameter are determined by the contents of the file. We include test cases so that each load-time exception is exercised at least once, and so that every instruction is loaded at least once. For instructions that take an operand, we apply the interval rule to the operand (either an address or a SHAM integer). Finally, we include a test case that completely fills up the available memory.

Test cases are stored in several files, with names chosen to distinguish files that should generate load-time exceptions and those that should not. For exam-

```
load 0
load 50
load 99
```

Figure 10.18 *load* test implementation—part of test case

```
void am_s_mem(a,i)
int a,i;
{
     mem[a] = i;
}

int am_g_mem(a)
int a;
{
     return(mem[a]);
}
```

Figure 10.19 *load* test implementation—stubs for **am_s_mem** and **am_g_mem**

ple, Figure 10.18 contains the first three lines of the file **instr**, which should not generate a load-time exception.

Part of the TI consists of the implementation of the stubs for *absmach* and *exec*. We use simple stubs that store the values loaded into memory in an array and that print out the contents of this array after the load phase is completed successfully. These stubs (1) provide adequate observability, and (2) can combine easily the output checking for the stubs with the output checking for *load*. To implement this scheme, the stubs for *absmach* maintain an array **mem** of **AM_MEMSIZ** characters. The stub for **am_s_mem** stores values in **mem**, and the stub for **am_g_mem** retrieves values from **mem**. Both stubs are shown in Figure 10.19. Note that the stubs are much simpler than the production implementations because there is no need to perform exception checking. Figure 10.20 shows the stub for **ex_s_exec**, which makes calls to the stub for **am_g_mem** to print out the memory contents as a ten-by-ten array. For example, Figure 10.21 shows the output that is produced for the test file **instr**. Note that the first six memory locations correspond to the object code for the first three lines of **instr** shown in Figure 10.18.

The UNIX commands shown in Figure 10.22 are used to perform a test run. For each file f in the directory **input**, BSHAM is run on f, output is redirected to **act**/f, and **act**/f is compared to **exp**/f with the UNIX utility *diff*.

```
void ex_s_exec()
{
    int i;

    for (i = 0; i < AM_MEMSIZ; i++) {
        printf("%4d",am_g_mem(i));
        if (i % 10 == 9)
            printf("\n");
    }
}
```

Figure 10.20 *load* test implementation—stub for **ex_s_exec**

```
   0   0   0  50   0  99   1   0   1  50
   1  99   2   0   2  50   2  99   3   0
   3  50   3  99   4   0   4  50   4  99
   5   0   5  50   5  99   6   0   6  50
   6  99   7   0   7 500   7 999   8   9
   0   0   0   0   0   0   0   0   0   0
   0   0   0   0   0   0   0   0   0   0
   0   0   0   0   0   0   0   0   0   0
   0   0   0   0   0   0   0   0   0   0
   0   0   0   0   0   0   0   0   0   0
```

Figure 10.21 *load* test implementation—expected output

```
foreach f (input/*)
    echo input file: $f
    bsham $f >act/$f
    diff act/$f exp/$f
end
```

Figure 10.22 *load* test implementation—shell commands

10.7.4 The *exec* TP and TI

Figure 7.7 shows the MIS semantics for *exec*. The BSHAM version of *exec* calls access routines from *absmach*. The ISHAM version produces output and calls access routines from *absmach*, *scndr*, and *keybdin*. For both versions, since it is hard to write a stub for **am_s_exec** that provides good controllability, we use the production code of *absmach*. Similarly, for the ISHAM version, stubs for *keybdin* would provide poor controllability, and stubs for *scndr* would provide poor observability. We therefore use the production code for both these modules. To generate manually the sequence of calls that loads the memory in *absmach* would be quite tedious, so we use the production code for *load* and *token* to load the memory from a file. Finally, since we use the production code for *load* and *token*, it becomes hard to use PGMGEN, and hence we use the *sham* Coordinator as a test driver.

In summary, to test *exec* we prefer to use the production code for all of SHAM. We therefore incorporate the testing of *exec* with the system testing; see Section 10.9. Note that this is not the only possibility, and that this decision influences not only the testing of *exec*, but also the system testing. During system testing, we now need to thoroughly exercise *exec*. For example, we should achieve 100 percent statement coverage for *exec*. As an alternative, we could provide separate testing for *exec*, in which case the system testing would be simpler.

10.7.5 The *sham* TP and TI

Although we can test *sham*, the SHAM Coordinator module, as a separate module, *sham* is so simple that testing it separately is not worthwhile. Therefore, just as for *exec*, we incorporate the testing of *sham* with the system testing.

10.8 ISHAM Test Plans and Implementations

10.8.1 The *keybdin* TP and TI

Figure 7.8 shows the MIS semantics for *keybdin*. Since *keybdin* reads input from the keyboard, it has controllability problems and cannot be tested with PGMGEN. To automate the testing requires a means for storing and replaying keystroke sequences. Although tools exist that provide these services, we can adequately test *keybdin* with a simple interactive driver. The interactive driver we use repeatedly waits for input. It displays the characters that are entered on the screen, and terminates when the character 'q' is entered.

Since there is no reason to believe *keybdin* treats any character differently from any other character, there are no special values to test for. We therefore test *keybdin* for just a few characters. Since we have to select a few characters, we use the fact that, in our case, the intended use for *keybdin* is to read the ISHAM commands from the keyboard. Therefore we include at least both ISHAM commands and one character that is not an ISHAM command in the test cases. Since we use an interactive driver to test *keybdin*, it is the tester's responsibility to run the test cases that are described in the TP. Similarly, it is the tester's responsibility to check that the behavior of the implementation is correct for those inputs.

10.8.2   The *scngeom* TP and TI

scngeom provides run-time access to the layout of the screen, and it has no abstract state (Figure 7.9). The service provided by *scngeom* is straightforward. If there were any faults in the MI, these most likely would either cause obvious errors, such as a missing or truncated screen field, or cause errors with minor impact, such as a field that is not displayed in its correct position on the screen. Moreover, the normal-case behavior of **g_row**, **g_col**, **g_len**, and **g_val** is easily and thoroughly tested in the testing of the *scndr* module; see Section 10.8.4. The testing of *scngeom* therefore contains only test cases for the exceptions of **g_row**, **g_col**, **g_len**, and **g_val**, and normal-case test cases for **g_legfld**, which cannot be tested from the *scndr* module. Since the exception checking for **g_row**, **g_col**, **g_len**, and **g_val** is the same, we further simplify the testing by testing the exceptions for only **g_row** thoroughly. To test **g_row**, we choose exceptional parameter values for all field names and for illegal row and column values determined by the interval rule. For **g_col**, **g_len**, and **g_val**, we include one test case to ensure that the MI does at least some exception checking. To test the normal-case behavior of **g_legfld**, we choose special parameter values for all field names and for both legal and illegal row and column values.

10.8.3   The *scnstr* TP and TI

The *scnstr* MIS semantics are shown in Figures 7.10 and 7.11. *scnstr* provides access routines that write a string to any screen position. Since the exception testing for *scnstr* does not pose any observability problems, we perform the exception tests with a PGMGEN script. The normal-case testing, on the other hand, poses observability problems because *scnstr* updates the terminal screen. Automating the testing of *scnstr* requires access to the screen contents. To provide such access with software is a complex task, and instead we test *scnstr* with a customized driver and check the output manually. To simplify the checking of the output, the customized driver displays patterns on the screen that are chosen to exercise special values and to be quickly recognizable as correct or not.

To select special values, note that only the position where strings are displayed is important, not the actual content of the string. We apply the interval rule to the row and column number for both the exception and normal-case testing. For the normal-case testing, we use a unique string for each special position on the screen.

The implementation for the exception testing is straightforward. The driver for the normal-case testing displays the unique strings in the special positions on the screen. To allow the tester time to verify the screen contents, the driver then waits for the tester to press a key. Once the tester has verified the screen contents, he or she can press any key, and the test driver terminates.

10.8.4   The *scndr* TP and TI

The *scndr* MIS semantics are shown in Figure 7.12. The purpose of *scndr* is to update the screen contents according to the information stored in *absmach*. Since it updates the screen contents, it has observability problems, and we test it with a customized driver.

scndr calls three other modules: *scngeom*, *scnstr*, and *absmach*. Since we test the normal-case behavior of *scngeom* while testing *scndr* (see Section 10.8.2), we must use the production code for *scngeom*. Thus, the tester must check the position of each screen field as well as its value. We could verify this by checking that the access routine **ss_s_str** of *scnstr* is called by *scndr* with the correct parameters. However, in this case, verifying this visually is easy enough, and hence we use the production code for *scnstr*.

To verify that *scndr* correctly displays the information in *absmach*, we provide stubs for **am_g_mem**, **am_g_pc**, and **am_g_acc**, that return a unique value for each memory cell, the program counter, and the accumulator. For example, the stub for **am_g_mem** returns $10 \times a$ as the content of memory address a.

After initializing various modules, the test driver calls **sd_s_mem** to update the screen contents according to the values returned by the stubs for *absmach*. The driver then waits for the tester to press a key, so that he or she can verify the screen contents.

10.9   System Testing

During system testing, we use production code for the entire system and, if possible, we test the system in its production environment. The most important goal in system testing is to test whether or not a system satisfies its RS. This includes testing performance and storage requirements, if these are part of the RS. Depending upon the size and complexity of the system, system testing may also include some or all of the following testing techniques.

Volume and stress testing: to test whether the system can handle large volumes of data and heavy loads.

Reliability testing: to test how reliable a system is. For example, to test whether a system meets a certain mean-time-to-failure requirement.

Recovery testing: to test how well the system can recover from errors such as hardware failures or data errors.

Acceptance testing: to test whether the system meets the needs of the end user. It is typically performed by the end user.

In the following, we will only test whether BSHAM and ISHAM meet their respective RSs.

10.9.1 BSHAM

In system testing, it is important to focus the testing on the parts of the system that were not tested during module testing. We have tested every SHAM module separately, except for *exec* and the *sham* Coordinator module. Since *sham* is so simple, the test case selection for system testing is dominated by the need to exercise the *exec* module thoroughly.

The **test environment** and **test case selection strategy** sections for the system TP of BSHAM are shown in Figure 10.23. In the testing of BSHAM, we distinguish test cases with command-line errors and test cases that read input from a file. Since BSHAM produces output for all the test cases, we store this output in a file so that we can use delta testing to automate the checking of the output. The expected output for the test cases with command-line errors is stored in the file `cmdlin.exp`, and the actual output is stored in the file `cmdlin.act`. For the other test cases, we use the same directory structure as for testing *load*: the directory `input` contains the input files, `exp` the expected output files, and `act` stores the actual output files for a test run.

Since the BSHAM system has no module state and no access routines, we cannot use these to select special values for test cases. In BSHAM, the special values that we want to test are determined by the command-line arguments and the contents of the input files. We test every command-line error once. For the other test cases, we distinguish three types: test cases that produce load-time exceptions, those that produce run-time exceptions, and those that do not produce any exceptions at all. For load-time exceptions, we note that we have already tested the *load* module. However, recall that in testing *load*, we use stubs for some of the modules in SHAM. We therefore include one test case with a load-time exception, to ensure that the replacement of stubs by production code has not introduced any errors.

Since we have not tested *exec* yet, we must test every run-time exception at least once. However, we have already tested that the access routine **am_sg_exec** from *absmach* signals the correct run-time exception, and so we only need to test whether or not *exec* prints the correct message for each exception. We therefore include no more than one test case for every run-time exception. Note that for run-time exceptions we can store only one test case per input file.

For the test cases that do not signal an exception, we also benefit from the previous testing of **am_sg_exec**. We assume that it returns the correct value and correctly changes the memory contents and the value of the accumulator and the program counter. We do need to test whether *exec* correctly deals with the return value of **am_sg_exec**. For return values other than **AM_HALT** and **AM_PRINT**,

test environment

    entire BSHAM system

    input stored in files

    output saved in files, checked with delta testing

    directory structure:

        `sham/`

            `input/` - test cases stored one per file

            `exp/` - expected results of test case (same file name)

            `act/` - actual results of test case (same file name)

        `sham/cmdlin.exp` - expected results for command-line test cases

        `sham/cmdlin.act` - actual results for command-line test cases

test case selection strategy

    special values

        command-line errors

            each command-line error once

        content of input file

            one load-time exception

            every run-time exception once

            SHAM instructions

                halt with pc $= \{0, \texttt{SY\_MEMSIZ}/2, \texttt{SY\_MEMSIZ} - 1\}$

                print with interval rule on content accumulator

    test cases

        command-line errors

            hard-coded in Makefile

        load-time exceptions

            `ldexc`: one load-time exception

        run-time exceptions

            `addrexc`: $mem[pc] = ADD.object, \, mem[pc + 1] = 100$

            `arithexc`: $acc = 500 + 500$

            `noopexc`: $pc = 99, \, mem[pc] = LOADCON.object$

            `objectexc`: $mem[pc] = 10$

        normal-case

            `halt[1-3]`: $HALT$ instruction, check with $PRINT$ instruction

            `print`: print special values

            `two+two,sum`: programs from Appendix of RS

Figure 10.23   BSHAM test plan—part 1

test implementation strategy
    target `runtestb` in `Makefile`
        test cases for command-line errors
        for each file f in `input/`
            `bsham` f `>act/`f
            `diff act/`f `exp/`f
    statement coverage for *sham* and *exec* measured using the UNIX utility *tcov*
        100% coverage for statements not associated with ISHAM

Figure 10.24   BSHAM test plan—part 2

this is tested by the test cases for the run-time errors. For **AM_HALT**, we apply the interval rule to the value of the program counter in which the halt instruction is executed, and we include three test cases. For **AM_PRINT**, we apply the interval rule to the value of the accumulator. Finally, we include some non-trivial normal-case test cases as a "sanity check" of the whole system. For this purpose, we use the two SHAM programs from the appendix of the RS.

The **test implementation strategy** section for the TP of BSHAM is shown in Figure 10.24. To run the test cases with command-line errors, we invoke BSHAM with the incorrect command-line arguments. To run the other test cases, we use the same UNIX commands as for *load* (see Section 10.7.3). After running the test cases, we use the UNIX utility *tcov* to check the statement coverage of *exec* and *sham*. Since these modules contain `#ifdefs`, the statements associated with ISHAM will not be executed. We do check that all statements associated with BSHAM have been executed at least once.

10.9.2 ISHAM

Although BSHAM has some controllability and observability problems, these are far worse in ISHAM. Besides reading the program from a file, ISHAM obtains input from the keyboard and prints information to the screen. However, in testing ISHAM, we use the fact that the command-line arguments and large parts of *exec* and *sham* are exercised in the BSHAM testing. Similarly, the keyboard input and screen output modules have also been tested separately. Therefore we only need to test that *exec* and *sham* correctly respond to the user commands entered at the keyboard. This requires only a few simple test cases, making it feasible to test ISHAM interactively: we manually provide the keyboard commands and manually verify the behavior.

The programs we use for testing ISHAM are a subset of the test cases for BSHAM. There are four programs we use to test ISHAM: one with a load-time exception, one with a run-time exception, and the two programs from the appendix of the RS.

For the program with the load-time exception, ISHAM should terminate after the load phase. For the program with the run-time exception, we step through the program until the exception occurs. We include only one load-time and one run-time exception because all we are testing is that ISHAM correctly responds to these. We have already tested that the exceptions are correctly signaled by `am_sg_exec` and that the correct exception message is produced by *exec*.

For each of the two programs from the appendix, we step though the entire program, checking that the screen contents are correctly updated. We also need to test the ISHAM command *EXIT*. For this, we use the simpler of the two programs of the appendix. We load the program three times, and execute the *EXIT* command (1) right after the program is loaded, (2) after several instructions have been executed but before the halt instruction is reached, and (3) when the halt instruction is reached.

After running the test cases, we use the UNIX utility *tcov* to check the statement coverage of *exec* and *sham*. This time, we check that every statement inside the `#ifdef`s for ISHAM has been executed at least once. All other statements in these modules are executed at least once in the testing of BSHAM.

10.10 Verification

In this section, we discuss the verification procedures for the TP and the TI.

10.10.1 Test plan

Since a TP is not executable, we can verify it only by inspection. Figure 10.25 shows the criteria for a TP. Since the test case selection is primarily based on the MIS, a thorough understanding of the MIS is required to understand the TP.

While it is easy to verify that a TP is well formed, it is a lot harder to verify the last three "additional criteria" for a TP. Dijkstra's Law of testing tells us that we can never do enough testing to guarantee that there are no more bugs remaining. We thus have to find a balance between the adequacy of the test inputs and the cost of maintaining and running the test cases. This means that the TP must be comprehensible enough to be able to estimate both the adequacy and the feasibility of the proposed testing. The adequacy and feasibility criteria indicate where the balance should lie. On the one hand, test cases should at least exercise the normal and exceptional behavior of every access routine, and typically 100 percent statement coverage is expected. On the other hand, it should be possible to implement the testing affordably.

10.10.2 Test implementation

Recall that the TI includes the test scaffolding, the test data files, and the procedures—both manual and automated—required to execute the tests. The

For the module under test, M:

- **Audience**. Those considering running or modifying M's testing.

- **Prerequisites**. A thorough understanding of M's MIS and some understanding of M's MID.

- **Purpose**. Serve as a planning tool for development and evaluation of the test case selection strategy. Document the TI.

- **Additional criteria**.

  1. *Well formed*. The TP follows the format described in Section 10.2.

  2. *Comprehensible*. The TP can be read and understood by the intended audience. It is sufficient to estimate the adequacy and the feasibility of the TI.

  3. *Adequate*. Test cases are planned to exercise the module as thoroughly as is practical. Tests are planned to invoke every access routine in normal and exceptional situations. 100% statement coverage is expected.

  4. *Feasible*. The TP can be implemented affordably.

Figure 10.25   Test plan criteria

verification criteria for a TI are shown in Figure 10.26. Since a TI is executable, we verify it both by inspection and by testing.

The only criterion that needs further explanation is the correctness criterion. Since the purpose of the TI is to implement the TP, we verify that it follows the TP as closely as possible. For example, in a PGMGEN test script, the order of the test cases should follow the order given in the TP. As shown in the *symtbl* test script (Figure 10.12), the correspondence between the TP and the TI can be clarified by using comments in the test script.

In addition, we verify that the tests run to completion, with correct results and 100 percent statement coverage. We measure the statement coverage with the UNIX utility *tcov*, which instruments a program with additional statements to keep track of how often every statement in the original program is executed. To measure statement coverage for an MI, it is compiled with a special option. This creates an instrumented object file, and a *tcov* data file. Each time the program is executed, coverage information is accumulated in the data file. Finally, the program *tcov* is run on the data file, which produces a version of the MI in which each statement is prefixed with the number of times it has been executed. To make them easy to find, statements that have never been executed are prefixed with the string "#####."

For the module under test, M:

- **Audience**. Those considering running or modifying M's testing.

- **Prerequisites**. A thorough understanding of M's MIS and some understanding of M's MID.

- **Purpose**. Implement the TP as simply and inexpensively as possible.

- **Additional criteria**.

  1. *Well formed.* The code in test scripts obeys the Code Format Rules shown in Appendix G. For each standalone module M, a simple interactive tester is provided, giving keyboard access to all access routines and displaying return values on the screen. In M.c, the testing access routine g_dump is implemented to display the module state on the screen.

  2. *Comprehensible.* The TI can be read and understood by the intended audience.

  3. *Correct.* The TI follows the TP. The tests run to completion, with correct results and 100% statement coverage.

Figure 10.26   Test implementation criteria

10.11   Summary

Controllability and observability dictate that we test many modules individually. We advocate the systematic testing of modules in which the testing is planned, documented, and maintained. Systematic testing is performed by maintaining two work products for each module tested: the TP serves as specification, outlining the test case selection and execution strategies, and the TI implements the TP.

We emphasize three ways to make the testing of modules affordable and effective.

1. *Select test cases most likely to expose errors.* Two methods for selecting test cases are functional testing and structural testing. With functional testing, test cases are based primarily on the specification of a module. With structural testing, test cases are based on the internal structure of the code. In testing SHAM, we use functional testing for test case selection: we base test cases on special values for access routine parameters, module state, and combinations of these. We use structural coverage, in particular statement coverage, as a check on the adequacy of the test cases.

2. *Automate repetitive and tedious tasks.* Where possible, automate the execution of test cases and the comparison of actual and expected outputs, because these steps are performed every test run. The execution of test cases is automated using the PGMGEN testing tool, customized test drivers, and UNIX scripts. The comparison of outputs is automated using PGMGEN

scripts and delta testing. Where automation is not possible, limit testing to a few cases for which the output is easy to check.

3. *Design for testability.* The key considerations in design for testability are controllability and observability. Typical problems with controllability and observability are caused by interaction with other modules and the environment. Although this interaction cannot be eliminated completely, we can limit the problems by isolating the module under test and by restricting the interaction with the environment to a few modules.

Although it is important to test each module in isolation, we also need to perform integration and system testing. In a top-down approach to integration testing, we start by testing a top-level module using stubs, and gradually replace the stubs by production code. In a bottom-up approach, we first test low-level modules using drivers, and gradually replace the drivers by higher-level modules. In testing SHAM, we use a mixture of top-down and bottom-up testing.

Dijkstra's Law of testing tells us that testing cannot guarantee the absence of faults. This means that during testing we have to find a balance between the adequacy of the test inputs and the cost of maintaining and running the test cases. The hardest part of verifying a TP and the corresponding TI is to determine whether the testing is both adequate and feasible.

10.12   Bibliographic Notes

Two general textbooks on software testing that cover most of the topics discussed in this chapter are [42] and [82]. However, most of the testing research has focused on test case selection. Functional testing was first proposed in [83] and discussed in detail in [43]. Structural testing techniques such as path testing are discussed in [84]. Due to the infeasibility of path testing, other structural testing techniques such as dataflow testing [85], mutation testing [86], and domain testing [87] have been proposed. Partition testing [88] mixes functional and structural testing in that it considers both the specification and the implementation for defining test cases. A recent text by Beizer [89] focuses on test case selection, and discusses many of the above, and other, test case selection techniques.

For test case execution, several tools similar to PGMGEN have been proposed in the literature. Panzl [90] reports on the regression testing of FORTRAN subroutines using an automated tool. The DAISTS system [91] performs module testing and describes test cases using traces. Given a formal algebraic specification of the module under test, DAISTS automatically determines the correct behavior for a given test and measures the coverage of the specification and the implementation. Frankl [92] has developed a tool for object-oriented testing using algebraic specifications. The Protest system [93] is similar to PGMGEN, except that test cases are defined by a PROLOG program. Finally, the ACE tool [94] is an enhancement of PGMGEN that supports the testing of Eiffel and C++ classes.

Although very little has been published about test documentation, the IEEE Standard for Software Test Documentation is an excellent source of information on this topic [95]. The standard proposes a set of basic test documents, which is substantially more elaborate than the TPs we use in SHAM. The standard also contains an example of how these documents can be used in practice.

Part III

Summary

Chapter 11

Conclusions

In this text we present an approach to software development based on well-defined phases and work products. Below we summarize the most important concepts and discuss the difficulties commonly encountered when applying this approach in practice.

11.1 Principles

As we have seen, basic principles play a key role in handling the difficult problems that arise in multi-version/multi-person programming. Perhaps the most important principle in software engineering is *separation of concerns* [9]. When facing a problem that is too complex to be solved directly, decompose the problem into subproblems, recursively. In addition to the general principle of separation of concerns, we have emphasized four broad themes.

1. *The central role of documentation.* We present a single set of documents supporting design, implementation, and maintenance. Precise system and module specifications play a key role, providing the foundation for the important practice of *implementation to specification.*

2. *Systematic verification.* We use two complementary methods of verification. Inspections are applied to all work products, and testing is applied to executable work products.

3. *Effective use of mathematics.* While we make frequent use of mathematical concepts and notations, our approach is not highly formal. We use both formal notations and prose, choosing whichever seems clearer and simpler. Our inspections are proof-based, in the sense that the reader's job is to present a convincing logical argument.

4. *Reducing the cost of maintenance.* Our design method is based on information hiding, whereby maintenance costs are reduced by planning for likely

1. Requirements Specification
   Specification of the required system behavior.
2. Module Guide
   Description of and motivation for the module decomposition.
3. Module Interface Specification
   Specification of the required behavior of each module.
4. Module Internal Design
   Specification of the module internal data structures.
5. Module Implementation
   Production source code.
6. Test Plan
   Strategy for selecting and executing tests.
7. Test Implementation
   Source code, data files, and manual procedures required for testing.

Figure 11.1   Work product summary

changes to the system. Our testing is automated so that the tests can be repeated after every change to the implementation.

11.2   Work Products

We illustrate the above principles with a software development approach based on the seven work products shown in Figure 11.1. For each work product, we present standard formats, design techniques, and verification procedures. Detailed examples serve to show how to use the approach in the development of non-trivial software systems.

We emphasize specification and verification especially. While not highly formal, our specifications are precise enough to support *implementation to specification*. The inspection procedures help find many errors long before code execution begins, and the test suites provide highly automated checks on run-time behavior.

11.3   Practical Considerations

In practice, software development rarely follows the step-by-step approach outlined in Figure 11.1. Numerous practical considerations interfere:

- *The end user does not know what is needed.* It is difficult for the user to envision the system before it is developed and to communicate this vision to the software developers. Users frequently overlook flaws in a proposed system when it is described solely by a Requirements Specification. Prototypes may be developed to give the users a concrete, though incomplete, model of a future system. Even with prototypes, serious flaws are often discovered after delivery.

- *Human errors occur.* Typically, the number of details is overwhelming. There are many design alternatives and no sure way of deciding which is best. Even with systematic verification procedures in place, many errors are first detected in later development phases or after delivery.

- *Design decisions are invalidated by change.* Large software development projects often take one or more years to complete. During that time, changes in user needs and in the underlying platform are inevitable. As a result, many work products that have been completed and verified must be changed and reverified. Extensive changes may be required; some work products may have to be discarded.

- *Design freedom is constrained by existing software.* There is a huge amount of software in existence. While it is flawed in many ways, it cannot be thrown away; the replacement cost is too high. Thus, most programmers spend their time making changes to existing systems with every change tightly constrained by its effects on the rest of the system. Even new software must interact closely with existing software, eliminating many otherwise desirable design alternatives.

- *Design methods are constrained by existing development practices.* Recent surveys [96] have confirmed what many software professionals have long believed: most developers use no explicit methodology. Code inspection and testing are in widespread use. However, specifications are rarely precise enough to be inspected effectively or to support implementation to specification. Almost no use is made of mathematics in software development. Thus, industrial adoption of the methods in this text may require substantial change in the work habits of some developers.

In summary, software development rarely follows the process outlined in Figure 11.1. However, documentation that simulates this ideal process can still be produced, with significant benefits. Readers of the documentation will be given a rational explanation of the system. Such a description is usually simpler, more comprehensible, and more useful than the actual history of the development. Also, having a model of the ideal process helps developers to come closer to it. Finally, in an organization with many projects, a standard process makes measurement and review simpler and more effective.

11.4   SHAM Development History

To illustrate the differences between the actual and ideal software development processes, we consider the development of the SHAM system. The SHAM work products are presented in this text as though the development proceeded smoothly through the six phases without backtracking. For three main reasons, this was not the case. First, the software development schedule was driven by the text writing schedule. Chapters 2, 3, 7, and 10—and the associated SHAM work products—were written first and submitted to various publishers for review. Only then were the remaining chapters written and the associated work products developed. Second, for most of the SHAM development, the authors were on different continents: North America and Australia. With modern electronic communication, such distributed development is feasible, but it is still difficult. Finally, before SHAM, five different systems were used as teaching examples. Many SHAM work products were derived from these systems. For example, the screen handling decomposition—*scnstr*, *scngeom*, and *scndr*—was developed earlier. All of the *token* and *scnstr* work products were taken from previous systems.

Due to the above constraints, the SHAM development did not follow the ideal chronology. Instead the development order was as follows:

1. The SHAM language was designed. The instructions were chosen, the syntax determined, and the semantics sketched. Several sample SHAM programs were coded.

2. The Module Guide was sketched.

3. All Interface Specifications, Test Plans, and Test Implementations were completed. Note that, with precise specifications, it is feasible to develop thorough testing before implementation begins.

4. The BSHAM and ISHAM Module Internal Designs and Implementations were completed, requiring many Interface Specification changes.

5. The BSHAM and ISHAM Requirements Specifications were written, a part at a time throughout development. Many inconsistencies were discovered between these specifications and other work products. Numerous changes to all work products were made to achieve consistency. It is now clear that developing the Requirements Specifications first would have significantly reduced the rework. It is not clear whether we could have done this without the understanding gained during design and implementation. As it was, the Requirements Specifications were important products of the design and implementation effort.

6. The Module Guide was completed.

In summary, the SHAM development was far from ideal, due to numerous practical considerations. Still, we present the work products rationally, because a chronological presentation would be extremely confusing. We relied heavily on the work products—especially the Requirements and Interface Specifications—to maintain control while the developers were separated by thousands of kilometers and an 18-hour time difference.

11.5 Object-Oriented Programming

11.5.1 OOP and BCOOP

Object-oriented programming (OOP) is based on *encapsulation, inheritance,* and *polymorphism,* as supplied by languages such as SmallTalk and C++. *Encapsulation* insulates parts of the system from changes in other parts. *Inheritance* is a mechanism by which the services of one object can be extended or changed, without having to reimplement the entire object. *Polymorphism* allows us to provide the same service for objects of different types.

In this text we take a conservative approach to object-oriented programming by using base class object-oriented programming (BCOOP). BCOOP uses only encapsulation and can be carried out using C, Pascal, and even FORTRAN; the separate compilation facilities of these languages provide adequate support for encapsulation. While inheritance and polymorphism are important concepts, there are significant advantages to BCOOP. From a teaching perspective, it is critical to recognize the complexity of full OOP. An entire course can easily be devoted to teaching just the required language features. Thus, we cannot teach full OOP without sacrificing essential Software Engineering material. Of the three concepts—encapsulation, inheritance, and polymorphism—encapsulation is certainly the most important concept and the one that should be taught first. However, before leaving the SHAM system for good, we take a brief look at full OOP, as supplied by the C++ programming language.

11.5.2 Classifying a set module

We begin our brief sojourn into C++ by converting a set module into a set class. The *sset* module is specified in Table H.2 and Figure H.1. Figure 11.2 shows the declaration for the **sset** class. Based on this declaration, any number of **sset** objects can be created. The constructor, **sset**, is called automatically at object creation. The other access routines are as in the C version. The concrete state variables, **s** and **scnt**, appear in the class declaration, as does the local function **findpos**.

The benefits of C++ are apparent even in this small example.

- The hidden and exported identifiers are specified explicitly. In C, static declarations and file scope can only approximate this interface information.

```
const int N = 10;

class sset {
public:
        sset();
    void s_add(int); // mem, full
    void s_del(int); // notmem
    int  g_mem(int);

protected:
    int  s[N];
    int  scnt;
    int  findpos(int);
};
```

Figure 11.2 **sset** class declaration

- The constructor invocation is generated automatically. In C, we must rely on the module user to invoke this routine.

- Objects of type **sset** can be created at will, at compile time, or run time. Only one instance of the *sset* module can exist in a C program.

Inheritance allows a programmer to provide a new class by building on an existing class. Figure 11.3 shows how an iterator can be added to the **sset** class. (See Table H.3 and Figure H.2 for a specification of the *iset* module.) Objects of type **iset** provide the functions shown in Figures 11.2 and 11.3. When **s_add** is called, the code provided by **sset** is executed; when **s_mod** is called, the new **iset** code is executed. Programmers are frequently required to provide many variations on the same service. Inheritance provides a way to do this while minimizing the amount of code to be written and maintained.

C++ provides another powerful mechanism for avoiding duplicate code. The **sset** class stores a set of integers. Suppose that a set of strings was required. The **sset** code could be copied and quickly modified to produce this new class. The same approach could be used to develop a variety of classes differing only in the type of the set elements. The same result can be achieved with far less code by using C++ templates. Figure 11.4 shows the class declaration for the **tset** class. The declaration is parameterized by **Element**, the data type of the set elements. **Element** can be a built-in or user-defined type.

While C++ is considerably more complex than C, with practice substantial benefits are available from base classes, inheritance, and templates, as well as the many features not mentioned here.

```
typedef enum {SET,SEQ} mod;

class iset : public sset {
public:
        iset();
    void s_mod(int);
    void sg_next(int); // end
    int  g_end();

private:
    mod   m;
    int   iscnt;
}
```

Figure 11.3 **iset** class declaration

```
const int N = 10;

template <class Element>
class tset {
public:
        tset();
    void    s_add(Element); // mem, full
    void    s_del(Element); // notmem
    int     g_mem(Element);

protected:
    Element s[N];
    int     scnt;
    int     findpos(Element);
};
```

Figure 11.4 **tset** class declaration

11.6   Parting Words

We have described a disciplined approach to multi-person/multi-version programming. We doubt that any reader will use this approach exactly as presented. Rather we intend our approach as a starting point. We expect that many of you are or will soon be working on large software projects and will face difficult problems. We hope that you will find help among the techniques presented here.

Part IV

Appendix

Appendix A

Requirements Specifications

A.1 BSHAM Requirements Specification

A.1.1 Overview

A.1.1.1 System overview

SHAM, the Strooper-Hoffman Abstract Machine, provides an interpreter for a toy assembly language. The underlying machine has only two registers and performs arithmetic on unsigned decimal integers. Ten instructions are provided. SHAM operates in a load-and-go fashion; in response to a single user command, a file of assembler instructions is translated to object code, loaded into main memory, and executed.

There are two versions of the SHAM system. BSHAM, the batch version, is specified in this document. ISHAM, the interactive version, is specified separately.

A.1.1.2 Hardware and software environment

BSHAM runs on Sun/3 and Sun/4 workstations running SunOS. It is implemented in the C programming language and requires the UNIX/C standard libraries [55].

A.1.1.3 Notation

All identifiers are shown in *italics*. The names of constants and abbreviations are all uppercase. The others are all lowercase, except for types, whose names end in 'T'.

A.1.1.4   Document overview

The details of BSHAM operation are presented in the sections below. Section A.1.2 declares the environment variables. Section A.1.3 describes how to invoke BSHAM from the UNIX shell and contains the finite state machines (FSMs) that specify how BSHAM loads and executes source programs. Sections A.1.4–A.1.6 declare a collection of constants, types, and functions used throughout this document. Section A.1.7 lists the changes to BSHAM likely to be requested in the future. Section A.1.8 contains two sample BSHAM programs; Section A.1.9 contains tables that specify the details of the BSHAM syntax, semantics, and exceptions.

A.1.2   Environment variables

A.1.2.1   Input variables

srcfil : *string*
> The file name passed on the command line.

A.1.2.2   Output variables

stdout : *string*
> UNIX stdout.

A.1.3   State machine

BSHAM behavior is specified using two FSMs: one for each of the load and execution phases. The load-phase FSM reads the source program a line at a time, and loads the object code version into BSHAM's main memory. Exception messages are issued as needed. If the load phase is exception-free, then the execution-phase FSM begins running. It continues until a *HALT* instruction is reached, or an exception occurs.

A.1.3.1   Command-line invocation

BSHAM is invoked by typing

```
bsham srcfil
```

on the command line. Input is read from *srcfil* and output is written to *stdout*.
If the *srcfil* argument is not present, $excmsg(NOFILEXC, 0, \text{""})$ is written to *stdout*. If *srcfil* is unreadable (or does not exist)

$$excmsg(FILSYSEXC, 0, srcfil)$$

is written to *stdout*. If there are any command-line exceptions, BSHAM execution terminates.

Inputs

Each input is a line from *srcfil*, read in the order it appears in *srcfil*.

Outputs

Normal-case output and exception messages are written to *stdout*.

States

$mem : sequence\ [0..MEMSIZ - 1]\ of\ shamintegerT$

Initial state

Every element of *mem* is set to 0.

Transitions and outputs

For line L, with line number n:

if the Load-phase Exc. Table (Table A.3) specifies an exception then

write the specified message to *stdout*

else

if no previous line had an exception then

if there is room in *mem* then

load the object code form of L into *mem*

else

write $excmsg(NOMEMEXC, n, "")$ to *stdout*

Figure A.1   Load-phase FSM

A.1.3.2   Load phase

The instructions and their arguments are shown in Table A.1. The first column contains the instruction mnemonic used in this document. Column two contains the string that must be used in source files read by BSHAM. Column three contains the object-code form generated by BSHAM. The last column shows the type of the instruction operand, if any. For an instruction with mnemonic I, $I.source$ and $I.object$ refer to I's source code string and object code integer, respectively.

At load time, the contents of *srcfil* are scanned a line at a time, converted to object code form, and loaded into main memory. Each line in *srcfil* must contain exactly one BSHAM instruction. Input lines must not exceed $MAXLINLEN$ characters—BSHAM behavior is unpredictable on longer lines. On each input line, tokens must be separated by one or more blanks. Object code instructions are loaded contiguously, beginning at address 0. Instructions without operands occupy a single memory location. Instructions with an operand occupy two consecutive memory locations; the instruction code is in the first location and the operand in the second. The load actions are described in detail in the FSM in Figure A.1. If there are any load exceptions, BSHAM execution terminates at the end of the load phase.

Inputs

   None.

Outputs

   Normal-case output and exception messages are written to *stdout*.

States

   $mem : sequence\ [0..MEMSIZ - 1]\ of\ shamintegerT$
   $acc : shamintegerT$
   $pc : shamaddrT$

Initial state

   $mem, acc, pc :=$ (the final value from the load phase FSM), $0, 0$

Transitions and outputs

   for the instruction beginning at $mem[pc]$:

      if the Execution-phase Exc. Table (Table A.4) specifies an exception then
         write the specified message to *stdout*
         terminate SHAM
      else if $mem[pc] = HALT.object$ then
         terminate SHAM
      else

         if $mem[pc] = PRINT.object$ then
            write to *stdout* : $acc\ ||$ newline
         modify *mem*, *acc*, and *pc* as shown in the Language Semantics Table

Figure A.2   BSHAM execution-phase FSM

A.1.3.3   Execution phase

The execution phase is based on Table A.2, the BSHAM Language Semantics
table. This table specifies the effect of each exception-free BSHAM instruction
on the values of *mem*, *acc*, and *pc*. The FSM itself is straightforward (see Figure A.2). The execution phase consumes no input; all the required information
has already been loaded into *mem*, *pc*, and *acc*. The FSM executes the instructions in $mem[pc]$ until an exception occurs or $mem[pc] = HALT.object$.

A.1.4   Constants

Name	Value
MAXLINLEN	100
MAXINT	999
MEMSIZ	100

A.1.5   Types

$shamaddrT = [0..MEMSIZ - 1]$
$shamintegerT = [0..MAXINT]$

$$sourceT = \{LOAD.source, STORE.source, ADD.source, SUBTRACT.source,$$
$$BRANCH.source, BRANCHZERO.source, BRANCHPOS.source,$$
$$LOADCON.source, PRINT.source, HALT.source\}$$
$$op0sourceT = \{HALT.source, PRINT.source\}$$
$$op1sourceT = sourceT - op0sourceT$$

$$objectT = \{LOAD.object, STORE.object, ADD.object, SUBTRACT.object,$$
$$BRANCH.object, BRANCHZERO.object, BRANCHPOS.object,$$
$$LOADCON.object, PRINT.object, HALT.object\}$$
$$op0objectT = \{HALT.object, PRINT.object\}$$
$$op1objectT = objectT - op0objectT$$

$$excidT = \{FILSYSEXC, NOFILEXC,$$
$$BLANKLINEXC, MISSINGOPEXC, NOMEMEXC,$$
$$OPFMTEXC, SOURCEEXC,$$
$$ADDREXC, ARITHEXC, NOOPEXC, OBJECTEXC\}$$

A.1.6 Functions

$excmsg : excidT \times integer \times string \to string$

if *id* is	then $excmsg(id, loc, tok)$ is
	Command-line messages
FILSYSEXC	`Command line error. Cannot open file:` *tok*
NOFILEXC	`Command line error. No file name specified`
	Load-phase messages
BLANKLINEXC	`Load exception at` *loc*`. Blank line illegal`
MISSINGOPEXC	`Load exception at` *loc*`. Operand missing`
NOMEMEXC	`Load exception at` *loc*`. Program too large`
OPFMTEXC	`Load exception at` *loc*`. Illegal operand:` *tok*
SOURCEEXC	`Load exception at` *loc*`. Illegal instruction:` *tok*
	Execution-phase messages
ADDREXC	`Execution exception at` *loc*`. Illegal operand:` *tok*
ARITHEXC	`Execution exception at` *loc*`. Arithmetic overflow`
NOOPEXC	`Execution exception at` *loc*`. Operand not accessible`
OBJECTEXC	`Execution exception at` *loc*`. Illegal instruction:` *tok*

A.1.7 Expected changes

Input/output format
- Command-line parameters besides *srcfil*.
- Different input format: new tokens, delimiters, and instruction formats.
- Handle overlength lines robustly.

Abstract machine
- Change in word size, number of words in main memory.
- New or extended data types, especially signed integers.
- More registers, e.g., index registers.

- More or different SHAM instructions.
- More addressing modes.
- Symbolic data and branch addresses.

Platform
- Different operating system: other UNIX platforms or MS-DOS.

Exception handling
- Limits on the number of exceptions reported or instructions executed.
- Changes in the conditions defining exceptions and in the message text.

A.1.8   Sample programs

Calculate 2 + 2 and display the result

```
loadcon 2
store 8
add 8
print
halt
```

Calculate $\Sigma_{i=0}^{n} i$ and display the result

```
loadcon 5          initial value of n
store 40           location 40: value of n, decremented each iteration
loadcon 0
store 41           location 41: value of sum
loadcon 1
store 42           location 42: 1, used for decrementing
load 40
brz 28             check if 0
add 41             add to the sum
store 41
load 40            subtract 1 from n
sub 42
store 40
br 14
load 41            print value of sum
print
halt
```

A.1.9   Tables

Table A.1   Language syntax table

Mnemonic	*I.source*	*I.object*	Operand type
Memory access			
LOAD	load	0	*shamaddrT*
STORE	store	1	*shamaddrT*
Arithmetic			
ADD	add	2	*shamaddrT*
SUBTRACT	sub	3	*shamaddrT*
Branch			
BRANCH	br	4	*shamaddrT*
BRANCHZERO	brz	5	*shamaddrT*
BRANCHPOS	brp	6	*shamaddrT*
Miscellaneous			
LOADCON	loadcon	7	*shamintegerT*
PRINT	print	8	
HALT	halt	9	

Table A.2   Language semantics table ($op = mem[pc + 1]$)

Instruction at $mem[pc]$	Effect on mem, acc, and pc
Memory access	
LOAD.object	$acc, pc := mem[op], (pc + 2) \bmod MEMSIZ$
STORE.object	$mem[op], pc := acc, (pc + 2) \bmod MEMSIZ$
Arithmetic	
ADD.object	$acc, pc := acc + mem[op], (pc + 2) \bmod MEMSIZ$
SUBTRACT.object	$acc, pc := acc - mem[op], (pc + 2) \bmod MEMSIZ$
Branch	
BRANCH.object	$pc := op$
BRANCHZERO.object	$pc := (acc = 0 \Rightarrow op$ $\mid acc > 0 \Rightarrow (pc + 2) \bmod MEMSIZ)$
BRANCHPOS.object	$pc := (acc > 0 \Rightarrow op$ $\mid acc = 0 \Rightarrow (pc + 2) \bmod MEMSIZ)$
Miscellaneous	
LOADCON.object	$acc, pc := op, (pc + 2) \bmod MEMSIZ$
PRINT.object	$pc := (pc + 1) \bmod MEMSIZ$
HALT.object	no change to acc, pc, mem

Table A.3   Load-phase exception table

Let L be the current line, with line number n (numbered one-relative).
Let $T_1, T_2, \ldots, T_K$ be the tokens in L.

Condition	Message
$K = 0$ (L is blank)	$excmsg(BLANKLINEXC, n, "")$
$K > 0$	
$T_1 \in op0sourceT$	**Normal case**
$T_1 \in op1sourceT$	
$K = 1$	$excmsg(MISSINGOPEXC, n, "")$
$K > 1$	
$T_1 = LOADCON.source$	
$T_2 \in shamintegerT$	**Normal case**
$T_2 \notin shamintegerT$	$excmsg(OPFMTEXC, n, T_2)$
$T_1 \neq LOADCON.source$	
$T_2 \in shamaddrT$	**Normal case**
$T_2 \notin shamaddrT$	$excmsg(OPFMTEXC, n, T_2)$
$T_1 \notin sourceT$	$excmsg(SOURCEEXC, n, T_1)$

Table A.4   Execution-phase exception table

Let $i = mem[pc]$ and $op = mem[pc + 1]$

Condition	Message
$i \in op0objectT$	**Normal case**
$i \in op1objectT$	
$pc \in [0..MEMSIZ - 2]$	
$i = LOADCON.object$	**Normal case**
$i \neq LOADCON.object$	
$op \in shamaddrT$	
$i = ADD.object$	
$acc + mem[op] \in shamintegerT$	**Normal case**
$acc + mem[op] \notin shamintegerT$	$excmsg(ARITHEXC, pc, "")$
$i = SUBTRACT.object$	
$acc - mem[op] \in shamintegerT$	**Normal case**
$acc - mem[op] \notin shamintegerT$	$excmsg(ARITHEXC, pc, "")$
$true$	**Normal case**
$op \notin shamaddrT$	$excmsg(ADDREXC, pc, op)$
$pc = MEMSIZ - 1$	$excmsg(NOOPEXC, pc, "")$
$i \notin objectT$	$excmsg(OBJECTEXC, pc, i)$

A.2 ISHAM Requirements Specification

A.2.1 Overview

A.2.1.1 System overview

This document specifies the behavior of ISHAM, the interactive version of SHAM. The ISHAM and BSHAM load phases are identical, as are the language syntax and semantics, but the execution phases differ in two ways. In ISHAM:

1. Object code execution is "single-stepped" under user control.

2. Output is through a formatted screen, with main memory and the registers displayed, and updated after each instruction execution.

A.2.1.2 Hardware and software environment

The *curses* function library is required to perform output to the terminal screen.

A.2.1.3 Notation

Nothing is added to the BSHAM Requirements Specification.

A.2.1.4 Document overview

Because ISHAM and BSHAM have much in common, this document is written as an addendum to the BSHAM Requirements Specification, describing only the differences between ISHAM and BSHAM. Section A.2.2 declares the new environment variables: *stdin* to model keyboard input and *scn* to model the terminal screen. A detailed format is provided to precisely describe screen updates. Section A.2.3 specifies the ISHAM execution-phase FSM; the BSHAM load-phase FSM is unchanged. Sections A.2.4–A.2.6 declare the constants, types, and functions used throughout this document. There are two new constants and no new types or functions. Section A.2.7 lists the changes to ISHAM likely to be requested in the future.

A.2.2 Environment variables

A.2.2.1 Input variables

stdin : *string*
    UNIX standard input

A.2.2.2 Output variables

scn : *sequence* [24][80] *of char*
    scn[*r*][*c*] is the character at screen row *r* and column *c*,
    with numbering zero-relative and beginning at the upper-left corner.

```
01234567890123456789012345678901234567890123456789012345678901234567890
***********************************************************************
                              SHAM


            0     1     2     3     4     5     6     7     8     9

Main    0   MEM   MEM   MEM   MEM   MEM   MEM   MEM   MEM   MEM   MEM
memory: 10  MEM   MEM   MEM   MEM   MEM   MEM   MEM   MEM   MEM   MEM
        20  MEM   MEM   MEM   MEM   MEM   MEM   MEM   MEM   MEM   MEM
        30  MEM   MEM   MEM   MEM   MEM   MEM   MEM   MEM   MEM   MEM
        40  MEM   MEM   MEM   MEM   MEM   MEM   MEM   MEM   MEM   MEM
        50  MEM   MEM   MEM   MEM   MEM   MEM   MEM   MEM   MEM   MEM
        60  MEM   MEM   MEM   MEM   MEM   MEM   MEM   MEM   MEM   MEM
        70  MEM   MEM   MEM   MEM   MEM   MEM   MEM   MEM   MEM   MEM
        80  MEM   MEM   MEM   MEM   MEM   MEM   MEM   MEM   MEM   MEM
        90  MEM   MEM   MEM   MEM   MEM   MEM   MEM   MEM   MEM   MEM



                  Program counter:  PC
                     Accumulator: ACC
              Last value printed: PRT


Enter command: 's' to single step; 'e' to exit
Message: MSG-----------------------------------------------------------
***********************************************************************
```

Figure A.3   Screen format

We divide *scn*, a 24-by-80 array, into parts, as shown in Figure A.3. The non-blank areas are divided into *screen fields*, either *fixed* or *varying*. The fixed fields are written when ISHAM execution begins and remain unchanged while ISHAM is running. The varying fields may change repeatedly during ISHAM execution. Each varying field has an identifier: *MEM*, *PC*, *ACC*, *PRT*, or *MSG*. The extent of each varying field on the screen is the character positions occupied by the field identifier, and the trailing –s if present. When a *MEM*, *PC*, *ACC*, or *PRT* value is shorter than the extent shown, it is right-justified and padded left with blanks; *MSG* values are left-justified and padded right with blanks. Because the *MEM* field occurs 100 times on the screen, a particular *MEM* occurrence is indicated by row and column subscripts, numbered zero-relative, top-down, and left-to-right. For example, $MEM[9, 0]$ is the leftmost and lowest occurrence.

A.2.3 State machine

A.2.3.1 Command-line invocation

ISHAM is invoked by typing

> `isham` *srcfil*

on the command line. Input is read from *srcfil* and *stdin*, and output is written to *stdout* and *scn*.

If the *srcfil* argument is not present,

$$excmsg(NOFILEXC, 0, "")$$

is written to *stdout*. If *srcfil* is unreadable (or does not exist),

$$excmsg(FILSYSEXC, 0, srcfil)$$

is written to *stdout*. If there are any command-line exceptions, ISHAM execution terminates.

A.2.3.2 Load phase

Same as in the BSHAM Requirements Specification.

A.2.3.3 Execution phase

The ISHAM execution-phase behavior is defined by the FSM in Figure A.4.

A.2.4 Constants

Name	Value
$EXIT$	'e'
$STEP$	's'
$CMDERRMSG$	"Illegal keyboard entry: type 's' or 'e'"
$HALTMSG$	"HALT instruction reached"

A.2.5 Types

Same as in the BSHAM Requirements Specification.

A.2.6 Functions

Same as in the BSHAM Requirements Specification.

Inputs

  Keystrokes from *stdin*.

Outputs

  All outputs are to *scn* and its fields.

States

  Same as for the load phase FSM.

Initial state

  $mem, acc, pc :=$ (the final value from the load phase FSM), $0, 0$

Transitions and outputs

  For each character, c, from *stdin*

  if $c = EXIT$ then

    clear *scn*

    halt ISHAM execution

  else if $c = STEP$ then

    if the BSHAM Execution-phase Exception Table specifies

    an exception for $mem[pc]$ then

      $MSG :=$ the specified message

    else if $mem[pc] = HALT.object$ then

      $MSG := HALTMSG$

    else

      $MSG := ""$

      if $mem[pc] = PRINT.object$ then

        $PRT := acc$

      modify mem, acc, pc, as per the BSHAM Language Semantics Table

  else

    $MSG := CMDERRMSG$

Notes on screen updating:

- Initially and between transitions, ensure that:
  1. The fixed fields shown in the ISHAM screen format are displayed.
  2. MEM, PC, and ACC are such that
     $$(\forall r, c \in [0..9])(MEM[r,c] = mem[10 \times r + c]) \ \wedge \ ACC = acc \ \wedge \ PC = pc$$
  3. $MEM[pc/10, pc \bmod 10]$ is displayed in inverse video.
- Initially the MSG and PRT fields are blank

Figure A.4   ISHAM execution-phase FSM

A.2.7 Expected changes

1. The field positions and the contents of the fixed fields will change.

2. *MEMSIZ* will exceed 100 and vertical scrolling will be supported.

3. Different forms of stepping through the instructions will be supported, such as executing a specified number of instructions or executing until a specified instruction is reached.

Appendix B

Module Guide

B.1 Module Summary

Each SHAM module has a unique *long name* and a *short name*, and may have a shorter *module prefix* used to avoid name conflicts in exported C identifiers.

format: long name (short name, prefix)

SHAM modules
    Behavior hiding
        Load (*load*, **ld_**)
        Token (*token*, **tk_**)
        Abstract Machine (*absmach*, **am_**)
        Screen Driver (*scndr*, **sd_**)
        Screen Geometry (*scngeom*, **sg_**)
    Software decision hiding
        SHAM Coordinator (*sham*)
        Execute (*exec*, **ex_**)
    Machine hiding
        Keyboard Input (*keybdin*, **ki_**)
        Screen String (*scnstr*, **ss_**)

UNIX modules
    ctype, *curses*, *stdio*, *string*, *strtod*

B.2   Module Service and Secret

B.2.1   Behavior-hiding modules

B.2.1.1   The *load* module

- **Service**. Performs the load phase. Issues exception messages for incorrect input and, for correct input, stores the resulting object code in the *absmach* module.

- **Secret**. The details of the load-phase user interface, including the source language concrete syntax and the exception messages.

B.2.1.2   The *token* module

- **Service**. Extracts tokens from a string supplied by the user. Tokens are retrieved sequentially, in the order they occur in the user's string. The user is given access to the token value (a string) and the token type (integer, identifier, or unknown).

- **Secret**. The rules governing token types and token separators.

B.2.1.3   The *absmach* module

- **Service**. Implements the *mem*, *acc*, and *pc* state variables, as well as the Language Semantics Table from the SHAM Requirements Specification. Following each instruction execution, the user is given a status indicator and access to the state variables.

- **Secret**. The SHAM language semantics, including the execution-phase exceptions.

B.2.1.4   The *scndr* module

- **Service**. Updates the terminal screen, using the values stored by *absmach* and according to the screen format described in the ISHAM Requirements Specification.

- **Secret**. The means used to accomplish screen updates.

B.2.1.5   The *scngeom* module

- **Service**. Provides the length, row, and column position for each screen field, as per the screen format in the SHAM Requirements Specification.

- **Secret**. Hides, until execution time, the length, row, and column values.

B.2.2 Software decision–hiding modules

B.2.2.1 The *sham* module

- **Service**. Uses the other modules to provide the load-and-go assembler specified in the SHAM Requirements Specification.

- **Secret**. The way in which the other modules are used and the handling of command-line parameters.

B.2.2.2 The *exec* module

- **Service**. Performs the execution phase, executing the program stored in *absmach* and managing the run-time user interface, batch or interactive.

- **Secret**. The way in which the other modules are used, and the format and content of the exception messages.

B.2.3 Machine-hiding modules

B.2.3.1 The *keybdin* module

- **Service**. Provides keyboard input, one character at a time, without echoing or waiting for carriage return.

- **Secret**. The UNIX system services used to accomplish this task.

B.2.3.2 The *scnstr* module

- **Service**. Provides write access to the terminal screen. A string may be written to any position on the screen, the cursor may be moved to any position on the screen, and any screen position may be highlighted. To allow for efficient screen control, *scnstr* calls are buffered. An "apply changes to screen" access routine is provided; *scnstr* calls have no visible effect on the screen until the apply routine is invoked.

- **Secret**. The UNIX system services used to accomplish this task.

Appendix C

Module Interface Specifications

C.1   Global Definitions

C.1.1   system.h

```
#include <stdio.h>
#include <string.h>

/*****constants*****/

#define SY_EXCFIL "SHAM.excfil"

/*****types*****/

/*sham instructions*/
typedef enum {
    SY_LOAD,SY_STORE,SY_ADD,SY_SUBTRACT,
    SY_BRANCH,SY_BRANCHZERO,SY_BRANCHPOS,SY_LOADCON,SY_PRINT,SY_HALT
} sy_instr;

/*****macros for number of operands*****/

#define SY_OP0(cmd) \
    ((int)cmd == (int)SY_PRINT || (int)cmd == (int)SY_HALT)
#define SY_OP1(cmd) \
    ((int)cmd >= (int)SY_LOAD && (int)cmd <= (int)SY_LOADCON)

/*****variables*****/

extern FILE *sy_excfilp; /*file for exception messages*/
```

C.2   BSHAM Modules

C.2.1   *absmach* MIS

C.2.1.1   Interface syntax

```
#define AM_MEMSIZ 100
#define AM_MAXINT 999

typedef enum {AM_NORMAL,AM_HALT,AM_PRINT,
    AM_ARITHEXC,AM_ADDREXC,
    AM_OBJECTEXC,AM_NOOPEXC
} am_stat;
```

Routine names	Inputs	Outputs	Exceptions
am_s_init			
am_s_acc	int		am_int
am_g_acc		int	
am_s_pc	int		am_addr
am_g_pc		int	
am_s_mem	int		am_addr
	int		am_int
am_g_mem	int	int	am_addr
am_sg_exec		am_stat	

C.2.1.2   Interface semantics

state variables
$mem : sequence$ [AM_MEMSIZ] of [0..AM_MAXINT]
$acc : $ [0..AM_MAXINT]
$pc : $ [0..AM_MEMSIZ $- 1$]

state invariant
none

assumptions
am_s_init is called before any other access routine.

access routine semantics
am_s_init:
     transition: $acc, pc, mem := 0, 0,$ all zeroes
     exceptions: none
am_s_acc(i):
     transition: $acc := i$
     exceptions: $exc := (i \notin$ [0..AM_MAXINT] $\Rightarrow$ am_int)
am_g_acc:
     output: $out := acc$
     exceptions: none
am_s_pc(a):

transition: $pc := a$

exceptions: $exc := (a \notin [0..\textsf{AM\_MEMSIZ} - 1] \Rightarrow \textsf{am\_addr})$

am_g_pc:

output: $out := pc$

exceptions: none

am_s_mem(a, i):

transition: $mem[a] := i$

exceptions: $exc := \quad (a \notin [0..\textsf{AM\_MEMSIZ} - 1] \Rightarrow \textsf{am\_addr}$
$\qquad\qquad\qquad\quad | \; i \notin [0..\textsf{AM\_MAXINT}] \Rightarrow \textsf{am\_int})$

am_g_mem(a):

output: $out := mem[a]$

exceptions: $exc := (a \notin [0..\textsf{AM\_MEMSIZ} - 1] \Rightarrow \textsf{am\_addr})$

am_sg_exec:

transition-output:

$\quad$ (an error is specified in the Exec. Phase Exception Table $\Rightarrow$
$\qquad out := $ the error identifier
$\quad | \; mem[pc] = \textsf{SY\_HALT} \Rightarrow out := \textsf{AM\_HALT}$
$\quad | \; mem[pc] = \textsf{SY\_PRINT} \Rightarrow out, pc := \textsf{AM\_PRINT}, pc + 1$
$\quad | \; true \Rightarrow \quad out := \textsf{AM\_NORMAL}$
$\qquad\qquad\qquad acc, pc, mem := $ values specified in the RS Lang. Sem. Table)

exceptions: none

C.2.1.3 Header file: absmach.h

```
/*****constants*****/

#define AM_MEMSIZ 100 /*memory size*/
#define AM_MAXINT 999 /*maximum integer value*/


/*****types*****/

typedef enum {AM_NORMAL,AM_HALT,AM_PRINT,
    AM_ARITHEXC,AM_ADDREXC,AM_OBJECTEXC,AM_NOOPEXC
} am_stat;


/*****access routines*****/

void am_s_init();

void am_s_acc();
/*  void am_s_acc(i)
*   int i;
*/

int am_g_acc();

void am_s_pc();
/*  void am_s_pc(a)
```

```
*      int a;
*/

int am_g_pc();

void am_s_mem();
/*   void am_s_mem(a,i)
*      int a,i;
*/

int am_g_mem();
/*   int am_g_mem(a)
*      int a;
*/

am_stat am_sg_exec();

void am_g_dump(); /*for testing purposes only*/

/*****exception handlers*****/

void am_addr();

void am_int();
```

C.2.2   *exec* MIS

C.2.2.1   Interface syntax

Routine names	Inputs	Outputs	Exceptions
ex_s_init			
ex_s_exec			

C.2.2.2   Interface semantics

environment variables
scn
      the terminal screen
stdout
      UNIX standard output

state variables
none

state invariant
none

assumptions

Before `ex_s_exec` is called, `ex_s_init` has been called and
    the *absmach* module has been initialized.
At compile time, exactly one of these preprocessor flags is defined:
`BSHAM, ISHAM`

access routine semantics
`ex_s_init`:
    transition:
        if flag `ISHAM` is set then
            initialize the screen
    exceptions: none
`ex_s_exec`:
    transition:
        if flag `BSHAM` is set then
            perform the execution phase as described in the BSHAM RS
        else if flag `ISHAM` is set then
            perform the execution phase as described in the ISHAM RS
        In either case:
            • Use the *mem*, *acc*, and *pc* values stored in the *absmach* module
            • Invoke `am_sg_exec` to execute the next instruction
            • Use the `am_sg_exec` return value to determine whether
              a normal case or exception output is needed
    exceptions: none

C.2.2.3   Header file: `exec.h`

`/*****constants*****/`

`/*****types*****/`

`/*****access routines*****/`

`void ex_s_init();`

`void ex_s_exec();`

`/*****exception handlers*****/`

C.2.3   *load* MIS

C.2.3.1   Interface syntax

`#define typedef enum {LD_NORMAL,LD_ERROR} ld_stat;`

Routine names	Inputs	Outputs	Exceptions
`ld_s_init`			
`ld_sg_load`	`FILE*`	`ld_stat`	`ld_fil`

C.2.3.2   Interface semantics

environment variables
stdout
     UNIX standard output

state variables
none

state invariant
none

assumptions
ld_s_init is called before any other access routine.
The *absmach* and *token* modules have been initialized.
The argument to ld_sg_load points to an open file control block.

access routine semantics
ld_s_init:
     transition: none
     exceptions: none
ld_sg_load(f): defined in terms of the SHAM Requirements Specification.
     transition/output:
               (file f has no load errors $\Rightarrow$
                    absmach.mem := the object code version of the program in f
                    out := LD_NORMAL
               | *true* $\Rightarrow$
                    write the appropriate messages to *stdout*
                    out := LD_ERROR)
     exceptions: *exc* := (error reading file $f \Rightarrow$ ld_fil)

considerations
In ld_sg_load(f), if f has load errors or if ld_fil occurs,
the value of *absmach.mem* is "dontcare."

C.2.3.3   Header file: load.h

```
/*****constants*****/

/*****types*****/

typedef enum {LD_NORMAL,LD_ERROR} ld_stat;

typedef FILE *ld_filptr;

/*****access routines*****/

void ld_s_init();
```

```
ld_stat ld_sg_load();
/*    ld_stat ld_sg_load(f);
*     ld_filptr f;
*/

/*****exception handlers*****/

void ld_fil();
```

C.2.4   *sham* **MIS**

There is no MIS for *sham*.

C.2.5   *token* **MIS**

C.2.5.1   **Interface syntax**

```
#define TK_MAXSTRLEN 100
#define TK_MAXIDLEN 10
#define TK_MAXINTLEN 5

typedef enum {TK_ID,TK_INT,TK_BADTOK} tk_toktyp;

typedef struct {
   char val[TK_MAXSTRLEN+1];
   tk_toktyp typ;
} tk_valtyp;
```

Routine names	Inputs	Outputs	Exceptions
tk_s_init			
tk_s_str	char*		tk_maxlen
tk_sg_next		tk_valtyp	tk_end
tk_g_end		*boolean*	

C.2.5.2   **Interface semantics**

state variables
toklist : sequence of string

state invariant
none

assumptions
tk_s_init is called before any other access routine.
All string parameters are legal C strings.

access routine semantics
tk_s_init:
      transition: *toklist* := ⟨⟩

exceptions: none

tk_s_str(s):

    transition: $toklist := tokens(s)$

    exceptions: $exc := (|s| > \text{TK\_MAXSTRLEN} \Rightarrow \text{tk\_maxlen})$

tk_sg_next:

    transition/output: $toklist, out :=$

        $toklist[1..|toklist| - 1],$

        $\langle toklist[0], toktyp(toklist[0])\rangle$

    exceptions: $exc := (toklist = \langle\rangle \Rightarrow \text{tk\_end})$

tk_g_end:

    output: $out := (toklist = \langle\rangle)$

    exceptions: none

local types

$idtoksetT = \{s \mid s$ is a string of alphabetic or numeric characters $\wedge$

    $s[0]$ is alphabetic $\wedge |s| \in [1..\text{TK\_MAXIDLEN}]\}$

$inttoksetT = \{s \mid s$ is a string of numeric characters $\wedge |s| \in [1..\text{TK\_MAXINTLEN}]\}$

local functions

$tokens : string \rightarrow sequence\ of\ string$

    $tokens(s)$ returns the sequence of tokens in s where

        1. a token is a non-empty subsequence $s[i..j]$ of s

        2. $s[i..j]$ contains no blanks

        3. $(i = 0 \vee s[i - 1] = \text{` '}) \wedge (j = |s| - 1 \vee s[j + 1] = \text{` '})$

$toktyp : string \rightarrow \text{tk\_toktyp}$

    $toktyp(s) :=$

        $(s \in idtoksetT \Rightarrow \text{TK\_ID}$

        $\mid s \in inttoksetT \Rightarrow \text{TK\_INT}$

        $\mid true \Rightarrow \text{TK\_BADTOK})$

C.2.5.3   Header file: `token.h`

```
/*****constants*****/

#define TK_MAXSTRLEN 100 /*maximum length of an input string*/
#define TK_MAXIDLEN 10 /*maximum length of an id token*/
#define TK_MAXINTLEN 5 /*maximum length of an integer token*/

/*****types*****/

typedef enum {TK_ID,TK_INT,TK_BADTOK} tk_toktyp;

typedef struct {
    char val[TK_MAXSTRLEN+1];
    tk_toktyp typ;
} tk_valtyp;
```

```
/*****access routines*****/

void tk_s_init();

void tk_s_str();
/*    void tk_s_str(str)
*     char *str;
*/

void tk_sg_next(); /*out value returned using call-by-reference*/
/*    void tk_sg_next(valtyp);
*     tk_valtyp *valtyp; NOTE: caller must allocate *valtyp
*/

/*boolean*/ int tk_g_end();

void tk_g_dump(); /*for testing purposes only*/

/*****exception handlers*****/

void tk_end();

void tk_maxlen();
```

C.3 ISHAM Modules

C.3.1 *keybdin* MIS

C.3.1.1 Interface syntax

Routine names	Inputs	Outputs	Exceptions
ki_s_init			
ki_sg_next		char	
ki_s_end			

C.3.1.2 Interface semantics

environment variables
stdin : string
        UNIX standard input

state variables
none

state invariant
none

assumptions
The *curses* module has been initialized.

Calls to *keybdin* obey the following pattern:
(ki_s_init.ki_sg_next * .ki_s_end)*, where $X*$ indicates zero or more occurrences of X

access routine semantics
ki_s_init:
>   **transition**: turn off keystroke echoing
>   **exceptions**: none

ki_sg_next:
>   **transition-output**: *out* := the next available character
>   **exceptions**: none

ki_s_end:
>   **transition**: turn on keystroke echoing
>   **exceptions**: none

considerations

- Keystrokes are returned by ki_sg_next in first-in–first-out order.
- Characters are returned immediately, without waiting for a newline.
- If, on entry, there is no new keystroke available, ki_sg_next will not return until another keystroke occurs.

C.3.1.3 Header file: keybdin.h

```
/*****constants*****/

/*****types*****/

/*****access routines*****/

void ki_s_init();

char ki_sg_next();

void ki_s_end();

/*****exception handlers*****/
```

C.3.2   *scndr* MIS

C.3.2.1   Interface syntax

Routine names	Inputs	Outputs	Exceptions
sd_s_init			
sd_s_clrscn			
sd_s_con			
sd_s_mem			
sd_s_pc			
sd_s_acc			
sd_s_prt	int		
sd_s_msg	char*		
sd_s_hlt	int *boolean*		

C.3.2.2   Interface semantics

environment variables

scn

      the terminal screen

state variables

state invariant

assumptions

sd_s_init is called before any other access routine.

The *absmach*, *scnstr*, and *scngeom* modules have been initialized.

The address passed to sd_s_hlt is a legal address.

access routine semantics

Note: *MEM*, *PC*, *ACC*, *PRT*, and *MSG* are screen fields from the ISHAM RS.

sd_s_init:
      transition: none
      exceptions: none
sd_s_clrscn:
      transition: clear terminal screen
      exceptions: none
sd_s_con:
      transition: display the fixed screen fields
      exceptions: none
sd_s_mem:
      transition:
$$(\forall r, c \in [0..9]) MEM[r, c] := \mathtt{am\_g\_mem}(10 \times r + c),$$
      converted to ASCII, right justified and padded left with blanks

      exceptions: none

sd_s_pc:

      transition: $PC :=$ am_g_pc, converted to ASCII,

          right justified and padded left with blanks

      exceptions: none

sd_s_acc:

      transition: $ACC :=$ am_g_acc, converted to ASCII,

          right justified and padded left with blanks

      exceptions: none

sd_s_prt(x):

      transition: $PRT := x$, converted to ASCII,

          right justified and padded left with blanks

      exceptions: none

sd_s_msg(s):

      transition: $MSG := s$, left justified and padded right with blanks

      exceptions: none

sd_s_hlt(a, f):

      transition:

          ($f = true \Rightarrow$ display $MEM[a/10, a\%10]$ in inverse video

          $| f = false \Rightarrow$ display $MEM[a/10, a\%10]$ normally)

      exceptions: none

considerations

For each field displayed by *scndr*, the value is truncated to the field length returned by *scngeom*.

C.3.2.3   Header file: scndr.h

```
/*****constants*****/

/*****types*****/

/*****access routines*****/

void sd_s_init();

void sd_s_clrscn();

void sd_s_con();

void sd_s_mem();

void sd_s_pc();

void sd_s_acc();

void sd_s_prt();
/*   void sd_s_prt(i)
```

```
*     int i;
*/


void sd_s_msg();
/*    void sd_s_msg(s)
*     char *s;
*/


void sd_s_hlt();
/*    void sd_s_hlt(a,f)
*     int a;
*     (boolean) int f;
*/


/*****exception handlers*****/
```

C.3.3   *scngeom* MIS

C.3.3.1   Interface syntax

```
#define SG_NUMROW 24
#define SG_NUMCOL 80

typedef enum {
    SG_MEM,SG_PC,SG_ACC,SG_PRT,SG_MSG,
    SG_SCNTTL,SG_MEMTTL1,SG_MEMTTL2,SG_MEMCOLHDR,SG_MEMROWHDR,
    SG_PCTTL,SG_ACCTTL,SG_PRTTTL,SG_PROMPTTTL,SG_MSGTTL
} sg_fldnam;

typedef struct {
    sg_fldnam nam;
    int row;
    int col;
} sg_fld;
```

Routine names	Inputs	Outputs	Exceptions
sg_s_init			
sg_g_legfld	sg_fld	*boolean*	
sg_g_row	sg_fld	int	sg_badfld
sg_g_col	sg_fld	int	sg_badfld
sg_g_len	sg_fld	int	sg_badfld
sg_g_val	sg_fld	char*	sg_badfld

C.3.3.2   Interface semantics

Identifier	Legal row values	Legal column values	Associated field in ISHAM RS
	Variable fields		
SG_MEM	[0..9]	[0..9]	*MEM*
SG_PC	0	0	*PC*
SG_ACC	0	0	*ACC*
SG_PRT	0	0	*PRT*
SG_MSG	0	0	*MSG*
	Fixed fields		
SG_SCNTTL	0	0	Screen title
SG_MEMTTL1	0	0	*MEM* title line 1
SG_MEMTTL2	0	0	*MEM* title line 2
SG_MEMCOLHDR	0	[0..9]	*MEM* column header
SG_MEMROWHDR	[0..9]	0	*MEM* row header
SG_PCTTL	0	0	*PC* title
SG_ACCTTL	0	0	*ACC* title
SG_PRTTTL	0	0	*PRT* title
SG_PROMPTTTL	0	0	Prompt title
SG_MSGTTL	0	0	Error message title

state variables
none

state invariant
none

assumptions
sg_s_init is called before any other access routine

access routine semantics
sg_s_init:
    transition: none
    exceptions: none
sg_g_legfld(fld):
    output: out := (fld is a legal field identifier)
    exceptions: none
sg_g_row(fld):
    output: out := starting screen row for fld, zero-relative
    exceptions: exc := (fld is not a legal field identifier $\Rightarrow$ sg_badfld)
sg_g_col(fld):
    output: out := starting screen column for fld, zero-relative
    exceptions: exc := (fld is not a legal field identifier $\Rightarrow$ sg_badfld)
sg_g_len(fld):
    output: out := length of fld
    exceptions: exc := (fld is not a legal field identifier $\Rightarrow$ sg_badfld)
sg_g_val(fld):
    output: out :=

       (*fld* is a fixed screen field $\Rightarrow$ as shown in the RS
       | *fld* is a variable screen field $\Rightarrow$ "")
   exceptions: *exc* := (*fld* is not a legal field identifier $\Rightarrow$ sg_badfld)

C.3.3.3   Header file: `scngeom.h`

```
/*****constants*****/

#define SG_NUMROW 24 /*number of rows on the screen*/
#define SG_NUMCOL 80 /*number of columns on the screen*/

/*****types*****/

typedef enum {
    SG_MEM,SG_PC,SG_ACC,SG_PRT,SG_MSG,
    SG_SCNTTL,SG_MEMTTL1,SG_MEMTTL2,SG_MEMCOLHDR,SG_MEMROWHDR,
    SG_PCTTL,SG_ACCTTL,SG_PRTTTL,SG_PROMPTTTL,SG_MSGTTL
} sg_fldnam;

typedef struct {
    sg_fldnam nam;
    int row;
    int col;
} sg_fld;

/*****access routines*****/

void sg_s_init();

/*boolean*/ int sg_g_legfld();
/*    int sg_g_legfld(fld)
 *    sg_fld fld;
 */

int sg_g_row();
/*    int sg_g_row(fld)
 *    sg_fld fld;
 */

int sg_g_col();
/*    int sg_g_col(fld)
 *    sg_fld fld;
 */

int sg_g_len();
/*    int sg_g_len(fld)
 *    sg_fld fld;
 */
```

```
char *sg_g_val();
/*   char *sg_g_val(fld)
*    sg_fld fld;
*/


/*****exception handlers*****/

void sg_badfld();
```

C.3.4   *scnstr* **MIS**

C.3.4.1   Interface syntax

```
#define SS_NUMROW 24
#define SS_NUMCOL 80
```

Routine names	Inputs	Outputs	Exceptions
ss_s_init			
ss_s_clrscn			
ss_s_str	int		ss_row
	int		ss_col
	char*		ss_len
ss_s_hlt	int		ss_row
	int		ss_col
	int		ss_len
	boolean		
ss_s_cur	int		ss_row
	int		ss_col
ss_s_ref			
ss_s_end			

C.3.4.2   Interface semantics

environment variables

scn : *sequence* [SS_NUMROW][SS_NUMCOL] *of char*

   scn[r][c] is the character at screen row r and column c,

   with numbering zero-relative and beginning at the upper-left corner

hlt : *sequence* [SS_NUMROW][SS_NUMCOL] *of boolean*

   hlt[r][c] is true if the position at screen row r and column c is highlighted,

   with numbering zero-relative and beginning at the upper-left corner

cur : *tuple of* (*row* : [0..SS_NUMROW $-$ 1], *col* : [0..SS_NUMCOL $-$ 1])

   the terminal cursor is at screen row *cur.row* and column *cur.col*

   with numbering zero-relative and beginning at the upper-left corner

state variables

scnbuf : *sequence* [SS_NUMROW][SS_NUMCOL] *of char*

hltbuf : *sequence* [SS_NUMROW][SS_NUMCOL] *of boolean*

$curbuf : tuple\ of\ (row : [0..\text{SS\_NUMROW} - 1], col : [0..\text{SS\_NUMCOL} - 1])$

state invariant
none

assumptions
The *curses* module has been initialized.

Calls to *scnstr* obey the following pattern:
$\quad\quad (\text{ss\_s\_init}.T * .\text{ss\_s\_end})*$, where
$\quad\quad\quad\quad T$ is any call other than ss_s_init or ss_s_end
$\quad\quad\quad\quad X*$ indicates zero or more occurrences of X
String parameters are legal C strings.

access routine semantics
ss_s_init:
$\quad\quad$ **transition:** none
$\quad\quad$ **exceptions:** none
ss_s_clrscn:
$\quad\quad$ **transition:** $scnbuf, hltbuf, curbuf := \text{all} \ ' \ ', \text{all}\,false, \langle 0, 0 \rangle$
$\quad\quad$ **exceptions:** none
ss_s_str(row, col, s):
$\quad\quad$ **transition:** $(|s| > 0 \Rightarrow scnbuf[row][col..col + |s| - 1] := s)$
$\quad\quad$ **exceptions:** $exc :=$
$\quad\quad\quad\quad (row \notin [0..\text{SS\_NUMROW} - 1] \Rightarrow \text{ss\_row}$
$\quad\quad\quad\quad | \ col \notin [0..\text{SS\_NUMCOL} - 1] \Rightarrow \text{ss\_col}$
$\quad\quad\quad\quad | \ |s| \notin [0..\text{SS\_NUMCOL} - col] \Rightarrow \text{ss\_len})$
ss_s_hlt(row, col, l, f):
$\quad\quad$ **transition:** $(l > 0 \Rightarrow hltbuf[row][col..col + l - 1] := f)$
$\quad\quad$ **exceptions:** $exc :=$
$\quad\quad\quad\quad (row \notin [0..\text{SS\_NUMROW} - 1] \Rightarrow \text{ss\_row}$
$\quad\quad\quad\quad | \ col \notin [0..\text{SS\_NUMCOL} - 1] \Rightarrow \text{ss\_col}$
$\quad\quad\quad\quad | \ l \notin [0..\text{SS\_NUMCOL} - col] \Rightarrow \text{ss\_len})$
ss_s_cur(row, col):
$\quad\quad$ **transition:** $curbuf := \langle row, col \rangle$
$\quad\quad$ **exceptions:** $exc :=$
$\quad\quad\quad\quad (row \notin [0..\text{SS\_NUMROW} - 1] \Rightarrow \text{ss\_row}$
$\quad\quad\quad\quad | \ col \notin [0..\text{SS\_NUMCOL} - 1] \Rightarrow \text{ss\_col})$
ss_s_ref:
$\quad\quad$ **transition:** $scn, hlt, cur := scnbuf, hltbuf, curbuf$
$\quad\quad$ **exceptions:** none
ss_s_end:
$\quad\quad$ **transition:** none
$\quad\quad$ **exceptions:** none

considerations
ss_s_str and ss_s_hlt may alter the value of *curbuf*.

C.3.4.3   Header file: scnstr.h

```
/*****constants*****/

#define SS_NUMROW 24 /*number of rows on the screen*/
#define SS_NUMCOL 80 /*number of columns on the screen*/

/*****types*****/

/*****access routines*****/

void ss_s_init();

void ss_s_clrscn();

void ss_s_str();
/*   void ss_s_str(r,c,s)
 *   int r,c;
 *   char *s;
 */

void ss_s_hlt();
/*   void ss_s_hlt(r,c,l,f)
 *   int r,c,l;
 *   (boolean) int f;
 */

void ss_s_cur();
/*   void ss_s_cur(r,c)
 *   int r,c;
 */

void ss_s_ref();

void ss_s_end();

/*****exception handlers*****/

void ss_row();

void ss_col();

void ss_len();
```

C.4 Demonstration Modules

C.4.1 *stack* MIS

C.4.1.1 Interface syntax

`#define PS_MAXSIZ 100`

Routine names	Inputs	Outputs	Exceptions
ps_s_init			
ps_s_push	int		ps_full
ps_s_pop			ps_empty
ps_g_top		int	ps_empty
ps_g_depth		int	

C.4.1.2 Interface semantics

state variables
s : *sequence of integer*

state invariant
$|s| \le$ PS_MAXSIZ

assumptions
ps_s_init is called before any other access routine.

access routine semantics
ps_s_init:
    transition: $s := \langle \rangle$
    exceptions: none
ps_s_push(x):
    transition: $s := s \parallel \langle x \rangle$
    exceptions: $exc := (|s| = $ PS_MAXSIZ $\Rightarrow$ ps_full$)$
ps_s_pop:
    transition: $s := s[0..|s| - 2]$
    exceptions: $exc := (|s| = 0 \Rightarrow$ ps_empty$)$
ps_g_top:
    output: $out := s[|s| - 1]$
    exceptions: $exc := (|s| = 0 \Rightarrow$ ps_empty$)$
ps_g_depth:
    output: $out := |s|$
    exceptions: none

C.4.1.3 Header file: stack.h

```
/*****constants*****/

#define PS_MAXSIZ 100 /*the maximum stack size*/
```

```
/*****types*****/

/*****access routines*****/

void ps_s_init();

void ps_s_push();
/*   void ps_s_push(i);
*    int i;
*/

void ps_s_pop();

int ps_g_top();

int ps_g_depth();

void ps_g_dump(); /*for testing purposes only*/

/*****exception handlers*****/

void ps_empty();

void ps_full();
```

C.4.2 *symtbl* MIS

C.4.2.1 Interface syntax

```
#define ST_MAXSYMS 50
#define ST_MAXSYMLEN 20
```

Routine names	Inputs	Outputs	Exceptions
st_s_init			
st_s_add	char* int		st_maxlen st_exsym st_full
st_g_exsym	char*	*boolean*	
st_s_loc	char* int		st_notexsym
st_g_loc	char*	int	st_notexsym
st_g_siz		int	

C.4.2.2 Interface semantics

state variables

tbl : set of tuple of (sym : string, loc : integer)

state invariant
1. $|tbl| \leq \text{ST\_MAXSYMS}$
2. $(\forall t \in tbl)(|t.sym| \leq \text{ST\_MAXSYMLEN})$
3. $(\forall t_1, t_2 \in tbl)(t_1 \neq t_2 \rightarrow t_1.sym \neq t_2.sym)$

assumptions
st_s_init is called before any other access routine.
All string parameters are legal C strings.

access routine semantics
st_s_init:
    transition: $tbl := \{\}$
    exceptions: none
st_s_add(sym, loc):
    transition: $tbl := tbl \cup \{\langle sym, loc \rangle\}$
    exceptions: $exc :=$ $(|sym| > \text{ST\_MAXSYMLEN} \Rightarrow \text{st\_maxlen}$
             $| (\exists loc_1)(\langle sym, loc_1 \rangle \in tbl) \Rightarrow \text{st\_exsym}$
             $| |tbl| = \text{ST\_MAXSYMS} \Rightarrow \text{st\_full})$
st_g_exsym(sym):
    output: $out := (\exists loc)(\langle sym, loc \rangle \in tbl)$
    exceptions: none
st_s_loc(sym, loc):
    transition: $tbl := (tbl - \{\langle sym, loc_1 \rangle\}) \cup \{\langle sym, loc \rangle\}$ where $\langle sym, loc_1 \rangle \in tbl$
    exceptions: $exc := (\neg(\exists loc_1)(\langle sym, loc_1 \rangle \in tbl) \Rightarrow \text{st\_notexsym})$
st_g_loc(sym):
    output: $out := loc$, where $\langle sym, loc \rangle \in tbl$
    exceptions: $exc := (\neg(\exists loc)(\langle sym, loc \rangle \in tbl) \Rightarrow \text{st\_notexsym})$
st_g_siz:
    output: $out := |tbl|$
    exceptions: none

C.4.2.3   Header file: symtbl.h

```
/*****constants*****/

#define ST_MAXSYMS 50 /*maximum number of symbols*/
#define ST_MAXSYMLEN 20 /*maximum symbol length*/


/*****types*****/

/*****access routines*****/

void st_s_init();

void st_s_add();
/*    void st_s_add(sym,loc);
 *    char *sym;
 *    int loc;
```

```
*/

int st_g_siz();

/*boolean*/ int st_g_exsym();
/*    int st_g_exsym(sym);
*     char *sym;
*/

void st_s_loc();
/*    void st_g_loc(sym,loc);
*     char *sym;
*     int loc;
*/

int st_g_loc();
/*    int st_g_loc(sym);
*     char *sym;
*/

void st_g_dump(); /*for testing purposes only*/

/*****exception handlers*****/

void st_exsym();

void st_maxlen();

void st_notexsym();

void st_full();
```

Appendix D

Module Internal Designs

D.1 BSHAM Modules

D.1.1 *absmach* MID

state variables
int acc,pc;
int mem[AM_MEMSIZ];

state invariant
1. acc $\in [0..$AM_MAXINT$]$
2. pc $\in [0..$AM_MEMSIZ$ - 1]$
3. $(\forall i \in [0..$AM_MEMSIZ$ - 1])(mem[i] \in [0..AM_MAXINT])$

considerations
Since the abstract and concrete states are identical, the abstraction function and
the access routine semantics are omitted.

D.1.2 *exec* MID

There is no MID for *exec*.

D.1.3 *load* MID

There is no MID for *load*.

D.1.4 *sham* MID

There is no MID for *sham*.

D.1.5   *token* **MID**

state variables
char buf[TK_MAXSTRLEN+2];
int cur;

state invariant
1. buf$[0..$TK_MAXSTRLEN$+1]$ contains a null.
2. cur $\in [0..leftnull(\text{buf})]$
3. cur $< leftnull(\text{buf}) \rightarrow (\text{buf}[\text{cur}] \neq$ ' ' $\wedge$ buf$[leftnull(\text{buf})-1] =$ ' ')

abstraction function
toklist = the sequence of tokens in buf$[\text{cur}..leftnull(\text{buf})-1]$

access routine semantics
tk_s_init:
    transition: buf, cur $:= $ "", 0
    exceptions: none
tk_s_str(s):
    transition:
        buf $:=$ (there is a token in $s[0..leftnull(s)-1] \Rightarrow rmblanks(s) \,||\,$ " "
             $|\ true \Rightarrow$ "")
        cur $:= 0$
    exceptions: $exc := (|s| >$ TK_MAXSTRLEN $\Rightarrow$ tk_maxlen)
tk_sg_next:
    transition/output:
        Let   *curtok* be the token beginning at buf[cur]
                curtoktyp be the token type of *curtok*
        out $:= \langle curtok, curtoktyp \rangle$
        cur $:=$ (there is a token, beginning at position i,
                in buf$[\text{cur} + |curtok| + 1..leftnull(\text{buf})-1]$
                    $\Rightarrow i$
            $|\ true \Rightarrow leftnull(\text{buf}))$
    exceptions: $exc :=$ (buf[cur] $= null \Rightarrow$ tk_end)
tk_g_end:
    output: *out* $:=$ (buf[cur] $= null$)
    exceptions: none

local functions
leftnull : *string* $\rightarrow$ *integer*
    leftnull(s) $:=$ (there is a null in $s \Rightarrow$ the index of the leftmost one)
rmblanks : *string* $\rightarrow$ *string*
    rmblanks(s) $:= s$, with leading blanks removed

D.2 ISHAM Modules

D.2.1 *keybdin* MID

There is no MID for *keybdin*.

D.2.2 *scndr* MID

There is no MID for *scndr*.

D.2.3 *scngeom* MID

There is no MID for *scngeom*.

D.2.4 *scnstr* MID

There is no MID for *scnstr*.

D.3 Demonstration Modules

D.3.1 *stack* MID

state variables
int stack[PS_MAXSIZ];
int siz;

state invariant
$\text{siz} \in [0..\text{PS\_MAXSIZ}]$

abstraction function
$|s| = \text{siz} \wedge (\forall i \in [0..\text{siz} - 1])(s[i] = \text{stack}[i])$

access routine semantics
ps_s_init:
    transition: $\text{siz} := 0$
    exceptions: none
ps_s_push(x):
    transition: $\text{stack}[\text{siz}], \text{siz} := x, \text{siz} + 1$
    exceptions: $exc := (\text{siz} = \text{PS\_MAXSIZ} \Rightarrow \text{ps\_full})$
ps_s_pop:
    transition: $\text{siz} := \text{siz} - 1$
    exceptions: $exc := (\text{siz} = 0 \Rightarrow \text{ps\_empty})$
ps_g_top:
    output: $out := \text{stack}[\text{siz} - 1]$
    exceptions: $exc := (\text{siz} = 0 \Rightarrow \text{ps\_empty})$

ps_g_depth:
    output: $out := $ siz
    exceptions: none

D.3.2   *symtbl* **MID**

state variables
```
struct {
    char sym[ST_MAXSYMLEN+1];
    int loc;
} tbl[ST_MAXSYMS];
int tblcnt;
```

state invariant
1. Every symbol in $\text{tbl}[0..\text{tblcnt} - 1]$ contains a null.
2. There are no duplicate symbols in $\text{tbl}[0..\text{tblcnt} - 1]$.
3. $\text{tblcnt} \in [0..\text{ST\_MAXSYMS}]$

abstraction function
$$tbl = \{\langle sym, loc \rangle \mid (\exists i \in [0..\text{tblcnt} - 1])(sym = \text{tbl}[i].\text{sym} \wedge loc = \text{tbl}[i].\text{loc})\}$$

access routine semantics
st_s_init:
    transition: $\text{tblcnt} := 0$
    exceptions: none
st_s_add(sym, loc):
    transition: $\text{tblcnt}, \text{tbl}[\text{tblcnt}] := \text{tblcnt} + 1, \langle sym, loc \rangle$
    exceptions: $exc := \quad (|sym| > \text{ST\_MAXSYMLEN} \Rightarrow \text{st\_maxlen}$
    $\mid findsym(sym) \neq \text{NOTFOUND} \Rightarrow \text{st\_exsym}$
    $\mid \text{tblcnt} = \text{ST\_MAXSYMS} \Rightarrow \text{st\_full})$
st_g_exsym(sym):
    output: $out := (findsym(sym) \neq \text{NOTFOUND})$
    exceptions: none
st_s_loc(sym, loc):
    transition: $\text{tbl}[findsym(sym)].\text{loc} := \text{loc}$
    exceptions: $exc := (findsym(sym) = \text{NOTFOUND} \Rightarrow \text{st\_notexsym})$
st_g_loc(sym):
    output: $out := \text{tbl}[findsym(sym)].\text{loc}$
    exceptions: $exc := (findsym(sym) = \text{NOTFOUND} \Rightarrow \text{st\_notexsym})$
st_g_siz:
    output: $out := \text{tblcnt}$
    exceptions: none

local constants

```
#define NOTFOUND -1
```

local functions

$findsym : string \rightarrow integer$

$$findsym(s) = \quad ((\exists i \in [0..\mathbf{tblcnt} - 1])(s = \mathbf{tbl}[i].\mathbf{sym}) \Rightarrow i$$
$$\quad\quad\quad\quad | \; true \Rightarrow \mathbf{NOTFOUND})$$

Appendix E

Module Implementations

E.1 BSHAM Modules

E.1.1 *absmach* MI

E.1.1.1 Module implementation: `absmach.c`

```
#include "system.h"
#include "absmach.h"

/*****constants*****/

/*****types*****/

/*****module state*****/

static int acc; /*accumulator*/
static int pc; /*program counter*/
static int mem[AM_MEMSIZ]; /*memory*/

/*****local functions*****/
/*out := (state invariant holds =>
*       (an exception is specified in Execution-phase Exception Table of RS
*            => the associated exception identifier
*       | true => AM_NORMAL))
*/
static am_stat execexc()
{
    sy_instr cmd;
    int op;

    if (SY_OP0(mem[pc]))
        return(AM_NORMAL);
```

```
        if (SY_OP1(mem[pc])) {
            cmd = (sy_instr)mem[pc];
            if (pc < AM_MEMSIZ-1) {
                op = mem[pc+1];
                if (cmd == SY_LOADCON)
                    return(AM_NORMAL);
                /*we know that cmd != SY_LOADCON*/
                if (op >= 0 && op <= AM_MEMSIZ-1) {
                    if (cmd == SY_ADD) {
                        if (acc+mem[op] <= AM_MAXINT)
                            return(AM_NORMAL);
                        else
                            return(AM_ARITHEXC);
                    } else if (cmd == SY_SUBTRACT) {
                        if (acc-mem[op] >= 0)
                            return(AM_NORMAL);
                        else
                            return(AM_ARITHEXC);
                    } else
                        return(AM_NORMAL);
                }
                /*we know that op not in shamaddrT*/
                return(AM_ADDREXC);
            }
            /*we know that pc == AM_MEMSIZ-1*/
            return(AM_NOOPEXC);
        }
        /*we know that mem[pc] not in objectT*/
        return(AM_OBJECTEXC);
}


/*****access routines*****/

void am_s_init()
{
    int i;

    acc = 0;
    pc = 0;
    for (i = 0; i < AM_MEMSIZ; i++)
        mem[i] = 0;
    return;
}


void am_s_acc(i)
int i;
{
    if (i < 0 || i > AM_MAXINT) {
```

```
            am_int();
            return;
      }
      acc = i;
      return;
}

int am_g_acc()
{
      return(acc);
}

void am_s_pc(a)
int a;
{
      if (a < 0 || a > AM_MEMSIZ-1) {
            am_addr();
            return;
      }
      pc = a;
      return;
}

int am_g_pc()
{
      return(pc);
}

void am_s_mem(a,i)
int a,i;
{
      if (a < 0 || a > AM_MEMSIZ-1) {
            am_addr();
            return;
      }
      if (i < 0 || i > AM_MAXINT) {
            am_int();
            return;
      }
      mem[a] = i;
      return;
}

int am_g_mem(a)
int a;
{
      if (a < 0 || a > AM_MEMSIZ-1) {
            am_addr();
```

```
            return(0);
      }
      return(mem[a]);
}

am_stat am_sg_exec()
{
      am_stat stat;
      sy_instr cmd;
      int op;

      stat = execexc();
      if (stat != AM_NORMAL)
            return(stat);
      cmd = (sy_instr)mem[pc];
      if (cmd == SY_HALT)
            return(AM_HALT);
      if (cmd == SY_PRINT) {
            pc = (pc+1) % AM_MEMSIZ;
            return(AM_PRINT);
      }
      op = mem[pc+1];
      switch (cmd) {
      case SY_LOAD:
            acc = mem[op];
            pc = (pc+2) % AM_MEMSIZ;
            break;
      case SY_STORE:
            mem[op] = acc;
            pc = (pc+2) % AM_MEMSIZ;
            break;
      case SY_ADD:
            acc = acc+mem[op];
            pc = (pc+2) % AM_MEMSIZ;
            break;
      case SY_SUBTRACT:
            acc = acc-mem[op];
            pc = (pc+2) % AM_MEMSIZ;
            break;
      case SY_BRANCH:
            pc = op;
            break;
      case SY_BRANCHZERO:
            if (acc == 0)
                  pc = op;
            else if (acc > 0)
                  pc = (pc+2) % AM_MEMSIZ;
            break;
```

```
        case SY_BRANCHPOS:
            if (acc > 0)
                pc = op;
            else if (acc == 0)
                pc = (pc+2) % AM_MEMSIZ;
            break;
        case SY_LOADCON:
            acc = op;
            pc = (pc+2) % AM_MEMSIZ;
            break;
        }
        return(AM_NORMAL);
}

void am_g_dump()
{
        int id;

        printf ("acc=%d!pc=%d!\n",acc,pc);
        for (id = 0; id < AM_MEMSIZ; id++) {
            if (id%10 == 0)
                printf("%d: ",id);
            printf("%d ",mem[id]);
            if ((id+1)%10 == 0)
                printf("\n");
        }
}
```

E.1.1.2 Default exception handlers: `absmach_e.c`

```
#include "system.h"
#include "absmach.h"

void am_addr()
{
        fprintf(sy_excfilp,"Exception am_addr occurred\n");
}

void am_int()
{
        fprintf(sy_excfilp,"Exception am_int occurred\n");
}
```

E.1.2 *exec* MI

E.1.2.1 Module implementation: `exec.c`

```
#include "system.h"
```

```
#include "absmach.h"
#include "exec.h"
#ifdef ISHAM
#include "keybdin.h"
#include "scngeom.h"
#include "scndr.h"
#endif

/*****constants*****/

#define STEP 's'
#define EXIT 'e'

/*****types*****/

/*****module state*****/

/*****local functions*****/

/*buf := the exception message corresponding to exception identifier
*     excid and program counter pc
*/
void excmsg(excid,pc,buf)
am_stat excid;
int pc;
char *buf;
{
    char tmpbuf[80];

    sprintf(buf,"Execution exception at %d. ",pc);
    switch (excid) {
    case AM_ADDREXC:
        sprintf(tmpbuf,"Illegal operand: %d",am_g_mem(pc+1));
        break;
    case AM_ARITHEXC:
        sprintf(tmpbuf,"Arithmetic overflow");
        break;
    case AM_NOOPEXC:
        sprintf(tmpbuf,"Operand not accessible");
        break;
    case AM_OBJECTEXC:
        sprintf(tmpbuf,"Illegal instruction: %d",am_g_mem(pc));
        break;
    }
    strcat(buf,tmpbuf);
}


/*****access routines*****/
```

```
void ex_s_init()
{
    return;
}

void ex_s_exec()
{
    am_stat stat;
    char buf[80];
#ifdef ISHAM
    char ch;
    int oldpc;
#endif

    am_s_acc(0);
    am_s_pc(0);
#ifdef BSHAM
    stat = am_sg_exec();
    while (stat == AM_NORMAL || stat == AM_PRINT) {
        if (stat == AM_PRINT)
            printf("%d\n",am_g_acc());
        stat = am_sg_exec();
    }
    if (stat != AM_HALT) {
        excmsg(stat,am_g_pc(),buf);
        printf("%s\n",buf);
    }
#else
    /*clear screen, display constants*/
    sd_s_clrscn();
    sd_s_con();
    /*display initial values*/
    sd_s_mem();
    sd_s_acc();
    sd_s_pc();
    /*highlight current instruction*/
    sd_s_hlt(am_g_pc(),1);
    ch = ki_sg_next();
    while (ch != EXIT) {
        if (ch == STEP) {
            oldpc = am_g_pc();
            stat = am_sg_exec();
            if (stat != AM_PRINT && stat != AM_NORMAL &&
                stat != AM_HALT) {
                excmsg(stat,am_g_pc(),buf);
                sd_s_msg(buf);
            } else if (stat == AM_HALT) {
```

```
                    sd_s_msg("HALT instruction reached");
            } else {
                /*update screen*/
                sd_s_msg("");
                if (stat == AM_PRINT)
                    sd_s_prt(am_g_acc());
                sd_s_mem();
                sd_s_acc();
                sd_s_pc();
                /*update highlighting of cursor*/
                sd_s_hlt(oldpc,0);
                sd_s_hlt(am_g_pc(),1);
            }
        } else
            sd_s_msg(
                "Illegal keyboard entry: type \"s\" or \"e\".");
        ch = ki_sg_next();
    }
    /*clear screen*/
    sd_s_clrscn();
#endif
}
```

E.1.2.2   Default exception handlers

There are no exceptions for *exec*.

E.1.3   *load* MI

E.1.3.1   Module implementation: `load.c`

```
#include "system.h"
#include "load.h"
#include "absmach.h"
#include "token.h"

/*****constants*****/

/*****types*****/

typedef enum
    {OPFMTEXC,SOURCEEXC,BLANKLINEXC,MISSINGOPEXC,NOMEMEXC} excid_t;

/*****module state*****/

/*****local functions*****/
/*out,instr :=
*    ((exists i)(s = i.source) => true,i
```

```
*       | true => false,SY_HALT)
*/
static int getinstr(s,instr)
char s[];
sy_instr *instr;
{
    static struct {
        char *src;
        sy_instr instr;
    } tbl[] = {
        {"load",SY_LOAD},
        {"store",SY_STORE},
        {"add",SY_ADD},
        {"sub",SY_SUBTRACT},
        {"br",SY_BRANCH},
        {"brz",SY_BRANCHZERO},
        {"brp",SY_BRANCHPOS},
        {"loadcon",SY_LOADCON},
        {"print",SY_PRINT},
        {"halt",SY_HALT},
        {NULL,SY_HALT} /*terminator*/
    };
    int i;

    i = 0;
    while (tbl[i].src) {
        if (!strcmp(s,tbl[i].src)) {
            *instr = tbl[i].instr;
            return(1);
        }
        i++;
    }
    *instr = SY_HALT;
    return(0);
}


/*write to stdout the message corresponding to the exception ide
*     in the first argument, with line number lin, and token tok
*/
static void excmsg(excid,lin,tok)
excid_t excid;
int lin;
char tok[];
{
    switch (excid) {
    case BLANKLINEXC:
        printf("Load exception at %d. Blank line illega
        break;
```

```
        case MISSINGOPEXC:
            printf("Load exception at %d. Operand missing\n",lin);
            break;
        case NOMEMEXC:
            printf("Load exception at %d. Program too large\n",lin);
            break;
        case OPFMTEXC:
            printf("Load exception at %d. Illegal operand: %s\n",lin,tok);
            break;
        case SOURCEEXC:
            printf("Load exception at %d. Illegal instruction: %s\n",
                lin,tok);
            break;
    }
}


/*(line number lin, consisting of the string buf, contains an error =>
 *    write the appropriate message to stdout
 *    out := LD_ERROR
 * | true =>
 *    *instr := SHAM instruction in buf
 *    *arg := argument, if any, to the instruction
 *    out := LD_NORMAL)
 */
static ld_stat parse(buf,lin,instr,arg)
char buf[];
int lin,*arg;
sy_instr *instr;
{
    tk_valtyp tok;

    tk_s_str(buf);
    if (tk_g_end()) {
        excmsg(BLANKLINEXC,lin,"");
        return(LD_ERROR);
    }
    /*we know that there is at least one token*/
    tk_sg_next(&tok);
    if (getinstr(tok.val,instr)) {
        if (SY_OP0(*instr))
            return(LD_NORMAL);
        /*we know that SY_OP1(*instr)*/
        if (tk_g_end()) {
            excmsg(MISSINGOPEXC,lin,"");
            return(LD_ERROR);
        }
        /*we know that there is more than one token*/
        tk_sg_next(&tok);
```

```
            if (tok.typ != TK_INT) {
                excmsg(OPFMTEXC,lin,tok.val);
                return(LD_ERROR);
            }
            *arg = atoi(tok.val);
            if (*instr == SY_LOADCON) {
                if (*arg >= 0 && *arg <= AM_MAXINT)
                    return(LD_NORMAL);
                else {
                    excmsg(OPFMTEXC,lin,tok.val);
                    return(LD_ERROR);
                }
            } else {
                if (*arg >= 0 && *arg < AM_MEMSIZ)
                    return(LD_NORMAL);
                else {
                    excmsg(OPFMTEXC,lin,tok.val);
                    return(LD_ERROR);
                }
            }
        }
        /*we know that tok.val not in sourceT*/
        excmsg(SOURCEEXC,lin,tok.val);
        return(LD_ERROR);
}

/*****access routines*****/

void ld_s_init()
{
        return;
}

ld_stat ld_sg_load(f)
ld_filptr f;
{
        char buf[TK_MAXSTRLEN+2]; /*extra characters needed for fget
        int index,lin,arg;
        ld_stat stat;
        sy_instr instr;

        index = 0;
        lin = 0;
        stat = LD_NORMAL;
        while (fgets(buf,TK_MAXSTRLEN+2,f) != NULL) {
            /*fgets stores newline character, which must be
            buf[strlen(buf)-1] = '\0';
            lin++;
```

```
            if (parse(buf,lin,&instr,&arg) == LD_ERROR)
                stat = LD_ERROR;
            else if (stat == LD_NORMAL) {
                if (index < AM_MEMSIZ-1 ||
                        (index == AM_MEMSIZ-1 && SY_OP0(instr))) {
                    am_s_mem(index++,(int)instr);
                    if (SY_OP1(instr))
                            am_s_mem(index++,arg);
                } else {
                    excmsg(NOMEMEXC,lin,"");
                    stat = LD_ERROR;
                }
            }
        }
    }
    return(stat);
}
```

E.1.3.2   Default exception handlers: `load_e.c`

```
#include "system.h"
#include "load.h"

void ld_fil()
{
    fprintf(sy_excfilp,"Exception ld_fil occurred\n");
}
```

E.1.4   *sham* MI

E.1.4.1   Module implementation: `sham.c`

```
#include "system.h"
#include "absmach.h"
#include "token.h"
#include "exec.h"
#include "load.h"
#ifdef ISHAM
#include "keybdin.h"
#include "scngeom.h"
#include "scnstr.h"
#include "scndr.h"
#endif

/*****constants*****/

/*****types*****/

/*****variables*****/
```

```
FILE *sy_excfilp;

/*****local functions*****/

/*****main*****/

main(argc,argv)
int argc;
char *argv[];
{
    FILE *fp;

    /*check command line arguments*/
    if (argc == 1) {
        printf("Command line error. ");
        printf("No file name specified\n");
        return(0);
    } else {
        fp = fopen(argv[1],"r");
        if (fp == NULL) {
            printf("Command line error. ");
            printf("Cannot open file: %s\n",argv[1]);
            return(0);
        }
    }

    /*initialize exception file pointer*/
#ifdef BSHAM
    sy_excfilp = stdout;
#else
    sy_excfilp = fopen(SY_EXCFIL,"a");
#endif

    am_s_init();
    tk_s_init();
    ld_s_init();
    ex_s_init();

    if (ld_sg_load(fp) == LD_NORMAL) {
#ifdef ISHAM
        /*initialize curses*/
        initscr();

        /*initialize keyboard and screen handling*/
        ki_s_init();
        sg_s_init();
        ss_s_init();
```

```
                sd_s_init();
#endif


                ex_s_exec();

#ifdef ISHAM
                /*terminate keyboard and screen handling*/
                ss_s_end();
                ki_s_end();

                /*terminate curses*/
                endwin();
#endif
        }

#ifdef ISHAM
        /*close exception file*/
        fclose(sy_excfilp);
#endif
        return(0);
}
```

E.1.4.2   Default exception handlers

There are no exceptions for *sham*.

E.1.5   *token* MI

E.1.5.1   Module implementation: token.c

```
#include <ctype.h>
#include "system.h"
#include "token.h"


/*****constants*****/

/*****types*****/

/*****module state*****/

static char buf[TK_MAXSTRLEN+2]; /*scanned string; space for sentinel*/
static int cur; /*current char in buf*/

/*****local functions*****/

/*****access routines*****/

void tk_s_init()
```

```
{
     buf[0] = '\0';
     cur = 0;
}

void tk_s_str(s)
char *s;
{
     if (strlen(s) > TK_MAXSTRLEN) {
          tk_maxlen();
          return;
     }
     while (*s == ' ') /*skip over leading blanks*/
          s++;
     strcpy(buf,s); /*copy in what remains*/
     if (*s != '\0')
          strcat(buf," "); /*add trailing blank as sentinel*/
     cur = 0;
}

void tk_sg_next(valtyp)
tk_valtyp *valtyp;
{
     enum {START,INT,ID,ERR,END} state; /*lexical analyzer state*/
     int tokstart,tokend,toklen;
     int i;

     if (buf[cur] == '\0') {
          tk_end();
          valtyp->val[0] = '\0';
          valtyp->typ = TK_BADTOK;
          return;
     }
     tokstart = cur; /*needed later to save value of token*/
     state = START;
     while (state != END) {
          switch (state) {
          case START:
               if (isalpha(buf[cur])) {
                    state = ID;
                    cur++;
               } else if (isdigit(buf[cur])) {
                    state = INT;
                    cur++;
               } else {
                    state = ERR;
                    cur++;
               }
```

```
                    break;
            case ID:
                if (buf[cur] == ' ') {
                    state = END;
                    tokend = cur-1;
                    valtyp->typ = TK_ID;
                } else if (isalnum(buf[cur]))
                    cur++;
                else {
                    state = ERR;
                    cur++;
                }
                break;
            case INT:
                if (buf[cur] == ' ') {
                    state = END;
                    tokend = cur-1;
                    valtyp->typ = TK_INT;
                } else if (isdigit(buf[cur]))
                    cur++;
                else {
                    state = ERR;
                    cur++;
                }
                break;
            case ERR:
                if (buf[cur] == ' ') {
                    state = END;
                    tokend = cur-1;
                    valtyp->typ = TK_BADTOK;
                } else
                    ++cur;
                break;
        }
    }
    /*check maximum lengths*/
    switch (valtyp->typ) {
    case TK_ID:
        if (tokend-tokstart+1 > TK_MAXIDLEN)
            valtyp->typ = TK_BADTOK;
        break;
    case TK_INT:
        if (tokend-tokstart+1 > TK_MAXINTLEN)
            valtyp->typ = TK_BADTOK;
        break;
    }
    /*copy token to valtyp*/
    toklen = tokend-tokstart+1;
```

```
    for (i = 0; i < toklen; i++)
        valtyp->val[i] = buf[tokstart+i];
    valtyp->val[toklen] = '\0';
    /*skip over blanks preceding next token*/
    while (buf[cur] == ' ')
        cur++;
}


/*boolean*/ int tk_g_end()
{
    return(buf[cur] == '\0');
}


void tk_g_dump()
{
    printf("cur=%d!\n",cur);
    printf("buf=!%s!\n",buf);
}
```

E.1.5.2 Default exception handlers: token_e.c

```
#include "system.h"
#include "token.h"


void tk_maxlen()
{
    fprintf(sy_excfilp,"Exception tk_maxlen occurred\n");
}


void tk_end()
{
    fprintf(sy_excfilp,"Exception tk_end occurred\n");
}
```

E.2 ISHAM Modules

E.2.1 *keybdin* MI

E.2.1.1 Module implementation: keybdin.c

```
#include <curses.h>
#include "system.h"
#include "keybdin.h"


/*****constants*****/


/*****types*****/
```

```
/*****module state*****/

/*****local functions*****/

/*****access routines*****/

void ki_s_init()
{
    cbreak();
    noecho();
}

char ki_sg_next()
{
    return(getch());
}

void ki_s_end()
{
    echo();
    nocbreak();
}
```

E.2.1.2   Default exception handlers

There are no exceptions for *keybdin*.

E.2.2   *scndr* MI

E.2.2.1   Module implementation: scndr.c

```
#include "system.h"
#include "absmach.h"
#include "scngeom.h"
#include "scnstr.h"
#include "scndr.h"

/*****constants*****/

/*****types*****/

/*****module state*****/

/*****local functions*****/

#define FLD(f,t,r,c) (f.nam = t, f.row = r, f.col = c)

/*print constant field with fieldname t, row r, and column c*/
```

```
static void prtcon(t,r,c)
sg_fldnam t;
int r,c;
{
    sg_fld f;

    FLD(f,t,r,c);
    ss_s_str(sg_g_row(f),sg_g_col(f),sg_g_val(f));
}

/*pad s on the left with blanks to length l
*     truncate s to l if longer than l
*/
static void rjust(s,l)
char *s;
int l;
{
    int shift;

    s[l] = '\0';
    shift = l-strlen(s);
    while (--l >= shift)
        s[l] = s[l-shift];
    while (l >= 0)
        s[l--] = ' ';
}

/*pad s on the right with blanks to length l
*     truncate s to l if longer than l
*/
static void ljust(s,l)
char *s;
int l;
{
    int i;

    for (i = strlen(s); i < l; i++)
        s[i] = ' ';
    s[l] = '\0';
}

/*****access routines*****/

void sd_s_init()
{
    /*do nothing*/
}
```

```
void sd_s_clrscn()
{
    ss_s_clrscn();
    ss_s_ref();
}

void sd_s_con()
{
    int i;

    prtcon(SG_SCNTTL,0,0);
    prtcon(SG_MEMTTL1,0,0);
    prtcon(SG_MEMTTL2,0,0);
    for (i = 0; i < 10; i++) {
        prtcon(SG_MEMCOLHDR,0,i);
        prtcon(SG_MEMROWHDR,i,0);
    }
    prtcon(SG_PCTTL,0,0);
    prtcon(SG_ACCTTL,0,0);
    prtcon(SG_PRTTTL,0,0);
    prtcon(SG_PROMPTTTL,0,0);
    prtcon(SG_MSGTTL,0,0);
    ss_s_ref();
}

void sd_s_mem()
{
    sg_fld f;
    int r,c;
    char s[SG_NUMCOL+1];

    for (r = 0; r < 10; r++) {
        for (c = 0; c < 10; c++) {
            FLD(f,SG_MEM,r,c);
            sprintf(s,"%d",am_g_mem(10*r+c));
            rjust(s,sg_g_len(f));
            ss_s_str(sg_g_row(f),sg_g_col(f),s);
        }
    }
    ss_s_ref();
}

void sd_s_pc()
{
    sg_fld f;
    char s[SG_NUMCOL+1];

    FLD(f,SG_PC,0,0);
```

```
      sprintf(s,"%d",am_g_pc());
      rjust(s,sg_g_len(f));
      ss_s_str(sg_g_row(f),sg_g_col(f),s);
      ss_s_ref();
}

void sd_s_acc()
{
      sg_fld f;
      char s[SG_NUMCOL+1];

      FLD(f,SG_ACC,0,0);
      sprintf(s,"%d",am_g_acc());
      rjust(s,sg_g_len(f));
      ss_s_str(sg_g_row(f),sg_g_col(f),s);
      ss_s_ref();
}

void sd_s_prt(val)
int val;
{
      sg_fld f;
      char s[SG_NUMCOL+1];

      FLD(f,SG_PRT,0,0);
      sprintf(s,"%d",val);
      rjust(s,sg_g_len(f));
      ss_s_str(sg_g_row(f),sg_g_col(f),s);
      ss_s_ref();
}

void sd_s_msg(msg)
char *msg;
{
      sg_fld f;
      char s[SG_NUMCOL+1];

      FLD(f,SG_MSG,0,0);
      strcpy(s,msg);
      ljust(s,sg_g_len(f));
      ss_s_str(sg_g_row(f),sg_g_col(f),s);
      ss_s_ref();
}

void sd_s_hlt(a,f)
int a,f;
{
      sg_fld fld;
```

```
        FLD(fld,SG_MEM,a/10,a%10);
        ss_s_hlt(sg_g_row(fld),sg_g_col(fld),sg_g_len(fld),f);
        ss_s_ref();
}
```

E.2.2.2   Default exception handlers

There are no exceptions for *scndr*.

E.2.3   *scngeom* MI

E.2.3.1   Module implementation: scngeom.c

```
#include "system.h"
#include "scngeom.h"


/*****constants*****/


/*NOTE: because the variable below is initialized and never changed
 *it is listed as a constant.
 */

static struct {
        int row,col,len;
        char *val;
} fldtbl[] = {
        /*SG_MEM*/           {5,15,3,""},
        /*SG_PC*/         {17,45,2,""},
        /*SG_ACC*/           {18,44,3,""},
        /*SG_PRT*/           {19,44,3,""},
        /*SG_MSG*/           {23,9,63,""},

        /*SG_SCNTTL*/        {0,33,4,"SHAM"},
        /*SG_MEMTTL1*/       {5,0,4,"Main"},
        /*SG_MEMTTL2*/       {6,0,7,"memory:"},
        /*SG_MEMCOLHDR*/     {3,15,3,""},    /*depends on row*/
        /*SG_MEMROWHDR*/     {5,9,3,""},     /*depends on column*/
        /*SG_PCTTL*/         {17,24,19,"   Program counter:"},
        /*SG_ACCTTL*/        {18,24,19,"       Accumulator:"},
        /*SG_PRTTTL*/        {19,24,19,"Last value printed:"},
        /*SG_PROMPTTTL*/     {22,0,46,
            "Enter command: \"s\" to single step; \"e\" to exit"},
        /*SG_MSGTTL*/        {23,0,8,"Message:"}
};


/*****types*****/
```

```
/*****module state*****/

/*****local functions*****/

/*out := (fld is a legal field identifier)*/
static int legfld(fld)
sg_fld fld;
{
    int maxrow,maxcol;

    if (fld.nam == SG_MEM || fld.nam == SG_MEMROWHDR)
        maxrow = 9;
    else
        maxrow = 0;
    if (fld.nam == SG_MEM || fld.nam == SG_MEMCOLHDR)
        maxcol = 9;
    else
        maxcol = 0;
    return(
        (int)fld.nam >= 0 && (int)fld.nam <= (int)SG_MSGTTL &&
        fld.row >= 0 && fld.row <= maxrow &&
        fld.col >= 0 && fld.col <= maxcol
    );
}

/*****access routines*****/

void sg_s_init()
{
    /*do nothing*/
}

int sg_g_legfld(fld)
sg_fld fld;
{
    return(legfld(fld));
}

int sg_g_row(fld)
sg_fld fld;
{
    if (!legfld(fld)) {
        sg_badfld();
        return(0);
    }
    return(fldtbl[(int)fld.nam].row+fld.row);
}
```

```
int sg_g_col(fld)
sg_fld fld;
{
     if (!legfld(fld)) {
          sg_badfld();
          return(0);
     }
     return(fldtbl[(int)fld.nam].col+fld.col*6);
}


int sg_g_len(fld)
sg_fld fld;
{
     if (!legfld(fld)) {
          sg_badfld();
          return(0);
     }
     return(fldtbl[(int)fld.nam].len);
}

char *sg_g_val(fld)
sg_fld fld;
{
     char str[4];

     if (!legfld(fld)) {
          sg_badfld();
          return(NULL);
     }
     if (fld.nam == SG_MEMCOLHDR) {
          sprintf(str,"%3d",fld.col);
          return(str);
     } else if (fld.nam == SG_MEMROWHDR) {
          sprintf(str,"%3d",10*fld.row);
          return(str);
     }
     return(fldtbl[(int)fld.nam].val);
}
```

E.2.3.2   Default exception handlers: scngeom_e.c

```
#include "system.h"
#include "scngeom.h"

void sg_badfld()
{
     fprintf(sy_excfilp,"Exception sg_badfld occurred\n");
}
```

E.2.4   *scnstr* MI

E.2.4.1   Module implementation: `scnstr.c`

```
#include <curses.h>
#include "system.h"
#include "scnstr.h"

/*****constants*****/

/*****types*****/

/*****module state*****/

/*****local functions*****/

/*instr(r,c,l,s)
*     load into s the string at positions (r,c) thru (r,c+l-1)
*/
static void instr(r,c,l,s)
int r,c,l;
char *s;
{
     int i;

     for (i = 0; i < l; i++) {
          move(r,c+i);
          s[i] = inch();
     }
     s[l] = '\0';
}


/*****access routines*****/

void ss_s_init()
{
     /*do nothing*/
}

void ss_s_clrscn()
{
     clear();
}

void ss_s_str(r,c,s)
int r,c;
char *s;
{
     if (r < 0 || r >= SS_NUMROW) {
```

```
            ss_row();
            return;
        } else if (c < 0 || c >= SS_NUMCOL) {
            ss_col();
            return;
        } else if (strlen(s) > SS_NUMCOL-c) {
            ss_len();
            return;
        }
        if (strlen(s) > 0) { /*handle the 0-length case neutrally*/
            move(r,c);
            addstr(s);
        }
}

void ss_s_hlt(r,c,l,f)
int r,c,l,f;
{
        char s[SS_NUMCOL+1];

        if (r < 0 || r >= SS_NUMROW) {
            ss_row();
            return;
        } else if (c < 0 || c >= SS_NUMCOL) {
            ss_col();
            return;
        } else if (l < 0 || l > SS_NUMCOL-c) {
            ss_len();
            return;
        }
        if (l > 0) {
            instr(r,c,l,s);
            if (f) {
                standout();
                move(r,c);
                addstr(s);
                standend();
            } else {
                move(r,c);
                addstr(s);
            }
        }
}

void ss_s_cur(r,c)
int r,c;
{
    if (r < 0 || r >= SS_NUMROW) {
```

```
        ss_row();
        return;
    } else if (c < 0 || c >= SS_NUMCOL) {
        ss_col();
        return;
    }
    move(r,c);
}

void ss_s_ref()
{
    refresh();
}

void ss_s_end()
{
    /*do nothing*/
}
```

E.2.4.2   Default exception handlers: scnstr_e.c

```
#include "system.h"
#include "scnstr.h"

void ss_row()
{
    fprintf(sy_excfilp,"Exception ss_row occurred\n");
}

void ss_col()
{
    fprintf(sy_excfilp,"Exception ss_col occurred\n");
}

void ss_len()
{
    fprintf(sy_excfilp,"Exception ss_len occurred\n");
}
```

E.3   Demonstration Modules

E.3.1   *stack* MI

E.3.1.1   Module implementation: stack.c

```
#include "system.h"
#include "stack.h"
```

```c
/*****constants*****/

/*****types*****/

/*****module state*****/

static int stack[PS_MAXSIZ]; /*stack elements*/
static int siz; /*number of elements in stack*/

/*****local functions*****/

/*****access routines*****/

void ps_s_init()
{
    siz = 0;
}

void ps_s_push(x)
int x;
{
    if (siz == PS_MAXSIZ) {
        ps_full();
        return;
    }
    stack[siz++] = x;
}

void ps_s_pop()
{
    if (siz == 0) {
        ps_empty();
        return;
    }
    --siz;
}

int ps_g_top()
{
    if (siz == 0) {
        ps_empty();
        return(0);
    }
    return(stack[siz-1]);
}

int ps_g_depth()
{
```

```
      return(siz);
}

void ps_g_dump()
{
      int i;

      printf("siz=%d\n",siz);
      for (i = 0; i < siz; i++)
          printf("stack[%d]=%d\n",i,stack[i]);
}
```

E.3.1.2 Default exception handlers: stack_e.c

```
#include "system.h"
#include "stack.h"

void ps_empty()
{
      fprintf(sy_excfilp,"Exception ps_empty occurred\n");
}

void ps_full()
{
      fprintf(sy_excfilp,"Exception ps_full occurred\n");
}
```

E.3.2 *symtbl* MI

E.3.2.1 Module implementation: symtbl.c

```
#include "system.h"
#include "symtbl.h"

/*****constants*****/

#define NOTFOUND -1

/*****types*****/

/*****module state*****/

static struct {
      char sym[ST_MAXSYMLEN+1]; /*symbol value*/
      int loc; /*symbol location*/
} tbl[ST_MAXSYMS]; /*one entry per symbol*/

static int tblcnt; /*number of symbols in tbl*/
```

```
/*****local functions*****/

/*out := (state invariant holds =>
            ((exists i in [0,tblcnt-1])(s = tbl[i].sym)) => i
            | true => NOTFOUND))
*/
static int findsym(sym)
char *sym;

{
    int i;

    for (i = 0; i < tblcnt; i++) {
        if (!strcmp(sym,tbl[i].sym))
            return(i);
    }
    return(NOTFOUND);
}

/*****access routines*****/

void st_s_init()
{
    tblcnt = 0;
}

void st_s_add(sym,loc)
char *sym;
int loc;
{
    if (strlen(sym) > ST_MAXSYMLEN) {
        st_maxlen();
        return;
    } else if (findsym(sym) != NOTFOUND) {
        st_exsym();
        return;
    } else if (tblcnt == ST_MAXSYMS) {
        st_full();
        return;
    }
    strcpy(tbl[tblcnt].sym,sym);
    tbl[tblcnt].loc = loc;
    tblcnt++;
}

int st_g_exsym(sym)
char *sym;
{
```

```
    return(findsym(sym) != NOTFOUND);
}

void st_s_loc(sym,loc)
char *sym;
int loc;
{
    int i;

    i = findsym(sym);
    if (i == NOTFOUND) {
        st_notexsym();
        return;
    }
    tbl[i].loc = loc;
}

int st_g_loc(sym)
char *sym;
{
    int i;

    i = findsym(sym);
    if (i == NOTFOUND) {
        st_notexsym();
        return(0);
    }
    return(tbl[i].loc);
}

int st_g_siz()
{
    return(tblcnt);
}

void st_g_dump()
{
    int i;

    printf ("tblcnt=%d!ST_MAXSYMS=%d!\n",tblcnt,ST_MAXSYMS);
    for (i = 0; i < tblcnt; i++)
        printf("tbl[%d].sym=%s!.loc=%d\n",i,tbl[i].sym,tbl[i].loc);
}
```

E.3.2.2 Default exception handlers: symtbl_e.c

```
#include "system.h"
#include "symtbl.h"
```

```
void st_exsym()
{
    fprintf(sy_excfilp,"Exception st_exsym occurred\n");
}

void st_maxlen()
{
    fprintf(sy_excfilp,"Exception st_maxlen occurred\n");
}

void st_notexsym()
{
    fprintf(sy_excfilp,"Exception st_notexsym occurred\n");
}

void st_full()
{
    fprintf(sy_excfilp,"Exception st_full occurred\n");
}
```

Appendix F

Test Plans and Implementations

F.1 BSHAM Modules

F.1.1 *absmach* TP and TI

F.1.1.1 Test plan

assumptions
> AM_MEMSIZ > 2
> AM_MAXINT $\geq 2 \times$ AM_MEMSIZ

test environment
> PGMGEN driver
> no stubs

test case selection strategy
> special values
> > module state
> > > based of content of *mem*, *pc*, and *acc*, test for:
> > > run-time exceptions
> > > > all exceptions for all instructions at least once
> > >
> > > AM_HALT
> > > > *HALT* instruction with $pc \in \{0, \text{AM\_MEMSIZ} - 1\}$
> > >
> > > AM_PRINT
> > > > *PRINT* instruction with $pc \in \{0, \text{AM\_MEMSIZ} - 1\}$
> > >
> > > AM_NORMAL
> > > > all instructions with one operand and $pc = \text{AM\_MEMSIZ} - 2$
> > > > all instructions with address argument:
> > > > > interval rule on address: $[0, \text{AM\_MEMSIZ}]$
> > > >
> > > > each instruction at least once

> access routine parameters
>> am_s_acc(i), am_s_pc(a), am_s_mem(a, i), and am_g_mem(a):
>>> interval rule for a: $[0, \text{AM\_MEMSIZ}]$
>>> interval rule for i: $[0, \text{AM\_MAXINT}]$
> test cases
>> exceptions
>>> am_s_mem and am_g_mem
>>>> generate am_addr
>>> am_s_acc, am_s_pc, and am_s_mem
>>>> generate am_int
>> normal case
>>> am_s_acc and am_g_acc
>>>> am_g_acc after am_s_init and after am_s_acc
>>> am_s_pc and am_g_pc
>>>> am_g_pc after am_s_init and after am_s_pc
>>> am_s_mem and am_g_mem
>>>> am_g_mem after am_s_init and after am_s_mem
>>> am_sg_exec
>>>> all special module states
>>>> in each case, check *pc* and *acc* afterwards
>>>> for commands that alter *mem*, check *mem* afterwards

test implementation strategy
> statement coverage measured using the UNIX utility *tcov*

F.1.1.2   Test implementation

PGMGEN script: `absmach.script`

```
module
    am_

accprogs
    <s_init,s_acc,g_acc,s_pc,g_pc,s_mem,g_mem,sg_exec>

exceptions
    <addr,int>

globcod
{%
#include "system.h"
#include "absmach.h"

int cmd;
%}


cases

/*****exceptions*****/
```

```
/*addr*/
<s_init().s_pc(-1000), addr, dc, dc, dc>
<s_init().s_pc(-1), addr, dc, dc, dc>
<s_init().s_pc(AM_MEMSIZ), addr, dc, dc, dc>
<s_init().s_pc(2*AM_MEMSIZ), addr, dc, dc, dc>
<s_init().s_mem(-1000,0), addr, dc, dc, dc>
<s_init().s_mem(-1,0), addr, dc, dc, dc>
<s_init().s_mem(AM_MEMSIZ,0), addr, dc, dc, dc>
<s_init().s_mem(2*AM_MEMSIZ,0), addr, dc, dc, dc>
<s_init().g_mem(-1000), addr, dc, dc, dc>
<s_init().g_mem(-1), addr, dc, dc, dc>
<s_init().g_mem(AM_MEMSIZ), addr, dc, dc, dc>
<s_init().g_mem(2*AM_MEMSIZ), addr, dc, dc, dc>

/*int*/
<s_init().s_acc(-1000), int, dc, dc, dc>
<s_init().s_acc(-1), int, dc, dc, dc>
<s_init().s_acc(AM_MAXINT+1), int, dc, dc, dc>
<s_init().s_acc(2*AM_MAXINT), int, dc, dc, dc>
<s_init().s_mem(0,-1000), int, dc, dc, dc>
<s_init().s_mem(0,-1), int, dc, dc, dc>
<s_init().s_mem(0,AM_MAXINT+1), int, dc, dc, dc>
<s_init().s_mem(0,2*AM_MAXINT), int, dc, dc, dc>

/*****normal case*****/
/*s_acc and g_acc*/
<s_init(), noexc, g_acc(), 0, int>
<s_init().s_acc(0), noexc, g_acc(), 0, int>
<s_init().s_acc(AM_MAXINT/2), noexc, g_acc(), AM_MAXINT/2, int>
<s_init().s_acc(AM_MAXINT), noexc, g_acc(), AM_MAXINT, int>

/*s_pc and g_pc*/
<s_init(), noexc, g_pc(), 0, int>
<s_init().s_pc(0), noexc, g_pc(), 0, int>
<s_init().s_pc(AM_MEMSIZ/2), noexc, g_pc(), AM_MEMSIZ/2, int>
<s_init().s_pc(AM_MEMSIZ-1), noexc, g_pc(), AM_MEMSIZ-1, int>

/*s_mem and g_mem*/
<s_init(), noexc, g_mem(0), 0, int>
<s_init(), noexc, g_mem(AM_MEMSIZ/2), 0, int>
<s_init(), noexc, g_mem(AM_MEMSIZ-1), 0, int>
<s_init().s_mem(0,0), noexc, g_mem(0), 0, int>
<s_init().s_mem(0,AM_MAXINT/2), noexc, g_mem(0), AM_MAXINT/2, int>
<s_init().s_mem(0,AM_MAXINT), noexc, g_mem(0), AM_MAXINT, int>
<s_init().s_mem(AM_MEMSIZ/2,3), noexc, g_mem(AM_MEMSIZ/2), 3, int>
<s_init().s_mem(AM_MEMSIZ-1,3), noexc, g_mem(AM_MEMSIZ-1), 3, int>

/*sg_exec: run-time exceptions*/
```

```
<s_init.s_mem(0,10), noexc, sg_exec(), AM_OBJECTEXC, int>
<s_init.s_mem(0,AM_MAXINT), noexc, sg_exec(), AM_OBJECTEXC, int>

{% for (cmd = 0; cmd <= 7; cmd++) %}
    <s_init.s_pc(AM_MEMSIZ-1).s_mem(AM_MEMSIZ-1,cmd),
        noexc, sg_exec(), AM_NOOPEXC, int>

{% for (cmd = 0; cmd <= 6; cmd++) { %}
    <s_init.s_mem(0,cmd).s_mem(1,AM_MEMSIZ),
        noexc, sg_exec(), AM_ADDREXC, int>
    <s_init.s_mem(0,cmd).s_mem(1,2*AM_MEMSIZ),
        noexc, sg_exec(), AM_ADDREXC, int>
{% } %}

<s_init.s_mem(0,SY_ADD).s_mem(1,2).s_mem(2,1).s_acc(AM_MAXINT),
    noexc, sg_exec(), AM_ARITHEXC, int>
<s_init.s_mem(0,SY_ADD).s_mem(1,2).s_mem(2,AM_MAXINT).s_acc(1),
    noexc, sg_exec(), AM_ARITHEXC, int>
<s_init.s_mem(0,SY_ADD).s_mem(1,2).s_mem(2,AM_MAXINT).
    s_acc(AM_MAXINT), noexc, sg_exec(), AM_ARITHEXC, int>

<s_init.s_mem(0,SY_SUBTRACT).s_mem(1,2).s_mem(2,1).s_acc(0),
    noexc, sg_exec(), AM_ARITHEXC, int>
<s_init.s_mem(0,SY_SUBTRACT).s_mem(1,2).s_mem(2,AM_MAXINT).
    s_acc(AM_MAXINT-1), noexc, sg_exec(), AM_ARITHEXC, int>
<s_init.s_mem(0,SY_SUBTRACT).s_mem(1,2).s_mem(2,AM_MAXINT).
    s_acc(0), noexc, sg_exec(), AM_ARITHEXC, int>

/*sg_exec: AM_HALT*/
<s_init().s_mem(0,SY_HALT), noexc, sg_exec(), AM_HALT, int>
< , noexc, g_pc(), 0, int>
< , noexc, g_acc(), 0, int>
<s_init().s_pc(AM_MEMSIZ-1).s_mem(AM_MEMSIZ-1,SY_HALT),
    noexc, sg_exec(), AM_HALT, int>
< , noexc, g_pc(), AM_MEMSIZ-1, int>
< , noexc, g_acc(), 0, int>

/*sg_exec: AM_PRINT*/
<s_init().s_mem(0,SY_PRINT), noexc, sg_exec(), AM_PRINT, int>
< , noexc, g_pc(), 1, int>
< , noexc, g_acc(), 0, int>
<s_init().s_pc(AM_MEMSIZ-1).s_mem(AM_MEMSIZ-1,SY_PRINT),
    noexc, sg_exec(), AM_PRINT, int>
< , noexc, g_pc(), 0, int>
< , noexc, g_acc(), 0, int>

/*sg_exec: AM_NORMAL*/
/*maximal pc*/
```

```
{% for (cmd = 0; cmd <= 7; cmd++) { %}
    <s_init().s_pc(AM_MEMSIZ-2).s_mem(AM_MEMSIZ-2,cmd),
        noexc, sg_exec(), AM_NORMAL, int>
    < ,noexc, g_pc(), 0, int>
{% } %}

/*full range of addresses*/
{% for (cmd = 0; cmd <= 6; cmd++) { %}
    <s_init().s_pc(1).s_mem(1,cmd).s_mem(2,0),
        noexc, sg_exec(), AM_NORMAL, int>
    <s_init().s_mem(0,cmd).s_mem(1,AM_MEMSIZ/2),
        noexc, sg_exec(), AM_NORMAL, int>
    <s_init().s_mem(0,cmd).s_mem(1,AM_MEMSIZ-1),
        noexc, sg_exec(), AM_NORMAL, int>
{% } %}

/*load*/
<s_init().s_mem(0,SY_LOAD).s_mem(1,2).s_mem(2,7),
    noexc, sg_exec(), AM_NORMAL, int>
< , noexc, g_pc(), 2, int>
< , noexc, g_acc(), 7, int>

/*store*/
<s_init().s_mem(0,SY_STORE).s_mem(1,2).s_acc(7),
    noexc, sg_exec(), AM_NORMAL, int>
< , noexc, g_pc(), 2, int>
< , noexc, g_acc(), 7, int>
< , noexc, g_mem(2), 7, int>

/*add*/
<s_init().s_mem(0,SY_ADD).s_mem(1,2).s_mem(2,AM_MAXINT-7).s_acc(7),
    noexc, sg_exec(), AM_NORMAL, int>
< , noexc, g_pc(), 2, int>
< , noexc, g_acc(), AM_MAXINT, int>

/*subtract*/
<s_init().s_mem(0,SY_SUBTRACT).s_mem(1,2).s_mem(2,7).s_acc(7),
    noexc, sg_exec(), AM_NORMAL, int>
< , noexc, g_pc(), 2, int>
< , noexc, g_acc(), 0, int>

/*branch*/
<s_init().s_mem(0,SY_BRANCH).s_mem(1,7), noexc, sg_exec(), AM_NORMAL, int>
< , noexc, g_pc(), 7, int>
< , noexc, g_acc(), 0, int>

/*branchzero*/
<s_init().s_mem(0,SY_BRANCHZERO).s_mem(1,7),
```

```
        noexc, sg_exec(), AM_NORMAL, int>
< , noexc, g_pc(), 7, int>
< , noexc, g_acc(), 0, int>
<s_init().s_mem(0,SY_BRANCHZERO).s_mem(1,7).s_acc(1),
        noexc, sg_exec(), AM_NORMAL, int>
< , noexc, g_pc(), 2, int>
< , noexc, g_acc(), 1, int>


/*branchpos*/
<s_init().s_mem(0,SY_BRANCHPOS).s_mem(1,7),
        noexc, sg_exec(), AM_NORMAL, int>
< , noexc, g_pc(), 2, int>
< , noexc, g_acc(), 0, int>
<s_init().s_mem(0,SY_BRANCHPOS).s_mem(1,7).s_acc(1),
        noexc, sg_exec(), AM_NORMAL, int>
< , noexc, g_pc(), 7, int>
< , noexc, g_acc(), 1, int>


/*loadcon*/
<s_init().s_mem(0,SY_LOADCON).s_mem(1,7),
        noexc, sg_exec(), AM_NORMAL, int>
< , noexc, g_pc(), 2, int>
< , noexc, g_acc(), 7, int>
```

Interactive driver: `absmach_i.c`

```c
#include "system.h"
#include "absmach.h"

#define QUIT 0
#define S_INIT 1
#define S_PC 2
#define G_PC 3
#define S_ACC 4
#define G_ACC 5
#define S_MEM 6
#define G_MEM 7
#define SG_EXEC 8
#define G_DUMP 9

#define BUFLEN 80

FILE *sy_excfilp = stderr;

int nextcall()
{
    int reply;
    char s[81];
```

```
      do {
            printf("\nEnter command:\n");
            printf("\t0:quit\n");
            printf("\t1:s_init\n");
            printf("\t2:s_pc\n");
            printf("\t3:g_pc\n");
            printf("\t4:s_acc\n");
            printf("\t5:g_acc\n");
            printf("\t6:s_mem\n");
            printf("\t7:g_mem\n");
            printf("\t8:sg_exec\n");
            printf("\t9:g_dump:");
            gets(s);
            if (sscanf(s,"%d",&reply) != 1)
                  reply = -1; /*user error - stay in loop*/;
      } while (reply < 0 || reply > G_DUMP);
      return(reply);
}

int readint(msg)
char *msg;
{
      int reply,found;
      char s[BUFLEN];

      found = 0;
      while (!found) {
            printf(msg);
            gets(s);
            if (sscanf(s,"%d",&reply) == 1)
                  found = 1;
      }
      return (reply);
}

main()
{
      int reply,i1,i2;

      while ((reply=nextcall()) != QUIT) {
            switch(reply) {
            case S_INIT:
                  am_s_init();
                  break;
            case S_PC:
                  i1 = readint("Enter pc:");
                  am_s_pc(i1);
```

```
            break;
       case G_PC:
            i1 = am_g_pc();
            printf("returns %d\n",i1);
            break;
       case S_ACC:
            i1 = readint("Enter acc:");
            am_s_acc(i1);
            break;
       case G_ACC:
            i1 = am_g_acc();
            printf("returns %d\n",i1);
            break;
       case S_MEM:
            i1 = readint("Enter addr:");
            i2 = readint("Enter val:");
            am_s_mem(i1,i2);
            break;
       case G_MEM:
            i1 = readint("Enter addr:");
            i2 = am_g_mem(i1);
            printf("returns %d\n",i2);
            break;
       case SG_EXEC:
            i1 = (int)am_sg_exec();
            printf("returns %d\n",i1);
            break;
       case G_DUMP:
            am_g_dump();
            break;
       }
    }
    return(0);
}
```

F.1.2   *exec* TP

F.1.2.1   Test plan

assumptions

test environment

test case selection strategy

test implementation strategy

considerations
    exec testing performed during SHAM system testing

F.1.3 *load* TP and TI

F.1.3.1   Test plan

assumptions
>   AM_MAXINT = 999
>   AM_MEMSIZ = 100

test environment
>   *sham* Coordinator used as driver
>   stubs for *absmach* and *exec*, production code for *sham* and *token*
>   input stored in files
>   output saved in files, checked with delta testing
>   directory structure:
>>   load/
>>>   input/ - test cases stored one per file
>>>   exp/ - expected results of test case (same file name)
>>>   act/ - actual results of test case (same file name)

test case selection strategy
>   special values
>>   module state
>>>   none
>>   access routine parameters
>>>   input file for ld_sg_load:
>>>>   every load-time exception for every instruction
>>>>   every SHAM instruction at least once
>>>>>   interval rule for instructions with an operand
>>>>   completely fill up memory
>   test cases
>>   load-time exceptions
>>>   ldexc1: all load-time exceptions except *NOMEMEXC*
>>>   ldexc2: *NOMEMEXC*
>>   normal case
>>>   instr: every SHAM instruction
>>>   fill: completely fill up memory

test implementation strategy
>   stubs print out name and parameters of access routines
>   target runtest in Makefile
>>   for each file *f* in input/
>>>   bsham *f* >act/*f*
>>>   diff act/*f* exp/*f*
>   statement coverage measured using the UNIX utility *tcov*

F.1.3.2   Test implementation

absmach **stubs:** absmach_s.c

```
#include "system.h"
```

```
#include "absmach.h"

/*****module state*****/
static int mem[AM_MEMSIZ];

/*****access routines*****/

void am_s_init()
{
}

void am_s_mem(a,i)
int a,i;
{
    mem[a] = i;
}

int am_g_mem(a)
int a;
{
    return(mem[a]);
}
```

exec **stubs: exec_s.c**

```
#include "system.h"
#include "absmach.h"
#include "exec.h"

/*****access routines*****/

void ex_s_init()
{
}

void ex_s_exec()
{
    int i;

    for (i = 0; i < AM_MEMSIZ; i++) {
        printf("%4d",am_g_mem(i));
        if (i % 10 == 9)
            printf("\n");
    }
}
```

Input file: `input/fill`

```
store 2
store 2
store 2
store 2
store 2
store 2
store 2
store 2
store 2
store 2
store 2
store 2
store 2
store 2
store 2
store 2
store 2
store 2
store 2
store 2
store 2
store 2
store 2
store 2
store 2
store 2
store 2
store 2
store 2
store 2
store 2
store 2
store 2
store 2
store 2
store 2
store 2
store 2
store 2
store 2
store 2
store 2
store 2
store 2
store 2
store 2
store 2
store 2
```

```
store 2
store 2
store 2
```

Expected output: exp/fill

```
1   2   1   2   1   2   1   2   1   2
1   2   1   2   1   2   1   2   1   2
1   2   1   2   1   2   1   2   1   2
1   2   1   2   1   2   1   2   1   2
1   2   1   2   1   2   1   2   1   2
1   2   1   2   1   2   1   2   1   2
1   2   1   2   1   2   1   2   1   2
1   2   1   2   1   2   1   2   1   2
1   2   1   2   1   2   1   2   1   2
1   2   1   2   1   2   1   2   1   2
```

Input file: input/instr

```
load 0
load 50
load 99
store 0
store 50
store 99
add 0
add 50
add 99
sub 0
sub 50
sub 99
br 0
br 50
br 99
brz 0
brz 50
brz 99
brp 0
brp 50
brp 99
loadcon 0
loadcon 500
loadcon 999
print
halt
```

Expected output: exp/instr

```
0    0   0  50   0  99   1    0   1  50
1   99   2   0   2  50   2   99   3   0
3   50   3  99   4   0   4  50   4  99
5    0   5  50   5  99   6    0   6  50
6   99   7   0   7 500   7 999   8   9
0    0   0   0   0   0   0    0   0   0
0    0   0   0   0   0   0    0   0   0
0    0   0   0   0   0   0    0   0   0
0    0   0   0   0   0   0    0   0   0
0    0   0   0   0   0   0    0   0   0
```

Input file: input/ldexc1

```
xxx
load
store
add
sub
br
brz
brp
loadcon
load x
load 100
load 200
store x
store 100
store 200
add x
add 100
add 200
sub x
sub 100
sub 200
br x
br 100
br 200
brz x
brz 100
brz 200
brp x
brp 100
brp 200
loadcon x
loadcon 1000
loadcon 2000
```

Expected output: `exp/ldexc1`

```
Load exception at 1. Blank line illegal
Load exception at 2. Illegal instruction: xxx
Load exception at 3. Operand missing
Load exception at 4. Operand missing
Load exception at 5. Operand missing
Load exception at 6. Operand missing
Load exception at 7. Operand missing
Load exception at 8. Operand missing
Load exception at 9. Operand missing
Load exception at 10. Operand missing
Load exception at 11. Illegal operand: x
Load exception at 12. Illegal operand: 100
Load exception at 13. Illegal operand: 200
Load exception at 14. Illegal operand: x
Load exception at 15. Illegal operand: 100
Load exception at 16. Illegal operand: 200
Load exception at 17. Illegal operand: x
Load exception at 18. Illegal operand: 100
Load exception at 19. Illegal operand: 200
Load exception at 20. Illegal operand: x
Load exception at 21. Illegal operand: 100
Load exception at 22. Illegal operand: 200
Load exception at 23. Illegal operand: x
Load exception at 24. Illegal operand: 100
Load exception at 25. Illegal operand: 200
Load exception at 26. Illegal operand: x
Load exception at 27. Illegal operand: 100
Load exception at 28. Illegal operand: 200
Load exception at 29. Illegal operand: x
Load exception at 30. Illegal operand: 100
Load exception at 31. Illegal operand: 200
Load exception at 32. Illegal operand: x
Load exception at 33. Illegal operand: 1000
Load exception at 34. Illegal operand: 2000
```

Input file: `input/ldexc2`

```
load 0
load 0
load 0
load 0
load 0
load 0
load 0
load 0
load 0
load 0
```

```
load 0
load 0
load 0
load 0
load 0
load 0
load 0
load 0
load 0
load 0
load 0
load 0
load 0
load 0
load 0
load 0
load 0
load 0
load 0
load 0
load 0
load 0
load 0
load 0
load 0
load 0
load 0
load 0
load 0
load 0
load 0
load 0
load 0
load 0
load 0
load 0
load 0
load 0
load 0
load 0
load 0
print
```

Expected output: exp/ldexc2

Load exception at 51. Program too large

F.1.4   *sham* TP

F.1.4.1   Test plan

assumptions

test environment

test case selection strategy

test implementation strategy

considerations
  sham module testing performed during SHAM system testing

F.1.5   *token* TP and TI

F.1.5.1   Test plan

assumptions
  TK_MAXSTRLEN $\geq$ 9
  TK_MAXIDLEN $\geq$ 3
  TK_MAXINTLEN $\geq$ 3

test environment
  PGMGEN driver
  no stubs

test case selection strategy
  special values
    module state
      number of tokens: $\{0, 1, 3\}$
      types of token:
        TK_ID - minimum and maximum length
        TK_INT - minimum and maximum length
        TK_BADTOK -
          overlength TK_ID and TK_INT tokens
          tokens that are "almost" legal TK_ID or TK_INT tokens
    access routine parameters
      tk_s_str(s):
        interval rule on $|s|$: [0, TK_MAXSTRLEN]
        number of blanks before/after tokens: $\{0, 1, 3\}$
  test cases
    exceptions
      tk_s_str
        generate tk_maxlen
      tk_sg_next
        generate tk_end for special number of tokens
    normal

$tk\_s\_str(s)$

        special values $|s|$

        special values number of blanks

            check using tk_sg_next

    special number of tokens

        check using tk_g_end

    special token types

        check token value and type using tk_sg_next

test implementation strategy

$mkvaltyp(v, t)$: returns $\langle v, t \rangle$ as a structure of type **tk_valtyp**

$cmp\_valtyp(a, e)$ and $prt\_valtyp(a, e)$: cmp_ and prt_ functions for tk_valtyp

$mkstring(n)$: returns a string of n *'s

    must be able to return a string much longer than **TK_MAXSTRLEN**

$mkid(n)$: returns a string with one alphabetic by $n - 1$ alphanumerics

$mkint(n)$: returns a string of n digits

statement coverage measured using the UNIX utility *tcov*

F.1.5.2   Test implementation

PGMGEN script: `token.script`

```
module
    tk_

accprogs
    <s_init,s_str,g_end,sg_next>

exceptions
    <end,maxlen>

globcod
{%
#include "system.h"
#include "token.h"

/***tk_valtyp functions: creation; pgmgen cmp_, prt_*/

static tk_valtyp valtyp1,valtyp2;
static tk_valtyp *vtp = &valtyp1;

tk_valtyp *mkvaltyp(val,typ)
char *val;
tk_toktyp typ;
{
    strcpy(valtyp2.val,val);
    valtyp2.typ = typ;
    return(&valtyp2);
}
```

```
int cmp_valtyp(actvtp,expvtp)
tk_valtyp *actvtp,*expvtp;
{
     if (!strcmp(actvtp->val,expvtp->val))
          return(actvtp->typ == expvtp->typ);
     else
          return(0);
}

void prt_valtyp(actvtp,expvtp)
tk_valtyp *actvtp,*expvtp;
{
     printf("Expected value:<%s,%d>. Actual value:<%s,%d>\n",
          expvtp->val,expvtp->typ,actvtp->val,actvtp->typ);
}
static char s[TK_MAXSTRLEN+2];
char *mkstr(n)
int n;
{
     int i;

     for (i = 0; i < n; i++)
          s[i] = '*';
     s[n] = '\0';
     return(s);
}

char *mkid(n)
int n;
{
     int i;

     for (i = 0; i < n; i++)
          s[i] = 'a';
     s[n] = '\0';
     return(s);
}

char *mkint(n)
int n;
{
     int i;

     for (i = 0; i < n; i++)
          s[i] = '9';
     s[n] = '\0';
     return(s);
```

```
}
%}

cases

/*****exceptions*****/
/*maxlen*/
<s_init().s_str(mkstr(TK_MAXSTRLEN+1)), maxlen, dc, dc, dc>
<s_init().s_str(mkstr(2*TK_MAXSTRLEN)), maxlen, dc, dc, dc>


/*end*/
<s_init().sg_next(vtp), end, dc, dc, dc>
<s_init().s_str("").sg_next(vtp), end, dc, dc, dc>
<s_init().s_str("abc").sg_next(vtp).sg_next(vtp), end, dc, dc, dc>
<s_init().s_str("a b c").sg_next(vtp).sg_next(vtp).sg_next(vtp).
    sg_next(vtp), end, dc, dc, dc>


/*****normal case*****/
/*s_str - length of string*/
<s_init().s_str(""), noexc, dc, dc, dc>
<s_init().s_str(mkstr(TK_MAXSTRLEN)), noexc, dc, dc, dc>


/*s_str - blanks before and after token*/
<s_init().s_str("abc").sg_next(vtp),
    noexc, vtp, mkvaltyp("abc",TK_ID), valtyp>
<s_init().s_str(" abc ").sg_next(vtp),
    noexc, vtp, mkvaltyp("abc",TK_ID), valtyp>
<s_init().s_str(" abc").sg_next(vtp),
    noexc, vtp, mkvaltyp("abc",TK_ID), valtyp>
<s_init().s_str("abc ").sg_next(vtp),
    noexc, vtp, mkvaltyp("abc",TK_ID), valtyp>
<s_init().s_str("   abc   ").sg_next(vtp),
    noexc, vtp, mkvaltyp("abc",TK_ID), valtyp>
<s_init().s_str("abc def").sg_next(vtp),
    noexc, vtp, mkvaltyp("abc",TK_ID), valtyp>
<s_init().s_str("abc def").sg_next(vtp).sg_next(vtp),
    noexc, vtp, mkvaltyp("def",TK_ID), valtyp>
<s_init().s_str("abc   def").sg_next(vtp),
    noexc, vtp, mkvaltyp("abc",TK_ID), valtyp>
<s_init().s_str("abc   def").sg_next(vtp).sg_next(vtp),
    noexc, vtp, mkvaltyp("def",TK_ID), valtyp>


/*special number of tokens*/
<s_init(), noexc, g_end(), 1, bool>
<s_init().s_str(""), noexc, g_end(), 1, bool>
<s_init().s_str("abc"), noexc, g_end(), 0, bool>
<s_init().s_str("abc").sg_next(vtp), noexc, g_end(), 1, bool>
<s_init().s_str("a b c").sg_next(vtp).sg_next(vtp),
```

```
        noexc, g_end(), 0, bool>
<s_init().s_str("a b c").sg_next(vtp).sg_next(vtp).sg_next(vtp),
        noexc, g_end(), 1, bool>

/*special token types: TK_ID*/
<s_init().s_str("a").sg_next(vtp),
        noexc, vtp, mkvaltyp("a",TK_ID), valtyp>
<s_init().s_str(mkid(TK_MAXIDLEN)).sg_next(vtp),
        noexc, vtp, mkvaltyp(mkid(TK_MAXIDLEN),TK_ID), valtyp>

/*special token types: TK_INT*/
<s_init().s_str("1").sg_next(vtp),
        noexc, vtp, mkvaltyp("1",TK_INT), valtyp>
<s_init().s_str(mkint(TK_MAXINTLEN)).sg_next(vtp),
        noexc, vtp, mkvaltyp(mkint(TK_MAXINTLEN),TK_INT), valtyp>

/*special token types: TK_BADTOK - overlength*/
/*TK_ID*/
<s_init().s_str(mkid(TK_MAXIDLEN+1)).sg_next(vtp),
        noexc, vtp, mkvaltyp(mkid(TK_MAXIDLEN+1),TK_BADTOK), valtyp>
/*TK_INT*/
<s_init().s_str(mkint(TK_MAXINTLEN+1)).sg_next(vtp),
        noexc, vtp, mkvaltyp(mkint(TK_MAXINTLEN+1),TK_BADTOK), valtyp>

/*special token types: TK_BADTOK - almost legal id or int*/
/*bad characters*/
<s_init().s_str("!").sg_next(vtp),
        noexc, vtp, mkvaltyp("!",TK_BADTOK), valtyp>
/*TK_ID*/
<s_init().s_str("!bc").sg_next(vtp),
        noexc, vtp, mkvaltyp("!bc",TK_BADTOK), valtyp>
<s_init().s_str("a!c").sg_next(vtp),
        noexc, vtp, mkvaltyp("a!c",TK_BADTOK), valtyp>
<s_init().s_str("ab!").sg_next(vtp),
        noexc, vtp, mkvaltyp("ab!",TK_BADTOK), valtyp>
/*TK_INT*/
<s_init().s_str("!23").sg_next(vtp),
        noexc, vtp, mkvaltyp("!23",TK_BADTOK), valtyp>
<s_init().s_str("1!3").sg_next(vtp),
        noexc, vtp, mkvaltyp("1!3",TK_BADTOK), valtyp>
<s_init().s_str("12!").sg_next(vtp),
        noexc, vtp, mkvaltyp("12!",TK_BADTOK), valtyp>
```

Interactive driver: token_i.c

```
#include "system.h"
#include "token.h"
#include <stdio.h>
```

```
#define QUIT 0
#define S_INIT 1
#define S_STR 2
#define G_END 3
#define SG_NEXT 4
#define G_DUMP 5

FILE *sy_excfilp = stderr;

int nextcall()
{
     int reply;
     char s[81];

     do {
          printf("\nEnter call name:\n");
          printf("\t0:quit\n");
          printf("\t1:s_init\n");
          printf("\t2:s_str\n");
          printf("\t3:g_end\n");
          printf("\t4:sg_next\n");
          printf("\t5:g_dump: ");
          gets(s);
          if (sscanf(s,"%d",&reply) != 1)
               reply = -1; /* user error - stay in loop */
     } while (reply < 0 || reply > G_DUMP);

     return(reply);
}

main()
{
     int reply;
     char s[80];

     tk_valtyp valtyp;

     while ((reply=nextcall()) != QUIT) {
          switch(reply) {
          case S_INIT:
               tk_s_init();
               break;
          case S_STR:
               printf("Enter string:");
               gets(s);
               tk_s_str(s);
               break;
```

```
      case SG_NEXT:
          tk_sg_next(&valtyp);
          printf("val=%s!typ=%d\n",valtyp.val,valtyp.typ);
          break;
      case G_END:
          reply = tk_g_end();
          printf("returns!%d!\n",reply);
          break;
      case G_DUMP:
          tk_g_dump();
      }
  }
  return(0);
}
```

F.2   ISHAM Modules

F.2.1   *keybdin* TP and TI

F.2.1.1   Test plan

assumptions

test environment
    keybdin_i customized interactive driver
    no stubs

test case selection strategy
    special values
        module state
            none
        access routine parameters
            return value for ki_sg_next:
                all valid ISHAM commands
                at least one invalid ISHAM command
    test cases
        enter special values one at a time

test implementation strategy
    keybdin_i:
        repetitively wait for input command
        if command is 'q' then quit
        else print command
    statement coverage measured using the UNIX utility *tcov*

F.2.1.2   Test implementation

Customized interactive driver: keybdin_i.c

```
#include <curses.h>
#include "system.h"
#include "keybdin.h"

main()
{
    char ch;

    /*initialize curses*/
    initscr();
    clear();
    refresh();

    ki_s_init();
    move(0,0);
    addstr("Enter character ('q' to quit).");
    move(1,0);
    addstr("Character entered: ");
    refresh();
    ch = ki_sg_next();
    while (ch != 'q') {
        move(1,strlen("Character entered: "));
        addch(ch);
        refresh();
        ch = ki_sg_next();
    }
    ki_s_end();

    /*terminate curses*/
    clear();
    refresh();
    endwin();
    return(0);
}
```

F.2.2 *scndr* TP and TI

F.2.2.1 Test plan

assumptions
> SY_MAXINT $\geq$ 990

test environment
> scndr_pic customized driver
> stubs for *absmach*, production code for *scngeom* and *scnstr*

test case selection strategy
> special values

module state
    ISHAM screen, with the following values
        $MEM(r, c) = 10 \times (10 \times r + c)$
        $MEM(0, 0)$ and $MEM(9, 9)$ highlighted
        $PC = 11$
        $ACC = 222$
        $PRT = 333$
        $MSG =$ "123456789012345678901234567890"
access routine parameters
    none
test cases
    exceptions
        no exception testing done
    normal case
        ISHAM screen

test implementation strategy
    stubs for *absmach*
        only get calls implemented
        return values indicated above for ISHAM screen
    scndr_pic: display ISHAM screen
        wait until return is hit
        clear screen and exit
        during execution, no exceptions should be recorded in the file `SHAM.excfil`
    statement coverage measured using the UNIX utility *tcov*

considerations
    The normal-case testing of *scngeom* is included in the testing of *scndr*.

F.2.2.2   Test implementation

Customized driver: `scndr_pic.c`

```
#include <curses.h>
#include "system.h"
#include "scngeom.h"
#include "scnstr.h"
#include "scndr.h"


FILE *sy_excfilp;

main()
{
    char buf[80];

    /*initialize exception file pointer*/
    sy_excfilp = fopen(SY_EXCFIL,"a");

    /*initialize curses*/
```

```
        initscr();

        /*initialize modules*/
        ss_s_init();
        sg_s_init();
        sd_s_init();

        /*create screen*/
        sd_s_clrscn();
        sd_s_con();
        sd_s_mem();
        sd_s_pc();
        sd_s_acc();
        sd_s_prt(333);
        sd_s_msg("123456789012345678901234567890");

        sd_s_hlt(0,1);
        sd_s_hlt(50,1);
        sd_s_hlt(50,0);
        sd_s_hlt(99,1);

        /*leave picture up until return*/
        gets(buf);

        sd_s_clrscn();
        ss_s_end();

        /*terminate curses*/
        endwin();

        /*close exception file*/
        fclose(sy_excfilp);

        return(0);
}
```

absmach **stubs:** absmach_s.c

```
#include "system.h"
#include "absmach.h"

/*access routines*/

int am_g_acc()
{
        return(222);
}
```

```
int am_g_pc()
{
    return(11);
}

int am_g_mem(a)
int a;
{
    return(10*a);
}
```

F.2.3   *scngeom* **TP and TI**

F.2.3.1   Test plan

assumptions

test environment
    PGMGEN driver
    no stubs

test case selection strategy
    special values
        module state
            none
        access routine parameters
            sg_g_row
                all field names
                interval rule for row and column numbers
            sg_g_col, sg_g_len, and sg_g_val
                one illegal field
    test cases
        exceptions
            sg_g_row, sg_g_col, sg_g_len, and sg_g_val
                generate sg_badfld
        normal
            none

test implementation strategy
    statement coverage measured using the UNIX utility *tcov*
        100% statement coverage for exception-code

considerations
    Only exception testing is included.
    Normal-case testing is performed while testing *scndr*.

F.2.3.2   Test implementation

PGMGEN script: `scngeom.script`

```
module
     sg_

accprogs
     <s_init,g_legfld,g_row,g_col,g_len,g_val>

exceptions
     <badfld>

globcod
{%
#include "system.h"
#include "scngeom.h"

sg_fld fld;
int nam;

#define FLD(f,t,r,c) (f.nam = t, f.row = r, f.col = c)
%}


cases

/*****exceptions for g_row, g_col, g_len, and g_val only*****/
/*****normal case handled elsewhere*****/
/*g_row*/
{%
for (nam = 0; nam <= SG_MSGTTL; nam++) {
%}
     <s_init().FLD(fld,nam,-1,0).g_row(fld), badfld, dc, dc, dc>
     <s_init().FLD(fld,nam,-100,0).g_row(fld), badfld, dc, dc, dc>
     <s_init().FLD(fld,nam,0,-1).g_row(fld), badfld, dc, dc, dc>
     <s_init().FLD(fld,nam,0,-100).g_row(fld), badfld, dc, dc, dc>
{%
     if (nam == SG_MEM || nam == SG_MEMROWHDR) {
%}
          <s_init().FLD(fld,nam,10,0).g_row(fld), badfld, dc, dc, dc>
{%
     } else {
%}
          <s_init().FLD(fld,nam,1,0).g_row(fld), badfld, dc, dc, dc>
{%
     }
%}
     <s_init().FLD(fld,nam,100,0).g_row(fld), badfld, dc, dc, dc>
{%
```

```
        if (nam == SG_MEM || nam == SG_MEMCOLHDR) {
%}
            <s_init().FLD(fld,nam,0,10).g_row(fld), badfld, dc, dc, dc>
{%
        } else {
%}
            <s_init().FLD(fld,nam,0,1).g_row(fld), badfld, dc, dc, dc>
{%
        }
%}
        <s_init().FLD(fld,nam,0,100).g_row(fld), badfld, dc, dc, dc>
{%
}
%}


/*g_col, g_len, and g_val*/
<s_init().FLD(fld,SG_MEM,-1,0).g_col(fld), badfld, dc, dc, dc>
<s_init().FLD(fld,SG_MEM,-1,0).g_len(fld), badfld, dc, dc, dc>
<s_init().FLD(fld,SG_MEM,-1,0).g_val(fld), badfld, dc, dc, dc>


/*****g_legfld normal case*****/
{%
for (nam = 0; nam <= SG_MSGTTL; nam++) {
%}
     <s_init().FLD(fld,nam,-1,0), noexc, g_legfld(fld), 0, bool>
     <s_init().FLD(fld,nam,0,-1), noexc, g_legfld(fld), 0, bool>
     <s_init().FLD(fld,nam,0,0), noexc, g_legfld(fld), 1, bool>
{%
}
%}
<s_init().FLD(fld,SG_MEM,10,0), noexc, g_legfld(fld), 0, bool>
<s_init().FLD(fld,SG_MEM,0,10), noexc, g_legfld(fld), 0, bool>
<s_init().FLD(fld,SG_MEM,9,9), noexc, g_legfld(fld), 1, bool>
<s_init().FLD(fld,SG_MEMROWHDR,10,0), noexc, g_legfld(fld), 0, bool>
<s_init().FLD(fld,SG_MEMROWHDR,9,0), noexc, g_legfld(fld), 1, bool>
<s_init().FLD(fld,SG_MEMCOLHDR,0,10), noexc, g_legfld(fld), 0, bool>
<s_init().FLD(fld,SG_MEMCOLHDR,0,9), noexc, g_legfld(fld), 1, bool>
```

Interactive driver: scngeom_i.c

```c
#include "system.h"
#include "scngeom.h"

#define QUIT 0
#define S_INIT 1
#define G_LEGFLD 2
#define G_ROW 3
#define G_COL 4
```

```
#define G_LEN 5
#define G_VAL 6

#define BUFLEN 80

FILE *sy_excfilp = stderr;

int nextcall()
{
    int reply;
    char s[81];

    do {
        printf("\nEnter command:\n");
        printf("\t0:quit\n");
        printf("\t1:s_init\n");
        printf("\t2:g_legfld\n");
        printf("\t3:g_row\n");
        printf("\t4:g_col\n");
        printf("\t5:g_len\n");
        printf("\t6:g_val:");
        gets(s);
        if (sscanf(s,"%d",&reply) != 1)
            reply = -1; /*user error - stay in loop*/
    } while (reply < 0 || reply > G_VAL);
    return(reply);
}

int readint(msg)
char *msg;
{
    int reply,found;
    char s[BUFLEN];

    found = 0;
    while (!found) {
        printf(msg);
        gets(s);
        if (sscanf(s,"%d",&reply) == 1)
            found = 1;
    }
    return (reply);
}

sg_fld readfld()
{
    sg_fld fld;
```

```
        fld.nam = (sg_fldnam)readint("Enter field name:");
        fld.row = readint("Enter row:");
        fld.col = readint("Enter column:");
        return(fld);
}

main()
{
    int reply;

    while ((reply=nextcall()) != QUIT) {
        switch(reply) {
        case S_INIT:
            sg_s_init();
            break;
        case G_LEGFLD:
            printf("returns %d\n",sg_g_legfld(readfld()));
            break;
        case G_ROW:
            printf("returns %d\n",sg_g_row(readfld()));
            break;
        case G_COL:
            printf("returns %d\n",sg_g_col(readfld()));
            break;
        case G_LEN:
            printf("returns %d\n",sg_g_len(readfld()));
            break;
        case G_VAL:
            printf("returns !%s!\n",sg_g_val(readfld()));
            break;
        }
    }
    return(0);
}
```

F.2.4   *scnstr* TP and TI

F.2.4.1   Test plan

assumptions

  SS_NUMCOL $\geq$ 9

  SS_NUMROW $>$ 0

test environment

  exception testing with PGMGEN driver

  normal case testing performed with scnstr_pic customized driver

  no stubs

test case selection strategy
>   special values
>   >   module state
>   >   >   none
>   >   access routine parameters
>   >   >   ss_s_str(r, c, s), ss_s_hlt(r, c, l, f), and ss_s_cur(r, c)
>   >   >   >   interval rule for r and c
>   >   >   ss_s_str(r, c, s)
>   >   >   >   interval rule for $|s|$
>   >   >   ss_s_hlt(r, c, l, f)
>   >   >   >   interval rule for l
>   >   >   >   turn highlighting on and off again
>   test cases
>   >   exceptions
>   >   >   ss_s_str, ss_s_hlt, and ss_s_cur
>   >   >   >   generate ss_row, ss_col, and ss_len
>   >   normal case
>   >   >   pattern consisting of
>   >   >   >   letters A, B, C, and D in four corners
>   >   >   >   letter V going down vertically in the middle
>   >   >   >   letter H going across horizontally in the middle
>   >   >   >   string YYYXXXYYY in center with the Y's highlighted
>   >   >   >   cursor in center of the screen

test implementation strategy
>   scnstr_pic:
>   >   display pattern on the screen
>   >   wait until return is hit
>   >   clear screen and exit
>   >   during execution, no exceptions should be recorded in the file **SHAM.excfil**
>   statement coverage measured using the UNIX utility *tcov*

F.2.4.2   Test implementation

PGMGEN script: scnstr.script

```
module
     ss_

accprogs
     <s_init,s_clrscn,s_str,s_hlt,s_cur,s_ref,s_end>

exceptions
     <row,col,len>

globcod
{%
#include "system.h"
#include "scnstr.h"
```

```
/*return an oversize string*/
char s[2*SS_NUMCOL+1];
char *str(l)
int l;
{
    int i;

    for (i = 0; i < l; i++)
        s[i] = '*';
    s[l] = '\0';
    return(s);
}
%}

cases

/*****exceptions only - normal case handled elsewhere*****/
/*s_str*/
<s_init().s_str(-100,0,""), row, dc, dc, dc>
<s_init().s_str(-1,0,""), row, dc, dc, dc>
<s_init().s_str(SS_NUMROW,0,""), row, dc, dc, dc>
<s_init().s_str(2*SS_NUMROW,0,""), row, dc, dc, dc>

<s_init().s_str(0,-100,""), col, dc, dc, dc>
<s_init().s_str(0,-1,""), col, dc, dc, dc>
<s_init().s_str(0,SS_NUMCOL,""), col, dc, dc, dc>
<s_init().s_str(0,2*SS_NUMCOL,""), col, dc, dc, dc>

<s_init().s_str(0,0,str(SS_NUMCOL+1)), len, dc, dc, dc>
<s_init().s_str(0,SS_NUMCOL-1,str(2)), len, dc, dc, dc>
<s_init().s_str(0,0,str(2*SS_NUMCOL)), len, dc, dc, dc>

/*s_hlt*/
<s_init().s_hlt(-100,0,0,0), row, dc, dc, dc>
<s_init().s_hlt(-1,0,0,0), row, dc, dc, dc>
<s_init().s_hlt(SS_NUMROW,0,0,0), row, dc, dc, dc>
<s_init().s_hlt(2*SS_NUMROW,0,0,0), row, dc, dc, dc>

<s_init().s_hlt(0,-100,0,0), col, dc, dc, dc>
<s_init().s_hlt(0,-1,0,0), col, dc, dc, dc>
<s_init().s_hlt(0,SS_NUMCOL,0,0), col, dc, dc, dc>
<s_init().s_hlt(0,2*SS_NUMCOL,0,0), col, dc, dc, dc>

<s_init().s_hlt(0,0,-100,0), len, dc, dc, dc>
<s_init().s_hlt(0,0,-1,0), len, dc, dc, dc>
<s_init().s_hlt(0,0,SS_NUMCOL+1,0), len, dc, dc, dc>
<s_init().s_hlt(0,SS_NUMCOL-1,2,0), len, dc, dc, dc>
```

```
<s_init().s_hlt(0,0,2*SS_NUMCOL,0), len, dc, dc, dc>

/*s_cur*/
<s_init().s_cur(-100,0), row, dc, dc, dc>
<s_init().s_cur(-1,0), row, dc, dc, dc>
<s_init().s_cur(SS_NUMROW,0), row, dc, dc, dc>
<s_init().s_cur(2*SS_NUMROW,0), row, dc, dc, dc>

<s_init().s_cur(0,-100), col, dc, dc, dc>
<s_init().s_cur(0,-1), col, dc, dc, dc>
<s_init().s_cur(0,SS_NUMCOL), col, dc, dc, dc>
<s_init().s_cur(0,2*SS_NUMCOL), col, dc, dc, dc>
```

Customized driver: scnstr_pic.c

```c
#include <curses.h>
#include "system.h"
#include "scnstr.h"

FILE *sy_excfilp;

main()
{
    int i;
    char buf[SS_NUMCOL+1];

    /*initialize exception file pointer*/
    sy_excfilp = fopen(SY_EXCFIL,"a");

    /*initialize curses*/
    initscr();

    ss_s_init();
    ss_s_clrscn();

    ss_s_str(0,0,"A");
    ss_s_str(0,SS_NUMCOL-1,"B");
    ss_s_str(SS_NUMROW-1,SS_NUMCOL-1,"C");
    ss_s_str(SS_NUMROW-1,0,"D");

    for (i = 0; i < SS_NUMROW; i++)
        ss_s_str(i,SS_NUMCOL/2,"V");
    for (i = 0; i < SS_NUMCOL; i++)
        buf[i] = 'H';
    buf[SS_NUMCOL] = '\0';
    ss_s_str(SS_NUMROW/2,0,buf);

    ss_s_str(SS_NUMROW/2,SS_NUMCOL/2-4,"YYYXXXYYY");
```

```
ss_s_hlt(SS_NUMROW/2,SS_NUMCOL/2-4,9,1);
ss_s_hlt(SS_NUMROW/2,SS_NUMCOL/2-1,3,0);

ss_s_cur(SS_NUMROW/2,SS_NUMCOL/2);
ss_s_ref();

/*leave picture up until return*/
gets(buf);

ss_s_clrscn();
ss_s_ref();
ss_s_end();

/*terminate curses*/
endwin();

/*close exception file*/
fclose(sy_excfilp);

return(0);
}
```

F.3   System Testing

F.3.1   BSHAM system TP and TI

F.3.1.1   Test plan

assumptions
>   SY_MAXINT = 999
>   SY_MEMSIZ = 100

test environment
>   entire BSHAM system
>   input stored in files
>   output saved in files, checked with delta testing
>   directory structure:
>>   sham/
>>>   input/ - test cases stored one per file
>>>   exp/ - expected results of test case (same file name)
>>>   act/ - actual results of test case (same file name)
>>   sham/cmdlin.exp - expected results for command-line test cases
>>   sham/cmdlin.act - actual results for command-line test cases

test case selection strategy
>   special values
>>   command-line errors
>>>   each command-line error once

content of input file
    one load-time exception
    every run-time exception once
    SHAM instructions
        halt with pc = $\{0, \mathtt{SY\_MEMSIZ}/2, \mathtt{SY\_MEMSIZ} - 1\}$
        print with interval rule on content accumulator
test cases
    command-line errors
        hardcoded in `Makefile`
    load-time exceptions
        `ldexc`: one load-time exception
    run-time exceptions
        `addrexc`: $mem[pc] = ADD.object, mem[pc + 1] = 100$
        `arithexc`: $acc = 500 + 500$
        `noopexc`: $pc = 99, mem[pc] = LOADCON.object$
        `objectexc`: $mem[pc] = 10$
    normal-case
        `halt[1-3]`: *HALT* instruction, check with *PRINT* instruction
        `print`: print special values
        `two+two,sum`: programs from Appendix of RS

test implementation strategy
    target `runtestb` in `Makefile`
        test cases for command-line errors
        for each file f in `input/`
            `bsham` f `>act/`f
            `diff act/`f `exp/`f
    statement coverage for *sham* and *exec* measured using the UNIX utility *tcov*
        100% coverage for statements not associated with ISHAM

F.3.1.2 Test implementation

Command-line test cases input commands

```
bsham >cmdlin.act
bsham foo >>cmdlin.act
```

Command-line test cases expected output: `cmdlin.exp`

```
Command line error. No file name specified
Command line error. Cannot open file: foo
```

Input file: `input/addrexc`

```
loadcon 100  % store bad address 100 as operand of add instruction
store 5
add 0
```

Expected output: exp/addrexc

```
Execution exception at 4. Illegal operand: 100
```

Input file: input/arithexc

```
loadcon 500
store 10
loadcon 500
add 10        % 500+500
```

Expected output: exp/arithexc

```
Execution exception at 6. Arithmetic overflow
```

Input file: input/halt1

```
halt
```

Expected output: exp/halt1

Input file: input/halt2

```
loadcon 8     % store "print, halt" in locations 50,51
store 50
loadcon 9
store 51
loadcon 5     % 5 should be printed once
br 50
```

Expected output: exp/halt2

```
5
```

Input file: input/halt3

```
loadcon 8     % store "print, halt" in locations 98,99
store 98
loadcon 9
store 99
loadcon 5     % 5 should be printed once
br 98
```

Expected output: exp/halt3

```
5
```

Input file: `input/ldexc`

```
loadcon 5
xxx
halt
```

Expected output: `exp/ldexc`

```
Load exception at 2. Illegal instruction: xxx
```

Input file: `input/noopexc`

```
loadcon 7      % store "loadcon" in location 99
store 99
br 99          % should cause NOOPERR
```

Expected output: `exp/noopexc`

```
Execution exception at 99. Operand not accessible
```

Input file: `input/objectexc`

```
loadcon 10    % store invalid command 10 in location 4
store 4
```

Expected output: `exp/objectexc`

```
Execution exception at 4. Illegal instruction: 10
```

Input file: `input/print`

```
print
loadcon 999
print
loadcon 500
print
loadcon 0
print
halt
```

Expected output: `exp/print`

```
0
999
500
0
```

Input file: `input/sum`

```
loadcon 5       % value of n
store 40        % location 40: value of n, decremented each iteration
loadcon 0
store 41        % location 41: value of sum
loadcon 1
store 42        % location 42: 1, used for decrementing
load 40
brz 28          % check if 0
add 41          % add to the sum
store 41
load 40         % subtract 1 from n
sub 42
store 40
br 14
load 41         % print value of sum
print
halt
```

Expected output: `exp/sum`

15

Input file: `input/two+two`

```
loadcon 2
store 20
loadcon 2
add 20
print
halt
```

Expected output: `exp/two+two`

4

F.3.2   ISHAM system TP and TI

F.3.2.1   Test plan

assumptions
> SY_MAXINT = 999
> SY_MEMSIZ = 100

test environment
> entire ISHAM system
> SHAM programs stored in files, ISHAM commands entered manually
> output checked manually

directory `sham/input/` contains test cases, one per file

test case selection strategy
> special values
> > one load-time exception
> > one run-time exception
> > user commands
> > > one invalid command
> > > *STEP* through entire program
> > > *EXIT* at beginning, in the middle, and at *HALT* instruction
> test cases
> > `ldexc`: one load-time exception
> > `arithexc`: one run-time exception
> > `two+two,sum`: programs from Appendix of RS

test implementation strategy
> test cases must be run manually
> > run four test cases described above
> > for `aritherr`, step through program until run-time exception
> > for `two+two` and `sum`, step through entire program
> > use `two+two` to test special user commands
> statement coverage for *sham* and *exec* measured using the UNIX utility *tcov*
> > 100% coverage for statements associated with ISHAM
> > *tcov* must be run manually after the test cases

considerations
> The testing of the ISHAM version of *exec* is included in the testing of ISHAM.

F.4   Demonstration Modules

F.4.1   *stack* TP and TI

F.4.1.1   Test plan

assumptions
> `PS_MAXSIZ` > 2

test environment
> PGMGEN driver
> no stubs

test case selection strategy
> special values
> > module state
> > > interval rule on size of stack: $[0, \texttt{PS\_MAXSIZ}]$
> > access routine parameters
> > > none
> test cases

> for each of the special module state values,
>> call ps_s_push, ps_s_pop, ps_g_top, ps_g_depth
>> check exception behavior
>> after set calls, check get call values

test implementation strategy
> load(n)
>> loads stack with $10, 20, \ldots, 10 \times n$
> statement coverage measured using the UNIX utility *tcov*

F.4.1.2   Test implementation

PGMGEN script: stack.script

```
module
    ps_

accprogs
    <s_init,s_push,s_pop,g_top,g_depth>

exceptions
    <empty,full>

globcod
{%
#include "system.h"
#include "stack.h"

static void load(n)
int n;
{
    int i;

    ps_s_init();
    for (i = 0; i < n; i++)
        ps_s_push((i+1)*10);
}
%}

cases

/*empty stack*/
<load(0).s_push(10), noexc, g_top(), 10, int>
<load(0).s_push(10), noexc, g_depth(), 1, int>
<load(0).s_pop(), empty, dc, dc, dc>
<load(0).g_top(), empty, dc, dc, dc>
<load(0), noexc, g_depth(), 0, int>

/*partially full stack*/
```

```
<load(2).s_push(30), noexc, g_top(), 30, int>
<load(2).s_push(30), noexc, g_depth(), 3, int>
<load(2).s_pop(), noexc, g_top(), 10, int>
<load(2).s_pop(), noexc, g_depth(), 1, int>
<load(2), noexc, g_top(), 20, int>
<load(2), noexc, g_depth(), 2, int>

/*full stack*/
<load(PS_MAXSIZ).s_push(0), full, dc, dc, dc>
<load(PS_MAXSIZ).s_pop(), noexc, g_top(), (PS_MAXSIZ-1)*10, int>
<load(PS_MAXSIZ).s_pop(), noexc, g_depth(), PS_MAXSIZ-1, int>
<load(PS_MAXSIZ), noexc, g_top(), PS_MAXSIZ*10, int>
<load(PS_MAXSIZ), noexc, g_depth(), PS_MAXSIZ, int>
```

Interactive driver: stack_i.c

```c
#include "system.h"
#include "stack.h"

#define QUIT 0
#define S_INIT 1
#define S_PUSH 2
#define S_POP 3
#define G_TOP 4
#define G_DEPTH 5
#define G_DUMP 6

#define BUFLEN 80

FILE *sy_excfilp = stderr;

int nextcall()
{
    int reply;
    char s[81];

    do {
        printf("\nEnter command:\n");
        printf("\t0:quit\n");
        printf("\t1:s_init\n");
        printf("\t2:s_push\n");
        printf("\t3:s_pop\n");
        printf("\t4:g_top\n");
        printf("\t5:g_depth\n");
        printf("\t6:g_dump:");
        gets(s);
        if (sscanf(s,"%d",&reply) != 1)
            reply = -1; /*user error - stay in loop*/;
```

```c
    } while (reply < 0 || reply > G_DUMP);
    return(reply);
}

int readint(msg)
char *msg;
{
    int reply,found;
    char s[BUFLEN];

    found = 0;
    while (!found) {
        printf(msg);
        gets(s);
        if (sscanf(s,"%d",&reply) == 1)
            found = 1;
    }
    return (reply);
}

main()
{
    int reply,i;

    while ((reply=nextcall()) != QUIT) {
        switch(reply) {
        case S_INIT:
            ps_s_init();
            break;
        case S_PUSH:
            i = readint("Enter element:");
            ps_s_push(i);
            break;
        case S_POP:
            ps_s_pop();
            break;
        case G_TOP:
            i = ps_g_top();
            printf("returns %d\n",i);
            break;
        case G_DEPTH:
            i = ps_g_depth();
            printf("returns %d\n",i);
            break;
        case G_DUMP:
            ps_g_dump();
            break;
        }
```

```
        }
        return(0);
}
```

F.4.2 *symtbl* TP and TI

F.4.2.1 Test plan

assumptions
> ST_MAXSYMLEN $\geq$ length of ST_MAXSYMS $- 1$ in string form
> ST_MAXSYMS > 0

assumptions
> PGMGEN driver
> no stubs

test case selection strategy
> special values
>> module state
>>> number of symbols in table: $\{0, 1, \text{ST\_MAXSYMS}/2, \text{ST\_MAXSYMS}\}$
>>> symbol length: short, ST_MAXSYMLEN
>> access routine parameters
>>> st_s_add: strings of length $\{0, \text{ST\_MAXSYMLEN} + 1, 2 \times \text{ST\_MAXSYMLEN}\}$
>>> st_s_add, st_s_loc, st_g_loc, st_g_exsym: empty string
> test cases
>> exceptions
>>> for each special module state
>>>> add overlength symbols
>>>> if the table is full
>>>>> add a symbol not in the table
>>>> set and get locations for symbols not in table
>>>> add every symbol in the table
>> normal
>>> check st_g_exsym for empty string in empty table
>>> add the empty string, check and change its location
>>> for each special module state
>>>> check table length
>>>> check that a very long symbol is not in table
>>>> for each i in $[0, \text{ST\_MAXSYMS} - 1]$
>>>>> if i in $[0, \text{t\_siz} - 1]$
>>>>>> check t_sym(i) in table with correct location
>>>>>> check st_s_loc resets location
>>>>> else
>>>>>> check t_sym(i) not in table

test implementation strategy
> C functions to support iterating over the special module states,
> viewed as a sequence:

void t_init: initialize to the first state

void t_next: load next state

int t_end: return *true* if no states remain

C functions to generate and check symbols in current state:

int t_siz: number of symbols in current state

char *t_sym(i): i-th symbol in current state

int t_loc(i): location of i-th symbol in current state

char *t_mksym(i, l): string consisting of i converted to ASCII, padded right with *'s to length l

statement coverage measured using the UNIX utility *tcov*

F.4.2.2 Test implementation

PGMGEN script: symtbl.script

```
module
     st_

accprogs
     <s_init,s_add,g_exsym,s_loc,g_loc,g_siz>

exceptions
     <exsym,maxlen,notexsym,full>

globcod
{%
#include "system.h"
#include "symtbl.h"

#define T_FILLCHAR '*'

static int i,cur;

static struct {
     int syms; /*number of symbols*/
     int symlen; /*symbol length*/
} tbl[] = {
     {0,0},
     {1,0},
     {1,ST_MAXSYMLEN},
     {ST_MAXSYMS/2,0},
     {ST_MAXSYMS/2,ST_MAXSYMLEN},
     {ST_MAXSYMS,0},
     {ST_MAXSYMS,ST_MAXSYMLEN},
     {-1,0} /*sentinel*/
};

static void t_init()
{
```

```
        cur = -1;
}

static char *t_mksym(i,len)
int i,len;
{
    static char buf[2*ST_MAXSYMLEN+1];
    int j;

    sprintf(buf,"%d",i); /*convert i to ASCII*/
    if (len > strlen(buf)) {
        for (j = strlen(buf); j < len; j++) /*pad right with '*'*/
            buf[j] = T_FILLCHAR;
        buf[len] = '\0'; /*add string terminator*/
    }
    return(buf);
}

static void t_next()
{
    int i;

    cur++;
    st_s_init();
    for (i = 0; i < tbl[cur].syms; i++)
        st_s_add(t_mksym(i,tbl[cur].symlen),10*i);
}

static int t_end()
{
    return(tbl[cur].syms == -1);
}

static int t_siz()
{
    return(tbl[cur].syms);
}

static char *t_sym(i)
int i;
{
    return(t_mksym(i,tbl[cur].symlen));
}

static int t_loc(i)
int i;
{
    return(10*i);
```

```
}
%}

cases

/*****exceptions*****/
{%
t_init();
t_next();
while (!t_end()) {
%}
      /*add overlength symbols*/
      <s_add(t_mksym(0,ST_MAXSYMLEN+1),0), maxlen, dc, dc, dc>
      <s_add(t_mksym(0,2*ST_MAXSYMLEN),0), maxlen, dc, dc, dc>

      /*if the table is full, add a symbol not in the table*/
{%
      if (t_siz() == ST_MAXSYMS)
%}
            <s_add("x",0), full, dc, dc, dc>

      /*set and get locations for symbols not in the table*/
      <s_loc(t_mksym(t_siz(),0),0), notexsym, dc, dc, dc>
      <s_loc("",0), notexsym, dc, dc, dc>
      <g_loc(t_mksym(t_siz(),0)), notexsym, dc, dc, dc>
      <g_loc(""), notexsym, dc, dc, dc>

      /*add every symbol in the table*/
{%
      for (i = 0; i < t_siz(); i++)
%}
            <s_add(t_sym(i),0), exsym, dc, dc, dc>
{%
      t_next();
}
%}


/*****normal case*****/
/*check g_exsym for empty string in empty table*/
<s_init(), noexc, g_exsym(""), 0, bool>
/*add the empty string, check and change its location*/
<s_init().s_add("",10), noexc, g_exsym(""), 1, bool>
< , noexc, g_loc(""), 10, int>
<s_loc("",20), noexc, g_loc(""), 20, int>

{%
t_init();
t_next();
```

```
while (!t_end()) {
%}
    /*check table length*/
    < , noexc, g_siz(), t_siz(), int>
    /*check that a very long symbol is not in table*/
    < , noexc, g_exsym(t_mksym(0,2*ST_MAXSYMLEN)), 0, bool>
{%
    for (i = 0; i < ST_MAXSYMS; i++) {
        if (i < t_siz()) {
%}
            /*check t_sym(i) in table with correct location*/
            < , noexc, g_exsym(t_sym(i)), 1, bool>
            < , noexc, g_loc(t_sym(i)), t_loc(i), int>
            /*check s_loc resets location*/
            <s_loc(t_sym(i),t_loc(-i)), noexc,
                g_loc(t_sym(i)), t_loc(-i), int>
{%
        } else {
%}
            /*check t_sym(i) not in table*/
            < , noexc, g_exsym(t_sym(i)), 0, bool>
{%
        }
    }
    t_next();
}
%}
```

Interactive driver: symtbl_i.c

```
#include "system.h"
#include "symtbl.h"

#define QUIT 0
#define S_INIT 1
#define S_ADD 2
#define G_EXSYM 3
#define S_LOC 4
#define G_LOC 5
#define G_SIZ 6
#define G_DUMP 7

#define BUFLEN 80

FILE *sy_excfilp = stderr;

int nextcall()
{
```

```
    int reply;
    char s[81];

    do {
        printf("\nEnter command:\n");
        printf("\t0:quit\n");
        printf("\t1:s_init\n");
        printf("\t2:s_add\n");
        printf("\t3:g_exsym\n");
        printf("\t4:s_loc\n");
        printf("\t5:g_loc\n");
        printf("\t6:g_siz\n");
        printf("\t7:g_dump:");
        gets(s);
        if (sscanf(s,"%d",&reply) != 1)
            reply = -1; /*user error - stay in loop*/;
    } while (reply < 0 || reply > G_DUMP);
    return(reply);
}

int readint(msg)
char *msg;
{
    int reply,found;
    char s[BUFLEN];

    found = 0;
    while (!found) {
        printf(msg);
        gets(s);
        if (sscanf(s,"%d",&reply) == 1)
            found = 1;
    }
    return (reply);
}

main()
{
    int reply,i;
    char s[80];

    while ((reply=nextcall()) != QUIT) {
        switch(reply) {
        case S_INIT:
            st_s_init();
            break;
        case S_ADD:
            printf("Enter sym:");
```

```
                gets(s);
                sscanf(s,"%s",s);
                i = readint("Enter loc:");
                st_s_add(s,i);
                break;
        case G_EXSYM:
                printf("Enter sym:");
                gets(s);
                sscanf(s,"%s",s);
                i = st_g_exsym(s);
                printf("returns %d\n",i);
                break;
        case S_LOC:
                printf("Enter sym:");
                gets(s);
                sscanf(s,"%s",s);
                i = readint("Enter loc:");
                st_s_loc(s,i);
                break;
        case G_LOC:
                printf("Enter sym:");
                gets(s);
                sscanf(s,"%s",s);
                i = st_g_loc(s);
                printf("returns %d\n",i);
                break;
        case G_SIZ:
                i = st_g_siz();
                printf("returns %d\n",i);
                break;
        case G_DUMP:
                st_g_dump();
                break;
        }
    }
    return(0);
}
```

Appendix G

Code Format Rules

G.1 Identifier names

1. Module prefix is used on all exported identifiers and on no others.

2. Naming is mnemonic and consistent.

3. Identifiers declared by `#define` are all uppercase. Other identifiers are all lowercase.

G.2 Coding style

1. *Whitespace.* Generally: minimize vertical and horizontal whitespace.

   Exception—add a blank line:

   - Following the last `#include`.
   - Following the last global declaration.
   - Between declarations and executable code in functions.
   - Between each adjacent pair of functions.
   - Between major blocks of code.

   Exception—add a space:

   - Around assignment, relational, and logical operators.
   - Following `for`, `while`, `if`, and `switch`.
   - Following ';' in for loop headers.
   - Before '{' and following '}'.

2. *Line breaks.* Generally: one statement per line.

   Specifically: '{' on same line as **if**, **else**, **switch**, **for**, **while**, and **do** but on a new line for the start of a function. In all cases, '}' on the start of a new line.

3. *Indenting.* Generally: indenting with tabs only.

   Indent one tab stop within functions, **struct**, **if**, **else**, **switch**, **for**, **while**, and **do**.

   Place the '}' at same level as the line containing the matching '{'.

4. *Comments.* Generally: only two forms: inline and block.

   Inline: no space after /* or before */.

   Block: /* to start, column of *'s in column 1, and */ to end.

5. *Local functions.* Specification at top of function.

   Defined and implemented before invocation, where possible.

Appendix H

Exercises

H.1 Chapter 2: Software Engineering Fundamentals

1. Name three serious problems with current software documentation.

2. What are the four roles associated with software specifications?

3. What is the difference between set, get, and set-get access routines?

4. What is the most important difference between a Module Interface Specification and a Module Internal Design?

5. In the specification trichotomy, what is the most important difference between exceptions and assumptions?

6. What are the key differences between faults and failures?

7. In inspection meetings, why doesn't the work product author also serve as reader?

8. Provide a justification for Dijkstra's Law of Testing.

9. Why is it important to use both inspection and testing on Module Implementations?

10. Frequently Module Implementations are tested in their production environments. Why does this approach lead to poor controllability and observability?

H.2   Chapter 3: Mathematical Fundamentals

Unless stated otherwise, assume x, y, and z are of type *integer* and b is of type *boolean*.

1. For each pair of sets S_1 and S_2, what is $S_1 \cap S_2$?

   (a) $S_1 = [3..7]$ and $S_2 = \{1, 3, 5\}$

   (b) $S_1 = [7..3]$ and $S_2 = \{1, 3, 5\}$

   (c) $S_1 = \{\langle x, y \rangle \mid x < y\}$ and $S_2 = \{\langle 1, 5 \rangle, \langle 2, 2 \rangle, \langle 3, -1 \rangle\}$

   (d) $S_1 = \{\langle x, y \rangle \mid y^2 = x\}$ and $S_2 = \{\langle 4, 2 \rangle, \langle 4, -2 \rangle, \langle -4, 2 \rangle\}$

2. For each relation R and domain value v, specify the set of range elements corresponding to v.

   (a) $R = \{\langle x, y \rangle \mid x < y\}$ and $v = 0$

   (b) $R = \{\langle x, y \rangle \mid y^2 = x\}$ and $v = -1$

   (c) $R = \{\langle x, y \rangle \mid y^2 = x\}$ and $v = 0$

   (d) $R = \{\langle x, y \rangle \mid y^2 = x\}$ and $v = 1$

3. Which of the following relations is also a function? If the relation is not a function, provide a domain element that has at least two range elements related to it.

   (a) $\{\langle x, y \rangle \mid x < y\}$

   (b) $\{\langle x, y \rangle \mid y^3 = x\}$

   (c) $\{\langle x, y \rangle \mid y = x^3\}$

   (d) $\{\langle \langle x, y \rangle, b \rangle \mid b = (x < y)\}$

4. For each function F and each element x of S, what is $F(x)$?

   (a) $F = \{\langle x, y \rangle \mid y^3 = x\}$ and $S = \{-8, 0, 8\}$

   (b) $F = \{\langle x, b \rangle \mid b = (x \neq 5)\}$ and $S = \{1, 5\}$

   (c) $F = \{\langle \langle x, y \rangle, b \rangle \mid b = (x < y)\}$ and $S = \{\langle 1, 5 \rangle, \langle 2, 2 \rangle, \langle 3, -1 \rangle\}$

5. For each pair of sets S_1 and S_2, what is $S_1 \cap S_2$?

   (a) $S_1 = \{x \mid x < 10 \wedge x \geq 0 \vee x < 5\}$ and $S_2 = \{-1, 3, 5, 12\}$

   (b) $S_1 = \{x \mid x < 10 \vee x \geq 0 \wedge x < 5\}$ and $S_2 = \{-1, 3, 5, 12\}$

   (c) $S_1 = \{x \mid x < 10 \rightarrow x > 0\}$ and $S_2 = \{0, 5, 10\}$

   (d) $S_1 = \{\langle x, y \rangle \mid (y = 1 \vee y = 2) \wedge x \geq 0 \wedge x < y\}$ and $S_2 = \{\langle 1, 1 \rangle, \langle 1, 2 \rangle, \langle 1, 3 \rangle\}$

6. For each logical expression below, is it *true* or *false*? If it is *true*, give a general formula for a value of y (in terms of the value for x) that satisfies the expression. If it is *false*, give a value of x for which no value of y exists that satisfies the expression.

   (a) $(\forall x)(\exists y)(x > y)$

   (b) $(\forall x)(\exists y)(y > 0 \wedge x > y)$

   (c) $(\forall x)(\exists y)(x > 0 \wedge x > y)$

   (d) $(\forall x)(\exists y)(y > 0 \wedge x > y)$

7. For each logical expression below and each element s of S, is the expression *true* or *false* for s?

   (a) $(\forall x \in s)(x > 0)$ and $S = \{\{\}, \{3\}, \{0, 3, 5\}\}$
       Assume S : *set of set of integer*.

   (b) $(\exists i \in [0..|s| - 1])(s[i] > 0)$ and $S = \{\langle\rangle, \langle 3\rangle, \langle 0, 3, 5\rangle\}$
       Assume S : *set of sequence of integer*.

   (c) $(\exists v \in s)(v.x > v.y)$ and $S = \{\{\}, \{\langle 3, 1\rangle\}, \{\langle 1, 3\rangle, \langle -3, 3\rangle\}\}$
       Assume S : *set of tuple of* $(x, y : integer)$.

8. For each of the informal expressions below, give an equivalent completely formal logical expression.

   (a) The element x is the largest element in the set S.
       Assume S : *set of integer*.

   (b) There exists an element in the set S that is larger than x.
       Assume S : *set of integer*.

   (c) The element x is the largest element in the sequence S.
       Assume S : *sequence of integer*.

   (d) There exists an element in the sequence S that is larger than x.
       Assume S : *sequence of integer*.

9. For each function F and each element x of S, what is $F(x)$? If x is not in the domain of F, write "$F(x)$ is not defined."

   (a) F : *set of integer* $\rightarrow$ *integer*

   $$F(x) = \text{the minimum element of } x$$

   $S = \{\{\}, \{5\}, \{3, 5\}\}$

   (b) F : *sequence of integer* $\rightarrow$ *integer*

   $$F(x) = x[|x| - 1]$$

   $S = \{\langle\rangle, \langle 5\rangle, \langle 3, 5\rangle\}$

(c) $F : tuple\ of\ (x, y : integer) \rightarrow integer$

$$F(v) = v.x + v.y$$

$S = \{\langle 1, 3\rangle, \langle -3, 3\rangle\}$

(d) $F : sequence\ of\ integer \rightarrow set\ of\ integer$

$$F(s) = \{x \mid x = s[i]\ \text{for some}\ i \in [0..|s| - 1]\}$$

$S = \{\langle\rangle, \langle 3, 5\rangle, \langle 1, 3, 5, 3, 1\rangle\}$

(e) $F : set\ of\ tuple\ of\ (id : integer, val : string) \rightarrow set\ of\ string$

$$F(s) = \{x \mid (\exists v \in s)(x = v.val)\}$$

$S = \{\{\}, \{\langle 3, \texttt{"cat"}\rangle, \langle 3, \texttt{"dog"}\rangle\}, \{\langle 1, \texttt{"cat"}\rangle, \langle 3, \texttt{"cat"}\rangle\}\}$

10. Assume that the state space consists of triples of values for variables x, y, and z. For each multiple assignment statement and each state value $s \in S$, determine the state resulting from executing the multiple assignment statement in state s.

    (a) $x, y := 2 \times x, z - y$ and $S = \{\langle 0, 1, 2\rangle, \langle 4, 4, 4\rangle, \langle 2, -1, 3\rangle\}$
    (b) $x, z := y, y$ and $S = \{\langle 0, 1, 2\rangle, \langle 4, 4, 4\rangle, \langle 2, -1, 3\rangle\}$
    (c) $x, y, z := y + z, 2 \times z, x + 1$ and $S = \{\langle 0, 1, 2\rangle, \langle 4, 4, 4\rangle, \langle 2, -1, 3\rangle\}$

11. Assume that the state space consists of triples of values for variables x, y, and z. For each multiple assignment statement and sequence of single assignment statements, determine whether the multiple assignment statement defines the same function as the sequence of single assignment statements. If not, give values for x, y, and z for which the two are different.

    (a) $x, y := z, x + z$ and $x := z; y := x + z$
    (b) $x, y := z, x + z$ and $y := x + z; x := z$
    (c) $x, y := x + y, x$ and $x := x + y; y := x$
    (d) $x, y := x + y, x$ and $x := x + y; y := x - y$

12. For each sequence of assignment statements, define an equivalent multiple assignment statement.

    (a) $x := z; y := z - y$
    (b) $x := y; y := x + y$
    (c) $x := 10; y := x + z; z := y - 10$
    (d) $x := x + y; y := x - y; x := x - y$

13. For each function F and each element x of S, what is $F(x)$? If x is not in the domain of F write "$F(x)$ is not defined."

    (a) $F : integer \rightarrow integer$

    $$F(x) = (x < 0 \Rightarrow -x \mid x > 0 \Rightarrow x)$$

    $S = \{-5, 0, 5\}$

    (b) $F : integer \rightarrow integer$

    $$F(x) = (x > 5 \Rightarrow (x < 10 \Rightarrow 2 \times x \mid true \Rightarrow 10) \mid true \Rightarrow 5)$$

    $S = \{0, 5, 10\}$

    (c) $F : integer \times integer \rightarrow integer$

    $$F(\langle x, y \rangle) = (x > y \Rightarrow x - y \mid x < y \Rightarrow y - x \mid true \Rightarrow 0)$$

    $S = \{\langle 2, 4 \rangle, \langle 4, 2 \rangle, \langle 3, 3 \rangle\}$

    (d) $F : sequence \ of \ integer \rightarrow integer$

    $$F(s) = (|s| > 0 \Rightarrow \text{minimum element of } s \mid true \Rightarrow 0)$$

    $S = \{\langle \rangle, \langle 3 \rangle, \langle 1, 3, 5, 3, 1 \rangle\}$

14. Rewrite each conditional rule below in tabular form. Then, for each conditional rule and each state value $s \in S$, determine the state resulting from executing the conditional rule in state s. Assume that the state space consists of triples of values for variables x, y, and z.

    (a) $(z > 0 \Rightarrow x := x + y \mid true \Rightarrow y := x + y)$
    $S = \{\langle 0, 1, 2 \rangle, \langle 1, 2, 0 \rangle, \langle 2, 3, -1 \rangle\}$

    (b) $x, y := (z > 0 \Rightarrow z \mid true \Rightarrow -z), z$
    $S = \{\langle 0, 1, 2 \rangle, \langle 1, 2, 0 \rangle, \langle 2, 3, -1 \rangle\}$

    (c) $(z > 0 \Rightarrow (x > y \Rightarrow z := x \mid true \Rightarrow z := y)$
    $\mid z < 0 \Rightarrow (x < y \Rightarrow z := x \mid true \Rightarrow z := y) \mid true \Rightarrow z := 0)$
    $S = \{\langle 0, 1, 2 \rangle, \langle 1, 2, 0 \rangle, \langle 2, 3, -1 \rangle\}$

15. Rewrite each conditional rule below in tabular form. For each pair of conditional rules, determine whether the two rules are equivalent. If they are not, give values for the variables for which the two rules differ. Assume that the state space consists of triples of values for variables x, y, and z.

    (a) $(x \le y \Rightarrow x \mid true \Rightarrow y)$ and $(x \le y \Rightarrow x \mid y \le x \Rightarrow y)$

    (b) $(x < y \Rightarrow x \mid true \Rightarrow y)$ and $(x < y \Rightarrow x \mid y < x \Rightarrow y)$

    (c) $(x > 5 \Rightarrow (x < 10 \Rightarrow 2 \times x \mid true \Rightarrow 10) \mid true \Rightarrow 5)$
    and $(x > 9 \Rightarrow 10 \mid x > 5 \Rightarrow 2 \times x \mid true \Rightarrow 5)$

Table H.1   Transition function for FSM exercise

Condition	$T(s, x)$
$x < 0$	
$s = -1$	s
$true$	$s - 1$
$x > 0$	
$s = 1$	s
$true$	$s + 1$
$x = 0$	s

(d) $(x < y \Rightarrow (x < z \Rightarrow x \mid true \Rightarrow z) \mid true \Rightarrow (y < z \Rightarrow y \mid true \Rightarrow z))$
and $(x \leq y \wedge x \leq z \Rightarrow x \mid y \leq x \wedge y \leq z \Rightarrow y \mid z \leq x \wedge z \leq y \Rightarrow z)$

16. Consider an FSM with the set of states $S = \{-1, 0, 1\}$, the initial state $s_0 = 0$, the set of inputs $I = integer$, the transition function T shown in Table H.1, the event-output function

$$E(s, x) = (s = 0 \Rightarrow Z \mid true \Rightarrow (x < 0 \Rightarrow N \mid x > 0 \Rightarrow P \mid true \Rightarrow Z))$$

and the condition-output function

$$C = \{\langle -1, N \rangle, \langle 0, Z \rangle, \langle 1, P \rangle\}.$$

For each state s and input element x below, what are the values for $T(s, x)$, $E(s, x)$, and $C(s)$?

(a) $s = -1$ and $x = -3$

(b) $s = -1$ and $x = 5$

(c) $s = 0$ and $x = 5$

(d) $s = 1$ and $x = -3$

(e) $s = 1$ and $x = 0$

17. For each FSM below, we define the set of states S, the initial state s_0, and the set of inputs I. We also give an informal definition for the transition function T, the event-output function E, and the condition-output function C. In each case, provide formal definitions for T, and for E and C when they are present.

(a) $S = \{0, 1, 2\}$, $s_0 = 0$, and $I = \{UP, DOWN\}$. If the input is UP, then the transition function increments the state modulo 3. For example, $T(2, UP) = 0$. If the input is $DOWN$, then the transition function decrements the state, unless it is 0; in that case the state is unchanged. There is no event-output function. The condition-output function returns the value of the state.

Table H.2   *sset* module state machine—access routines

Routine name	Inputs	Outputs	Exceptions
s_init			
s_add	*integer*		full
			mem
s_del	*integer*		notmem
g_mem	*integer*	*boolean*	

(b) $S = sequence$ [3] *of integer*, $s_0 = \langle 1, 2, 3 \rangle$, and $I = \{L, R\}$. If the input is L, then the transition function rotates the elements of the sequence to the left, and places the first element of the sequence at the end. For example, $T(\langle 1, 2, 3 \rangle, L) = \langle 2, 3, 1 \rangle$. If the input is R, the transition function rotates the elements of the sequence to the right, and places the last element of the sequence at the front. The event-output function returns the first element of the old sequence if the input is L, and otherwise it returns the last element of the old sequence. There is no condition-output function.

18. Consider the *sset* (simple set) module, which provides access to a set of at most N integers. The access routines for *sset* are shown in Table H.2, and the **access routine semantics** are shown in Figure H.1. For each of the traces below, show the corresponding execution table, assuming that $N = 3$.

    (a) s_init.g_mem(10).s_add(10).g_mem(10).s_del(10).g_mem(10)

    (b) s_init.s_add(10).s_add(20).s_add(30).s_add(40).g_mem(40).s_del(40)

    (c) s_init.s_add(10).s_init.g_mem(10)

19. Consider the *iset* (iterator set) module, an extension of *sset* from the previous exercise that allows sequential access to the elements of the set. The access routines for *iset* are shown in Table H.3, and the **access routine semantics** are shown in Figure H.2. For each of the traces below, show one possible execution table assuming that $N = 3$.

    (a) s_init.s_add(10).s_mod(SEQ).g_end.sg_next.g_end.sg_next

    (b) s_init.s_add(10).s_add(20).s_mod(SEQ).sg_next.sg_next

    (c) s_init.s_add(10).sg_next.g_end

    (d) s_init.s_add(10).s_mod(SEQ).g_mem(10).s_del(10).sg_next.g_end

state variables
s : *set of integer*

access routine semantics
s_init:
    transition: $s := \{\}$
    exceptions: none
s_add(x):
    transition: $s := s \cup \{x\}$
    exceptions: $exc := (|s| = N \Rightarrow \mathtt{full} \mid x \in s \Rightarrow \mathtt{mem})$
s_del(x):
    transition: $s := s - \{x\}$
    exceptions: $exc := (x \notin s \Rightarrow \mathtt{notmem})$
g_mem(x):
    output: $out := x \in S$
    exceptions: none

Figure H.1 *sset* module state machine—semantics

Table H.3 *iset* module state machine—access routines

Routine name	Inputs	Outputs	Exceptions
s_init			
s_add	*integer*		full
			mem
			mod
s_del	*integer*		notmem
			mod
g_mem	*integer*	*boolean*	
s_mod	$\{SET, SEQ\}$		
sg_next		*integer*	nonext
			mod
g_end		*boolean*	mod

state variables
$s, is : set\ of\ integer$
$m : \{SET, SEQ\}$

access routine semantics
s_init:
    transition: $s, is, m := \{\}, \{\}, SET$
    exceptions: none
s_add(x):
    transition: $s := s \cup \{x\}$
    exceptions: $exc := (m = SEQ \Rightarrow \mathtt{mod} \mid |s| = N \Rightarrow \mathtt{full} \mid x \in s \Rightarrow \mathtt{mem})$
s_del(x):
    transition: $s := s - \{x\}$
    exceptions: $exc := (m = SEQ \Rightarrow \mathtt{mod} \mid x \notin s \Rightarrow \mathtt{notmem})$
g_mem(x):
    output: $out := x \in s$
    exceptions: none
s_mod(mod):
    transition: $(mod = SEQ \Rightarrow is, m := s, SEQ \mid mod = SET \Rightarrow is, m := \{\}, SET)$
    exceptions: none
sg_next:
    transition-output: $is, out := is - \{x\}, x$ where $x \in is$
    exceptions: $exc := (m = SET \Rightarrow \mathtt{mod} \mid is = \{\} \Rightarrow \mathtt{nonext})$
g_end:
    output: $out := (is = \{\})$
    exceptions: $exc := (m = SET \Rightarrow \mathtt{mod})$

Figure H.2   *iset* module state machine—semantics

H.3   Chapter 5: Requirements Specification

1. What problems are likely to arise if a large system is developed without an RS?

2. Why is it important to record expected changes in the RS?

3. For each of the SHAM programs below, what is the exact output specified by the BSHAM RS?

    (a)
```
loadcon    1
store     99
loadcon   10
print
sub       99
brp        6
halt
```

(b)
```
    load      5
    store     6
    loadcon   3 ?

    loadcon 105
    store   105
```

(c)
```
    load      2
    store    99
    load      3
    store    98
    store     0
    load      9
    print
    add      99
    store     9
    load     98
    br        8
```

4. Write a SHAM program to compute the sum of three integers. Assume that you are given the following code fragment:

```
    loadcon   x
    store     97
    loadcon   y
    store     98
    loadcon   z
    store     99
```

Also assume that x, y, and z are non-negative and that $x + y + z \in shamintegerT$. Your task is to complete the program by writing code to print the value of $x + y + z$.

5. Write a SHAM program to compute the minimum of two integers. Assume that you are given the following code fragment:

```
    loadcon   x
    store     98
    loadcon   y
    store     99
```

Also assume that x and y are in $shamintegerT$. Your task is to complete the program by writing code to print the value of $min(x, y)$.

6. Write a SHAM program to compute the product of two integers. Assume that you are given the following code fragment:

```
    loadcon   x
    store     98
```

```
loadcon  y
store    99
```

Also assume that x and y are non-negative and that $x \times y \in shamintegerT$. Your task is to complete the program by writing code to print the value of $x \times y$.

7. Prove that the specification for the BSHAM load phase is complete. Show that, for each *srcfil* line that is exception-free and not overlong, the object code to be generated is clearly specified.

H.4   Chapter 6: Module Decomposition

1. Suppose that you have been asked to modify SHAM for French users. Name the modules that must be modified to change the exception messages to French.

2. In the current design, exception message text is contained in several modules. State the pros and cons of having an Exception Message module that contains all of the exception message text.

3. For each change named in the BSHAM Expected Changes section, name the module(s) that would be affected if that change were made.

4. For each change named in the ISHAM Expected Changes section, name the module(s) that would be affected if that change were made.

5. In the current design, command-line parameters are handled by the Sham module. Discuss the pros and cons of having a Command Line module which does all handling of command-line parameters.

6. In the current design, adding a new instruction is likely to affect the *load* and *absmach* modules, and perhaps others as well. Is there a way to encapsulate this change in a single module?

H.5   Chapter 7: Module Interface Specification

1. What are the main disadvantages of using the implementation of a module as its interface specification?

2. What is the most important difference between the interface syntax and the interface semantics?

3. In the SHAM approach to exceptions, how must the MI signal the occurrence of exception E?

4. Which access routine idiom corresponds most closely to the service provided by the C standard input function **getc**?

5. Why are two access routine idioms provided for tuples? Isn't one idiom sufficient?

6. Which of the five quality criteria is the most important?

7. This question is based on the *stack* MIS. For each of the traces below, provide an execution table. For this question, assume that **MAXSIZ** $= 3$.

   (a) s_init.s_pop.g_top.s_pop.s_push(1).g_top

   (b) s_init.s_push(1).s_push(2).g_top.s_pop.g_top

   (c) s_init.s_push(1).s_push(2).s_push(3).g_top.s_push(4).g_top

   (d) s_init.s_push(1).s_pop.s_push(2).s_pop.g_top

8. This question is based on the *symtbl* MIS. For each of the traces below, provide an execution table. For this question, assume that **MAXSYMS** $= 3$ and **MAXSYMLEN** $= 4$.

   (a) s_init.s_add("cat", 10).s_add("dog", 20).g_siz.g_loc("dog").
       g_exsym("cat").g_exsym("bat").g_exsym("mouse").

   (b) s_init.s_add("cat", 10).s_add("dog", 20).s_add("mouse", 30).
       g_loc("mouse").g_loc("dog").g_siz.g_exsym("dog")

   (c) s_init.s_add("cat", 10).s_add("dog", 20).s_add("cat", 30).
       g_loc("cat").g_siz

   (d) s_init.s_add("cat", 10).s_add("dog", 20).s_add("bat", 30).
       s_add("orca", 40).g_loc("orca").g_siz

   (e) s_init.s_add("cat", 10).s_add("dog", 20).s_loc("cat", 20).
       g_loc("cat").s_loc("bat", 40).g_loc("bat")

This question is based on the *token* MIS. For each of the traces below, provide an execution table. For this question, assume that

$$\texttt{MAXSTRLEN} = 100, \texttt{MAXIDLEN} = 3, \text{ and } \texttt{MAXINTLEN} = 2$$

Also assume that variable **vt** is of type **valtyp**. In your execution table, represent **vt** in the **Output** column with a term of the form $\langle \texttt{vt.val}, \texttt{vt.typ} \rangle$. For example, for token "abc", the **Output** column should contain $\langle \texttt{"abc"}, \texttt{ID} \rangle$.

9. (a) s_init.s_str(" 14 2\$x 147 ").sg_next(&vt).g_end.
      sg_next(&vt).g_end.sg_next(&vt).g_end.
      sg_next(&vt).g_end

   (b) s_init.s_str("ab1 1ab").sg_next(&vt).g_end.
      s_str("ab1 1ab").sg_next(&vt).g_end

H.6 Chapter 8: Module Internal Design

1. What are the benefits of the MID as an intermediate work product between the MIS and the Module Implementation?

2. When is there little or no benefit to having an MID?

3. What are the roles of the state invariant and the abstraction function in an MID?

4. This question is based on the *symtbl* MID. For each of the traces below, provide an execution table. For this question, assume that PS_MAXSIZ = 3. To represent the concrete state, use a term of the form

$$\langle\langle\langle s[0], l[0]\rangle, \langle s[1], l[1]\rangle, \langle s[2], l[2]\rangle\rangle, n\rangle$$

   where $s[i]$ represents the string stored in tbl[i].sym, $l[i]$ represents the location stored in tbl[i].loc, and n represents the value of tblcnt. Use ? to indicate no value is specified by the MID.

   (a) s_init.s_add("cat", 5).g_loc("cat")

   (b) s_init.s_add("cat", 5).s_add("dog", 3).s_loc("cat", 1)

5. This question is based on the *token* MID. For each expression below, indicate whether or not it is a state invariant for *token*. If it is a state invariant, briefly explain why. If it is not a state invariant, show a trace that falsifies the expression.

   (a) cur $\in [0..leftnull(\text{buf})]$
       cur $< leftnull(\text{buf}) \rightarrow$
       $(\text{buf}[\text{cur}] \neq \text{' '} \wedge \text{buf}[leftnull(\text{buf}) - 1] = \text{' '})$

   (b) buf$[0..\text{TK\_MAXSTRLEN} + 1]$ contains a null
       cur $\in [0..leftnull(\text{buf})]$
       buf$[\text{cur}] \neq \text{' '} \wedge \text{buf}[leftnull(\text{buf}) - 1] = \text{' '}$

   (c) buf$[0..\text{TK\_MAXSTRLEN} + 1]$ contains a null
       cur $\in [0..leftnull(\text{buf})]$
       cur $< leftnull(\text{buf}) \rightarrow$
       $(\text{buf}[\text{cur}] \neq \text{' '} \vee \text{buf}[leftnull(\text{buf}) - 1] = \text{' '})$

6. This question is based on the *token* MID. For each of the traces below, provide an execution table. For this question, assume that

   $$\text{TK\_MAXSTRLEN} = 5, \text{TK\_MAXIDLEN} = 3, \text{ and } \text{TK\_MAXINTLEN} = 2$$

   To represent the concrete state, use a term of the form

   $$\langle\langle b[0], b[1], \ldots b[6]\rangle, c\rangle$$

   where $b[i]$ represents the i-th character in buffer buf, and c represents the value of cur. Use ? to indicate no value is specified by the MID.

(a) `s_init.s_str(" ").sg_next`

(b) `s_init.s_str("a3").sg_next`

(c) `s_init.s_str(" a3 ").sg_next`

(d) `s_init.s_str("1 a ").sg_next.sg_next`

(e) `s_init.s_str(" 1 a").sg_next.sg_next.sg_next`

7. Change the *token* MID so that it does not use a sentinel blank character, and so that it does not advance to the next token by skipping over leading blanks. For example, the **transition** entry for `tk_s_str` is simplified to

    `tk_s_str`(s):
        transition: $\text{buf}, \text{cur} := s, 0$

8. Consider the *sset* (simple set) module, which provides access to a set of at most N integers. The access routines for *sset* are shown in Table H.2, and the **access routine semantics** are shown in Figure H.1. Assume that the concrete state of *sset* is defined as

    state variables
    `int set[N];`
    `int siz;`

where the array **set** is used to store the elements of the set, **siz** represents the size of the set, and the set elements are stored in $\text{set}[0..\text{siz} - 1]$.

(a) Define an MID for the *sset* module with the above concrete state.

(b) For each of the traces below, show the corresponding execution table, assuming that $N = 3$. Use a similar state representation to the one for *stack*.

    i. `s_init.s_add`(10)`.g_mem`(10)`.s_del`(10)`.g_mem`(10)

    ii. `s_init.s_add`(30)`.s_add`(10)`.s_add`(20)

    iii. `s_init.s_add`(10)`.s_add`(20)`.s_add`(30).
        `s_del`(20)`.s_del`(10)`.s_del`(30)

9. Repeat the above exercise, but in this case maintain the elements in the array **set** in sorted order with the smallest element in $\text{set}[0]$.

10. Consider the *iset* (iterator set) module, an extension of *sset* from exercise 8 that allows sequential access to the elements of the set. The access routines for *iset* are shown in Table H.3, and the **access routine semantics** are shown in Figure H.2. Assume that the concrete state of *iset* is defined as

```
state variables
int set[N];
int siz,cur;
enum {SET,SEQ} mod;
```

where the array `set` is used to store the elements of the set, `siz` represents the size of the set, `cur` is used to iterate over the elements of the set, and `mod` is the current mode of operation (`SET` or `SEQ`). New elements should be added to the end of the array `set`. To iterate over the elements of the set, initialize `cur` to 0 every time `s_mod(SEQ)` is called and increment it in every call to `sg_next`.

(a) Define the MID for the *iset* module with the above concrete state.

(b) For each of the traces below, show the corresponding execution table, assuming that $N = 3$. Use a similar state representation to the one for *stack*.

     i. `s_init.s_add(10).s_mod(SEQ).g_end.sg_next.g_end.sg_next`

     ii. `s_init.s_add(10).s_add(20).s_mod(SEQ).sg_next.sg_next`

     iii. `s_init.s_add(10).s_add(20).s_del(10).s_mod(SEQ).sg_next`

11. Prove the correctness of the *sset* MID for exercise 8 using the verification techniques discussed in Section 8.7.

H.7   Chapter 9: Module Implementation

1. What are the advantages and disadvantages of enforcing the Code Format Rules?

2. Why do we use *stdout* for the reporting of error messages in BSHAM, while we use a file in ISHAM?

3. Using stepwise refinement, derive the implementation of `s_pop` from its specification in the *stack* MID.

4. Using stepwise refinement, derive the implementation of `g_loc` from its specification in the *symtbl* MID.

5. What are the advantages and disadvantages of using conditional compilation in the implementations of *exec* and *sham*?

6. This question is based on the *symtbl* MID and MI. Prove the correctness of the implementation of `s_add` using the verification techniques discussed in Section 9.6.2.

7. This question is based on the *symtbl* MID and MI. Prove the correctness of the implementation of `g_loc` using the verification techniques discussed in Section 9.6.2.

8. Prove that there are no *subscript out of range* errors in the *symtbl* MI. Note that an array is used to store each string in the symbol table and also to store all the symbol/location pairs.

9. Prove that there are no *endless loop* errors in the *token* MI. Note that there are four loops in the *token* MI.

H.8   Chapter 10: Testing

1. If we were to test BSHAM in a strictly top-down fashion, we would first test the *sham* Coordinator module using stubs for all the other modules. Define a TP for testing the BSHAM version of *sham* in this fashion.

2. Define the smallest possible number of PGMGEN test cases that still achieve statement coverage for the *stack* module. Do these test cases adequately test *stack*?

3. How many paths are there through the *token* access routine s_str? How many of those paths are feasible?

4. This question is based on the *stack* TI.

   (a) Modify the *stack* TI so that it does not make any calls to s_init, except for one call at the beginning of the script.

   (b) How would the TI of *stack* have to be changed if exceptions were signaled by printing a message rather than by calling an exception handler?

5. This question is based on the *symtbl* TP and TI. Modify the TP and TI so that it adequately tests an implementation that uses binary search (instead of linear search) to look up the symbols in the table.

6. This question is based on the *absmach* TP and TI. Currently, to test the behavior of sg_exec we test the return value, the value of the program counter, and the value of the accumulator with three separate test cases. Define cmp_ and prt_ functions so that these three tests can be performed with a single test case. Modify the *absmach* TP and TI to make use of these two functions.

7. Consider the *sset* (simple set) module, which provides access to a set of at most N integers. The access routines for *sset* are shown in Table H.2, and the **access routine semantics** are shown in Figure H.1. Assume that the concrete state of *sset* is defined as

```
int set[N];
int siz;
```

where the array **set** is used to store the elements of the set, **siz** represents the size of the set, and the set elements are stored in **set**$[0..\textbf{siz}-1]$. Define a TP for the above module.

8. Implement the TP from the previous exercise.

9. Currently the TP and TI of *scngeom* only test the exception behavior. The normal-case behavior is tested while testing *scndr*. Modify the *scngeom* TP and TI so that the normal-case behavior is also tested.

10. Define a TP and TI for the system test of **BSHAM**, assuming that no module testing is performed for any of the **BSHAM** modules.

Bibliography

[1] D. L. Parnas and P. C. Clements. A rational design process: how and why to fake it. *IEEE Trans. Soft. Eng.*, SE-12(2):251–257, February 1986.

[2] J. A. Hager. Software cost reduction methods in practice. *IEEE Trans. Soft. Eng.*, 15(12):1638–1644, December 1989.

[3] R. C. Linger, H. D. Mills, and B. I. Witt. *Structured Programming: Theory and Practice*. Addison-Wesley, 1979.

[4] M. Dyer. *The Cleanroom Approach to Quality Software Development*. John Wiley & Sons, 1992.

[5] D. M. Hoffman. Practical interface specification. *Software—Practice and Experience*, 19(2):127–148, February 1989.

[6] D. M. Hoffman and P. A. Strooper. A case study in class testing. In *Proc. CASCON'93*, pages 472–482. IBM Toronto Laboratory, October 1993.

[7] G. C. Murphy, P. Townsend, and P. S. Wong. Experiences with cluster and class testing. *Commun. ACM*, 37(9):39–47, September 1994.

[8] D. L. Parnas. Some software engineering principles. In *Structured Analysis and Design*. Infotech International Limited, 1978.

[9] E. W. Dijkstra. *A Discipline of Programming*. Prentice Hall, 1976.

[10] D. Teichrow and E. A. Hershey. PSL/PSA: A computer-aided technique for structured documentation and analysis of information processing systems. *IEEE Trans. Soft. Eng.*, 3(1):41–48, January 1977.

[11] J. M. Spivey. *The Z Notation: A Reference Manual*. Prentice Hall, 1989.

[12] C. B. Jones. *Systematic Software Development Using VDM*. Prentice Hall, 2d edition, 1990.

[13] B. W. Boehm. *Software Engineering Economics*. Prentice Hall, 1981.

[14] B. P. Lientz and E. B. Swanson. *Software Maintenance Management.* Addison-Wesley, 1980.

[15] F. P. Brooks. *The Mythical Man-Month.* Addison-Wesley, 1975.

[16] R. W. Selby, V. Basili, and F. Baker. Cleanroom software development: an empirical evaluation. *IEEE Trans. Soft. Eng.*, SE-13(9):1027–1038, November 1987.

[17] J. Guttag, J. Horning, and J. Wing. The Larch family of specification languages. *IEEE Software*, 2(5):24–36, September 1985.

[18] W. Bartussek and D. L. Parnas. Using traces to write abstract specifications for software modules. In *Information Systems Methodology*, pages 211–236. Springer-Verlag, 1978. *Proc. 2nd Conf. European Cooperation in Informatics*, October 10–12, 1978.

[19] T. J. McCabe. A complexity measure. *IEEE Trans. Soft. Eng.*, SE-2(4):308–320, December 1976.

[20] M. H. Halstead. *Elements of Software Science.* North-Holland, 1977.

[21] R. S. Pressman. *Software Engineering: A Practitioner's Approach.* McGraw-Hill, 3d edition, 1992.

[22] C. Ghezzi, M. Jazayeri, and D. Mandrioli. *Fundamentals of Software Engineering.* Prentice Hall, 1991.

[23] T. DeMarco. *Structured Analysis and System Specification.* Yourdon Press, 1978.

[24] E. Yourdon and L. Constantine. *Structured Design.* Prentice Hall, 1979.

[25] P. T. Ward and S. J. Mellor. *Structured Development for Real-Time Systems.* Yourdon Press, 1985.

[26] B. W. Boehm, T. E. Gray, and T. Seewaldt. Prototyping versus specifying: a multi-project experiment. *IEEE Trans. Soft. Eng.*, 10(3), 1984.

[27] B. W. Boehm. A spiral model of software development and enhancement. *Computer*, 21(5), 1988.

[28] A. Goldberg and D. Robson. *SmallTalk-80: The Language and Its Implementation.* Addison-Wesley, 1983.

[29] G. Booch. *Software Components with Ada—Structures, Tools, and Subsystems.* Benjamin/Cummings, 1987.

[30] B. Meyer. *Object-Oriented Software Construction.* Prentice Hall, 1988.

[31] B. Stroustrup. *The C++ Programming Language*. Addison-Wesley, 1991.

[32] W. S. Humphrey. *Managing the Software Process*. Addison-Wesley, 1989.

[33] R. B. Grady. *Practical Software Metrics for Project Management and Process Improvement*. Prentice Hall, 1992.

[34] W. A. Babich. *Software Configuration Management: Coordination for Team Productivity*. Addison-Wesley, 1983.

[35] G. W. Russell. Experience with inspection in ultralarge-scale developments. *IEEE Software*, 8(1):25–31, 1991.

[36] E. W. Dijkstra. Structured programming. In *Proc. Conf. NATO Science Committee*, 1969.

[37] P. J. Courtois and D. L. Parnas. Documentation for safety critical software. In *Proc. 15th Intl. Conf. Soft. Eng.*, pages 315–323. IEEE, 1993.

[38] S. D. Hester, D. L. Parnas, and D. F. Utter. Using documentation as a software design medium. *Bell System Technical Journal*, 60(8):1941–1977, October 1981.

[39] A. J. Jackson and D. M. Hoffman. Inspecting module interface specifications. *Journal of Software Testing, Verification and Reliability*, pages 101–117, October 1994.

[40] W. W. Royce. Managing the development of large software systems. In *Proc. Ninth Intl. Conf. Soft. Eng.* IEEE, 1987.

[41] M. E. Fagan. Design and code inspections to reduce errors in program development. *IBM Systems Journal*, 15(3):182–211, 1976.

[42] G. J. Myers. *The Art of Software Testing*. John Wiley & Sons, 1979.

[43] W. E. Howden. *Functional Program Testing*. McGraw-Hill, 1987.

[44] M. Piff. *Discrete Mathematics—An Introduction for Software Engineers*. Cambridge University Press, 1991.

[45] P. R. Halmos. *Naive Set Theory*. Springer-Verlag, 1974.

[46] W. Hodges. *Logic*. Penguin Books, 1977.

[47] H. B. Enderton. *A Mathematical Introduction to Logic*. Academic Press, 1972.

[48] D. F. Stubbs and N. W. Webre. *Data Structures with Abstract Data Types and Pascal*. Brooks/Cole Publishing Company, 2d edition, 1989.

[49] H. Ehrig and B. Mahr. *Fundamentals of Algebraic Specification 1*. Springer-Verlag, 1985.

[50] R. Milner. A theory of type polymorphism in programming. *Journal of Computer and System Sciences*, 17(3):348–375, 1978.

[51] J. E. Hopcroft and J. D. Ullman. *Introduction to Automata Theory, Languages, and Computation*. Addison-Wesley, 1979.

[52] R. J. Nelson. *Introduction to Automata*. John Wiley & Sons, 1968.

[53] D. M. Hoffman and G. Jones. Module state machines. Technical Report DCS-167-IR, University of Victoria, Dept. Comp. Sci., 1991.

[54] V. C. Hamacher, Z. G. Vranesic, and S. G. Zaky. *Computer Organization*. McGraw-Hill, 1978.

[55] R. N. Horspool. *The Berkeley UNIX Environment*. Prentice Hall Canada, 2d edition, 1992.

[56] K. L. Heninger. Specifying software requirements for complex systems: new techniques and their applications. *IEEE Trans. Soft. Eng.*, SE-6(1):2–13, January 1980.

[57] K. L. Heninger, J. W. Kallander, and J. E. Shore. *Software Requirements for the A-7E Aircraft*. Naval Research Laboratory, Washington, DC, 1978.

[58] M. W. Alford. A requirements engineering methodology for real-time processing requirements. *IEEE Trans. Soft. Eng.*, SE-3(1):60–69, January 1977.

[59] D. Harel, H. Lachover, A. Naamad, A. Pnueli, M. Politi, R. Sherman, A. Shtull-Trauring, and M. Trakhtenbrot. Statemate: A working environment for the development of complex reactive systems. *IEEE Trans. Soft. Eng.*, 16(4):403–414, April 1990.

[60] J. B. Dreger. *Function Point Analysis*. Prentice Hall, 1989.

[61] A. M. Davis. A comparison of techniques for the specification of external system behavior. *Commun. ACM*, 31(9):1098–1115, September 1978.

[62] O. J. Dahl, E. W. Dijkstra, and C. A. R. Hoare. *Structured Programming*. Academic Press, 1972.

[63] E. W. Dijkstra. The structure of THE multiprogramming system. *Commun. ACM*, 11(5):341–346, May 1968.

[64] D. L. Parnas. On the criteria to be used in decomposing systems into modules. *Commun. ACM*, 15(12):1053–1058, December 1972.

[65] D. L. Parnas, P. C. Clements, and D. M. Weiss. The modular structure of complex systems. In *Proc. 7th Intl. Conf. Soft. Eng.*, pages 408–417. IEEE, 1984.

[66] N. Wirth. Program development by stepwise refinement. *Commun. ACM*, 14(4):221–227, April 1971.

[67] D. L. Parnas. On the design and and development of program families. *IEEE Trans. Soft. Eng.*, SE-2(1), March 1976.

[68] G. A. Blaauw and F. P. Brooks. Computer architecture (draft). Computer Science Department, University of North Carolina, Chapel Hill, NC, 1989.

[69] D. L. Parnas. A technique for software module specification with examples. *Commun. ACM*, 15(5):330–336, May 1972.

[70] K. Britton, A. Parker, and D. L. Parnas. A procedure for designing abstract interfaces for device interface modules. In *Proc. 5th Intl. Conf. Soft. Eng.*, pages 195–204. IEEE, 1981.

[71] J. V. Guttag and J. J. Horning. The algebraic specification of abstract data types. *Acta Informatica*, 10(1):27–52, 1978.

[72] D. M. Hoffman and R. Snodgrass. Trace specifications: methodology and models. *IEEE Trans. Soft. Eng.*, 14(9):1243–1252, September 1988.

[73] B. Meyer. Applying "design by contract." *IEEE Computer*, 25(10):40–51, October 1992.

[74] Rational. *The C++ Booch Components—Class Catalog*, 1991.

[75] C. A. R. Hoare. Proof of correctness of data representations. *Acta Informatica*, 1(4):271–281, 1972.

[76] J. D. Gannon, R. G. Hamlet, and H. D. Mills. Theory of modules. *IEEE Trans. Soft. Eng.*, 13(7):820–829, 1987.

[77] T. Nipkow. Non-deterministic data types: models and implementations. *Acta Informatica*, 22:629–661, 1986.

[78] B. W. Kernighan and D. M. Ritchie. *The C Programming Language*. Prentice Hall, 1978.

[79] C. A. R. Hoare. An axiomatic basis for computer programming. *Commun. ACM*, 12(10):576–583, 1969.

[80] D. Gries. *The Science of Programming*. Springer-Verlag, 1981.

[81] C. Morgan. *Programming from Specifications*. Prentice Hall, 1990.

[82] B. Beizer. *Software System Testing and Quality Assurance.* Van Nostrand Reinhold, 1984.

[83] W. E. Howden. Functional program testing. *IEEE Trans. Soft. Eng.*, 6(2):162–169, 1980.

[84] W. E. Howden. Reliability of the path analysis testing strategy. *IEEE Trans. Soft. Eng.*, 2(3):208–215, 1976.

[85] S. Rapps and E. J. Weyuker. Selecting software test data using dataflow information. *IEEE Trans. Soft. Eng.*, 11(4):367–375, 1985.

[86] R. A. DeMillo, R. J. Lipton, and F. G. Sayward. Hints on test data selection: help for the practicing programmer. *Computer*, 11(4):34–41, 1978.

[87] L. J. White and E. I. Cohen. A domain strategy for computer program testing. *IEEE Trans. Soft. Eng.*, 6(3):247–257, 1980.

[88] D. J. Richardson and L. A. Clarke. Partition analysis: a method combining testing and verification. *IEEE Trans. Soft. Eng.*, 11(12):1477–1490, 1985.

[89] B. Beizer. *Software Testing Techniques.* Van Nostrand Reinhold, 2d edition, 1990.

[90] D. J. Panzl. A language for specifying software tests. In *Proceedings AFIPS '78*, pages 609–619, 1978.

[91] J. Gannon, P. McMullin, and R. Hamlet. Data-abstraction implementation, specification, and testing. *ACM Trans. Program. Lang. Syst.*, 3(3):211–223, 1981.

[92] P. G. Frankl. Tools for testing object-oriented programs. In *Proc. Pacific Northwest Software Quality Conf.*, pages 309–324, 1990.

[93] D. M. Hoffman and P. A. Strooper. Automated module testing in PROLOG. *IEEE Trans. Soft. Eng.*, 17(9):934–943, 1991.

[94] P. Wong. Automated class exerciser (ACE) user's guide. Technical Report TR92-0655, MPR Teltech Ltd., September 1992.

[95] IEEE Computer Society. *IEEE Standard for Software Test Documentation*, 1983.

[96] D. H. Kitson and S. M. Masters. An analysis of SEI software process assessment results: 1987–1991. In *Proc. 15th Intl. Conf. Soft. Eng.*, pages 68–77. IEEE, 1993.

Index